WORKS BY
ZHU YONGXIN
ON
EDUCATION

My Vision on Education

ZHU YONGXIN

New York   Chicago   San Francisco   Athens   London
Madrid   Mexico City   Milan   New Delhi
Singapore   Sydney   Toronto

Beijing Jinghua Hucais Printing, Co., Ltd.

ISBN   978-0-07-182755-3
MHID   0-07-182755-2

e-ISBN   978-0-07-182757-7
e-MHID   0-07-182757-9

McGraw-Hill Education books are available at special quantity discounts to use as premiums and sales promotions or for use in corporate training programs. To contact a representative, please visit the Contact Us pages at www.mhprofessional.com.

Contents

Foreword

The sparks of new experiments in education have caused me, a publisher who has not been interested in Chinese education for very long, to have always hoped to meet Zhu Yongxin, but we had never met before.

In the late autumn of 2010, on a sunny morning near Beijing's Sanyuan, in that office that was swelling with passion and a bustling, literary atmosphere, I was finally able to see Zhu Yongxin, whom I have long admired.

What sort of person did I see?

A government official? Scholar? Teacher? He was all of these and yet also none of these. This person who looked simple and honest, willful and easygoing, wise and farsighted, sensitive and profound. His gestures were calm, his words were occasionally mild, passionate, or simple and unadorned, his laugh was mellow and rich and his clear gaze occasionally flashed with a trace of tiredness. This is the image of a person who possesses great love and compassion. I was deeply shocked. On listening to him casually say a few words, I vaguely understood why it would be possible for his works to have so many readers and why he would have so many followers in his single-handed push for new experiments in education. I went straight up to him and said: Professor, I would like to publish an anthology of your works.

I was blunt in so doing, but I did not act on impulse. Before meeting Zhu Yongxin, I had previously endeavored to read a large proportion of Professor Zhu's works and earnestly searched for anything on the Internet that was related to his opinions and views on education, as well as all kinds of actions in which he has delved deeper into the frontlines of education as if he were an itinerant monk looking for the direction of China's education. After three decades, despite the wind and the rain, Zhu Yongxin walks steadily onward bearing the luggage that is education.

The first edition of *My Vision on Education* in 2000 is without a doubt Professor Zhu Yongxin's most well known work. Over the past decade, this work has been hailed as "the most stunning educational masterpiece, the most moving educational classic." It has been looked up to by the entire nation's primary and secondary school teachers as a set of standards, has been entirely reprinted more than 20 times, and has received plenty of good reviews. This book pushes Zhu Yongxin's consistent thoughts and creative passion to its peak, and in the past decade, he has used the passion of his own spirit and his unparalleled love of Chinese teachers and students to enable Chinese education, which had been gravely ill for a long time, to be full of vitality. What is undeniable is that in the first decade of the twenty-first century, Zhu Yongxin has stood majestically at the summit of Chinese education.

The ideal traction often possesses an inconceivable power. The new experiments in education that began in 2002 and Zhu Yongxin's take on the ideal education possess an inseparable intrinsic connection. This experiment was aimed at "giving children something that is useful to them for the rest of their lives" and used the founding of the public not-for-profit website Education Online as a starting point and "the building of scholarly campuses, the composition of writing by teachers and students, the listening to the voices outside of the classroom, the cultivation of outstanding eloquence, the construction of ideal classrooms, and the building of digital communities" as its content. In nearly a decade up to the present, it has been extended to more than 20 provinces and introduced into 1,141 schools. In this unprecedented experiment within the Chinese education sector, Zhu Yongxin's thoughts as an "itinerant monk" were published and announced to the world in *New Education China*, and this text, which was full of practical style, appropriately conveyed another extraordinary scene for Chinese education.

Following the ideal route, walking along the path of new experiments in education, even though Zhu Yongxin is not in the least bit vigorous and dynamic, he does however possess a rare sort of calm. Apart from his personal charisma, I think that an even more profound reason is that he had previously clearly and furthermore quite completely sorted through the basic thoughts in the history of Chinese educational ideologies. The course of writing the three works: *The History of Ancient Chinese Educational Ideologies*, *The History of Modern Chinese Educational Ideologies*, and *The History of Contemporary Chinese Educational Ideologies*, gave him profound learning and cultivation and also appears to have enabled him to find the historical basis for the benign development of Chinese education. This sort of advance preparation of theory and historical materials has enabled him to engage in in-depth thinking on all kinds of problems facing present-day Chinese education and furthermore to propose solutions with apparent ease and skill.

In reading the 150,000 words of "The Chronology of Zhu Yongxin's Academic Activities" (published within the current edition of *Recommendations for Chinese Education*), you will discover that at the time when Zhu Yongxin was in university, he already had a keen interest in academic research. In the 1980s, in the years when dreams take flight and ideals reign supreme, the keen and perceptive Zhu Yongxin read extensively and was open and broad-minded to the world. His articles on all sorts of categories, which mainly drew on psychology, often made the headlines. Within more than a decade, from the time he was in university all the way till his postdoctoral years, his rigorous mental training and rich research of knowledge enabled him to later on write the two works of substantial weight: *Studies on Educational Psychology* and *Research on Chinese Local Psychology*. These books established Professor Zhu Yongxin's academic status and influence within the field of educational psychology.

Many gifted people are often immersed in their own talents and time hurriedly passes them by. However, Zhu Yongxin's hard work has been publicly recognized, and people who have met him or worked with him know that Zhu Yongxin's main characteristic is that he has never let himself go. This professor who has had the dual identity of being both a scholar and an administrative leader for a long period of time, with perseverance and consistency, the results of his administrative work have been brilliant and his academic research has also never been remiss. He often accepts interviews with journalists and calmly voices a variety of viewpoints on Chinese education. He never lets an opportunity to observe Chinese or foreign education slip by and furthermore will use his diligent penmanship to record these observations down in a book. Hence the birth of such works as *Observations on Chinese Education, Observations on Foreign Education, Review of Chinese Education, Recommendations for Chinese Education,* and so on.

There are many things in this world that cannot be described, such as Zhu Yongxin's new experiments in education with which he devotes all his passion and talents to achieving a state of operations that far exceeds that of an ordinary person; many things in this world cannot be explained, such as how can Zhu Yongxin achieve such brilliant academic work outside of his administrative work?

An author once said that Zhu Yongxin has the "passion of a poet, depth of a sage, purity of an infant, the simple-mindedness of an old farmer, and the mischievousness of a naughty child"; a journalist who deeply understands him also said that "behind all the efforts of Zhu Yongxin, the struggles, hesitations as well as the awakening of Chinese education over the past century, is faintly discernible"; famous author Zhao Lihong once said that Zhu Yongxin is "an itinerant monk, an observer, a thinker and a practitioner." However to me, Zhu Yongxin himself and his achievements in work are like a riddle, which I cannot possibly provide a satisfactory answer to.

This is precisely the reason why we have compiled and published Zhu Yongxin's *Works on the New Education.* The author is like the book. No commentary whatsoever can be like this basically complete set of works and be able to convey the wholeness and uniqueness of Zhu Yongxin on a practical and spiritual level. Of course, not one book among this complete set of works can explain on its own what heights Zhu Yongxin has reached in the field of education.

Hu Yanhua
Langlang Study

Preface I

Professor Zhu Yongxin asked me to write a preface for his forthcoming collection, probably because he knows I pay attention to education and publish my views from time to time or because both he and I are successors of such people as Ma Xulun, Zhou Jianren, Ye Shengtao, and Lei Jieqiong, all of whom are members of the China Association for Promoting Democracy. Although I'm not an expert in education, I agreed out of my admiration for his academic achievements, my favor of this young scholar, and my interest in education regardless of his thought. Maybe I can express my views and opinions on the collection and the author from the perspective of a layman paying attention to the education industry in a sober and more objective way.

I once said all people can talk about and comment on Chinese education because education is too complicated, and in particular Chinese education. China runs the largest-scale education in the world as a developing country and is in a period of transformation characterized by serious imbalance between urban and rural areas and between eastern and western areas, and by mutual frictions and agitations of ideologies rarely seen in the world. With education becoming increasingly popular, more and more people express comments on education and nearly all households frequently discuss it, thus raising for education-related research many problems that may not be prominent in other countries. In my opinion, the following two problems are most important and urgent. First, education has a butterfly effect. We can neither discuss education for the sake of education nor discuss one aspect of education while ignoring others. Our discussion must be different from daily discussions and talks by the common people. Second, how will educational science walk out of the narrow circle of educational theories to be understood, commented on, and practiced by more people and to test whether educational theories are accepted by the people on a larger scale so as to avoid the divorce of experts from society? Because of these two problems, I'm gratified by this collection by Professor Zhu Yongxin.

The author investigates and ponders the issues of Chinese education from extensive perspectives of domestic and international situations, politics, economy, culture, society, ancient times, and modern times. His expositions cover nearly the whole educational process of all students. He conscientiously ponders, systematically surveys, and earnestly tests all aspects of education ranging from educational ideas to curriculum reform and extracurricular activities, to upgrade them to the level of theory. Moreover, he also pays attention to psychology that is closely related to education and studies and analyzes foreign education while researching Chinese education.

Professor Zhu Yongxin is not a "pure" scholar, although research on educational theories is forever the core of what he does. He is a teacher, official, and researcher and became a father as his child was born and grew up. As a result, he must research the educational system in an all-dimensional, multiperspective, and graded way instead of observing one section or aspect of the educational system. Now he serves as the vice chairman of the Central Committee of the China Association for Promoting Democracy. As his colleague, after seeing he was extremely exhausted, I once wondered whether his hard work was a test assigned by God to a great man or something he was doomed to do. As a matter of fact, he obtains an excellent research environment and conditions inaccessible to others: he has gradually developed unique research methods and style by frequently changing roles, changing angles and methods of thinking, and naturally combining macro and micro perspectives.

It is difficult for us to creatively do a good job in research on anything if we are only rationally driven but don't have a great enthusiasm based on profound knowledge of the thing, namely vast devotion. Professor Zhu Yongxin throws himself into educational research. Physically, his three roles and one identity naturally take up all of his time and efforts. The distinctive loving heart running through all his job tasks and embodied in all his works is the best evidence of his invisible heart.

He has said, "education is a poem." He often praises education and expresses his educational thoughts in poetic language.

Education is a poem named ardent love;
A mother's heart is found in the eyes of all children.
Education is a poem named the future;
A wave-breaking boat is found in the long river of civilization's continuation.

How could the thought of a poem occur to Professor Zhu Yongxin if he was purely rational, without abundant and insuppressible emotions? However, he is not a romantic scholar. He was very busy but took the lead to launch an education website at his own expense and opened an education blog and Weibi to bring together numerous netizens and friends struggling at the front lines of education reform throughout China. Every day, he has to browse and respond to all posts and letters on the website one by one after returning home fatigued. Someone said he asks for trouble. However, in his opinion, he "is travelling together with poetry and ideal" and "is enjoying happiness." He once worked and lived in Suzhou, hailed as a paradise on earth where 12-year compulsory education was made universal at an early date and the goal of universal university education is being realized. However, this deputy mayor who once took charge of culture and education was concerned about West China and kept pondering over and calling for narrowing the education gap between the eastern and western areas. How can he keep doing so for a long time? In my opinion, his biggest driving force is great love. A seamless connection of emotion and reason represents the biggest difference between Professor Zhu and those people who regard education and theoretical study as an occupation, and it represents a success factor.

Education is the fundamental guarantee for the continuation and development of human society. In a sense, humans differ from other animals because humans receive education of varying degrees and content through different channels. For a country, education constitutes a basic project guaranteeing development and expansion. These are common views. However, education is a huge and complicated system that involves a large number of education theorists and management experts. Those engaged in education are content with their work, but in the eyes of outsiders, research on educational theories is boring and burdensome, evidenced by too many education works, and management leaves a complicated, miscellaneous, and trivial impression on people. Such an impression generally becomes one of the reasons for estrangement between theorists, management staffs, and education participants (including parents, students, and bystanders). Scholars who are engaged in both theoretical research and management and who can convey their love for education to the society are needed to share with people the pleasure and happiness in the ocean of education. However, there are few scholars of this kind. Do we misunderstand humanistic and social science such as educational theory and argue that academism is only characterized by a lot of jargon and hard-to-understand sentences in a specific industrial language? Are there a few people who are good at expressing a complicated thing in the clearest language? Are educational theories indeed too abstruse to be expressed in a language "transcending" social conventions? I firmly believe truth is always plain and simple. A genuine "master" is able to express profound reflections and complicated laws in easy-to-understand and vivid language. There have been many such masters in history.

As an educational theorist, Professor Zhu Yongxin is moving toward this goal and begins to develop his own style characterized by a combination of exposition, emotional expression and Q&A, logical and rational language, a vernacular to be easily understood by common people, active thinking, and passionate verses. Readers are serious when they read some articles by Professor Zhu, applaud enthusiastically when reading others, and repeatedly read and taste other articles. Commendably, the articles show his nature rather than being painstaking. Such nature is attributed to his love for education and love for the people in the final analysis.

Any new style is always deemed "alien" when one style already is pervasive in the society and permeates many people's subconscious. I don't know whether Professor Zhu Yongxin has such an experience. I hope he can stick to his style even though his articles are not considered "papers," because whether an academic life is strong or weak is finally judged by the people instead of being identified by a small academic circle. I also hope he will keep improving and exercising his style to continue this refreshing breeze in educational theory.

Like all things closely related to people's livelihood, education must sensitively keep abreast of the times, meet people's needs, and change with time and different conditions. This collection mainly includes works and papers by Professor Zhu

Yongxin from his engagement in the education field to 2010, reflecting the process of theoretical research and practice in education since the reform and opening up in China. "The struggle will go on and on." Endless problems in education will appear and be solved in two decades, from a primarily well-off society to an overall well-off society, so we must keep observing, pondering, and researching. Education with Chinese characteristics will develop and grow up in this process and may take shape in this period. Professor Zhu Yongxin is in the prime of his life. As indicated by his name, he will certainly seize the once-in-a-hundred-years opportunity to deepen and expand his research, contribute more talents and wisdom to Chinese education and educational theory, and write more and better articles. We are looking forward to it.

Xu Jialu
December 14, 2010
Riduyijuan Book House

Preface II

I met Zhu Yongxin in the 1990s. At that time, I received a letter from Zhu Yongxin at Suzhou University inviting me to attend an education seminar held by him as entrusted by the Japan International Education Society. I thought he was an old comrade but found he was a young scholar when I met him. He was in his thirties and had returned from Japan where he studied psychology. My first impression of him was that he was very warm and passionate and wanted to contribute to Chinese education. A little later, he worked with the Jiangsu Education Publishing House to compile the *World Education Encyclopedia* and invited me to act as editor-in-chief. I was a bit hesitant because I didn't want to take over such a huge project after the *Education Dictionary*, which took me 12 years. However, I accepted the invitation, bewitched by his enthusiasm and persuaded by many young scholars including Yuan Zhenguo. The compilation of the book took nearly five years, during which time Zhu Yongxin made great efforts as associate editor-in-chief, and I found he was pragmatic and easygoing.

Later, I was in frequent contact with Zhu Yongxin. When he served as deputy mayor of Suzhou, the Chinese Education Society cooperated with the Jiangsu Provincial Education Department and the Suzhou Municipal Government to hold the Twenty-First Century Education Forum in 2001 to discuss education internationalization, digitization, and basic education. The successful forum featured expert dialogue, novel form, and rich content, and was specially reported on CCTV several times. Later, the Chinese Education Society convened the nineteenth annual academic meeting in Suzhou, and the Central Committee of the China Association for Promoting Democracy and the Ye Shengtao Research Society convened the Cross-Strait Education Seminar in Suzhou. Both Zhu Yongxin and I attended these forums and seminars, which were very smooth and successful thanks to his thoughtful arrangements.

Zhu Yongxin has a passion for education and can chase down his education dream. He said, "an ideal teacher must be discontented with life and have a dream." He published *My Education Ideals in 2000*, published *Dreams of New Education*, and began the experiment of new education in 2002 which now involves more than 800 schools nationwide. Hundreds and thousands of teachers participate in every seminar convened by Zhu Yongxin and have warm discussions. As a result, his educational ideals and dreams become actions. Where are the ideals and dreams of new education? He summarizes the following four ideals and dreams: (1) to change the environment of Chinese students—to become an ideal paradise where students enjoy the pleasure of growth; (2) to change the path of Chinese teachers—to become an ideal stage for their professional development; (3) to reshape the humanistic spirit of Chinese education—to become an ideal platform for improvement in schools' education quality; (4) to create a "community of new education" in China—to become a spiritual home of education and an ideal village of growth. In a word, we must change outdated ideas of traditional education, overcome present educational shortcomings, and return to the essence of education. Education is an activity making students grow up happily and a stage for teachers' professional growth instead of making teachers and students dance in shackles and suffer from such a dance.

Teachers are essential to any educational undertaking and critical to educational success. In our opinion, education must enlighten students' subjectivity and rely on teachers. Therefore, teachers' growth is crucial. According to Zhu Yongxin, teachers must read books and take reading notes. He said to me that to participate in his experiment, teachers have to read and write every day and then they will certainly have thoughts and apperceptions. Therefore, he opened the network blog to talk with teachers and inspire them to experience education. He asks teachers, students, parents, and all nationals to read books so as to improve our quality. When he acted as a member of the Chinese People's Political Consultative Congress and deputy to the National People's Congress, he several times proposed the establishment of National Reading Day and reading by all people. Zhu Yongxin is very diligent. He keeps reading, teaching, and researching amid busy official affairs. He is doctoral supervisor at Suzhou University, undertakes national scientific education research projects, and launches the new education experiment. He goes to the grassroots and delivers speeches throughout China to publicize his new education ideals and dreams. I hope his ideals and dreams will come true in China at an early date. He is diligent in writing and takes notes of his experiences and feelings. As a result, he has a collection made up of dozens of volumes of millions of words to be published.

His articles are characterized by a combination of theories and practices. He expresses theories of educational laws to teachers in an easy-to-understand language and lists cases full of educational philosophy that are easily understood and accepted by teachers. Therefore, his books have numerous readers.

Zhu Yongxin asked me to write something for his revised and enlarged education collection. I'm not very good with words and can't use many rhetorical and laudatory words and terms. However, Zhu Yongxin is indeed admirable for his enthusiasm, diligence, and productivity. I would like to conclude my preface with verses from the recent poem *Seed of New Education* by Zhu Yongxin:

I'm a seed, a seed of new education;
I come from a blooming flower by idea and passion;
I can't choose the soil to be landed in—fertile or barren, North or South;
I'll finally pass through the soil and move toward the light no matter how deep
I'm buried . . .

Gu Mingyuan
March 12, 2011

My Vision on Education

PART 1

This volume has five chapters that were completed at the commission of the editor in chief of the *New China Education Weekly*, Zong Ping. In the summer of 2000, beside the beautiful Taihu Lake, I gave a lecture to the teachers who were attending a forum for innovation in education: "My Take on the Ideal Teacher." Based on the feedback from the lecture during my presentation and after the forum concluded, the positive reception that I received far exceeded my expectations. A revised version of this lecture was published and also evoked a strong response, with the *Chinese Education Daily* republishing a short summary of the article on its front page. Everyone believes that we strongly need these types of theoretical articles that are full of passion and poetic sentiments. With the encouragement of my colleagues, I wrote a series of articles including the subjects of my take on the ideal school, the ideal principal, the ideal parents, and the ideal student. Afterward, in response to the fervent requests of numerous readers, I wrote five articles about my take on the ideal moral education, intellectual education, physical education, aesthetic education, and technical education. The overarching theme in all ten articles is my educational ideals, and obviously an idealistic tone is unavoidable. However, after all is said and done, I believe that without the ideal educationalist, it would be impossible to possess the spirit of pursuing excellence; impossible to be bursting with passion, poetic sentiments, and energy during educational activities. "We may gaze up to the mountain's brow / We may travel along the great road / Signifying that although we cannot hope to reach the goal / Still we may push on thitherward in spirit." Let us use the great ideals of education to embrace the light of the new century!

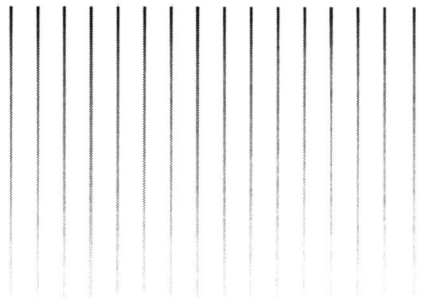

1

My Take on Moral Education

In the past few years, the distorted personalities and the moral degeneracy prevalent in some youth have sounded alarm bells across the entire society. From the Jinhua middle school student Xu Li's matricide case in Zhejiang province to the Central Conservatory of Music university student Chen Guo's case of self-immolation, from the 14-year-old boy's cruel murder of his classmate's sister in Beijing to a delinquent student's crazed killings of four relatives of the school principal by hacking them to death—when faced with such horrible acts, people cannot help but ask: have our children's many years of education even sunk into their psyche? What has happened to our moral education?

Professor Lu Jie once wrote in an article titled "The Return to True Education": "The entire twentieth century illustrates that humankind has suffered from 'schizophrenia.' From a materialistic point of view, humankind has already attained the level of God, with practically nothing being impossible, with humankind having free reign to do whatever they please. However from a spiritual and moral point of view, in terms of such areas as understanding oneself and knowing one's own capabilities, our growth has also in turn been stunted and standards lowered." Chinese people lacking in great wisdom are in reality ruining themselves through the application of petty wisdom. "This makes the plight of humankind especially dangerous, similar to a one-year-old child raising a loaded gun."[1] One important route toward the return to genuine education that Professor Lu speaks of is to value moral education.

All educationalists, whether ancient or modern, Chinese or otherwise, fully value moral education and fully place moral education in a special vaunted

3

position. The esteemed German educator Johann Friedrich Herbart once said, "The attainment of morals is generally seen as the ultimate goal of humankind, it is therefore also education's ultimate goal." Esteemed physicist Albert Einstein pointed out in an article commissioned by the editor in chief of the *New York Times* titled "Education for Independent Thought" that "it is not enough to teach a man a specialty. Through it he may become a kind of useful machine but not a harmoniously developed personality. It is essential that the student acquire an understanding of and a lively feeling for values. He must acquire a vivid sense of the beautiful and of the morally good. Otherwise he—with his specialized knowledge—more closely resembles a well-trained dog than a harmoniously developed person."

Our country's well-regarded educator Tao Xingzhi once said, "Morals are the essential link to how one should conduct oneself, even if you were to have knowledge and skills, they are of no use without morals. Otherwise, for those who have no morals, the greater their knowledge and skills base, the greater their propensity for evil, that is why I proposed the idea not so long ago of the Great Wall of Integrity, requiring us all to 'construct a great wall of integrity.' It is only through this means that students will consciously create personalities that are truly virtuous and good." The educators who have written about the importance of moral education are not limited to these few, but it is evident to us just from these three articles that they place moral education in a position that is surpassed by no other in terms of importance. Moral education truly should be the essence of education in its entirety.

1. Allow Students to Develop Moral Character Through Unstructured Activities

My take on the ideal moral education is that it should place importance on developing a student's moral character through unstructured activities, allowing students to experience and come to their own realizations about the realms of morality through games and various independent activities.

The most important part of moral education is the research into the principles that govern the formation of a person's moral character. One basic principle is that it must be formed through unstructured play. Abstract moral principles cannot truly penetrate deep into a person's heart and soul, and they cannot be fully comprehended by humankind, through preaching alone.

For example, in the past, families generally had three children who would self-consciously come to realize their own rights, duties, and responsibilities through growing up within the atmosphere of positive home education. When eating an apple, children would comply with the rules of priority: older children eating less and offering part of their share to the younger children so that they could eat more. In the distribution and execution of household chores, they would distribute the amount of work among themselves, allowing each person's rights, responsibilities, and duties to be in agreement. This itself is a form of auto-matic implementation of morals. These kinds of unstructured activities can allow children to learn several moral guidelines, resolving many issues of morality without parents having to resort to repetitive preaching. However, within the current society, most children are from single-child families. These children lack the chance to interact with others, are kept in an "iron cage" before starting school, and for the most part are isolated from the outside world. Even within an envi-ronment surrounded by peers, students attend school from seven or eight o'clock in the morning till four or five o'clock in the afternoon, with the bulk of their time spent at school mainly focused on classwork and homework, and so they are still unable to freely communicate and engage in activities with others.

There is one point that is certain, though: these students lack a type of funda-mental moral character for interacting with others—they do not know how to deal with conflicts, face setbacks, or handle conflicts. This type of fundamental moral character is not something that can be nurtured simply through preaching alone.

In our work we have always been keen to tackle the problem of moral edu-cation, to write its teachings down in words and put together a proper syllabus. In actuality, the effects of this type of moral education are very weak and lack-luster. Moral education should instead exist within people's own lives, within children's interactions with their peers, and within children's interactions with their teachers. It is only through these avenues that moral education can achieve favorable results.

In our actual lives, we often discover the phenomenon of culture and morals being mutually separate from one another. There are some people in our society who, although their level of cultural refinement and character is not high, possess high levels of morality. These people are philanthropic, possess a love of helping others, and are dedicated and hardworking. The cause of the formation of moral character in these people is without a doubt, different from the section of the school curriculum dedicated to moral education. From this example it is also evident that although knowledge and morals are similar at a certain level, they are definitely not the same. Therefore, favorable educational conditions and a bene-ficial environment must be created in order to implement moral education so that unstructured "free" moral activities can be fashioned through which good moral conduct can be cultivated in students.

Within his own teachings, Sukhomlinsky placed great emphasis on the impor-tance of allowing students to cultivate their own moral conduct through unstruc-tured activities, so that their spirits can be refined and their characters molded and educated within these familiar environments. Sukhomlinsky once described his teaching experiences involving placing students within naturally occurring envi-ronments and having them engage in unstructured "free" activities in *On the Issue of the Overall Development of Education*. He wrote:

After experiencing our first autumn on-campus, we came to firmly believe that marveling at the fiery red rosa multiflora hips; appreciating the few remaining yellow leaves on the well-shaped branches of the small apple tree and feeling sorrow for the tomatoes frozen by the cold early winter winds are all scenes that awaken feelings in children of familiarity, love and protection toward all things beautiful and living. Within children's hearts, a plant becomes a living object that will tremble and shiver in the biting cold winter winds, therefore they will want to protect it and help it to ward off the bitter cold. Educators' most important mission is to allow children, teenagers and young adults to formulate ideas on the transcendent and divine things related to a person's beauty and within a person's thoughts, feelings and experiences. We need these ideas to take on a more substantial form in their minds by using vivid actual examples of virtuous and moral behavior as a means of adding weight to these ideas.

Unfortunately, there are already very few examples of moral education around us that will stir the hearts of children, teenagers, and young adults in such a way.

2. Enable Students to Regard Books as Their Allies and to Converse with the Great Literary Masters

My take on the ideal moral education is that it should enable students to regard books as their allies and allow them to converse with the great literary masters, to have their spirits refined and their character elevated due to humankind's exquisite cultural heritage.

Reading is an extremely important means of refining a child's spirit and elevating a child's character. The above section emphasizes cultivating a student's moral character through the use of unstructured "free" activities mainly to stress allowing students to experience and come to understand moral standards from an emotional perspective. Reading for the purpose of refining a student's spirit emphasizes the elevation in perception of moral lessons learned through experience and moral understandings to morality's levels of rationality, raising these to a state of self-realization.

In actuality, many literary works and writings related to the social sciences themselves are highly influential, infused with the strength of a type of intangible moral education. For example, if you were to discuss what is beauty or benevolence, you need only have read such famous works by Victor Hugo as *The Hunchback of Notre Dame* and *Les Miserables* or flipped through Charlotte Bronte's *Jane Eyre*, *The Making of a Hero* by Nikolai Alexeevich Ostrovsky, or *The Common World* by Lu Yao. Reading these great works will inevitably impact students' hearts and minds, with students using the vaunted and much revered moral states found within these works as a type of personal goal. This kind of strength in terms of internalizing moral education is something that is quite difficult to accomplish using any other methods. Therefore, the effective implementation of moral education requires the establishment of "literary societies" and "literary campuses," allowing students to develop a love of reading. If children love reading, then through these literary works they will be able to gain comfort for their souls, guidance for how to live their lives, and refinement for their spirits. The characters in these works will often become the standard by which they live and the principles found in these works, mapping coordinates for their lives.

Regrettably, most of our students today hardly have any time to read anything besides their school textbooks, especially junior high students who spend their entire day surrounded by "standardized" textbooks; this is a definite education blunder of ours. The time in which one is a student is the golden age for studying. Schools must adopt definite steps to encourage students to read more, to read well, and to flip through human civilization's top classics and works with the finest content. This is no longer purely a way to read but has profound significance for the cultivation of a student's benevolent moral character.

3. Nurture a Student's Healthy Lifestyle and Creative Talents
My take on the ideal moral education is that it should place importance on nurturing a student's healthy lifestyle and creative talents, enriching a student's mental and spiritual state.

Within an ideal environment, the push for the development of one's moral character through good quality education, interest in a healthy lifestyle, and one's creative talents is extremely important. In the past, we often viewed lifestyle interests and creative talents as skills, things that have no connection with moral character; we very easily overlook their use as a means of cultivating moral character, for example with painting, calligraphy, music, and dance. In actual fact, what is truly virtuous and good is an organically whole entity and indeed, moral character, intellect, physical fitness, art, and work are also such an inseparable whole entity. It is only for the sake of convenience in terms of discussion that they have been separated. Genuine education is an entire entity, harmonious and compatible. In ancient times, gifted scholars were required to be well acquainted with The Four Books and Five Classics and to be proficient in lute playing, chess, calligraphy, and painting. People from ancient times brought forth these demands because they had already come to the realization that these types of healthy lifestyle interests and creative talents were not just technical skills but in fact served a didactic function during the process of cultivating one's moral character. We can therefore understand that when these healthy lifestyle interests and creative talents occupied all of people's time, would they still have the time to scheme and plot against one another? Would they still have time to run amok and cause utter chaos? So instead of giving students numerous rules of "don't do such and such," why not use these elegant and healthy activities to enrich our students' lives and have them voluntarily not go and do "such and such"?

In regard to the practice of moral education in this area, Sukhomlinsky was someone we should indeed learn from. He once proposed three measures for enriching the spiritual and mental aspect of students' lives. First, while at the same time students are inspired and enticed to finish their study obligations in various subjects, they must have one other subject that they themselves particularly like. Allow them to venture outside of the standard curriculum requirements and delve deeply into the studies of their subject to come up with even more profound questions. Second, attempt to have every student possess a favorite work task and science and technology–related activity, allowing them to undertake their own inventing and experimenting in their free time. Third, have every student possess a favorite book, a much-loved text outside of school-endorsed reading. Sukhomlinsky believed that if our students immerse their whole bodies and minds into these activities and possess rich spiritual and mental lives, is there anything about them that is cause for us to worry? Therefore, nurturing students' creative talents in a particular area is definitely desirable not only because it imparts a skill but also because it serves an important purpose in cultivating a person's moral character.

4. Use Real and Touching Images of Morality to Inspire Students

My take on the ideal moral education is that it should attach importance to searching out role models for students on how to live one's life, using real and touching images of morality to inspire students and cultivate within them the spirit of heroism.

Some people claim that we are at present living in an era without heroes, and more and more people believe that heroes such as Lei Feng, Zhang Haidi, and Kong Fansen are becoming increasingly distant from us. This makes it very difficult for students to establish an image of a contemporary hero within their hearts and in turn greatly influences the implementation of moral education. This is due to the fact that the formation of individuals' moral character is largely dependent on their version of what a hero should be like and also the role models that they have had in life. Upon researching the world's greatest people, we can discover evidence of the explicit and implicit impression that heroes have had on these people on their paths to success. Thus it is imperative that we call out to the heroes out there and have our children strive toward being heroes. Regarded from a purely biological viewpoint, humans easily grow lazy, are easy to satisfy, and are quick to come to a standstill. However, those who have established a vaunted image of a hero within their hearts are able to find the gap between themselves and their hero, giving themselves the strength to move forward through their image of the ideal hero, endowing themselves with the courage to overcome hardships and to incite enthusiasm, passion, and energy. Through being inspired by one's hero, one is able to gain the impetus to exert oneself and work hard. If teachers are able to consciously guide students into establishing their own version of the ideal hero within their hearts, then the results of this kind of moral education are much more positive than having teachers in classrooms explaining until their voices go hoarse.

The famous French author Romain Rolland writes in the preface of *Beethoven the Creator*:

> Let them not complain too piteously, the unhappy ones, for the best of men share their lot. It is for us to grow strong with their strength. If we feel our weakness, let us rest on their knees. They will give solace. From their spirits radiate energy and goodness. Even if we did not study their works, even if we did not hearken to their voices, from the light of their countenances, from the fact that they have lived, we should know that life is never greater, never more fruitful—never happier—than in suffering.[2]

If everyone could rest for a while on the knees of heroes and feel their breaths on us, could continually use heroes as our role model in life, then each person's life would in turn become great and remarkable. In reality, heroism is not such an unattainable goal; every single person has the ability to become a hero. If everyone can continually draw strength from our heroes, be inspired by them, and face life each day with heroic sentiments, then we ourselves will eventually become heroes. Within our teachings of moral education, teachers should consciously use heroes to reform students, using their hometowns and familiar and touching examples on campus. We should allow students to treat heroes as people they hold in high regard and to internalize their noble morality and conduct as moral cultivation. However, without heroes in these times, bringing up a new generation of heroes is quite difficult.

5. Establish a Scientific System of Incremental Moral Education Goals

My take on the ideal moral education is that it should establish incremental moral goals in a scientifically sound way, combining the two viewpoints—realism and idealism—and forming a moral education system that is constantly improving in progressive stages.

One major problem facing the school's moral education system is the issue of setting out objectives, that is, what moral standards and criteria students must grasp at each stage of their learning. Generally speaking, moral education can be separated into three stages. The first stage is the essential stage and the most basic goal of moral education at this present time, requiring students to comply with the fundamental morals in our society, that is, the moral "baseline." The second stage is the enrichment stage, wherein the goal is to use ideas such as collectivism, patriotism, humanism, altruism, and a respectful attitude toward the elderly and care for the young as the fundamental lesson content. The third stage is the stage of pursuit, wherein the foundations are rooted in a Marxist perspective and the ideals of communism. It is not a mandatory stage for all students to reach. These three stages are interconnected, with the progress students make from the lowest to the highest stage providing the link between the three stages. Our moral education needs only to follow this goal-oriented scientific system through the progression of stages to be able to make this type of moral education a reality.

However, at the present time, there is indeed within our school's moral education system an evidently unclear division of stages, even to the point of being the complete opposite of the scientific system as described above, that is severely affecting moral education. An example is demanding primary school students to be the successors of communism, although primary school students draw a blank when it comes to what communism actually is. We also require junior high students to love socialism and senior high students to make full use of collectivism. However, many university students do not possess even the fundamental morals in our society, and so teachers must carry out supplementary classes on these fundamental morals. Therefore, the establishment of scientifically sound goals in moral education must begin its practical implementation with the students.

Sukhomlinsky was very concerned with reinforcing students' moral education by using the students' real world around them as a basis. Every year at the Pavlysh Secondary School, the school where he taught, there is a large banner that hangs on the wall directly facing the main entrance that reads: "Love your mother!" When Sukhomlinsky was questioned as to why he did not write a more common slogan on the banner such as "love your homeland" or "love your people," he would reply: "You cannot speak of abstract concepts to seven-year-old children, moreover, if a child does not even love their mother, would they still love others, their hometown or their homeland? Loving one's mother is easy to comprehend and do and can also lay out the foundation for future teachings on loving one's homeland and its people."

Therefore, the decision to use as goals the fundamental moral standards of "patriotism and observance of the law; courtesy and honesty; unity and camaraderie; frugality and ceaseless self-improvement and dedication and industry" as proposed by the Central Committee of the Communist Party of China (CPC) in their proclamation "Program for Improving Civic Morality" to focus on cultivation of socialist citizens who have ideals, morals, culture, and discipline, is precise and rational.

Research on the psychology of moral education shows that the lesson content covered is restricted in breadth and depth due to the specific traits belonging to each student age group. In terms of breadth, different age groups should cover different lesson content in moral education. In terms of depth, different age groups covering the same lesson content should not be covering it to the same degree. For example, in order to cultivate respect for others among primary school students, one primary school in Japan repeatedly angles moral education teaching toward nurturing this particular moral characteristic throughout the entire primary schooling period, but the moral education requirements differ at each grade level. The main theme in first grade is "friendship." From second to sixth grade, the main themes respectively are "harmony," "to do no harm onto others through slander," "understanding," "respect for human dignity," and "the happiness of all." The goal of first-grade students is "to not bully and look down on others, stand united through camaraderie with your classmates." The goals of students in second grade through sixth grade respectively are "to be able to put yourself in someone else's shoes, to not be self-centered"; "to not talk behind someone's back and do detestable things that will make others dislike you"; "to comprehend human dignity, to respect both yourself and others"; and "to mutually understand each other, to work as one to strive towards happiness." The success that this Japanese school has had in terms of the formulation and implementation of moral education goals is indeed something that is worth our learning from.

In short, the school moral education curriculum should establish a system that has ideals, but moreover uses realistic goals that progressively move from elementary to advanced levels of difficulty and are ceaselessly developing.

6. Place Importance on Communication with the Psyche and Establishing the Setting for Intimate Dialogue

My take on the ideal moral education is that it should place importance on communication with the psyche and establish a setting for these intimate dialogues to occur, allowing mental health education and counseling activities to take root in education in schools.

Moral education is different from intellectual education. For example, if we were to oppose the implementation of monodirectional knowledge transference, then moral education would be even more incapable of implementing monodirectional teaching. The progress of moral education is quiet and unobtrusive, carried out through the mental and spiritual communication between teacher and student from positions of equal footing. Feng Enhong, a teacher of distinction from Shanghai, raised the issue of "traces of watered down education" in moral educational theory as early as the 1980s. He believes that the past process of moral education had roles that were too clearly defined: teachers were the educators and students were the ones to be educated. In reality, teachers may know more than students in terms of knowledge, but teachers and students should be equal in issues of morality. Some students' moral character and conduct may even surpass that of their teachers.

Students are most dissatisfied with teachers who use two particular ways of speaking to them in the classroom and administrative office. They are most dissatisfied with teachers who use arguments that even they themselves do not believe to "put students in their place." Students also do not take kindly to teachers who are overbearing and consider themselves to be advisors. They will use their own eyes to observe and their own minds to think; they welcome interactions that are unrelated to education, conversations that are free of psychological barriers, and atmospheres that are conducive to heart-to-heart conversations. In short, they wish for teachers to become their intermediaries between school and society; someone who can guide them, whom they can discuss things with, who they can call upon and become their own friend. They do not wish for teachers to put distance between themselves and others, give out orders arbitrarily, act as lecturers and overseers, and become the students' own "teachers." During the process of moral education, teachers must have communications and conduct educational investigations with students on an equal footing to cultivate moral character together through educational activities.

Moral education in particular needs a relaxing, tolerant, and comforting environment, one that is not too overly critical about students' occasional mistakes and mishaps, as even teachers will occasionally deviate from words and deeds that are moral. Students especially need their teachers' encouragement and praise during the process of forming good moral conduct. The power of encouragement and praise greatly outweighs that of criticism and punishment. By receiving their teachers' praise and commendations, students will self-consciously develop their strengths to limitless heights, demonstrate great self-confidence, and spur themselves on to be even better as some unsavory elements of their moral conduct unconsciously disappear.

However, in real educational activities, many teachers of moral education often assume the role of "the police officer," their most commonly used weapon being class meetings that are "public criticisms of another's mistakes," openly criticizing a student's unbecoming conduct or a certain tendency. These teachers take a student's flaws and greatly magnify them, yet rarely do they discover and unearth a student's merits, which would incite an internal strength to improve within these students' inner selves. Students who are frequently subjected to their teachers' criticisms and punishments will most likely only be able to see their own flaws and unable to find their own merits. Such students will develop the thinking of "in for a penny, in for a pound," giving up their inherent good qualities and instead constantly existing in a negative state of precaution.

American educational psychologists Cage and Berliner point out in *The Psychology of Instruction* that "for teachers, praise is the easiest-to-use, most natural and most effective way of creating motivation. The most important thing is for the praise accompanying certain behavior to increase along with the frequency with which such behavior occurs." They also state: "at times, teachers forget how important their comments regarding students are. We have seen teachers who have never spoken a positive word to students. This sort of behavior is unforgivable!" Is this not the best advice for those teachers who only play the role of the police officer?

In addition, strengthening moral education also requires fully placing importance on students' mental health education. In the past, we often confused students' behavioral problems with psychological problems. The two admittedly are closely related to one another, but when all is said and done, they are still different. Many mistakes that people make throughout their lives are viewed as problems of moral character when in fact they are psychological issues. For example, if a student takes someone else's things, it has always been seen as a problem related to moral behavior, but according to research, many such cases are actually problems related to mental health. This is because although many students are not lacking in possessions, through taking someone else's things they are able to gain a sense of satisfaction. If we were to take these mistakes made due to psychological problems and expose them to the public, moving to treat them as corruptions of moral character, it would instead severely lower students' self-esteem and hinder the normal development of their character. Teachers must accurately analyze the causes of a student's problems from perspectives such as the student's psychological state and the student's actions. This then raises a new requirement of our education system: to universally implement mental health education.

In an article issued by the Ministry of Education, "Comments on the Consolidation of Health Education for College Students," every education department and every tertiary education institution must take the work of reinforcing the mental health education of university students as further strengthening and improving the work of tertiary mental health education and put in place important measures to comprehensively carry forth quality education. Through mental health education for university students, we can help them establish an awareness of their mental health, optimizing their mental strength and increasing their ability to mentally adjust and socially adapt to lifestyle changes while preventing and alleviating mental health problems. We can also help them deal with problematic issues such as adapting to their environment; self-management; studying; interacting with other people; friendships and relationships; employment and career choices; character development and regulating their emotions. Through the undertaking of mental health education, its relevance, applicability in the real world, and the level of initiative of tertiary moral education are increased, making the management system of moral education in schools robust. This sufficiently shows that our country has already begun valuing the use of mental health education as a means of developing students' moral character. Mental health education should be strengthened not only in universities but also in high schools and primary schools.

7. Teach Students to Teach Themselves

My take on the ideal moral education is that it should teach students self-education methods such as how to self-monitor and how to be self-disciplined and self-motivated, allowing students to form the autonomous habit of "learning without being taught" through the process of cultivating their character and sharpening their will.

When all is said and done, cultivation of a student's moral character is dependent upon what the students themselves have self-learned. Sukhomlinsky once said, "real education is self-education." This is certainly the case. In my opinion, "learning without being taught" is the pinnacle stage of education and is attained through the students teaching themselves. This notion contains two key concepts.

The first is that moral education has to place importance on cultivating a student's good conduct and habits, as "habit becomes nature" for many things.

Ye Shengtao once said that education is the cultivation of habits, teaching is the nurturing of students to develop the habit of seeking knowledge, and moral education is the nurturing of students to develop the habit of striving toward improvement. Teachers need to constantly encourage students and reinforce the effects of striving toward improvement during the process, allowing students' tendencies toward improvement to constantly be shaped into distinctive moral qualities. Having students engage in "moral long-distance running" is another important means of cultivating students' virtuous moral conduct. It is not difficult for one to commit a few good deeds; what is difficult is for one to commit a lifetime of good deeds and to never commit any evil ones. In order to accomplish this, students will have to constantly police and advise themselves, and this requires teachers to help students cultivate a type of self-learning habit so that they can constantly remind themselves on how to conduct themselves. Many people write their own motto upon their walls at home or on top of a desk, and people in ancient times engraved their own motto on jade pendants they wore on their chests, reminding themselves at any given time how one should conduct oneself; all are methods of self-education. In addition, keeping a journal is also a very effective means of "moral long-distance running." It is not only a form of literary study but also an important means of morally educating oneself. Through the use of a journal, one can continuously reflect on one's conduct and deeds and also make oneself attain new insights.

Students cannot forever be on the receiving end of a teacher's teachings and guidance, and eventually they will have to grow up and leave their teachers. Therefore, genuine moral education should achieve the effect of "learning without being taught" and, as much as possible, allow students to live independently, to constantly reflect on their own words and actions, and to continually improve themselves.

8. Establish a Moral Education Network with the Family, School, and Society

My take on the ideal moral education is that it should form the general consensus of "conducting oneself with integrity foremost" in all aspects of society, establishing a cooperative moral education network that consists of the three sectors: family, school, and society, allowing the strength of each sector to form a superior kind of moral education whose power can influence and cross space and time.

As early as the 1980s, Japanese prime minister Yasuhiro Nakasone criticized Japanese education's tendency toward being "abundant in knowledge but lacking in morals." Up till now, our educational activities are still shrouded by the shadow of "intellectualism," and the phenomenon of "a beautiful appearance covers up many defects" is still widespread. Families, schools, and society are concerned with students' academic performance, with "results, results and more results being the students' lifeblood; exams, exams and more exams being the teachers' magical wand." The school awards the title of "hero" to those who have achieved top academic results and frequently has little regard for the development of the students' personalities and cultivation of their moral character. For many, the teachings at home are even the antithesis of moral education. For example, when teaching their own children, some parents, with their decades of experience, warn their children not to trust other people or help people so readily. Such teachings have a negative impact on the cultivation of virtuous moral conduct in students. The effects of a few years of being taught moral education at schools can possibly be destroyed in an instant by a few words from their parents.

We should really rethink the role of social factors in students' moral education. At present, allowing students to go and find a games center or Internet cafe is very easy, but it is still quite difficult to find a place that would honestly allow teachers and parents not to worry. In the past, numerous Homes for Young People were the important bases of operation for moral education, but many now have become gaming and entertainment venues. On the eve of the war of resistance, patriotic students cried out in alarm: "Although China is as large as it is, there is no longer anywhere for us to place a desk down"; at present, although China is as large as it is, it is surprisingly very difficult to find a venue that is beneficial to students and not worrisome to teachers and parents.

Furthermore, the role of social media in promoting, inculcating, and influencing students' development of moral character has also not been fully utilized. Our media today are mostly filled with content such as pornography and violence in order to attract viewers or readers and raise their revenues, are lacking in proper guidance, and have produced many negative effects. The *China Youth Daily* in the 1980s reported on crimes committed by three 19-year-old offenders whose modus operandi was a combination of those found in *The Adventures of Sherlock Holmes* and *Garrison's Gorillas*. When a reporter asked these three students if their school had an after-school activity for students to review a few novels, television series, or movies, one of the offenders, Han Xu, replied that the school did not care about these things at all and at the senior high level only cared about studies; no one cared at all about what the students were thinking. Upon graduating from senior high, Han Xu was confused about many issues such as life and ideals, but there was hardly anyone who gave him proper help in terms of his thinking. Han Xu's father is an engineer, and in his letters to his son who was studying at university he often wrote: "Having accumulated 30 years of experiences, I advise you, do not speak the truth to others so readily." Was it not the combined negative factors of mass media, influences from school, and teachings at home that resulted in these three youths descending down the path of crime?

Therefore, to improve the effects of moral education, we must establish a cooperative moral education network that consists of the three sectors: family, school, and society, allowing the strength of each sector to form a superior kind of moral education whose power can influence and cross space and time. The family home is the first place where people receive any form of moral education. Moral education must start from a child's infancy and, when children are able to comprehend, begin with teaching them moral principles in layman's terms, guiding them skillfully, patiently, and sensibly, depending on their context. Parents must influence their children through their own virtuous words, deeds, and bearing. Schools must increase their correspondence with parents and help raise their educational level, forming good atmospheres conducive to teaching moral education at home. Schools should also pay attention to the content and direction of information circulating through society and resist and remove adverse effects of some information. They will need to make choices and adjustments to the various social environmental influences and strive to create a favorable social atmosphere, allowing those being educated to advance in the direction that society hopes they will develop.

"Two things fill the mind with ever-increasing wonder and awe, the more often and the more intensely the mind of thought is drawn to them: the starry heavens above me and the moral law within me" (Immanuel Kant). The refinement of morals is the vehicle for the constant evolution of civilization; properly undertaking students' moral education is every educator's sacred mission and also the shared responsibility of all society.

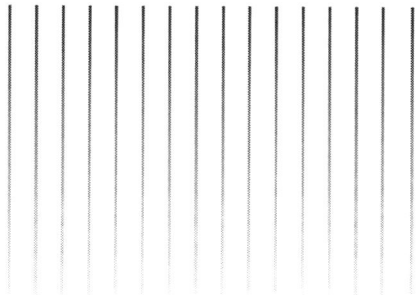

2

My Take on Intellectual Education

In the Chinese education sector, intellectual education has rarely received such a high level of regard. "Focus on Teaching" has become a resounding slogan for all primary and high schools; results of junior high and university entrance exams have simultaneously become the lifeblood of teachers and schools. Finding the means to fund a child's education has become a willing investment for all parents, even if it means plunging themselves into financial despair. Coaching classes and private tutors in all subjects have become the industry with the biggest marketing potential, with all types of reference books, exercises, and accompanying teaching materials becoming top sellers. Some have theorized this rise of intense competition for school advancement examinations as "examination results are the absolute truth!"

In Chinese society, intellectual education has rarely been met with such intense dissatisfaction as it has now. Because of the rise of "intellectual education," other school subjects have become merely window dressing, and students' holistic education has become no more than empty words. Due to "intellectual education" students have become study and examination machines. Although their minds are full of knowledge and all sorts of abilities due to "intellectual education," such knowledge and abilities amount to naught. Studying has become the only activity in a student's life, with examination results becoming a student's only honor or disgrace. Due to "intellectual education," students' bodies and minds suffer severe damage; their personalities are subjected to distortion, with the occurrence of tragedies such as suicide or even occasional patricide and matricide. This type of distorted intellectual education is summed up as "exam-oriented education."

On one hand, intellectual education has received unprecedented attention, but on the other hand, it has been subjected to fierce verbal assaults. This phenomenon appears to be full of contradictions, but it clearly, unmistakably conveys to each and every educator: intellectual education must be reformed!

Therefore I present to you my take on intellectual education.

1. Surpass Knowledge, Advance Toward Wisdom, and Stimulate Creativity

My take on the ideal intellectual education is that it should surpass knowledge, advance toward wisdom, and stimulate innovation. It should strengthen character and lay down a solid foundation of knowledge and skills so that students can enjoy a lifetime of spiritual, cultural, and intellectual happiness in the future.

Within the entire educational sector, intellectual education undoubtedly holds an extremely important place. However, what are the objectives of intellectual education? Countless educators believe that the transfer of knowledge encompasses all aspects of intellectual education or at least is its main objective. This understanding is clearly one-sided, and it is due in part to this one-sided understanding that distorted types of intellectual education based on theories regarding the emphasis on and pursuit of "knowledge" and "marks" have been allowed to inundate the educational sector. Intellectual education naturally cannot separate itself from the transfer of knowledge, but the transfer of knowledge is not the real objective of intellectual education.

The acclaimed scientist Einstein once spoke these thought-provoking words at the 300-year anniversary celebration of higher education in America: "Education is what remains after one has forgotten what one has learned in school." In UNESCO's publication "Learning: The Treasure Within," when "learning for the sake of knowing" is mentioned, the text indicates: "This type of learning is more concerned with the methods of mastering knowledge as opposed to acquiring cataloged systematic knowledge. It can be viewed as both a way to live and as a motive for living. As a way to live, it should allow all to learn to understand the world around them; at the very least it allows them to live with dignity, to be able to develop their own professional competence and be able to socialize with others. As a motive for living, the foundations lie in a willingness to understand, to know and to realize."

In traditional agrarian and industrial societies, knowledge was mostly related to knowledge gained through "experience." Therefore at that time the main aim, or even the only aim of intellectual education, was the transfer of knowledge, to allow the knowledge gained from the experiences of one generation to be passed down to the next. However, in the information era of today with its relentless development of science and technology, the probability of students directly applying the majority of the knowledge they learn at school in the future is very low. Although there remains some knowledge that is "useful" to students, generally speaking, the main motive for students' learning is no longer for the sake of practical future application but rather the process of learning itself—through the act of learning, one can become an intelligent and civilized person who lives a dignified life.

In terms of the current situation of Chinese education, the main motive for students to learn is for the sake of passing school examinations. As these exams are a prerequisite for students to advance in their schooling, this motive originally gave no cause for criticism, but the problem is that at present the intellectual education offered at many junior high schools is completely tailored to meet the demands of these scant few days' worth of examinations. This type of intellectual education improves students' ability to undertake examinations but at the same time it deprives students of their right to an education that develops their minds. Even if they pass the school examinations, a large number of students that have been brought up with this type of intellectual education have lost the chance to further develop their latent potential and abilities. Having the passing of examinations as a motive for living, using entrance into university as the end goal as opposed to the genuine starting point, is a major feature of education in China, and it is also the reason why many people prefer to read *Harvard Girl Liu Yiting*. Without a doubt this is a type of intellectual education that focuses on "quick success and short term benefits." This type of intellectual education is harmful to children and brutal to their development; in terms of the progress of a country, its impact is frightening.

English philosopher and mathematician Alfred North Whitehead was quoted once as saying: "Before you have lost your textbooks, incinerated your lecture notes, forgotten all the tiny details that you have painstakingly memorized for the sake of passing an exam, remember that your studying is useless." This means that ideal intellectual education transforms knowledge into wisdom, and it is only under the guidance of wisdom that we can possibly partake in genuine intellectual activity.

Generally speaking, knowledge focuses on ready-made answers, formulas, and summaries of historical events. Wisdom focuses on the unknown world and is the process of pursuing knowledge. Therefore, we must update our concept of intellectual education.

What needs to be made clear is that knowledge is simply the means of acquiring intellectual education. The learning of knowledge is admittedly important to students, but what is even more important is the ability to acquire knowledge that students gain through the acquiring of knowledge. The teacher's transfer of knowledge is for the purpose of providing students with intellectually stimulating exercises. The aim of these exercises is to allow children to develop their ability to think, imagine, and create. Through intellectual education, students' good study habits and ability to self-study are nurtured. Intellectual education also equips students with long-term interests, deep affections, and resilience for learning in order to establish a solid foundation built on intelligence and ability for their future learning paths.

In *The Education Reference Manual* (2001, vol. 4), a guest contributor submitted the following words: "Education is all about mankind's spiritual education, and has nothing to do with the accumulation of rational knowledge and understanding. Educational activities are concerned with how best to awaken and help realize a person's latent capabilities and bring forth a person's internal intellect and potential." These words are the best interpretation of the purpose of intellectual education.

It is only through understanding the position of intellectual education and its role in the development of students that our intellectual education is truly able to become the ideal intellectual education.

2. Embody the Philosophy of "Students as the Main Focus"

My take on the ideal intellectual education is that it should be brimming with the spirit of democracy, be truly "people-oriented," and embody the philosophy of "students as the main focus" in the entire teaching process.

In traditional intellectual education, teachers were the embodiment of truth and knowledge, omnipotent sages whose mission was to fill the empty minds of their students with knowledge. Therefore, the concept of "a tutor for a day is a father for a lifetime" was expected, and teaching methods such as "force-feeding" and "chalk plus talk" were a natural consequence of this. Thus, as a matter of course, teachers replaced their students' thinking with their own and students took their teachers' ideas and used them as their own.

My take on the ideal intellectual education will first have to reexamine the relationship between teachers and students and establish a democratic teacher-student relationship.

In regard to the teacher-student relationship, Sukhomlinsky believed that teachers and students should be like-minded peers who work together to seek out the truth; this therefore places teacher-student interactions on an equal footing that must be implemented during the course of teaching. On this, he particularly stresses: "Firstly, learning is not just the transferal of knowledge from teacher to student, but rather the living relationship between teachers and children."[1]

Additionally, in the past people often said, "To give a student a bowl of water, teachers must first have a bucket of water." This saying stresses the importance of teachers' continuous improvement of their own character's view toward education, and from this idea's perspective it is, without a doubt, correct. However, in view of the present situation, this phrase does have its limitations. First, in this information age it is not possible for teachers to possess knowledge in all areas that surpasses that of students. At times, students may have attained knowledge that far surpasses that of their teachers in a particular area. Second, the students' minds are not empty receptacles but rather deep wells containing abundant reserves of water. A teacher's mission is precisely that of guiding students to excavate these wells and to have each student become a "well" that gushes with the water of knowledge. It is only through the establishment of these views on students and teachers that our intellectual education can truly become one that has "students as the main focus." Classroom teaching that is brimming with the spirit of democracy should transform the process of a teacher's "teaching" into the process of a student's "learning." In the past, when preparing our lessons, some of us teachers would often spend a considerable amount of time working out how we were to teach this lesson and would rarely place ourselves in the position of the students and think: if I were a student, what problems might I encounter? Similarly, when these teachers are teaching, they mainly "guide" students by following their own thoughts on teaching, often cleverly drawing students into their own teaching designs in accordance with their own teaching wants and ignoring the learning processes whereby students are to study, understand, and experience for themselves. This is the so-called replacement of "learning" with "teaching." Or perhaps this can be called a "teaching performance" based on a previously prepared "script." With this kind of teaching, what we consider more is how to "teach," but even if the teachers' thoughts on teaching are extremely clear and the way they convey themselves in the classroom easy to understand, this is also only a replacement of students' thinking with that of the teachers' thinking.

At present, we should be pondering more about how students learn; that is, making the students' learning needs our main focus and pursuing the engagement of teachers and students in collaborative investigations of knowledge and teacher-student dialogues on equal footing. During the process of this kind of teaching, teachers strive to link two different "trails": the students' learning (undertaking experiences, questioning, studying, taking part in discussions, making connections, and so on) and a teacher's "teaching" (challenging claims, exchanging opinions, debating ideas, dispelling doubts, and summarizing information). These two trails are woven together through the teachers' training of students' thinking, their experiencing of emotions, and the influences on their personalities. Here, the crucial point is still the repositioning of the role of the teacher. Using the words of Learning: The Treasure Within, teachers must "adapt their relationship with learners, switching roles from 'soloist' to 'accompanist,' and shifting the emphasis from dispensing information to helping learners seek, organize and manage knowledge, guiding them rather than molding them."

Presently, more and more teachers advocate teaching students how to acquire knowledge; this is of course the right course of action. However, my so-called teaching for others still cannot be a hollow and isolated form of "imparting one's knowledge" but allows students to learn to study through studying, learn to research through researching, and learn to create through creating. Currently, project learning, which is popular both domestically and abroad, is worth promoting. During the process of project learning, students transform their original prescribed way of learning, which placed a strong emphasis on memorization and understanding and was based upon the passive acceptance of knowledge transferal from teachers, into a type of active learning that actively seeks knowledge and values realistic problem solving. This method is conducive to lifelong learning and the development of learning. During this learning process, students naturally grasp and utilize several methods of learning and researching. This method not only transforms the knowledge-transferal approach into a hands-on training approach; it also truly takes the concept of "students as the main focus" and makes it a reality.

Starting in September 2000, Taicang County Senior High School in Jiangsu Province began offering courses that use project learning and in less than a year had already achieved a modicum of success. Not only have the courses raised teaching efficiency, but they have also made teachers and students more resilient. After implementing project learning, teachers have come to appreciate a whole new realm of teaching; some teachers have stated: "I feel like I have gone back to the days of my childhood; there's a sense of freshness that I haven't felt in a long time"; other teachers have said: "I now truly understand the real meaning of the slogan 'unity is strength'; I feel the charm that is created from closely associating oneself with scholars and the positive cooperation"; other teachers yet again have felt the "joy of growing up together with the students." As for the students, generally they agree that project learning has made the learning process no longer dull and boring but has greatly aroused the students' sense of curiosity and urge to investigate, allowing them to truly become masters of learning.

3. Respect Individuality, Teach in Line with Students' Abilities, and Allow Students to Relish Learning

My take on the ideal intellectual education is that it should face individuality head on and unearth hidden potential. It should truly be able to "teach in line with the students' abilities" and allow students to happily learn. It should also allow every student to experience success in learning and relish the joy of learning.

Within the best-selling book *The Learning Revolution*, which has caused quite a stir, there are admittedly many "myths" related to education, but there are still some ideas that hit the mark. Authors Gordon Dryden and Jeannette Vos wrote in their book: "The best system in the world is one that leads to success." They also wrote: "The majority of the education systems today lead to failure. They do not plan to lead every person to failure, but they have led a large percentage of students towards failure, in some cases up to 50% of students."

In a separately conducted survey, a Chinese middle school teacher more or less "verified" the claims of these two scholars. In September 2000, at a certain middle school, a form master conducted a survey with newly enrolled first-year senior high students regarding their attitudes toward learning. The results were: 46 percent of students were not interested in learning, 33 percent expressed an obvious dislike for learning, and a mere 21 percent genuinely had a positive attitude toward learning. When a few students explained the reason why they disliked learning, they frequently offered reasons such as "low grades," "studying is tiring," and "I've never done well in a test before." In short, the experiences of failure that students have had throughout their careers as school students has already completely destroyed their self-confidence toward learning. At the same time they are being struck down by "marks," they have already mentally struck themselves down in their own minds.

In actual fact, even if we were to ignore the results of this survey, pretty much all of us teachers have felt, at some point in our teaching, the indifferent attitude toward learning that countless students possess. It should be acknowledged that traditional intellectual education unduly emphasized the use of selection; therefore this form of education necessitated repeatedly examining students and eliminating most of the "weaker students" in order to create a handful of "university entrance examination champions" and "Olympic champions." Therefore, at the same time they were creating a handful of success stories, they were also creating a large number of failures, with the majority of students feeling mentally inferior and becoming "emotional dwarfs" whose personalities atrophied. This honestly goes against the inclusivity and universality of fundamental education. Even Confucius advocated that "instruction knows no class distinction." I am definitely not against teachers nurturing students who academically excel above others; I am merely opposed to education's gaze being fixed on only a handful of elites and the strange phenomenon of the student majority "accompanying" the studies of the elite minority. I believe that an intellectual education that embodies the principles of democracy, equality, and equity should allow every student to enjoy the sense of accomplishment in learning.

Where does a student's sense of accomplishment in learning come from? From the teachers' teaching in line with students' abilities. "Education must face individuality" is not an empty phrase; it should point us toward every student that we face on a daily basis. Sukhomlinsky had a famous saying: "Let every child lift up their head!" He further elaborated on this by writing:

> People's talents, possibilities, capabilities and preferences are indeed limitless and every person's manifestations in these areas are unique . . . the wisdom and genuine humanity of communist education lies within: discovering the source of every person's (every single person without exception) creative labors that are unique to every person; to assist each person to be able to view themselves, to see, comprehend and detect the spark of humanity's pride that lies within them, thus transforming them into mentally strong individuals, individual soldiers that will safeguard their own dignity.

Tragedies in education are often created when a single standard is required of all students, but it is only through focusing on each student's application of what he has learned in education and allowing each student to be able to continuously develop her foundation that education and also students are able to attain true success.

Teaching in line with students' abilities is particularly of great significance to "underachievers." Some teachers believe that the reason why underachievers are poor at learning is because of bad behavior and habits. This understanding is certainly correct, but not comprehensive enough. During the "Eighth Five-Year

Plan" period, I was in charge of the issue of underachievers' mentality and education. After surveying close to 10,000 students and interviewing some exceptional teachers, I discovered that a considerable portion of weak students' poor conduct and bad habits actually resulted from poor academic performance. Try putting yourself in these students' shoes—when faced with the knowledge taught to them during the teachers' lectures, they do not comprehend a single word; when faced with homework prescribed to them by their teachers, they are completely helpless; and every time they sit for an exam, they fail. Are these students able to gain an interest in studying? Are they able to be full of self-confidence? Since they are unable to experience success in learning and have fun, they will inevitably hate learning. Therefore, if we want to transform the underachiever, besides reinforcing the thorough and meticulous ideological education and implementing scientific and intensive training in standards of conduct, we should also assist weak students to attain a sense of success in learning, thus establishing a kind of healthy and stable mental pursuit. As long as our teachers truly face every specific student and teach according to their abilities and allow every student to feel the joys of seeking out knowledge, thinking, and creativity, then every student can become a success in learning.

In this regard, Shanghai's Zhabei Eighth Middle School's "success education" is an excellent model. The school principal, Liu Jinghai, explained "success education" in simple terms by saying, "We use success to motivate students to attain even more, even greater success." He believes that children are naturally partial to success, and repeatedly having success can raise one's motivation to achieve. Success is also the "mother" of success, and the essence of the education and teaching process is the pursuit of success. Success is a means, but it is more an objective than it is a means. Under the guidance of this idea, Zhabei Eighth Middle School formed three classroom teaching methods that were suitable to the realities facing the school: "assisting success (with 'low,' 'small,' 'many,' and 'fast' being its basic features); attempting to attain success (having students attempt to explore and investigate through organizing problem-solving situations); and autonomous success." All three of these methods achieved positive results.

4. Focus on the Holistic Development of Students

My take on the ideal intellectual education is that it should focus on coordinated harmonization, integrating morality, intelligence, physical fitness, aesthetic sense, and technical skills into a single entity. It should set its eyes on the students' holistic development and focus on cultivating personalities that are "qualified" and "have special skills."

Intellectual education is, without a doubt, extremely important, but any type of effective education, including intellectual education, cannot be isolated. A school's moral education, intellectual education, physical education, aesthetic education, and technical education are all organically interconnected and closely related to one another. For example, it goes without saying that a student's main obligation is to learn and a school's central task is the overall improvement of the quality of education. However, intellectual education is not simply the imparting of knowledge to others, and during the intellectual education process, there are factors such as moral education, aesthetic education, physical education, and technical education that relate to teaching students the proper outlook on life, portraying the pursuit of one's true beliefs, nurturing an appreciation for aesthetics, cultivating the strength of perseverance, and putting into practice training that targets their abilities. By the same token, apart from the classroom lessons on intellectual education, the school's moral education, physical education, aesthetic education, and technical education are all capable of permeating the element of intellectual education. Successful education in these same areas is completely brimming with the elements of knowledge and, in addition, embodies the spirit of science.

Even with regard to the transfer of knowledge, this method should automatically accompany the nurturing of abilities. Knowledge is of course the foundation of ability. Since ancient times, all great scientists, educators, politicians, and academics have been people who seemed to be "encyclopedic," but knowledge itself does not equate to ability. At present, there are some teachers who possess a certain misunderstanding: they believe that ability is the use of knowledge, meaning that for students the use of knowledge is something to consider in the future and at present it would be best to concentrate on laying out good knowledge foundations. This sort of thinking is most definitely one-sided.

It should instead be said that since primary and middle school is the stage when a child's knowledge foundations are established, it is also the stage when the foundations in their abilities take shape. From 1986 to 1989, America promoted a four-year study undertaken by its science promotion associations; when the research was completed, a report titled *Science for All Americans—Project 2061* was published. The researchers on this project believed that the urgent problem facing American education is how to popularize the laying out of the foundations of scientific knowledge while improving students' skills in various other areas. The project emphasizes that at the same time as imparting knowledge to students, we should also pay attention to these skills: the ability to call something into question; the ability to put something into practice; the ability to gather, organize, and use evidence; the ability to clearly express one's thinking; the ability to communicate with and cooperate with others; the ability to conduct scientific research; and the ability to innovate.

If America, the world leader in science and technology, has these sorts of reservations regarding the nurturing of abilities through education, then every one of us, every Chinese educator, should be even more inclined to feel a sense of crisis. Chinese intellectual education can no longer produce "bookworms" who are good at scoring on exams but poor at putting theories into practice!

Our intellectual education needs to properly address the relationship between "lightening one's load" and "adding to one's load." Quality education focuses on lightening the students' overwhelming workload, undoubtedly the correct course of action. However, the so-called lightening of the load is definitely not just lessening prescribed homework and cutting back on lesson hours. In actual fact, the essence should be to allow students to change from passive learning to active learning, to lessen the ineffective tasks of teachers and students in education, and to increase the students' development objectives. Specifically speaking, at the same time as lightening students' overwhelming school workload we should be increasing students' mental training "load."

For a long time, there existed the phenomenon of "three weighty burdens and one light burden" in students' learning conditions: students had weighty psychological burdens, stress on their memory recall was taxing, and homework workload was heavy, but the mental training load during the learning process was too light. This is just as Einstein claimed in his declaration written at the request of the *New York Times*: "It is also vital to a valuable education that independent critical thinking be developed in the young human being, a development that is greatly jeopardized by overburdening him with too much and with too varied subjects. Overburdening necessarily leads to superficiality."

Therefore, after lightening their load, we should turn training in exam skills into fostering of the ability to learn; the important point is to change the three weighty burdens and one light burden into three light burdens and one weighty burden.

Furthermore, while lightening the students' school workload we should add to the students' workload in terms of fostering their abilities. In the above section we have already mentioned the importance of fostering students' abilities. Reforming intellectual education necessitates enabling students to take the initiative in their learning and to learn in a relaxed manner, so they will have more time and energy to expand their horizons in various other fields and develop their own abilities. This requires teachers to simultaneously raise the level of students' learning efficiency and increase the cultivation of the students' other talents, especially in terms of their ability to innovate and put things into social practice.

It should be noted that at the same time we are emphasizing students' coordinated harmonization and holistic development, we must not "raise the banner of holistic development, but carry out the terrible deeds that do quite the opposite." In terms of the development of the students' latent potential, every student is a unique individual with the possibility of developing spectacularly and attaining remarkable results in a particular aspect. However, under the education system of "unification," with unified objectives, syllabus, curriculum, and assessments, many students have undoubtedly had their zest for life, passion for innovation, and open expression of their individuality stifled, causing them to become "carbon copies" of one another, "clones" without any sense of individuality.

Therefore, I very much admire the educational philosophy "to be qualified and have special skills" as proposed by Shanghai's Jianping Junior High School's principal, Feng Enhong. I believe that the true meaning of education is to help people become their own person, to realize the value of their own lives, and to bring out their own unique qualities and develop them to their fullest, thus making their own unique contribution to this nation and humankind.

5. Cultivate Students' Scientific Spirit and Human Feelings

My take on the ideal intellectual education is that it should move teaching activities away from the misconception of focusing on marks and cultivate students' scientific spirit and human feelings, allowing them to become the torchbearers for the "flame" that lights human civilization.

To this very day, there are some teachers who believe that intellectual education should focus on students' test scores and that test scores are the only standard for measuring the level of one's intellectual education. This perception is incorrect. It is true that intellectual education must pursue high standards including ideal test scores; however, the achievements of intellectual education lie not only in test scores but in students' development—in their way of thinking, their wisdom, their thirst for knowledge, their creativity, and so forth. Therefore, Deng Xiaoping equally applied the view of "development is the absolute principle" in regard to intellectual education.

Renowned scholar Xu Weicheng wrote in the preface of Li Zhenxi's *Love and Education*:

> [Educators] must first recognize the objective of their own educational activities—it is not the stacks of report cards, the pile of test scores or the enrollment notices from more advanced schools but rather real living people, talented people that will have the ability to stand on their own feet in future societies, talented people that will start up their own businesses and careers. These sorts of talented people must not only study at school and through studying gain a solid grasp on knowledge, but will more importantly need to have a life-long interest in studying, a desire to seek knowledge and furthermore, be able to self-study, to find the knowledge they require and to absorb this knowledge.

Singapore's primary and middle schools' educational foundations are solid. Students have repeatedly gained top marks in international subject tests. In 1996, the Third International Mathematics and Science Study tested approximately 500,000 students from 41 different countries and regions, the largest subject test that has ever been held. Results showed that Singaporean students ranked first in both mathematics and natural sciences, with average test scores of 643 points and 607 points respectively, well ahead of second-place holders South Korea and the Czech Republic. Most of the students from developed countries such as the United Kingdom and the United States attained scores that ranked lower than the top 20. At the time when the public in Singapore were widely promoting their students' success in attaining top scores, the Singaporean government was not so complacent, clearly recognizing that the top scores attained by its students in an international subject test were a double-edged sword. If the students' top scores cannot be reflected in improvements in student innovativeness and, on the contrary, become an obstacle to their creativity, then these sorts of top scores are harmful to students. Singapore's Deputy Prime Minister Lee Hsien Loong specially gave a speech saying that educators needed to reexamine the way in which they assess students. He believes that merely using test scores as a means of measuring a student's academic performance and as a criterion for the quality of national education is a one-sided way of thinking. Singapore's current teaching methods suit the demands of examinations, but what is missing, exactly, is the encouragement and fostering of independence and creativity. Lee Hsien Loong's speech injected a shot of lucidity into the Singaporean educational world, driving them to shift their thinking and focus from high marks to creativity.

Misteaching in China's current intellectual education is quite similar. Our country's middle school students gain gold medals almost every time they participate in the International Mathematical Olympiad. However, ever since 1949 no scholar from China has won the Nobel Prize until 2012, when Mo Yan received the prize in Literature. This is very much connected to our foundations in education being purely the pursuit of high test scores. Even now, some local administrative education departments still use school test scores as the main criterion of assessment, creating elaborate rankings based on test scores. I believe that our intellectual education should move the main focus of our pursuits from attaining high scores to attaining creativity. We must allow our advanced students to continuously consolidate their grasp on subject knowledge and furthermore be capable in all areas, especially in terms of their creativity and international competitiveness. The educator A. Mona Arsenishvili from the former Soviet Union believes: "Scores themselves cannot illustrate a child's specific academic performance. . . . Children do not need scores because they will only inhibit their thirst for knowledge and their happy and carefree lives at school." This educator does not give parents school reports at the end of every semester but instead gives them a paper bag. Inside this paper bag are examples of the students' intellectual and physical classwork: their calligraphy, the stories they have compiled, selected pieces of their completed homework in every subject, their drawings and paintings, the research information they have collected and organized, and their written compositions as well as Principal Arsenishvili's signed evaluation. This evaluation does not contain even one empty word or clichéd phrase; instead it is full of analyses of the students' intellectual ability and words of enthusiastic encouragement for the students. Without a doubt, compared with a few abstract scores, this paper bag truly and comprehensively reflects the students' learning situation, their learning achievements as well as their intellectual ability and the development of their capabilities. I fervently hope that we in China can also use this kind of method of assessing intellectual education, which is truly scientific and comprehensive and full of human feelings.

Intellectual education that merely reflects test scores is undoubtedly shortsighted and has forgotten the real mission of education. For students, their main task is to study; however, apart from their textbooks, students nowadays seldom read any other books. Students who achieve good academic results spend their days caught up pondering over numerous problems and issues and have no time to spare to peruse any other books. For students who do not achieve good academic results, the learning workload given to them by teachers and parents is even heavier—makeup classes and additional homework—meaning that they have even less time to read books outside of the school-prescribed texts and textbooks. The *Wenhui* Book Review once published a survey regarding the junior high students' extracurricular reading situation; the results showed that the number of junior high students who partake in extracurricular reading is pitifully low. The greatest irony is that a considerable number of junior high students know the names of renowned authors and literary works, both of Chinese origins and otherwise, like the back of their hand, and yet know absolutely nothing about the actual contents of these literary pieces!

Some educators may believe that extracurricular reading is a supplemental task for students, but I believe that a copious amount of reading falls squarely within the scope of our intellectual education's duties. This is because extensive reading not only plays the role of expanding university students' horizons but, more importantly, it can directly boost the students' learning in class.

Sukhomlinsky believed that for students to master deep and solid knowledge, we must allow learning to have a reinforced "major back-up"; in other words, we need to construct knowledge upon a vast "backdrop of intellectual ability." Sukhomlinsky was very adept at combining teaching materials used in the classroom with the students' extracurricular reading, thus causing both aspects to mutually boost the students' learning and raise their interest level in both aspects. He says, "For students who read a lot, any new concepts learned in the classroom can be incorporated into the knowledge system that they have absorbed from the various books that they have read. During this period, the scientific knowledge taught in class is particularly appealing to these students, and students will feel that this type of knowledge is something that they cannot lack as it will assist them in clarifying the knowledge that already resides within their minds." In order to do this, Sukhomlinsky clearly defined students' extracurricular reading and also had this definition classified as the Second Teaching Program. Particularly worth mentioning is that in terms of improving the academic results of underachievers, Sukhomlinsky's Second Teaching Program has played an incredible role. He says that:

> [Thirty] years of teaching has led me to believe that for these sorts of students, it is precisely the aforementioned Second Teaching Programme which can be of particularly important use to them. To these children, having learning limited to merely the memorization and recitation of school-prescribed teaching materials is particularly harmful, as this method will cause them to develop rote-learning habits, and cause them to become even more slow-witted. I have previously attempted several strategies to try to lessen the mental strain placed on these students with results that have led me to arrive at one conclusion: the most effective strategy is to expand the scope of their reading.

It is due to this reasoning that Sukhomlinsky regarded the establishment of libraries and promotion of reading as the essence of school education.

Therefore, I once again appeal to our teachers to set aside more time for children to read. Through guiding students' reading, teachers are able to open up windows into literature, civilization, and culture for them and ultimately allow students to develop the habit of reading on their own initiative. What we must make students understand is that reading is an integral part of life; the reason why we read is not merely for the sake of exams but because we want to live. We need to allow reading to accompany students' lifelong learning habits and let reading become the spiritual and mental path that students must walk upon on their life's journey. Whether it be from ancient or modern times, whether it be of Chinese or foreign origin, whether it be science and technology or humanities, all reading material that have condensed the best features of humanity and culture should enter the students' field of vision, allowing them to value fine cultural works through the process of reading, to raise their appreciation of the arts, to enrich the nourishment of their spirit and improve the shaping of their personalities. Ultimately, we should transform these features of culture into the torch that bears the inner fire of our own lives, allow ourselves to become the torchbearers of the "flame" that lights human civilization.

Based on these considerations, in the 1990s we organized the large-scale Anthology of New Century Educational Works (with approximately 400 titles), which included renowned specialists, scholars, and researchers from both China and abroad. It showcases and makes recommendations on the best features of humanity and culture for our teachers and students, allowing teachers and students, within a limited amount of time, to embrace the texts, converse with the literary masters, and communicate with the sublime spirit of humanity. We strongly believe that what lies ahead is a competitive and challenging era, one that is brimming with life and vitality and, simultaneously, also one that should be devoted to reading and studying. As the saying goes: "Listen to the sounds of the wind, rain, and recitation—let each sound enter your ears. Be involved in personal affairs, national affairs, and global affairs—let each affair enter your heart." Only in this way can we pitch ourselves between heaven and earth, fashion a generation of new talents who have a brand-new image and strength of spirit, and bring about the mighty rejuvenation of the Chinese nation.

6. Value Putting Theory into Practice, Allowing Students to Have an Interest in Life and Society

My take on the ideal intellectual education is that it should possess an openness and practicality, be connected to our lives, and communicate with society, allowing students to have an interest in the world outside of their classroom windows, a concern for the sky that is separate from the one they find on their school campus.

"Pay no attention to what is going on beyond one's study and bury oneself in the classics" was what teachers required of students at traditional private schools in ancient China. These circumstances still exist in our schools today; "read outdated books, read aimlessly and read mechanically" is a phrase that summarizes these sorts of misteaching. Many teachers and parents are fond of sequestering a child in a room (school or home) so that they will "concentrate solely" on studying, believing that this is the path to success for a child. Little do they know that this sort of intellectual education that involves confinement will only stifle a child's wisdom and talents.

In regard to education's (particularly intellectual education's) openness and practicality, China's great educator Tao Xingzhi had an extremely insightful analysis. Focusing on the long-standing form of confinement and isolation of education, he distinctly advocated: "Life is education, society is school." He asserted that we are "to release birds from their cages and place them in the skies above, allowing them to fly freely, to have everything in schools promoted to being a part of the natural world."

In order to do this, he beseeched the public to give children "Six Liberations":

> Under the current circumstances, it is paramount that the Six Liberations are carried out, returning to students the basic freedoms of learning: (1) the liberation of his mind, so that he can think; (2) the liberation of his hands, so that can do; (3) the liberation of his eyes, so that he can see; (4) the liberation of his mouth, so that he can speak; (5) the liberation of his space, so that he can attain even more knowledge from visiting the natural world and society and (6) the liberation of his time, requiring teachers to: not fill up his homework schedule, not force him to take exams and to not join forces with his parents to attack him from both sides regarding his homework. Teachers must give him some free time to digest what he has learned, furthermore, he must be allowed to learn something that he truly desires to learn, to do something he truly has an interest in.[2]

The main focus of quality education is the cultivation of students' creativity and practicality, and no matter if it is cultivating creativity or practicality, it is imperative that they are mutually connected to society and to our lives, as it can only be truly effective if it is done in such a way. In this respect, many overseas practices are worth using as a reference.

In Japan, there is a type of teaching and learning activity called "school field trips" (*shuugakuryokou*), which are regularly organized trips by the school to take students outside of the classroom on tours to learn more about other places, a type of learning activity that takes the form of collectively traveling with others, a type of open, extracurricular learning. Its goal is to broaden students' horizons, increase their practical knowledge, and cultivate students' spirit of participation and capabilities.

In Australian primary and secondary schools, field practice and observation classes are specially set up. Prior to departure, students are given an excursion handout containing a drawn map, items for observation, cloze problem-solving exercises, and related information. This is a large-capacity, highly comprehensive practical lesson touching upon such fields as hydrology, geology, environmental protection, construction building, economics, culture, and history.

In the American coastal city of Mystic, Connecticut, there is a large-scale oceanography teaching program for all levels of schooling. This program has not only a strong cohort of teaching staff but also its own laboratories, classrooms, and fishing boats. The actual teaching process involves taking students out into the ocean to fish. Under the guidance of their teachers, students partake in activities such as casting nets to catch fish, extracting water samples to carry out analyses, learning about the different types of fish as well as how to differentiate species of fish, and undertaking hands-on dissections of fish.

What needs to be particularly noted is that I advocate for the mutual linkage of intellectual education with our lives and for the mutual connection of intellectual education to our society. I am most certainly not opposed to the system of knowledge gained through book learning, but I hope that teachers will be able to guide students to apply the knowledge that they have learned in the classroom to the real world and at the same time have students transform this type of dynamic knowledge into their own abilities, especially the ability to innovate. Of course, the reason why I promote the practicality and openness of intellectual education is not merely because a mutual connection between knowledge and social life is the only way for students to internalize knowledge and truly make it their own, but because social life itself is also an important means of attaining knowledge. What is even more important is that it is only when students are attaining, consolidating, and utilizing knowledge through putting theory into practice by living in society that they are able to turn knowledge into accomplishments, breathe conviction into themselves, and mold their own personalities. While this is taking place, students are gradually forming the ability to change their lives and society.

7. Let Classrooms Be Full of Energy, Fun, and Wisdom

My take on the ideal intellectual education is that it allows classrooms to be full of energy, fun, and wisdom; teaching programs to be enriching, recursive, relevant, and rigorous; and students to truly become the masters of their educational activities.

For students, the classroom is as significant as a field is to farmers, a workshop is to workers, or a battlefield is to soldiers. Furthermore, for students the classroom not only possesses meaning in terms of intellectual education but, more importantly, is meaningful to their lives.

Professor Wu Kangning once profoundly indicated in *Sociology of the Classroom Teaching* that the classroom itself is indeed a "microcosm." Within this microcosm exist special social organizations (classes and small groups); special social characters (teachers who act as authority figures, and students from different family and community backgrounds; a special social culture (the "legal culture" being the teaching content and the subcultures being the teaching culture and the students' culture of collectivism); special social activities (planned, purposeful, educational interpersonal exchanges); and specific social standards (a system of classroom regulations as well as the occurrence of various forms of basic social behavior). Therefore, "in the past, we spoke of students learning course content within their classrooms, nowadays, we can still say that they are within the classroom, or, more precisely that within the society of the classroom, they are, for the first time, personally experiencing life, experiencing for themselves the joys and sorrows of life such as: obedience, keeping silent, rebellion, competition, cooperation, revelations, setbacks, success and failure." So, what is the ideal classroom? What sort of classroom can be full of energy, fun, and wisdom? We believe that it should have the following characteristics.

The first is participation, namely, the students' complete and effective participation from start to end. In the Oxford English Resource Books for Teachers there is a book entitled *Learner-Based Teaching*. The authors of this book believe that classroom teaching requires "the promotion of students' participation in the decision-making process regarding the teaching content, to strive towards having the students' own input as the main resource for teaching content, as well as have it become the focus of the entire teaching activity." In other words, if the "force-feeding method" is used in the classroom and there is no student participation, then it absolutely cannot stimulate students' thinking. Under this definition, I advocate for general classrooms to have no less than half their time spent on student discussions and activities.

The second is a positive bond between teachers and students, with both parties happily communicating and exchanging knowledge. Jill Hadfield writes in *Classroom Dynamics*: "The class may be full of joy, friendship, cooperation and dreams, but it may also be one that is full of silence, sadness, conflicts and hostilities." The former is undoubtedly an example of a positive bond between teachers and students, which is also the foundation for success in classroom teaching.

The third is freedom. Our classrooms are like army barracks: emphasizing ironclad discipline and having students sit ramrod straight and still. Students act as if they are skating on thin ice, trembling with fear and trepidation. They lack a feeling of ease, humor, joyous laughter, and high spirits. The classroom requirements, especially ones such as having students answer in unison, not allowing them to whisper to one another, and forbidding them to dispute what a teacher says are undoubtedly shackling students' mental and physical freedom of development.

The fourth is integration, as in an overall grasp of the system of subject knowledge. Classroom teaching with a low degree of integration often fragments knowledge into many small pieces, such as language and literature teachers segmenting letters and words from their specific language context or history teachers disassociating historical incidents from their historical background and context. What students attain is a dismembered form of knowledge and not a truly integrated form of wisdom.

The fifth is practice, that is, the degree to which students exercise their minds, hands, and mouths in the classroom. According to Vygotsky's theory, students learn by interacting and by participating in activities through the use of collaborative activities with teachers and peers, observation, imitation, and experience.

How effective the learning is and also what results are attained is dependent on whether or not students are able to fully use their functioning organs during interactions and activities. Therefore, a good lesson does not depend on whether it has been methodically arranged, nor does it depend on whether it has run smoothly, but rather in whether it has genuinely allowed students to practice and put what they have learned into practice.

The sixth is extensibility, that is, extending the breadth and depth of the foundations of knowledge integration and extending classroom teaching to social life. During the process of teaching intellectual education, addressing any important issues that come up in the classroom takes precedence over the curriculum. Presently, discussions on "nation-based curricula," "region-based curricula," and "school-based curricula" are increasing on a daily basis, but it could be said that there are many differing opinions on what exactly constitutes the ideal curriculum.

A curriculum that possesses richness, recursion, relation, and rigor, the so-called 4Rs, is the viewpoint that is put forward in *A Post-modern Perspective on Curriculum* by Professor William E. Doll Jr. of Louisiana State University's Curriculum and Instruction Department in the United States. The *richness* of a curriculum refers to its depth, with multiple layers of meaning and multiple possibilities of interpretation; *recursion* refers to having dialogue give rise to the reflective interaction with the environment, others, and culture, thus adding to the experiences that teachers and students already have; *relation* refers to the connection between the curriculum and education and culture; and *rigor* refers to purposefully seeking out different options, relationships, and connections, "consciously seeking out the assumptions that we and others hold, as well as the channels of coordination between these assumptions, promoting dialogue that is meaningful and transformative."

These 4Rs are somewhat hard to understand in writing but their meaning is the same as the aforementioned "six liberations"; their purposes are to activate students' thinking, to grasp the world in its entirety, to focus on caring for the living, and to have students truly become masters of their own learning.

8. Use Modern Information Technology and Broaden Channels of Intellectual Education

My take on the ideal intellectual education is that it should make full use of modern information technology, update learning tools, broaden the channels of intellectual education, and allow students to run freely in cyberspace.

Modern information technology, characterized by computer technology, microelectronics technology, and communications technology, has already become widely used in every aspect of society and is currently in the process of changing the way in which people produce, live, work, and study. The digital era today has presented a new challenge for intellectual education. It requires students of this new century to possess the following new capabilities:

- *New literacy skills.* Reading not only involves traditional forms of text but also includes images and text on screens, requiring students to learn through text in multimedia and to select the necessary information from within these new forms of text.
- *New searching and navigational skills.* While browsing through books at the library or surfing the Net, we often discover something new. Therefore, learning does not only occur through listening and attending a lecture, but also through discovery and experimentation.
- *New inference skills.* Making inferences is not only the abstract interpretation of logical reasoning; instead, it is more related to search capabilities with search objectives, tools, codes, and documents being used in a new way, transferring their usage onto new text types.
- *New skills of evaluation.* It is reasonable to say that textbooks and news reports are still justifiably trustworthy, but the same cannot be said for several pieces of information on the Internet; evaluation appears to be even more crucial today than ever before.

Our education cannot ignore the growing trends of this era and should instead put forth a positive response. In 2000, the Education Department issued a document entitled "Advice on Accelerating the Establishment of Information Technology Courses in Primary and Secondary Schools (Draft)" which explicitly states: "to actively push for information technology education in primary and secondary schools throughout the nation; to promote reform in terms of primary and secondary school curricula, teaching resources and teaching; to implement the mentality indicated by Deng Xiaoping's 'Three For's,' to achieve need for modernization in education; to put into practice the '21st Century Education Revitalization Action Plan' and intensify reforms in elementary education as there is a need for the full implementation of quality education; to face the international competition of the 21st century, to improve the overall national strength and to improve the quality of people, thus there is a need for the cultivation of new talented individuals who possess the spirit of innovation and practicality."

The problem now is that many students have already come into contact with the Internet and, furthermore, have been positively or negatively affected by the Internet, yet many of our teachers have yet to understand how to operate a computer, which is cause for concern. The growing trend of the Internet is not something that one should defy, and its allure for students is even harder to resist. We should deal with this by using scientific research and guide students on the basis of this, maximizing its positive factors and limiting its negative influences. I believe that our intellectual education should treat carrying out modern information technology education for students as our own duty.

The development of modern information technology has injected our intellectual education with content that is full of the flavors of our modern era and, at the same time, has updated our teaching methodology as well as broadened our students' quest for knowledge and channels to put theory into practice. The duty of intellectual education today is already no longer merely the imparting of knowledge from traditional textbooks and the cultivation of traditionally meaningful abilities; rather, it also now includes the nurturing of students' interest in and awareness of information technology, to have them understand or grasp the basic knowledge and skills regarding information technology, allowing them to possess the ability to access, evaluate, transfer, process, and apply information. This forms good cultural qualities and lays the necessary foundations for them to adapt to learning, working, and living in an information society.

The emergence of the Internet has had a big impact on traditional education, offering a new challenge to both the teachers' "teaching" and the students' "learning." In traditional education, teachers had an advantage in terms of educational resources compared to students, but in the present day, teachers and students are both confronted with the Internet and the teachers' advantage in terms of educational resources no longer exists. On the contrary, students sometimes know even more about something than the teacher because students can freely use the Internet to obtain any information. At the same time, if we were to say that students' learning in the past was mainly accumulation of knowledge, then being confronted by the bombardment of information today has meant that students' learning now is mainly the selection of knowledge. Under these circumstances, the role of the teacher has inevitably changed. In terms of facing the Internet, teachers should be guides. The Internet is a huge database, and how to guide students to identify and select the most valuable information is a duty that teachers cannot shirk. At the same time, teachers should also be guardians. The Internet also contains a lot of information that is useless or even harmful to teenagers. This requires teachers to guide students not to deviate in their way of thinking through communicating with students and allowing them to mature in a healthy way.

Therefore, teachers must first be familiar with and, more importantly, be able to use Internet technology. If teachers cannot use a computer or use the Internet, then teaching and guiding students is out of the question. At the same time, teachers should be extremely sensitive to and have a comprehensive understanding and original insights on the latest in contemporary information and knowledge. It is only through doing so that teachers are able to grasp the initiative to guide students. Additionally, the emergence of the Internet has meant that teachers and students have gained equal footing in terms of educational resources. Teachers need to shift their perception and completely put down their mantle of authority. They are to be the students' learning partners, collaboratively investigating and exchanging ideas and truly achieving the democratization of teaching and learning.

Sukhomlinsky once likened education to a flower, with intellectual education being just one of its petals. This is indeed true, in a sense; intellectual education is not an end in itself, but rather a means to allow people to become "humans." Francis Bacon said: "Histories make men wise; poets, witty; the mathematics, subtle; natural philosophy, deep; moral, grave; logic and rhetoric, able to contend. *Abeunt studia in mores* (Studies permeate and shape manners)."

Therefore, it can be said overall that in terms of a fundamental purpose, intellectual education serves as a means of molding a student's character. Through harmoniously matching intellectual education with other types of education such as moral education, physical education, aesthetic education, and technical education, our students will have a lifelong scientific attitude, mentality, and worldview, and they will possess a proper understanding of themselves, others, human society, and the natural world. Furthermore, they will possess the qualities and abilities to properly handle the harmonious relationships between all of these elements mentioned above. Finally, they will possess a mind that is full of wisdom and become people who are spiritually and mentally eternally happy.

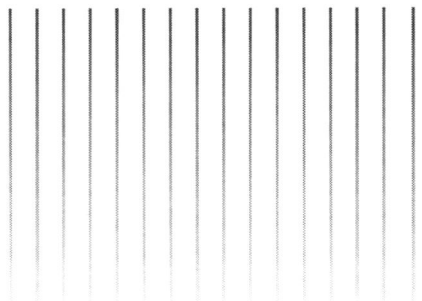

3

My Take on Physical Education

Sport is the power of the race; when two armies confront each other, whoever is able to gain supremacy will shake others to their core.

Sport is a contest of wisdom and military formations; whoever has a masterful plan will be unpredictable to others.

Sport is a beautiful display, strong and gentle combined; whoever comes out on top will be a delight to look upon.

From the gladiatorial slave fights in the ancient Roman arena to the modern competitions between athletes on the Olympic racetrack, sport has always been the exciting aspect of human society and has always been a subject of interest in education.

Following the evolution of human history, social progress, and the development of civilizations, the position and mission of sports in the development of humanity are continuously changing, and the function and value of sports are also constantly moving toward maturity and perfection. Especially in modern society, the increasingly difficult demands made regarding the quality of people and their harmonious development of their mind and body have caused sport to thrive. The impact that sport has on society, culture, and people's lives is also becoming bigger.

However, in schools the nature and function of physical education have been weakened and displaced. With the pressure of taking school advancement exams, sport and physical education at some schools has become a nonessential minor subject or a "vase decorating a shop front." Physical education at these schools merely satisfies the imparting of skills and improvement of physical fitness, but the spiritual meaning and lofty realms of physical education have been watered down and forgotten. This will undoubtedly cause physical education to hit a dead end. Therefore, it is necessary to reexamine physical education and call out our "take" on the ideal physical education.

1. Cultivate Students Who Will Pursue the Motto "Faster, Higher, Stronger"

My take on the ideal physical education is that it should embody the Olympic spirit. It should cultivate students who will pursue the motto "faster, higher, stronger" and are able to improve themselves and reflect the loftiness of human nature.

Constantly adapting to and changing nature, continuously pursuing new achievements and breakthroughs, reflects the nature of humanity. This inherent nature is able to emerge and be enhanced because of sports and is also able to develop, improve, and refine itself because of the existence of the Olympics.

The Olympic motto "faster, higher, stronger," was proposed by Reverend Father Henri Martin Didon, head of the Arcueil College in Paris, France, and close friend of the founder of the modern Olympic Games, Pierre de Coubertin. It was later borrowed by Coubertin to be used as the motto for the Olympic Games. In 1920, the International Olympic Committee officially recognized it as the motto for the Olympic Games, and it was used for the first time at the seventh Olympic Games in Antwerp. The pursuit of "faster, higher, stronger" is a limitless yearning for infinite strength, constantly challenging the limits of human ability, reflecting the value of competitive sports and also the goal that the Olympics must pursue.

In regard to Western cultural concepts, the body and the mind are inseparable. Without a robust physical body, it would be difficult to be strong in spirit. In order to have a robust physical body that is able to house a strong spirit, we have sporting events such as the marathon and discus as well as bullfighting, boxing, and wrestling. It is precisely in these sporting events that seem almost merciless that one's spirit of competition, struggle, and adventure as well as one's pioneering spirit can be nurtured and developed.

When mountaineers take their lives in their hands and conquer one mountain after another; when the first whitewater rafters at the Yangtze River thrust themselves into the raging waters; when bungee jumpers leap off from tall cliff faces; when weightlifting athletes smash world records and progress toward a new goal, what exactly are they trying to do? They have only one objective, and that is to be "faster, higher, stronger." For competitive athletes' never-ending quest, every improvement of 0.01 second, every emergence of new technology, and every brilliant performance is a concentrated manifestation and vivid portrayal of this spirit.

Isn't this spirit what modern society wants to advocate and carry forth? Is it not essential to the survival and development of the human race?

This pursuit of the Olympic spirit of "faster, higher, stronger," is extremely important to the growing student. It is only through continually striving for excellence and challenging oneself that one is able to produce extraordinary results and lead a glorious life. "There is no best, only better" is not only an advertising slogan spoken by Lang Ping for Aucma electrical appliances but a portrayal of the spirit of Chinese women's volleyball as well as an accurate way to describe the life that this outstanding athlete and coach leads. During the teaching of physical education, encouraging students to charge forward toward the goal of being "faster, higher, stronger" and encouraging students to go onward and upward, in a sense, is much more important than mastering certain sporting skills and attaining certain sporting results.

The pursuit of "faster, higher, stronger" challenges the limits of human ability and is the spirit advocated by the Olympic Games, but it is not their only objective. What the modern Olympic Games emphasize is the embodiment of a spirit of the humanities that will present itself in the form of respect for humanity, human rights, and human nature. Through the use of physical activities, it will promote caring for others and a respect for the value of human life. Within the scope of a humanist approach toward sports, physical education does not only mold a person in a powerful way but also places one's feelings, attitudes, and ideals into important domains that are educationally oriented, thus reflecting the goodness and elegance of human nature. The fundamental reason why Coubertin revived the Olympic Games was not merely to promote the popularity of competitive sports but to have it incorporated into the scope of education and humanities so as to achieve the goals of education and humanities through the science of exercise and fair competition. Therefore, the sporting spirit is also a spirit of the humanities.

First, sport is an important form of self-improvement and self-development for humanity. Sport uses the human body itself as its target. Under the guidance of the scientific principles of training and exercise and by partaking in a series of regular physical exercises, one finds that sport can have a direct influence on the human body. It will be able to positively transform the anatomical structure and physiological functions of the human body, thus gaining the effects of muscle development, a sharpening of reflexes, and an increase in energy levels, reflecting the perfect union between strength and beauty. These capabilities and values cannot be found in any other form of human activity.

Second, sport not only has an impact on the human body but is simultaneously an important influence on people's spiritual world. During physical exercise, the manifestations of the spirit of enterprise, the fighting spirit, the spirit of fair competition and solidarity, and the spirit of patriotism and internationalism are all reflections of the beautiful human nature. Therefore, whether from a physiological or spiritual point of view, sport is able to promote the self-perfection of humanity and reflect the noble character of human nature.

For a long time, the aforementioned roles and functions of physical education have, without a doubt, been ignored by education. In the encyclopedic dictionary *Ci Hai*, the definition of physical education goes no further than to merely state that it is "education that strengthens the body and one's inner qualities and raises the levels of one's physical fitness." The *Encyclopedia of China*, Education Volume, also defines physical education as "to impart the knowledge and skills of physical fitness onto those being taught; activities that strengthen the physique and cultivate a habit of consciously exercising one's body; it is an important part of the comprehensive development of education." Thus, in this way, the state of sports as a pursuit of the motto "faster, higher, stronger" and the embodiment of the noble character and charm of human nature has had its value greatly reduced in education. However, it is precisely these ideals that physical education should pursue.

2. Hone Students' Willpower and Have Them Develop Qualities of Tenacity and Perseverance

My take on the ideal physical education is that it should hone students' willpower and have them develop qualities of tenacity and perseverance, so that they never give up nor stop to rest.

In Lu Xun's article "The First and the Last," he writes, "When we watch sporting events, we often think: the winner is certainly worthy of our respect, however, those runners who fall behind yet still press on to their goal, together with those spectators who do not laugh at them, will some day be the backbone of China." The most important quality of these competitors is their indomitable will.

One's willpower is the conscious determination of a purpose, the adjustment of one's internal and external activities in accordance with this purpose, and the psychological process of overcoming various difficulties. Activities that promote an active and healthy willpower will have the following qualities.

First is self-awareness—systematically taking effective action in accordance with one's own understanding of the objective law of development and the purposes of one's self-determined actions, thus increasing self-awareness and lessening ignorance. The second is determination—not hesitating when making decisions and acting decisively; additionally, when decisions need to be postponed, being able to consider and think ahead until such time as the situation is ripe for taking appropriate measures. The third is perseverance and tenacity—the ability to persevere in carrying out decisions and to not veer from their path due to distractions. Additionally, one will not be intimidated by various difficulties and setbacks; neither will one be complacent due to success, nor discouraged by failure. The fourth is the maintenance of self-control—the ability to achieve the intended purpose by doing such things as controlling one's emotions, restraining one's words and deeds, and doing what must be done without hesitation; additionally, being adept at using rationality to steer one's emotions, using far-reaching goals to curb excessive desires, and using self-control to gather together one's scattered attention.

Clearly, sports are a powerful form of exercise and require participants to be equipped with these outstanding qualities of willpower. Additionally, it is precisely because sports are powerful that they will play a unique role in the cultivation of an individual's qualities of willpower. One of the draws of sports is that it reflects the capabilities of human willpower. Whether it be training in the classroom or in the competition arena, it requires students or athletes to challenge their own physical capabilities, their pasts, and their limits. It also requires students or athletes to endure with dogged will, to contend against adversaries, and to persevere until the very last minute. As the saying goes, "when Greek meets Greek, then comes the tug of war"; in a situation where two evenly matched adversaries meet, it is often the strength of one's willpower that is the key to deciding the outcome of the match.

We could see at the Sydney Olympic Games in 2000 that every winning of a medal is closely related to the participating athletes' tenacity and determined will that has been cultivated through long-term physical training. At the moment when Zhan Xugang struggled to lift a weight that he had never lifted before, when Kong Linghui gritted her teeth and prevailed over world champion Waldner, when the two young badminton players Zhang Jun and Gao Ling fearlessly faced the powerful world number one team, and when racewalker Wang Liping reached the finishing point by relying on patience and perseverance, the glittering medals were no longer that important in the eyes of the spectators. Furthermore, aren't these demonstrations of extraordinary talent and skill, which have caused people to be excited to the point of remembering them for the rest of their lives, precisely the type of self-improvement, perseverance, tenacity and indomitable spirit, and faith that athletes possess?

A friend who returned from America said, "In America, many children do not know Bill Clinton, but few do not know Michael Jordan." Love of the sport, pursuit of strength, participation in competitions, and hero worship—these elements of the sporting culture take root in a child's mind from an early age.

It is precisely because of this that every country attaches great importance to physical education. For example, within Germany's decade of consistent schooling system, the number of classes allocated to physical education in the school's teaching program is ranked third, after German and mathematics. In countries such as Cuba and France, the national stipulations are that if primary and secondary students fail their physical education classes or do not satisfy the curriculum requirements, then those students are unable to move to the following grade or to graduate. In British public schools, students even have the whole afternoon set aside to carry out various sport activities, the purpose being to train students to adapt to various living environments in the future and to also adapt to undertaking a variety of heavy and arduous work. Many of Britain's Conservative Party ministers, 87 percent of the royal military generals, 83 percent of the Church's archbishops, 65 percent of judges, and 88 percent of diplomats have all graduated from these sorts of schools. Because our nation in recent years has been pursuing the impact of students' promotion rate, physical education appears to be shrinking. Due to the "singular nature" of only children, opportunities and atmospheres that are conducive to cultivating admirable qualities of willpower such as children's ability to endure hardships and withstand setbacks, as well as decisiveness, self-control, and perseverance, are difficult to come by. Children are fed, coddled, and spoiled from their youth, with some becoming "little fatties," others becoming "little bean sprouts," and still others becoming "little medicine pots." This current development is incompatible with people's requirements of a healthy and strong physique.

Physical education in schools must undertake the duty and responsibility of honing students' willpower. I personally have had experiences regarding this that have left a deep impression on me. When studying at university, I was not good at sports but participated in the school's long-distance running team in order to work on my stamina. I pretty much had to run 10 laps of the oval every morning (more than 4,000 meters). After I finished running, I would rest for a bit and have a cold bath, and I would play a game of basketball in the afternoon. Although this sort of training was unlikely to turn me into a professional athlete, it did give me plenty of energy and perseverance and even earned me the nickname "eager beaver" in terms of my studies.

When Sang Xinmin's *Educational Philosophy: A Conversation* mentions issues related to modern physical education, he states that modern physical education needs a bit of Spartan spirit, that is, an emphasis on sports training and strengthening the honing of the body and mind. What needs to be installed is some rough, crude, fierce, and strict semimilitary-style exercise courses. We need to consciously have students go through hard times, undertake arduous training, gain sturdy muscles and bones, and strengthen their physique. Therefore, it is only through the implementation of physical activities that require strength and are considered tough, having students' minds "suffer" and their bodies "toil," continuously having them experience joy and pain and success and failure, that students' tenacious perseverance and conviction can be cultivated. It is also only then that they are able to assume great undertakings.

What must be noted is that willpower is not merely the embodiment of the allure of sports, but rather the key to the success of a great person. As renowned American inventor Thomas Edison stated: "The most obvious sign of a great man is a strong will. It doesn't matter how the environment changes, his original intentions and hopes will not have changed in the slightest and he will finally overcome obstacles and reach his desired goal." If the willpower that has been nurtured throughout the course of physical education is extended to other subjects and one's future work and life, then it will definitely assist one in gaining success, allowing one's life to be even more fulfilling.

2. Nurture Students' Spirit of Cooperation and Feelings of Collectivism and Patriotism

My take on the ideal physical education is that it should pay attention to the nurturing of students' spirit of cooperation and feelings of collectivism and

patriotism, allowing sporting activities to become an important means for cultivating good moral character.

American scientist Harriet Zuckerman has calculated statistics regarding the
first 25 years of Nobel Prize laureates and found collaborative research accounting
for only 41 percent of the winners. In the second 25-year period, collaboration
accounted for 65 percent, and in the third 25-year period, 79 percent. Nowadays,
there are extremely few who "fly solo" and bask in the glory of success alone. The
U.S. Apollo Space Program cost 25 billion U.S. dollars, and the scientists and staff
that were directly involved amounted to 420,000 people. Cooperation has become
a basic form of scientific research. Learning to work together is one of the basic
concepts of modern education. In 2001, it was the theme of the World Conference
on Education in Sweden, where it was also determined as the basic objective of
twenty-first-century education.

Treating sports as a competitive activity is an effective means of developing
a student's sense of competition. At the same time, sporting activities can also
develop an individual's sense of cooperation as well as attempt to seek an internal
unity between the two. Practice proves that an accomplished sporting team does
not only require that its athletes have excellent athleticism and high-caliber athletic skills, but more importantly, that the sporting team these athletes belong to is
able to provide an atmosphere of collectivism in which they can fully unearth and
show their sporting prowess. Particularly in terms of competitive team events, it
is even more necessary that all athletes effectively exhibit their individual level of
strength and also compete as a coordinated entity at a collective level. Even if it is
an individual competition event, athletes' success is also the crystallization of collective wisdom. At the 2000 Sydney Olympic Games as well as the 2008 Beijing
Olympic Games, the Chinese men's gymnastics, table tennis, badminton, weightlifting, and other teams achieved remarkable results that have received worldwide
attention, and all these achievements are closely related to the spirit of cooperation, feelings of collectivism, and patriotism.

Every kind of sport will always involve comparisons between competitors;
however, when competing, individuals and teams not only cross swords in the
match but their thinking and feelings will blend with one another. Whether it be
track and field, ball sports, gymnastics, or swimming, besides being influenced by
their own mental and physical factors, they will also be influenced by teammates,
coaches, referees, and spectators, as well as by factors such as the sporting rules,
stadium atmosphere, and the roles and responsibilities among team players.

It is precisely under the influence of these comprehensive factors that the athlete's sporting conduct is already no longer purely an individual's own behavior.
They should cultivate good moral traits such as friendship, compassion, understanding, cooperation, unity, and courtesy as well as establish team spirit and
feelings of collectivism. With this team spirit and these feelings of collectivism,
team members will be able to mutually understand each other's thoughts and
feelings and mutually trust one another, and in terms of their actions they will

coordinate and support one another, making it easier for tactical coordination of the whole team to be effective. With this team spirit and these feelings of collectivism, team members are able to form a common, mentally supportive atmosphere so that in times of hardship they can mutually motivate each other and in times of victory, mutually celebrate with one another. In addition, the team spirit and feelings of collectivism play a powerful role as psychological support in terms of the team members' individual matches, enabling them to better maintain their mental state during the competition and to increase their self-confidence, courage, and sense of honor toward the competition, strengthening the individual's sense of responsibility and cooperation, as is evident in the mottoes "I am but a tree in a forest" and "one tree does not make a forest."

If the spirit of cooperation that is found in sporting activities is extended to other areas of work, it would undoubtedly unleash a tremendous number of capabilities. Sun Jinfang, former captain of the Chinese women's volleyball team, once used team spirit and cooperation to defeat opponents from Japan and other countries, remaining at the top of their game for more than 10 years. When she took up her new position as director of the National Sports Lottery Centre, she said, "Long-term collective training and competitions cultivate the athletes' team spirit. In the work of running the lottery, it is reflected in the way one mutually learns from and helps one another, the exact compliance of the instructions, the way everyone works harmoniously as a single entity and the way everyone takes the whole situation into account." The reason why the National Sports Lottery Centre did not encounter many problems during the process of integrating the computer network in 1997 was because the already-established regional computer networks resolutely complied with the decisions made by the National Sports Lottery Centre, abandoning their own independent networks and incorporating themselves into the nationally unified network, consciously accepting the unified control and management of the National Sports Lottery Centre.

Therefore, in the physical education offered at school, teachers not only have to teach students how to master basic sports skills and to pursue the Olympic spirit, they must also allow students to learn how to cooperate with others. Teachers must guide students to set up their own freely organized sporting interest groups or clubs and encourage students to start up rich and varied extracurricular sporting activities. When guiding students on facing off against other teams in competition, they must encourage students on one hand to "put their all" into the fight and struggle, but on the other hand to tacitly coordinate with one another and to oppose individual heroism.

At interregional and multinational sporting competitions, athletes' spirit of cooperation and feelings of collectivism are often elevated to noble feelings of patriotism and internationalism. From the 1950s, when Chinese women's volleyball was at a very low starting point, till the 1980s when they reached the world's peak in women's volleyball, the fact that the team scrupulously abode by the belief "bravely scale new heights, bring glory to our nation" throughout this process is closely linked to their success. Famous writer Yan Wenjing writes in a poem dedicated to the Chinese women's volleyball team: "No matter how much of a proud legacy is left behind by our ancestors, we must craft new things with our own hands that will make us sufficiently proud." On the world table tennis stage, the Chinese table tennis team demonstrates extraordinary talents, makes outstanding contributions to the matches, and has endured for a long period in this position, the fruits of generations of proud table tennis athletes who are willing to brave the struggle for their country. Each time the national anthem is played and the national flag is raised, the tears of excitement that spring from their eyes are not just due to the joy of victory, but to the sincere inner pride that they feel for their motherland, which manifests itself as feelings of happiness. It is also that exact moment that evokes countless people's feelings of patriotic fervor.

Physical education teachers must take full advantage of all sorts of activities and opportunities so that they may carry out the teaching of patriotic education to students. When the Chinese Olympic Committee won over the hearts of the judging panel members and successfully gained the right to host the 2008 Olympic Games; when the Chinese soccer team defeated Oman in Shenyang and became qualified for the next round as an Asian team; when news of the success Chinese athletes have had in competitions reaches our ears and victory songs are sung, physical education teachers should seize the opportunity to host a variety of activities so that students can learn about various pieces of sporting knowledge, form patriotic feelings, and develop a sense of identity and pride for the motherland, inspiring them henceforth to study and work diligently for the sake of bringing glory to the nation.

3. Cultivate Students Who Abide by the Rules and Learn About Justice and Fairness

My take on the ideal physical education is that it should place an emphasis on cultivating students who abide by the rules, establish the concept of justice and fairness, and steer clear of fraudulent practices so as to develop the quality of honesty in students.

Sport, as a competitive activity, is regulated, involves cooperation, and is organized. Every sporting event and movement is subject to strict regulations and competition rules. These regulations are "commandments" for the athletes' behavior, acting as a means of order, control, and restriction, reflecting the scientific nature and fairness of sports. Sports training should first develop a sense of these regulations, guiding students to put these regulations into practice and abide by them, and gradually have these sorts of actions become habitual.

Especially given the present trend of continually improving the level of sports within the scope of this world, the regulations for sporting competitions have gradually become stricter and more complicated. Athletes and coaches must conduct research into the regulations of various sports and competitions and the trends in the development of technology and then formulate and implement scientifically sound training methods and measures that meet the required specifications and technical requirements. Physical education teachers must firmly establish students' compliance with rules and regulations through physical exercise and training and develop and bring forth their subjective sense of initiative and creativity within the limits of these objective rules and regulations.

The awareness of regulations and the cultivated sense of discipline that students or athletes, coaches, and referees possess during a competition demonstrate who is civilized and cultured, reflections of the high degree of responsibility in the sporting industry and a type of moral obligation. Our country's outstanding athlete Rong Zhixing played soccer with great sportsmanship for 18 years. He has never deliberately harmed others, and even when subjected to purposeful infringements by others, he never retaliated, creating "the Zhixing style" that has been praised by others and has influenced generations of athletes. At the third Volleyball World Championships, when the referee made an error of judgment, former captain of the Chinese women's volleyball team Sun Jinfang raised her hand and complied with the referee's decision with a smile on her face. At the end of the competition, she was awarded the "Outstanding Athlete" prize and "Best Athlete" prize.

With improvements in science and technology, the material life and standards of consumption in human society have rapidly increased. At the same time, the pursuit of material interests has also become the principal means of value orientation. Under this influence, sport, as a type of competitive activity, has also seen the distinct emergence of a phenomenon that places importance on the materialistic and disregards the spiritual and mental. It has had a negative impact on the sporting spirit of competitions, which should originally have been fair and just, leading to all sorts of bad conduct and feelings and unsavory practices in sporting competitions such as jealousy, vanity, and fraud.

The chief of Jiangsu Province's Sports Bureau, Kong Qingpeng, said when analyzing the "phenomenon of dissimilation" between athletes' identities and eligibilities:

> There are some people, who, in order to court publicity, commit cheating to gain results, glory and benefits. They will resort to any means possible to rig participating athletes' qualifications to the point that the competition is changed beyond recognition. Traditional grass-roots sporting matches have become regional school competitions; competitions between youths have become matches between elder siblings and younger siblings, transforming into matches between those with beards, and those without; there are even competitions between elders and juniors; provincial competitions have become mini national games with most of the participants in the secondary school competitions, university competitions, staff competitions and farmers competitions being fake students, fake employees and fake farmers, who assume these guises to deceive so that they snatch gold, grab silver and divvy up the medals among themselves.

In various major competitions, a small number of athletes and coaches who are looking only for a fast return take the risk of taking performance-enhancing drugs and engage in behind-the-scenes match fixing; there are also a handful of referees who are enticed by materialistic benefits and make arbitrarily biased decisions during the match and so on. I am sure you can imagine the negative influence that these evils, which run counter to the modern spirit of sport, have on the hearts and minds of the youths.

The purpose of sports today should be based on promoting the harmonious development of a person's body and mind. Regulations and standards found in various sports, as well as the "code" of athletes, referees, and coaches, besides functioning as limits and controls are simultaneously also turning human behavior toward a noble nature and assigning a system of values to the sports that is both just and fair.

On the regulations front, there are no differences between individuals in terms of their rank, the country they come from, their race, or the amount of wealth and property that they own. It is for this reason that justice and fairness have become the ethics and morals of sports worldwide. To use competitive sports to promote the worldwide spread of humanism as well as to seek out the common interests of and peaceful exchanges between every country are the ideals of the founder of the Olympic movement. In 2001, after Jacques Rogge took up the position of president of the International Olympic Committee, he pointed out that in the new century, perhaps in terms of sports what is even more necessary is a new motto: cleaner, more humane, more united. We look forward to this ideal being turned into a reality through being put into practice countless times in school sports, social sports, common sports, and competitive sports.

School sports need to take the lead and set an example. We must have our numerous sport teachers and students consciously abide by the basic public ethics of society and the basic rules and regulations of competitive sports. We must enable students to recognize that one of the essential features of sports is competition and that to lose fairness in a competition is to lose the essential meaning of sports and thus, lose the unique charm and vitality of sports. In physical education and competitions between all types of students, schools, and districts, we should steer clear of fraudulent practices and encourage students to always use their own strengths to win glory and respect, whether it is at a sporting competition or in their journey through life starting from now on.

4. Train Students to Calmly Face Competition and to Nurture Their Mental Strength

My take on the ideal physical education is that it should train students to calmly face competition and to have the attitude of being neither dizzy with success nor discouraged by failure. It should also enable students to conduct their own psychological adjustments and scientific training and to nurture their mental strength.

The famous British philosopher and physician John Locke had a famous saying: "A sound mind in a sound body." In regard to the definition of health, the World

Health Organization clearly treats as an integral part of being healthy the elements of a healthy psychological state, such as energy and vibrancy, quick thinking, broad mindedness, and a positive emotional state of mind. In our modern society, possessing a healthy mind has already become an important prerequisite to the survival, development, and success of a modern-day person.

First, from looking at the development of the times, the impact that modern society has had on people is mainly geared toward the structure of people's psychology. The increasingly severe issues of habitat and survival, the high-tech demands of the labor market, the intensification of competition, the intricacies of interpersonal relationships, and so on are all matters that increase people's psychological burden, with people remaining continuously in an anxious state of emergency. This requires the modern person to possess fine psychological qualities to adapt to the needs of social development. In terms of the growth of adolescents and children, both the adolescents' physical and psychological development are going through a period of intense change, at the same time that they find themselves in the midst of a confusing social environment and are surrounded by the burdens of heavy studying, which can easily lead to psychological problems or mental illness. Therefore, carrying out psychological "quality education" for students, conducting mental health guidance, and nurturing students' robust personalities are the urgent and important duties and missions of modern education.

Sport as a part of education plays a unique role during the process of promoting the formation of students' mental strength. At the same time, sport itself is a powerful form of training. It requires athletes to bear not only a certain amount of physical strain but also a certain amount of psychological strain or mental testing. This is because without mental strength, an athlete who already possesses a high level of skill would not be able to perform properly, leading to failure; however, an athlete who possesses sound psychological qualities will be able to perform better than usual and achieve victory. Cases like these are a common occurrence in sporting competitions.

"Train my body and relax my mind." Both a healthy body and a healthy mind, both a strong physique and a rousing spirit—these are the functions of values possessed by competitive sport since the day of its inception. Therefore, in the past two to three decades every country's training programs in sports, besides the training of skills and stamina, also offer specialized psychological training courses. This is used to solve the issue of athletes' psychological barriers in competitive sports. Through psychological training, the exhibition of athletes' psychological strength is also facilitated, thus improving their athletic performances. At the same time, this form of training enables sports to be used to strengthen one's body through physical exercise, which is conducive to the harmonious development of a students' physical and mental state.

In sports, athletes' good psychological quality is reflected not only in a technical level of play but also in how athletes properly approach success and failure in competitions. To be neither dizzy with success nor discouraged by failure is an essential quality for elite athletes as well as the mental quality that physical education in schools should first train their students in. At the twenty-second World Gymnastics Championships' men's team event, China's top gymnasts smoothly cleared the first five rounds. When their overall score was ranked in first place, Li Ning accidentally fell from the horizontal bar, causing the following gymnast Tong Fei to have to score above 9.85 in order to prevail in this tense situation. However, it was exactly in these tense conditions that Tong Fei was able to remain calm and levelheaded, gaining the high score of 9.90 by possessing the outstanding psychological quality of being "neither dizzy with success, nor discouraged by failure" and enabling the Chinese gymnastics team to ascend to the international throne of competitive gymnastics for the first time. At the 2000 Sydney Olympic Games' women's gymnastics individual all-around competition, Russian gymnast Svetlana Khorkina fell during her uneven bars routine, causing her score to be affected; however, after a brief moment to psychologically adjust herself, she, in a calm state of mind, once again leaped up onto the uneven bars and further showcased her exquisite, almost impeccable, skill to the spectators, winning the entire world's praise and admiration. And finally, world table tennis champion Jan Ove-Waldner's steady psychological state of mind has daunted opponents and is a continual source of envy for all.

Physical education in schools must urgently solve problems like how to enable students to have the courage to compete for first place and dare to struggle, as well as have students properly treat rankings and achievements and attain the mindset of "humble in victory while cheerful in defeat." Teachers must also find how best to guide students so that they are able to be fully prepared before a game, tournament, or competition; exhibit their own strengths at the level that they are already at; calmly accept all kinds of results; and treat sports and tournaments as a kind of "process."

Currently at domestic major sporting competitions, when the host team wins, many spectators will be "over the moon," but this joy will often reach the point of being uncontrollable; however, when the host team loses, spectators are grief stricken and often "sent into a towering rage," even committing such uncivilized acts as throwing bottles and smashing cars. This more or less reflects that in terms of cultivating the future spectators, our schools' physical education teaching is still not doing enough. This requires that we must update physical education teachers' knowledge structure and strengthen the teachers' own psychological quality and the cultivation of their human sentiments.

5. Enable Students to Sense the Harmony of Strength and Beauty While Focusing on Physical Training

My take on the ideal physical education is that it should open the window of world sports for students and enable them to sense the harmony of strength and beauty while they are focusing on physical training.

In ancient Greece, prior to the convening of the Olympic Games, people often held a sacred ceremony beside the temple of Zeus at Olympia. They would light a torch at the altar and then raise the torch aloft and run to every city-state in ancient Greece shouting as they ran: "Stop all battles, go and participate in the Games!" Wherever the torch arrives, the flames of war are extinguished, and even if both sides are in a state of mutual hostility or are city-states with intense close-quarter fighting, they will begin a "sacred truce." With people seemingly having forgotten their hatred and conflict, they throw their whole selves, mentally and physically, into the competitions of the Olympic games. Thus, Olympics have become an emissary of peace.

In modern society, sports have also made an important contribution to the friendly exchanges between people from every country. The famous "Ping-Pong diplomacy" created history with the "little ball" moving the "big ball" and made an everlasting contribution to the thawing of Sino-U.S. relations.

Even though the competitiveness in competition sports is very strong, it also opens a window of world understanding for our students and community, becoming a "display window" for a country and its people's comprehensive political, economic, cultural, scientific, and technological strengths. This type of competitive sports enables students to experience for themselves the rich cultural meanings that are contained within multinational and cross-regional sports. Through different perspectives and the use of a variety of methods, these cultures complement one another in order to provide students with a variety of cultural landscapes, inspiring their pursuit of truth, virtue, and beauty, imperceptibly enhancing their spiritual state. These are precisely the manifestations of the human spirit in modern sports.

The modern Olympic Games have already integrated sport and culture. They have taken the mutual understanding, mutual respect, high regard for heroes, and struggle against adversity between all countries and regions and used them to enhance the moral code that is acknowledged by all of humanity. The Olympic Charter points out: "The activity of the Olympic Movement is universal and permanent. It covers the five continents. It reaches its peak with the bringing together of athletes of the world at the great sports festival, the Olympic Games." The Olympic Movement merges with the Olympic Games, using the universally appealing medium of sports to spread the richly contemporary humanistic spirit to all corners of the world.

With the development of modern society, the trend toward the globalization of humanity is increasing on a daily basis with exchanges, such as those between people, information, and culture, becoming even closer. Likewise, the trend toward mutual influence and interaction between every country and every region and between people with different skin colors and different languages is becoming increasingly obvious. Thus the world is in the process of becoming an interdependent entity. Reality also shows that the main bulk of sport competitions involves differentiating between countries, but sporting activities themselves as well as the appreciation of sports transcends national borders. Jordan's superb basketball skills, Maradona's well-nigh perfect soccer footwork, the outstanding and incomparable NBA, Italian Serie A and English Premier League—in every corner of the world, I'm afraid that one would be hard pressed to resist their visual allure.

In this context, there is an urgent need for students' global awareness to be cultivated and enhanced through education, to rouse students' attention regarding global common interests. On this point, physical education in schools, which act as the educational component of sports, is even more duty bound. At various multinational, cross-regional sporting events and competitions, it should enable students to learn to respect "differences," to focus on taking in and learning from points of cultural and sporting excellence displayed by other countries, and finally to appreciate any points of uniqueness.

Overall, sports nowadays, especially the Olympic sports, have gradually centralized the universal meanings of truth, virtue, and beauty, and they possess an aesthetic value that transcends both regional borders and time. Among them is the Olympic rings logo, which symbolizes the unity of the five continents, humanity's pursuit of glory and radiance, and the ideal Olympic torch. Emblems of past Olympic Games that document the year the Games took place or the venue where they were hosted, as well as distinctive Olympic mascots and so on, have already become symbols of the world's culture of sports. The Olympic Games, this international sporting festival, as well as other transnational sporting competitions, have become a global wonder for humanity where people from different countries and regions, who speak different languages, are from different races, or possess different skin colors from all over the world band together as one to "sing the same song" (unite together in harmony for a common purpose).

During sports activities, it is possible to attain full movement and gain a series of the most basic sensations in every organ of the human body. These sensations are often the first step toward a state of aesthetic appreciation. In sports, every system and sensory receptor in the human body is intensely stimulated through running, jumping, sprinting, sliding, spinning, somersaulting, rolling, swaying, colliding, lifting and lowering oneself, and so on, arousing the athlete's movement sense, muscle sense, sense of rhythm, spatial and temporal sense, and depth perception, thus causing shock due to their strength, amazement at their speed, and admiration for their bravery, leading us to enter the beauty of the spiritual realm.

Modern sports push this beauty to even further extremes. Competitions such as rhythmic gymnastics, team gymnastics, artistic gymnastics, ballet on ice, surfing, and synchronized swimming have shown us countless split-second moments of beauty and fixed numerous frames of eternal beauty in our minds.

Physical education in schools should guide students into the splendid world of beauty in sport, fostering their ability to perceive beauty, to appreciate, to perform, and to create. Physical education teachers should endeavor to change students' vices such as having a lack of discipline and being out of practice, to have students influenced by beauty through the gracefulness of their own speech, the elegance of their actions, the honest simplicity in their lives, the tidiness of their clothing, the positivity in their outlook, the progressiveness in their thinking, and the propriety in their bearing. When modeling an example for students, teachers must have students experiencing the feeling of beauty through the use of superb technology, stunning images, and flawless skills. We must fully and vividly demonstrate the aesthetic features of physical education to students.

6. Enable Students to Discover and Enjoy Themselves Through Sporting Activities

My take on the ideal physical education is that it should respect students' individuality as well as their personal strengths. It should not use physical education as a means of punishing students, but enable students to discover themselves through partaking in sporting activities and enjoying themselves.

At school, physical education is often one of the students' favorite subjects. This is not only because in physical education classes they are able to engage in their favorite games and activities, but also because it can liberate students from the heavy burdens of the classroom, with fresh air and warm sunshine enabling them to enjoy the delights of nature. However, what is unexpected is the fact that at some schools, many students' most troublesome, most hated subject is physical education. This is because certain physical education teachers use physical education as a means of punishing students, forcing them to engage in sporting activities that they are not good at and do not like. This is especially the case for students who have poor physical fitness or are overweight. These students are forced to do physical activities that are not suitable for their level of physical fitness, to satisfy universal standards of physical fitness as well as being forced to wallow in the miseries of their own sporting failures.

In actual fact, students have countless individual differences. Respecting these differences and meeting the different needs of every student is the fundamental feature of modern physical education in schools.

With improvements in social development standards, all sectors of society are currently developing in the direction of meeting the customization needs of the individual. Trends in individualization such as customizing one's lifestyle, work, and consumption are on the rise. Modern physical education, which is closely linked to the spirit of humanity, should unify the development and training of the physical body with the cultivation and refinement of one's personality. Physical education should enable an individual's enjoyment of sports to be a right; it should become one of our individual needs, an avenue and method for individuals to reveal themselves and to undergo self-discovery.

In American primary schools, physical education focuses primarily on sports games, with formal classes in physical education only beginning when students enter high school. Students seek their own points of interest from within the numerous kinds of sports, choosing their own sport that will develop their intellect and cultivate their moral character. At various high schools across America, there are approximately 20,000 sporting teams whose purpose is to raise the competition levels of various sports. In our opinion, although we find them disorganized, it is precisely at these sporting activities for leisure where real, live people with individual personalities are fostered. Moreover, when students have entered university, there are basically no physical education classes like the ones they would have undertaken in high school, with students choosing activities of their own interests and joining club activities. Every year universities offer high school students thousands upon thousands of sports scholarship placements, with every prestigious university offering an average of 200 scholarships per year. For most high school students and their families, these scholarships are extremely appealing. These sorts of activities not only guarantee the strengthening of students' physiques but also allow students' individuality to freely develop to its fullest and create conditions for the development of students' initiative, creativity, and uniqueness.

When modern physical education was introduced in China, it was precisely during a period when Western physical education was being distorted for use as a political tool due to armed conflicts and colonial expansion. China, which was weak at the time, was under the influence of Japanese militarist ideology, thus affecting the way physical education was conducted and allowing military drills to be introduced in schools. These drills suppress individuality, promote obedience, and ruthlessly deny and ignore an individual's sense of freedom and desires. This sort of physical education, which lacks the spirit of humanity, still exists in physical education classes in today's schools.

Some schools treat physical education activities as a means of "straightening out" classroom discipline and a way of training students to obey rules and regulations, with physical education teachers becoming political instructors in disguise. Some schools often spend from a third to as much as half of their physical education lesson time carrying out drills that emphasize discipline and compliance. Some even force training upon students who do not comply with their instructions as a means of punishing them; for example, being forced to run however many meters or to stand for however many hours and so on as a form of punishment. In so doing, physical education not only loses its unique appeal, it also becomes a feared "devil" for students; it is no longer an emissary for improving one's physical fitness, but degenerates into a tool for ruining one's humanity. What I would like to bluntly say here is this: Whoever defiles and comprehends physical education like this should take leave of its hallowed halls.

At this point it is necessary to analyze an important form of evaluation that is used in physical education—"standards-based testing." Standards-based testing originated from the country's standards for students' sporting capabilities and prowess, an expectation of what the students could accomplish. Some schools have equated standards-based testing with physical education, limiting physical education to merely training for the sake of passing testing. This has caused some students who struggle to meet these standards to forgo sports that they themselves are interested in or have an affinity toward and to devote their entire efforts to meeting these standards.

In reality, the physical fitness and physique of each student is vastly different. There are some students who simply do not need to exert much effort and can meet the set standards, while others will find it difficult to raise their results or reach the set standards no matter how often they train. This being the case, it is not the least bit peculiar that physical education—which should have revealed students' strengths, caused people's spirits to relax, and allowed students' dynamism and vitality to shine—would instead incur students' boredom and even fear. Therefore, I advocate for the use of standards-based testing in schools, but not for this type of testing to be the sole evaluation. For students who are unable to meet these standards due to various reasons, we must offer them a realistic evaluation based on their attitude toward sports, their physical condition, and other particular sporting activities. It is only in so doing that we are able to not use standards-based teaching in physical education as the fundamental objective of assessing teaching and learning in this subject.

In terms of physical education itself, any sports activity has its own regulations and standards based on its structure and form, but the principle of "one size fits all" does not apply to these regulated structures and forms, which are neither inflexible nor repetitive. These regulations and rules are precisely that which can reflect the individuality of each sport as well as the unique beauty that can be determined from these individualities. For example, gymnastics reflects the beauty of form, structure, and movement; track and field events reflect the beauty of speed and strength; and so on.

Therefore, no matter the learning objectives or curriculum that is set up, physical education in schools is still organized in structure and didactic in form. It should be diversified, multidimensional, and relevant, enabling students to reveal their strengths and individuality through a variety of sporting activities and thereby discover and enjoy themselves. Some of our schools do not only focus on a teaching program that is set up according to the students' interests and hobbies, thus reflecting a physical education model that simultaneously runs multiple classes, but instead are able to offer elective and specialist classes in accordance with the students' study majors. For example, geological colleges increase lesson content on subjects such as mountaineering and loaded marches, and commerce colleges increase lesson content on subjects such as bowling and billiards. These are not only effective forms of fitness and entertainment but also embody the principle of "teaching within students' capabilities," enabling students to adapt to their work and personal life after graduation.

In primary and secondary schools, it is even more pressing to closely integrate students' personalities and their individual strengths, capitalizing on these in a relevant manner and helping students to know their own strengths, develop their own hidden potential, and make their individuality known. There is also a need to organize students to take sporting activities that complement their interests and personal strengths, and for the results of assessments and evaluations in physical education to have more flexibility and diversity, enabling all students to be able to find their "own place" in sports activities and for them to find their own joy in the physical education classroom.

Only physical education classes that are full of fun will be popular with students and genuinely effective. Similarly, only sports training and competitions that are full of happiness will be able to completely bring out the athletes' latent capabilities. In 2002, the Chinese soccer team were able to distinguish themselves at the World Cup qualifiers due mainly to the "Happy Soccer" philosophy established by main coach Milutinovic. He once said, "From now on, I will imbue players with all the happiness that I myself have experienced. I will have all players who participate in training close their eyes and carefully visualize: once we have placed ourselves in the World Cup stadium and hear the deafening cheers coming from the crowd of soccer fans from all over the world, imagine a raging fire being ignited within your bodies which will create the feeling of extreme excitement in your innermost being. Who would not want to enjoy this sort of happiness? We play soccer precisely for the sake of realizing this happy dream."

In regard to the future direction of physical education reform, Professor Mao Zhenming from the Capital Institute of Physical Education summarized his point of view in two sentences: "Enable physical education to be even more wonderful in children's minds and to be more useful to children's future lives. If our physical education can truly be guided by these two phrases, then its unique appeal will reach even more teachers and students."

7. Integrate School Sports with Community Sports, Enabling Physical Education to Become a Lifelong Activity

My take on the ideal physical education is that it should enable school sports and community sports to be organically linked together, making full use of community or nongovernment sporting resources and at the same time opening up schools' sporting facilities to the community, embodying physical education's trend toward developing into something that will become a part of our society, our lives, and a lifelong activity.

Having sporting activities become a part of our society and our lives is an important element of physical education reform in schools. At present, there is a strange phenomenon occurring: after graduating from school, "ace students" in physical education do not exercise, with the majority of students having participated in sports for the sake of physical education meeting the criteria set by standards-based testing. This phenomenon is heavily linked to physical education in schools becoming excessively "school-centric" and "curriculum-centric." Yet the sporting activities that have persevered have become an indispensable part of life for a modern person's mental and physical well-being.

In modern society, the degree to which automation is used in the production process is increasing, and the physical exertion required of workers is decreasing on a daily basis; as a result, their leisure time is increasing. At the same time, the production process is becoming increasingly more and more streamlined, with workers' mental strain and psychological burden during production also increasing. The development of science and technology in particular (which has simultaneously given humanity many salvations at the same time as some negative effects such as the exacerbation of environmental pollution), the decrease in the amount of physical activity people undertake, and the increase of "diseases of the modern civilization" will undoubtedly drive workers, in their spare time, to extensively pursue and rely more and more on various sporting activities that strengthen the body, improve one's health, and regulate one's mental and physical well-being. In addition, middle-aged people's pursuit of physical beauty and elderly people's yearning for a healthy body are even more intense. All of this has led to sports having an even more important status than ever before in people's modern-day lives. The trend toward having sports become a part of our society, our lives, and a lifelong activity is gradually intensifying, with sport already having expanded from an activity enjoyed for its leisure and entertainment by a few workers in specialized sporting fields and a few members of society, to an important part of our modern lives as well as a lifelong activity that is necessary and habitual.

Turning again to the essence of sports, it not only improves our health and fitness but also, at the same time, has entertainment value and is worth our viewing and admiration. In the sporting arena, elite athletes show a fusion of strength and beauty, a clash between courage and intellect, superb artistry, beautiful posture, style, an indomitable will, and so on, with all these features becoming examples of glory and models of success that will attract even more people to participate in sports. Conversely, it will also stimulate and spur the popularity and improvement of various nongovernment sporting competitions and recreation sports, facilitating the integration of competition sports, school sports, popular sports, and community sports, thus enabling sporting activities to have vast foundations in the populace.

In the past, people were accustomed to considering physical education classes as something that occurs exclusively within the grounds of the school campus, completely separate from society and home. The result was that students would attend more than a decade of physical education classes, participate in numerous extracurricular sporting activities, and yet, upon graduating, would not exercise. Professor Shen Jianhua from the Shanghai Institute of Physical Education points out that there is a need to transform the enclosed and isolated nature of physical education activities in schools into something of a more open nature with recreation sports, sports for health and well-being, lifestyle, and competition sports channeled into extracurricular activities. At the same time, we must obliterate the boundary between school sports and social sports and establish a new model for conducting sporting activities, that is, school district sports, such as setting up a system of club activities. This is perhaps one of the main directions for reform in physical education.

In order to adapt to the trend of sports becoming a lifelong activity and a part our society and lives, schools drawing up teaching objectives and setting up the teaching curriculum should take full advantage of the position of sports in modern society to set up and adjust a physical education model for schools that is based on the principle of "sports for life." It should organically integrate school and popular sports, fully capitalizing on community and nongovernment sports resources and, at the same time, open up school sporting facilities to the community. Finally, it should establish a sports culture and lifestyle in schools that is rich in variety based on raising and improving the overall mental and physical qualities of the nation.

The State General Administration of Sports and the Ministry of Education once jointly released the document "Notification on the development of hundreds of millions of children and adolescents' health and fitness activities," clearly demanding the widespread participation of children and adolescents in field and outdoor sporting activities. This is to be put into practice in every district, fully capitalizing on winter and summer holidays and actively organizing rich and various extracurricular sporting activities and various forms of summer (or winter) sport and fitness camping activities, such as long-distance running in winter, field trips in spring, swimming in summer, and mountain climbing in autumn. These will enable children and adolescents to hone their willpower, to improve their physical fitness, and develop their character in the midst of Mother Nature.

In this regard, we already have a successful example. There are some primary and secondary schools in Shanghai whose physical education classes focus particularly on traditional sports and folk sports passed on through folk customs, introducing them simultaneously alongside a new model for teaching physical education and fitness, doing all they can to embody the human, fundamental, entertaining, and diverse nature of sports. For example, the subjects introduced in this new model for the mental and physical development of people in the modern era include cross-country, bowling, billiards, golf, and soft volleyball; folk sports introduced include Chinese boxing, swing kicks, metal hoops, and climbing. Many of these city schools also regularly open up their playgrounds, gymnasiums, swimming pools, and so on to the public, where a multitude of men and women, the elderly, and the young, come together as a family to improve their fitness. Amid scenes of joyous laughter and sweat, these school campuses of today have already transformed into unique landscapes.

When school sporting facilities are opened up to the public, of course they will come across specific issues such as school safety and the maintenance of facilities, but as long as this process is scientifically managed and reasonably arranged, it should not be a major issue. In actual fact, many schools overseas do not have walls, and sporting facilities are open to members of the community to use for free. This not only increases the usage of these sporting facilities but also strengthens the close relationship between the school and community and imperceptibly influences students' love of sports; thus their combined effect is remarkable.

There is a maxim inscribed on the banks of the Alpheus River in Olympia in ancient Greece:

If you want to be smart, run!
If you want to be strong, run!
If you want to be healthy, run!

I would like here to slightly modify this maxim and to dedicate it to my readers:

If you want to have a healthy mind, participate in sports activities!
If you want to have a strong body, participate in sports activities!
If you want to have a successful life, participate in sports activities!
If you want to have the habit of participating in sports activities, start during your time as a student!

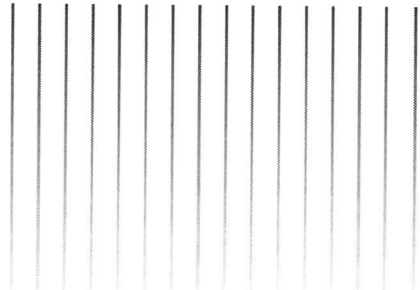

4

My Take on Aesthetic Education

Dear friends, would you delight in the first quietly blooming branch of greenery in the early spring? Would you cheer as the first rays of sunshine surge forth from the light of dawn? Were your thoughts ever shaken to their core by Shakespeare, Victor Hugo, Tolstoy, and Romain Rolland? Did your emotions ever soar because of Beethoven, Chopin, Tchaikovsky, Xian Xinghai, and A Bing? Are you equipped with a broad mind so that you can laugh and defy all the turmoil throughout your journey through life? Do you possess a beautiful and kind soul so that you can help others set sail on the ocean of life? The way we enjoy and experience these types of beauty, which come from the natural world, society, and our lives, constitutes exquisiteness in our lives.

However, all this aforementioned exquisiteness would be inconceivable if one were to depart from the ideal aesthetic education.

1. Cultivate Students' Love of Nature

My take on the ideal aesthetic education is that it should be a type of natural aesthetic education. It should focus on cultivating students' love of nature, enabling students to be fond of nature and to peacefully coexist with nature.

The twentieth century was the century that saw the most brilliant achievements in humankind's conquests over nature. Our scientific and technological achievements were practically a sum all the past centuries. However, the twentieth century was also the most prominent century in terms of humankind's destruction of nature's "profits"—the pollution of rivers and the air, the destruction of forests, the devastating effects of acid rain, the damage done to the ozone layer . . . have all reached the pinnacle of their "achievements" in this century. All this, without a doubt, is related to our lack of fondness and aesthetic feelings for nature.

When Engels was admiring natural beauty, he once felt a "blissful thrill," writing, "Then climb on to the rigging of the bowsprit and gaze on the waves, how, cleft by the ship's keel, they throw the white spray high over your head, and look out, too, over the distant green surface of the sea, where the foaming crests of the waves spring up in eternal unrest, where the sun's rays are reflected into your eyes from thousands of dancing mirrors, where the green of the sea merges with the blue of the sky and the gold of the sun to produce a wonderful color, and all your trivial cares, all remembrance of the enemies and their treacherous attacks disappear, and you stand upright, proudly conscious of the free, infinite mind!"[1]

I do not know if this keenly felt and created "blissful thrill" for natural beauty is one of the spiritual driving forces behind Engels's devotion to the cause of humankind's beauty, but in Kuomintang's Nanchang prison in May 1935, Fang Zhimin, who was facing execution, recalled "China's natural scenery" outside of his iron window, which "can look down upon others for a life time and make people cry out with envy" and where there is "no place that is not beautiful," such as "the imposing Mount Emei, the charming West Lake, the serene and elegant Yandang Mountains and Guilin, the world's most beautiful landscape." These further aroused glorious feelings of incomparable love for the motherland and incomparable faith toward his beliefs, and as a result he feelingly wrote "Beloved China," a famous piece of writing. Ultimately, he calmly died a martyr, choosing to die rather than to submit.

The ideal aesthetic education should be one that combines as one with nature, being in harmony and feeling its aura. Ancient Chinese landscape painter Wang Wei explained the significance of natural beauty in regard to spiritual detachment and the liberation of the mind: "Seeing autumn clouds the soul rises and flies; responding to spring breeze many a thought rolls along." French Enlightenment thinker Rousseau had the utmost regard for nature. He believed that nature is the source of notions on beauty, beauty exists within nature, and natural beauty is greater than artificial beauty. He also believed that people are born with an intimate connection with nature and have a deep and ardent love for nature. People are the most adept connoisseurs for sensing beauty in the natural world.

Indeed, the plants, trees, rivers, and mountains of the natural world all have connotations of beauty; thus they are all objects of aesthetics, being able to make people forget the troubles in their lives or to arouse desires for life and love. The ideal aesthetic education needs to move away from the "small world" of books and to merge with the natural world, to enjoy nature's warmth within its embrace and to feel its aura.

It is true that natural beauty is able to provide joy for people's minds and even nourishment for people's lives. Those beautiful, elegant, and gentle landscapes such as moonlight on water, dark green vegetable fields, trickling streams, and the light yellow willow twigs allow people to feel calm and comfortable; those magnificent and rugged landscapes such as turbulent seas, the surging Yangtze, and steep cliffs enable people to feel carefree and relaxed, a type of majestic beauty that springs up unbidden to the mind and people cannot help but admire nature's generous heart and open boldness.

However, our students today are far too removed from the natural world! When we shut students up in a classroom to carry out so-called aesthetic education, they already do not know what "two golden orioles singing in the green willows" means, nor do they know about "villages enveloped in cooking smoke," or "terrifying waves lashing against the shore," or "the gentle spring breeze kissing the grassland," or "the bitter autumn rain beating on the leaves."

The natural world is an incomparable aesthetics teaching resource, the water from the fountainhead of aesthetic education. A master of the study of aesthetics, Zong Baihua, wrote in "After Appreciating Rodin's Sculptures": "Nature has an inconceivable vitality, pushing the Azoic eon, which was devoid of any life forms, into the Archean eon and from the Archean eon to the point where we have reached the highest form of life, rationality, emotions and feelings. This vitality is the source of all life and is also the source of all beauty."[2] In Sukhomlinsky's "To Children I Give My Heart" he wrote:

> I tried to get the children, before they opened a book to read their first word syllable by syllable, to read the pages of the most miraculous book of all, the book of nature. . . . Go to the fields, to the park. Drink from the source of thought, and this living water will make your pupils wise researchers, inquisitive, curious people and poets. I am convinced a thousand times over that without poetic, emotional-aesthetic outbursts, it is impossible fully to develop the intellectual capabilities of the child. The very nature of the child's thoughts demands poetic creativity. Beauty and living thought are as organically interconnected as the sun and flowers. Poetic creativity begins with a vision of beauty. The beauty of nature sharpens perception, wakes up creative thought, and adds individual experience to the word.[3]

Therefore, I strongly appeal to you all: allow students to enter the natural world, to throw their whole selves, mentally and physically, into "reading and comprehending" nature. If our innermost selves do not evolve to be close to nature or if we are not in perfect harmony with the natural world, then we will not be able to have the true ideal aesthetic education!

Currently, in terms of issues related to natural aesthetic education, there are two long-standing misunderstandings. The first is the concern for students' safety that may arise when students head out into the natural world, hence the "ban" on all field trips and activities that come into close proximity with the natural world. Some places even use documents from the administrative department of education to stipulate that schools are not allowed to organize such activities. The second is the constant desire for all field activities to be "educational," such as "to understand the immense changes that have occurred in the hometown," "to experience the beauty of the rivers and mountains of the motherland," or "to recognize the importance of environmental protection." Furthermore, for students, these sorts of field trips always entail the "important task" of writing a composition. In this way, experiencing the beauty of nature becomes a heavy burden. There is actually no need for so much design because, in a sense, the feeling of closeness to nature and being able to experience the beauty of nature *is* education.

Whether it be the feelings of serenity and elegance of "a small bridge over the flowing water" or the majestic grandeur of "a great river rolling eastward," a dewdrop on the grass at dawn or a wisp of smoke on the plains at dusk, feelings of intimacy and a sense of the sublime for nature and the universe will spring up unbidden in us, just as Bing Xin writes in *A Myriad of Stars*: "We are all the babies of nature, lying in the universe's cradle."

2. Guide and Teach Students to Love, Cherish, and Enjoy Life

My take on the ideal aesthetic education is that it should be aesthetic education on life. It should guide and teach students to love, cherish, enjoy, enhance, and invigorate life.

Renowned poet Gu Cheng wrote this widely read two-line poem: "Even with these dark eyes, a gift of the dark night / I go to seek the shining light." This phrase was once used by Fudan University's debating team as the perfect concluding remark at the Singapore College's debating competition, where they were able to win first place. It has also given courage and strength to many youths who had once lost the confidence to live. However, this person who sang about life was eventually reduced to a murderer who ruins life—he hacked his wife to death and then hanged himself from a tree on Waiheke Island in New Zealand. He was a person who produced beautiful poetry and literary works, and yet he lost track of the beauty of life; his innate character still lacked a true awareness of life.

With scientific advancements, the extent to which modern humanity attaches value to their own lives has reached unprecedented proportions. The successful cloning of "Dolly the sheep" has not only impelled the rapid development of life sciences as a natural science but has also elicited strong reactions from the social sciences. New branches of science are still on the rise, such as bioethics, biolaw, and life aesthetics, with life aesthetics combining with creative arts appreciation studies and quality education to open up new horizons for aesthetic education, that is, aesthetic education on life. In the words of one of the founders of this discipline, Yao Quanxing, aesthetic education on life "enables people to pay more attention to our awareness of life and the state of our lives, it also allows us to focus on the power and beauty of life and for our understanding of the artistic and philosophical realms of life and to reach newer and greater heights."

Through the teaching of aesthetic education on life, we must enable students to understand that life itself is beautiful, that their lives are the masterpieces of beauty, and thus they should take pride in the fact that they possess life. Despite the fact that we were all born with different facial features and body shapes and were all born into different families and regions, we are all "people," incomparable in our greatness, and this is enough of a reason to be proud! Indeed, in terms of every specific person in this vast universe, their lives are not only short but also insignificant; however, the individual personalities molded by every life are definitely unique. Furthermore, every person's life is most definitely irreplaceable and from this, the sacredness of every person's life is evident. It is precisely because of the existence of countless lives brimming with individuality that this world is so rich with vitality and color.

We must also allow students to experience the course that the development of their lives takes and have them enjoy the beauty that occurs at different stages of their lives. About 30 years ago, in the novel entitled *When Rosy Clouds Vanish*, the protagonist makes the following comments:

> People have all sorts of different experiences at different stages of their lives. They can form different kinds of happiness, which are all equally as precious and tremendous in value. The love and affection of their parents during their infancy, the satisfaction of their curiosity during their childhood, the establishment of their reputations during their youth, the passionate love during their teenage years, the fervour of the struggles of their prime, the joy of success when they are middle-aged, the honour of being given respect by younger generations during their elderly years as well as the feeling of serenity and satisfaction when looking back on their entire life and feeling no regret or remorse during their declining years—all these constitute the possible forms of happiness in one's entire life. They are all capable of giving us great joy and leaving behind precious memories in our lives.

These forms of happiness, which occur at different stages of our lives, are at the same time also different forms of the beauty in life that are unique to different stages of our lives.

In recent years, there has been more and more media coverage of increasingly shocking suicides and murders of primary and secondary students. Oftentimes a few details that seem trivial to an adult are enough to cause a child to give up a blossoming life or to deprive others of a life that should not be taken in the first place.

In the face of this phenomena, educators and experts often carry out analyses in terms of education system, ideological education, psychological quality training, and so on. This is of course the correct course of action, but I believe that it is not enough. We should also analyze this problem in terms of what is lacking in aesthetic education on life. If a person does not even love or cherish life, then that person is extremely frightening.

Our present education too readily "confronts reality head-on," with too many "live broadcasts" of more negative aspects of society. In terms of the survival skills that children are trained in during the process of undertaking harsh and competitive school advancement exams, even if they have had a so-called ideal education they are also guided by personal ideals such as "no pain, no gain" and "one studies for the sake of earning big dollars and marrying a beautiful woman." Furthermore, children are being influenced by all sorts of violent homicide in movies, television series, cartoons, and comics and thus, in the skies of a child's mental landscape, there are no birds chasing the clouds; in the open fields of a youngster's mind, there are no flowers that freely dance in the wind. As a result, within children's consciousness, there is no sincerity, no fairy tales or dreams; no devoted love or care for life as well as no longing or yearning for a deep attachment to life. As a result, a primary school student stabbed his classmate in the heart and a high school student raised a hammer to his mother's head!

Knife-wielding, homicidal children are of course an extremely small minority, although they are so young, they "see through the world" and "are disillusioned with the human realm" and thus start to become callous. In this present day, there are quite a few children like this. At an age when they should instead be enjoying their life, these children are displaying a shocking numbness and even contempt for life! If people are willing to "risk their life" at the drop of a hat, do you still have hope that they will cherish something or have at least some sense of responsibility toward themselves, their loved ones, and the people around them?

An ardent love of life is not only the love that one has for people's lives but includes the care and affectionate love for all living things on this planet. I often see naive and innocent children enjoying a fight between two insects, the struggles of an earthworm after it has been split into two segments, or the helpless trembling of an injured bat. No matter how these children excel at being "paragons of virtue and learning" at school, I believe that the structure of their personalities is flawed, because if one is to depart from a love of life itself, then it would be very difficult to form the truly beautiful mind that we hope for.

A Taiwanese website for adopting stray dogs has these words written on the home page: "The long-term use of killing methods for dealing with the issue of stray dogs such as inducing fatal falls, premature burial, electrocution and so on, has set an extremely vile example for the public: one can bully and harm a weak and vulnerable life at will; anything that is not pleasing to the eye—kill it; anything that interferes with the structure of our lives—kill it; anything that we believe has no value—kill it! Supposing that one has been guided by this concept, they would not only be indifferent to the cries and screams of an injured life, but will even expect it as a matter of course." Therefore, people who truly appreciate the beauty of life will not abuse animals; they will even go beyond the general sense of the human-centered notion of "environmental protection" and treat all living things as an object of beauty.

The purpose of aesthetic education on life is to have students understand the extreme value of the beauty of life, and in particular to have them accept themselves, treat themselves well, revel in the joy of the growth and development of life, as well as to respect the lives of others and other forms of life. Only in so doing will our students not be so ready to give up their lives regardless of what setbacks they may encounter in the future. No matter what stage of life they might be at, they will be able to enjoy the fun that comes with their own lives. This is the highest state that our aesthetic education on life should be able to reach.

3. Guide and Teach Students to Love Living and to Be Survivors in Life

My take on the ideal aesthetic education is that it should be aesthetic education on living. It should guide and teach students to love living, to create their own lives, and to be survivors in life and masters of their own lives.

To this day, Beethoven's symphonies still shake humanity's soul to its core. The Beethoven who created such magnificent melodies was first and foremost a person who appreciated and enjoyed the beauty of living. He said, "Oh how beautiful it is to live—and live a thousand times over!" What one needs to know is that when Beethoven spoke these words, he had already lost his hearing in both ears. We can imagine, if it were not for a yearning for the beauty of living, it would be very difficult for Beethoven to compose immortal symphonies such as Symphony no. 5 (the Symphony of Destiny) or Symphony no. 3 (the *Eroica*).

Such is the beauty of living, but it would be difficult for those who do not ardently love living to be moved and excited by the beauty of living. French writer Albert Camus's novel *The Stranger* describes an ordinary company worker called Meursault. He is indifferent and apathetic toward everything in his life; even in love and at the time of his death, he remains the same. This kind of sensory sluggishness and psychological "apathy sickness" causes people's lives to become exceptionally lacking, monotonous, and dull and also causes people to increasingly distance themselves from others, society, nature, and the entire world. Our education system must prevent the development of present-day "Meursaults"!

My understanding of aesthetic education on living is that it steers students' appreciation of aesthetics toward the concept of living itself, enabling students to experience beauty within their everyday lives, thus having them come to love living and, furthermore, to create in them a desire for living a life that is even more beautiful. However, our current aesthetic education precisely overlooks the aesthetics of living. At present, many students have already lost confidence in living at a young age and feel that everything in life is "boring"; furthermore, when faced with setbacks, they will sigh deeply and say, "this is boring, it is really tiring to be alive!" At a time when their lives have not yet truly begun, these students' spirits have already withered up. In terms of dealing with these students, we can of course implement the ideal education and carry out "resilience education," but we can also guide students from the perspective of aesthetic education on living to face joys and sorrows, successes and failures, favorable circumstances and unfavorable circumstances, going forward and going backward.

The French artist Rodin said, "There is no lack of beauty in life but lack of the eyes to discover it." A person who is adept at appreciating the beauty in living is invincible, even in the face of adversity. Within German concentration camps during the Second World War, the prison guards forced every prisoner to do menial labor such as weaving women's straw hats. Before long, many people who were doing the same repetitive work every day in their single prison cells died from sickness, which stemmed from dejection and depression. However, there was one revolutionary who did not complete his daily quota in this sort of depressed manner; instead, he would anxiously await the day's end, full of interest and high spirits and creatively engrossed in the weaving, feeling that weaving itself is also a part of living that is worth sampling. As a result, he prevailed against loneliness and monotony and was able to energetically wait out his time in prison and, upon release, was once again able to throw himself into his work as a revolutionary.

When faced with the same situation, the different feelings one has toward living will enable different people to reach different states of being.

What we must make our students understand is that beauty in living is in the act of living itself and not in anything beyond living. In Wei Wei's *Who Are the Most Lovely People*, the conclusion has the following famous parallelism: "Dear friends, when you get on the first morning tram to go to the factory, when you heft your plow and hoe onto your shoulders and head towards the fields, when you have finished your cup of soy milk and start heading towards school whilst carrying your school bag, when you sit yourself down in front of your office desk and begin the day's work, when you stuff a piece of apple into your child's mouth, when you are strolling with your spouse . . . are you aware that you are in the midst of happiness?" This is the beauty of living. We must also inform our children that the beauty of living does not equate to perfection in living, as trauma, dilemma, twists and turns are also a part of life and are part of the proper characteristics of life, and each and every one of us creates beauty in our lives through our own actions.

In Italian writer Edmondo De Amicis's *Heart*, when faced with his son Enrico, who is unwilling to brave the bitter cold in the morning to go to school, the father says the following:

> Reflect in the morning, when you set out, that at that very moment, in your own city, thirty thousand other boys are going like yourself, to shut themselves up in a room for three hours and study. Think of the innumerable boys who, at nearly this precise hour, are going to school in all countries. Behold them with your imagination, going, going, through the lanes of quiet villages; through the streets of the noisy towns, along the shores of rivers and lakes; here beneath a burning sun; there amid fogs, in boats, in countries which are intersected with canals; on horseback on the far-reaching plains; in sledges over the snow; through valleys and over hills; across forests and torrents, over the solitary paths of mountains; alone, in couples, in groups, in long files, all with their books under their arms, clad in a thousand ways, speaking a thousand tongues, from the most remote schools in Russia, almost lost in the ice to the furthermost schools of Arabia, shaded by palm-trees, millions and millions, all going to learn the same things, in a hundred varied forms. Imagine this vast, vast throng of boys of a hundred races, this immense movement of which you form a part, and think, if this movement were to cease, humanity would fall back into barbarism; this movement is the progress, the hope, the glory of the world. Courage, then,

little soldier of the immense army. Your books are your arms, your class is your squadron, the field of battle is the whole earth, and the victory is human civilization. Be not a cowardly soldier, my Enrico.[4]

Observe, such a trivial and common occurrence such as going to school in the morning, yet the father is able to make his child feel that this is a grandiose and majestic beauty to be enjoyed, and at the same time, it is also a beauty that produces improvements in humankind. In this way, the child is guided through his careless actions in life to feel the reverberations of beauty in life, and from this arises the courage to endeavor, this is aesthetic education on living.

Therefore, I very much advocate making aesthetic education a part of life, so that we can enable our lives to be eternally bright. I once participated in an evening creative arts concert hosted by the Suzhou School for the Deaf-mutes with the theme of "bathing in sunlight together and offering our compassion together." There was one performance, "Imagination on Red Color," that sent intense shock waves to my very core. It expressed the desire and long-held yearning for red color of a group of children with hearing disabilities and three children with visual disabilities. It also expressed the yearning and true love that children with physical disabilities have for a beautiful life. The red color, which symbolizes a beautiful life, often appears before my eyes, inspiring me to cherish and love life.

Li Fan highly praised the significance of aesthetic education on living in terms of improving the quality of people's lives in *The Modern Mission of Aesthetic Education*: When the day comes when life has become the best work of art, when living becomes the best form of enjoyment in one's life, living will no longer be laborious, nor will it be painful. Even if there is pain and there are challenges and even disasters, people will not run away but instead be filled with courage and full of steadfast belief. At these times, "Suffering and disasters become ways to display human dignity and the best stage for confirming and developing a person's own strength, thus showing its positive side. Life will become an artistic life. This kind of life will be the highest state of living."

4. Guide and Educate Students to Love Art and to Have a Particular Artistic Talent

My take on the ideal aesthetic education is that it should be an aesthetic education on art and should guide and educate our students to love art, to appreciate art, and to have a particular artistic talent.

The ideal aesthetic education will of course draw support from the use of artistic skills as its carrier. In terms of holistic development, apart from the fact that young students should have an abundant amount of textbook knowledge and a healthy physique, it is also extremely necessary for them to possess some artistic skill, because this is essential for enriching a student's spiritual life and forming healthy lifestyle interests.

From the perspective of school education, apart from imparting basic knowledge on aesthetics such as art and music, it is also necessary to cultivate some real artistic skill in students, enabling them to personally experience beauty through the process of participating in artistic activities and not just be an observer of beauty. Therefore, the ideal aesthetic education does not wait until students become adults and "are sensible" before passing on artistic knowledge but starts from infancy—society ought to create favorable conditions for them and attach importance to their creative arts education. Many better-off families should view this from the perspective of molding a child's character. They should make full use of spare time and have students learn various artistic skills such as the piano, the violin, calligraphy, and painting and thus put their artistic talents to use through various channels.

At a regular primary or secondary school, creative arts education is mainly carried out from the perspective of quality education, with training conducted for students on some artistic skills. Comparatively more well-off schools can fully utilize after-school time to set up literature reading groups, calligraphy groups, rhythmic gymnastics teams, vocal ensemble teams, school bands, dance teams, and so on, and through these activities mold students' character and develop students' artistic talents such as in piano, chess, calligraphy, and painting, thereby enriching students' leisure lifestyle and creating a beautiful artistic mood.

However, the aesthetic education on the creative arts that I yearn for does not stop there because, forgive my directness, teaching a student how to play a musical instrument is not necessarily an aesthetic education on the creative arts. It is just as the vice chairman of the Chinese Musicians Association, Wang Liping, says: "The main objective of aesthetic education is not to cultivate skills in playing an instrument or singing, but to give people good cultural living habits. Some people say that 'no day should go by without music' whilst others say 'no day should go by without fine food', the difference between the two is also a matter of habits, whose formations are connected to parents, the school and their environment. What we should be the most afraid of is that some utilitarian elements can also be blended in."

If educators only teach students various skills in playing musical instruments, I believe that this is not aesthetic education on the creative arts but is only a type of artistic skills training. What do we mean by "aesthetic education on the creative arts"? What do we mean by "artistic skills training"? It would be better for me to illustrate by quoting a story that occurred when Professor Yu Qiuyu was recruiting research students in the field of creative arts. One year, Professor Yu attached a modern European painting to the application papers for research students and asked candidates to write a piece on the spot on their thoughts after viewing and appreciating the painting. Some candidates clearly wrote down the period in which the painting was produced, its genre, and a short biography of the author's life, but as for their appreciation of the artwork, they only wrote a few phrases such as "brushstrokes are flexible and colors are clear-cut." However, there was one candidate who simply did not know which country the painting was from or who the artist was, and instead threw himself completely into writing his appreciation, relying on his impromptu feelings to grasp what the artist was feeling, even mentally associating the painting with opportunities he had as a child and encounters he had beneath an old tree. As a result, Professor Yu decided to accept this candidate, commenting, "I applaud this candidate's own realistic, heartfelt and genuine feelings towards art." The "realistic, heartfelt and genuine feelings towards art," as described by Professor Yu, are exactly the feelings that we must teach students in our "aesthetic education on art."

At present, students who are able to perform art but do not "understand" art are in the majority. I believe the cause lies within this type of "artistic skills training" that is more or less tainted with utilitarianism; for example, training for the purpose of being the head of some sort of "family" in the future or for the purpose of "adding marks" in junior high and university entrance exams. Even if schools run interests classes related to the creative arts, some parents and teachers will still approach these from a utilitarian perspective.

Currently, many adults do not have clear motives for pursuing art and treat the learning and mastery of artistic skills as a means of making a living, treating it as a shortcut to make a name and reputation for oneself. As long as there is the possibility of "becoming successful," they will not hesitate to offer anything in return and will even be willing to do another's bidding. However, when they discover that an artistic skill will most likely not become "valuable," they immediately stop their children's practice of such a skill. Therefore, the phenomenon of looking only for short-term benefits is extremely serious. Other parents wish to make up for their own shortcomings by having their children invest in these areas, so that they may "retrieve" what they themselves lack from their children. However, one's own wishful thinking can be spoiled by excessive enthusiasm. Rather than saying that forcing children to learn the creative arts such as playing the piano or calligraphy is a way of molding a child's character, why not instead say that parents are fulfilling their "artistic dream" through the torments of their own offspring. Children, who have not yet stepped into the hallowed halls of the creative arts, or have yet to even find the road leading to creative arts, are impatiently required by some parents to participate in various forms of "grade examinations," forced to embark on the wrong path for learning an artistic skill. This type of utilitarian approach severely holds back children's desires to innovate and obstructs the development of their innovativeness.

Please do not misunderstand. I am not at all against children's mastery of some artistic skills, but I am opposed to the fact that at the same time as we blatantly make these skills utilitarian, we are departing from proper artistic cultivation and appreciation. I advocate for children to be able to enter the hallowed halls of the creative arts with relaxed steps while harboring the purity of childish innocence.

Under the premise of doing away with the yoke of utilitarianism, it is of course an excellent thing that children are able to play an instrument, do calligraphy, dance, and paint artworks, but the aesthetic education on creative arts that

I look forward to will instead wish for them, in this era that is clamoring with popular culture, to enter into the world of Li Bai, Du Fu, Rabindranath Tagore, Victor Hugo, and Shakespeare; to become acquainted with Xu Beihong, Qi Baishi, Picasso, Renoir, and Rodin; and to be intoxicated by pieces such as "A Moonlit Night on the Spring River," "The Moon Reflected by Two Springs," *The Butterfly Lovers*, "The Blue Danube," and "Symphony no. 6 (the *Pastoral*).

At this point, I must particularly emphasize that we should be guiding our students to learn how to appreciate traditional Chinese operas such as Kunqu opera, Shaoxing opera, and Peking opera, known as the quintessence of culture and art. They are treasures that have been polished over hundreds of years and are steeped in the cultural essence of our nation. Our aesthetic education on the creative arts should allow our children to become the new generation of opera fans and "amateur performers."

In terms of the beauty in the creative arts, its foundations are genuine and its premise is good. Therefore, the purpose of aesthetic education on the creative arts is to direct students to seek the truth for the sake of the realm of good and beauty through beauty in the creative arts.

5. Establish Aesthetic Education as a Major Concept and Construct a Rich Aesthetic Atmosphere

My take on the ideal aesthetic education is that it should be a multilayered aesthetic education. It should establish aesthetic education as a major concept and become a multilayered and networked model for aesthetic education, constructing a rich aesthetic atmosphere.

Traditional models of aesthetic education are often unilateral and flat; this form of aesthetic education could only be carried out through the art and music classes offered at school. I believe that this is far from being sufficient. Beauty exists in every aspect of our lives and thus aesthetic education should be offered everywhere.

At every stage of the school's education process, every aspect of society, the family and school are filled with elements of aesthetic education; therefore, my take on the ideal aesthetic education is one that should be holistic and multilayered. As Sukhomlinsky points out, "We strive to enable those thoughts of cherishing and loving beauty to link with all spheres of a student's spiritual life: to link their mental and physical labors, their innovativeness, social activities, moral and aesthetic attitude, friendship and love." In my opinion, these "spheres" also include all aspects of space and time in a student's life.

A multilayered aesthetic education first and foremost implies the mutual integration of aesthetic education with the other various forms of education: moral, intellectual, physical, and job skills. Apart from specialized aesthetic education (which is also necessary), we should also meld aesthetic education with moral education, intellectual education, physical education, and technical education. In moral education, teachings on aesthetics need to be carried out for the purpose of transforming abstract preaching in moral education to using vivid images of beauty as an influence, and through guiding students to appreciate beauty, have this appreciation refined into a pursuit of truth and virtue. In intellectual education, teachings on aesthetics need to guide students to experience beauty in science, wisdom, and innovation and have them personally experience the joy of discovery and the sense of beauty in reason while at the same time imparting knowledge to students and cultivating their abilities. In physical education, teachings on aesthetics need to have students, through a variety of sporting activities and exercise, directly experience the distinct charms of sport such as the beauty of health, form and structure, and strength while they are, at the same time, learning to grasp the rules and methods of play for various sporting activities. In technical education, teachings on aesthetics need to have students experience and understand what Marx called "the beauty of labor production" as well as the beauty created through practices of labor with one's own hands, by having students undertake practices of labor.

A "multilayered aesthetic education" also implies paying attention to the development of the hidden aesthetic education. The so-called hidden aesthetic education is the beauty that educators pursue throughout the process of teaching and education. The various elements of beauty that are created or aroused during education enable students to enjoy the beauty of the educational process or to be unconsciously influenced by beauty. If the beauty of the classroom teacher's decorous appearance, his refined and elegant speech, her relaxed and harmonious human relations in the classroom, an abundantly interesting teaching process, and a lively and vivacious teaching atmosphere are able to allow students to be influenced by this atmosphere of beauty, then it allows their intellectual and nonintellectual qualities to receive the best form of cultivation within a learning atmosphere that is brimming with beauty. Even in specialized creative arts classes such as music and art classes, we still cannot just impart basic knowledge to students but should instead use the process of teaching and learning itself (including necessary training processes) to have some sort of attractive beauty for students.

A multilayered aesthetic education also includes beautiful environments that influence a student's sense of aesthetics, such as the campus and the classroom. A beautiful environment is a subtle and silent form of aesthetic education.

Unfortunately, at present some of our luxury schools are becoming more and more like hotels or shopping centers: there is a lack of natural green vines on the terrazzo or marble columns, and on the bright corridor walls are often hung photographs and inscriptions of leaders and inspectors for the school from all levels of government as opposed to elegant Chinese art or oil paintings.

Sukhomlinsky once proudly introduced his Pavlysh Secondary School by saying: "We devote considerable time to providing children with a wide range of aesthetic impressions; indeed that is the starting point of our efforts to give them an aesthetic environment. Everything a child sees, once he has crossed the threshold of our school, and everything he encounters is beautiful. The general view of the school is beautiful, as it stands hidden in a sea of greenery; so are the green vines with their amber grapes, and the climbing roses along the path from one building to the next. The trees in the school garden are beautiful at any season of the year. The porch of the school's main entrance framed in wild vines is also beautiful."

The Pingjiang Experimental School in Suzhou is another model of a school that places an emphasis on environmental aesthetics. The entire campus is studded with soaring ancient trees and lush green trees to provide shade, floral garden features, rock gardens, and ponds; everything is visually intermingled, with simple, unadorned, and majestic halls contrasting pleasantly with 18 ginkgo trees over two hundred years old. Every school path has been given an elegant name, every building has a sign that is full of poetic sentiments, and every classroom has a signboard hung up that is unique in style. The school has set up an artistic troupe with "Ginkgo Babies" as its main theme, as well as "The Song of the Ginkgo Babies" and "The Dance of the Ginkgo Babies"; this rich cultural and artistic environment has enabled the school's aesthetic education to flourish and has also enabled the school's quality of teaching to continuously improve and its reputation to soar.

One can imagine what a beautiful spiritual world these children will have living and learning in this sort of enchanting environment! I hope that there will be increasingly more beautiful campuses like this one.

A multilayered aesthetic education should also be a coordinated integration of the aesthetics of the school, home, and society. The isolated teaching of aesthetic education in schools will be hard pressed to achieve truly tangible results; instead, it must be complemented by home and social aesthetics in order to be successful. Parents should be their child's instructors on aesthetics, not simply to accompany a child while practicing the piano but to provide an elegant aesthetic home environment for their child, to allow well-known classical music pieces to reverberate throughout the living room, to allow their bookshelves to be fully lined with literary masterpieces, and to allow world-famous paintings to be hung from the walls. Our society must, as much as possible, provide children with spiritual nourishment for beauty: Would it be possible for art galleries and museums to open up to children for free? Would it be possible for artists to be obliged to organize some lectures on aesthetics for children? Would it be possible for students to also be allowed to participate in the design process of urban planning? Would it be possible to build some artistic theme parks? Would it be possible to set up streets that have special artistic characteristics and environments? Multilayered aesthetic education also has an important implied meaning, that is, to allow our students not only to be the objects of aesthetic education but at the same time to also be the carriers or incarnation of beauty. In other words, at the same time students are undergoing an education in aesthetics, to become a part of the aesthetic environment or even a source of aesthetics through the beauty in their own appearance.

The multilayered aesthetic education that I imagine also includes enrichment of the lesson content in aesthetic education, networking of the channels of aesthetic education, diversification of the form of aesthetic education, and so on.

Only in so doing can our aesthetic education become ubiquitous, like the air, sunshine, and water.

6. Rely on Teachers with a Cultivated Sense of Aesthetics and Highlight Demonstrative Aesthetic Education

My take on the ideal aesthetic education is that it should be a type of demonstrative aesthetic education, closely relying on teachers who possess a cultivated sense of aesthetics and enabling students to progress toward a beautiful life under the guidance of their teachers.

As the German philosopher Hegel once said, in children's hearts, teachers are the perfect idol. The most effective form of aesthetic education should be the educators' natural impact and influence on and demonstrations of beauty for their students. It would be impossible for any other forms of aesthetic education to be truly effective if one were to depart from the use of teachers of "beauty." My take on the ideal aesthetic education calls out to teachers who possess a beautiful personality, are beautiful in their appearance, are adept at teaching the creative arts, and are full of interests in aesthetics.

These sorts of teachers should first possess a pure and beautiful personality. Beautiful facial features are something that one is born with; they are external and also temporary. Only a pureness in one's personality can enable educators to be forever beautiful.

Beauty in one's personality has many connotations, but for the primary and secondary teachers who all come into contact with children on a daily basis, I would like to put great emphasis on the fact that they must possess a childlike innocence—a simple, honest, natural, and straightforward childlike innocence. Life experiences have given us maturity, experiences in society have given us a worldly wisdom, cultural knowledge has given us gentility, and setbacks in life have given us wisdom; however, for the unyielding pursuit of truth, virtue, and beauty and the uncompromising stance on falsities, evil, and the ugly, a fiery passion and feelings of integrity will always be part of the power of an educator's personality!

When teachers meet their students for the first time, they begin to expose themselves to the scrutiny of dozens of students; even signs of pretense, slyness, worldly wisdom, perfunctoriness, apathy, and cynicism would not be able to escape the students' bright, pure, and innocent eyes, furthermore casting a shadow over the students' pure hearts. Sincerity can only be evoked by sincerity, benevolence can only be cultivated by benevolence, and so beauty can only rely on beauty for nourishment. It is precisely because of this that Rousseau warns educators in *Emile, or On Education*: "Beware of playing the tempter in this world, which nature intended as an earthly paradise for men, and do not attempt to give the innocent child the knowledge of good and evil."

Teachers like these should also possess an appropriate amount of beauty in their appearance. What do I mean by "an appropriate appearance"? I mean an outward appearance that is appropriate to an educator's status, an appropriateness in the substance being taught, and an appropriateness in the learning environment's makeup.

In Makarenko's "On Communist Education", he writes: "Outward appearances hold great significance in a person's life. It is hard to imagine a dirty and sloppy man would actually be able to pay attention to his own actions." Traditional teachers did not pay much attention to their appearances, to the point that they gave people the feeling that they were "antiquated"; present-day teachers are not only disseminators of the truth (knowledge) and guides to goodness (morals), but are also the embodiments and transmitters of beauty and ought to pay attention to their own appearance. In the profession of teaching, what determines the appearance of a teacher is not simply a matter of "personal taste," because in a sense, the teacher's appearance is also a part of the makeup of an aesthetic environment, to the extent that it can be considered a source of aesthetics. If teachers' outward appearance is not appropriate, such as female teachers wearing heavy makeup and over-the-top jewelry or male teachers dressing in an undignified, even scruffy, manner, they will have many negative effects on education. A vibrant, neat, simple, dignified, and stylish appearance should be the proper and "pleasing" appearance for teachers.

These sorts of teachers must also have superb teaching skills. Having a wealth of professional knowledge and proficient teaching skills does not necessarily mean that they also possess the beauty of teaching aesthetics. If teachers are unwilling to become "pedagogues," then they should put all their efforts into pursuing superb teaching skills.

Beauty in teaching skills refers to the beauty in the language of instruction, the resourcefulness displayed in teaching, the feelings related to education and the educational environment. We often say that listening to such-and-such a teacher teach a lesson is practically "a type of pleasure," not only because she explains various kinds of knowledge clearly, but more importantly, because at the same time, she brings us beauty that is like the spring breeze.

One year, Tsung-Dao Lee visited China to give a lecture on the art of learning entitled "Modern Trends in Technology and Recent Developments." He spoke freely, spontaneously talking about different things; at times he would transport everyone to remote ancient times and at other times take us to the other side of the Pacific Ocean. Everyone forgot that they themselves were still in a classroom; their hearts were soaring along with his words. After class, one student commented, "His words are like a boat, carrying and navigating his audience through his rivers of passionate knowledge. Throughout this, he is still just as elegant, graceful and refined. He likes to laugh, and the slight upturn of his lips carry with it a touch of humor. He likes to move about and his lively eyes seem to be speaking to us; at times he would stand still without speaking, but we students still knew what he wanted to say, bursting forth with a laughter like the spring rain at his silent expressions. We were truly intoxicated!"

These sorts of teachers must also have a refined sense of aesthetics. Requiring all teachers to have some sort of artistic talent is unrealistic, but if a teacher is able to possess at least one sort of artistic talent, then this would most definitely be beneficial to his teaching, and it is also a subtle form of aesthetic education. In Sichuan in the 1980s, a young teacher ran his class in a very distinctive manner; the way he organized and ran his recreational activities in particular was quite impressive. In actual fact, this teacher himself did not have any great artistic talents at all, but when he worked as an educated youth, he learned how to play the harmonica and furthermore liked to listen to famous pieces of world music and choral music, so he could also be considered a lover of music. He had each of his students buy a harmonica and utilized after-school hours to teach students how to play; later on, all the students in this class were able to play the harmonica and created a class harmonica group. Using this as a basis, he also guided students to appreciate famous pieces of world music and organized them to participate in choral ensemble competitions (with himself as the conductor). Under the guidance of the famous composer Gu Jianfen, he and his students composed their own class song. It is precisely music that promoted the development of his students in all aspects and his collectivist approach to teaching. His class later became nationally renowned as "the class of the future." This teacher is Professor Li Zhenxi, the very teacher who won the "Best Works Award" and the "Bing Xin Literature Award," established for the purpose of national spirit and culture, with educational works such as "Love and Education" and "To Enter the Mind."

This once again confirms what Sukhomlinsky says in *100 Pieces of Advice for Teachers*: "Education without beauty or art is inconceivable. If you can play a musical instrument, then as a teacher, you are already superior to other teachers; if you possess even a small spark of musical genius within you, then you are a king, a ruler of education, because music is able to draw the hearts of teachers and students closer together and is able to allow the most secretive corners of a student's heart to reveal itself in front of an educator."

7. Enable Students to Form Perfect Personalities and to Have Beautiful Souls Through Aesthetic Education

My take on the ideal aesthetic education is that it should be a spiritual aesthetic education. It should place emphasis on enabling students to form perfect personalities and have beautiful souls through aesthetic education.

Zhu Guangqian has a famous saying: "To ask for the purification of one's conscience, we must first ask for the beautification of one's life." Our aesthetic education should not stop at just teaching students to appreciate art. It has been said: "A child who can play the piano will not morally degenerate." I believe this notion is unilateral because beauty in the creative arts does not become internalized as beauty of the soul; one's humanity can morally degenerate in the same way.

It has been said that during the Second World War, many German Nazi officers would play Beethoven on the piano. In the film *Red Cherry*, the dehumanized German general is also a person who is highly accomplished and artistic. He has a passion for tattoo art and actually uses the Chinese girl Chuchu's skin as material for his artistic creations and tattoos the emblem of the Nazi party onto Chuchu's back! It can clearly be seen that a simple appreciation for the arts does not necessarily lead humanity toward honesty and the sublime.

Without a doubt, the ultimate goal of aesthetic education is to guide humanity. By today's standards, education in ancient China was mainly moral education, and the Chinese moral education from the time of Confucius was mainly achieved through aesthetic education, or it could be said that moral education at that time was more or less aesthetic education. Confucius says: "poetry makes a man, courtesy develops a man, while music fully matures a man," meaning that poetry can arouse a person's ambition, etiquette can steady a person's character, and music can mold a person's temperament.

Starting from the time of Confucius, ancient Chinese education began to attach great importance to the role of the creative arts in educating a person. One of the main representatives of the Song dynasty school of Neo-Confucianism, Cheng Yi, also comments: "People from ancient times entered themselves into primary school at age 8 and began studying 'Great Learning' at age 15. They were provided with literary talents to cultivate their eyes, voices to cultivate their ears, etiquette to cultivate their limbs, song and dance to cultivate their vigor and principles to cultivate their hearts." In the eyes of the ancient Chinese sages, education that departs from aesthetic education is practically impossible.

In modern times, aesthetic education began to separate itself from moral education. In regard to this, a pioneer of modern aesthetic education in China, Cai Yuanpei, explains: "It is because people in recent times have largely overlooked aesthetic education. According to the two classical arts of rites and music in our country's ancient times, aesthetic education has the benefit of solemn elegance. Western education also places great importance on aesthetics. For the purpose of having society be particularly alerted to this fact, I put forward aesthetic education in particular to be combined together with physical education, intellectual education and moral education to form the four disciplines of education."[5]

When former vice premier Li Lanqing stressed the significance of aesthetic education, he pointed out even more clearly that "aesthetic education, is an important part of educational policy and an important element of the comprehensive quality education for young people. This is because aesthetic education is not only an important means for humanity to understand and transform the world, but also an important channel for bringing about humanity's own culture and moulding perfect personalities." In a certain sense, the beauty of human nature, the beauty of the human conscience, and the beauty of the spirit are the fundamental pursuits and highest states of aesthetic education.

The spiritual aesthetic education is the formation of beauty in a student's soul through aesthetic education and furthermore externalizes this beauty in one's daily life through the beauty in one's speech and actions.

A beautiful soul includes benevolence, honesty, and strength, while at the same time associating itself with idealism, patriotism, and heroism. The indomitable heroic spirit that Beethoven's Symphony no. 5 is filled to the brim with, the stunning national spirit that rushes forth in the *Yellow River Oratorio*, the pure and

majestic love that flows throughout *The Butterfly Lovers*, the crystal clear innocence and love that is contained in De Amicis's *Heart*, the beauty of humanity
that emerges in *Les Miserables*, as well as the eternal smile of *Mona Lisa*, and the
profound poetry of *Stray Birds*, are all features that we cannot allow students to
"understand" only objectively; instead we should sow the seeds of truth, virtue,
and beauty and have the most beautiful flowers of human civilization bloom
within the wilderness of their spirits.

A beautiful soul must be embodied through language because beauty in language is the perfume that is emitted by one's soul. The "rhetoric dominated by sincerity" was proposed by ancient people in *The Book of Changes*. *The Book of Rites*
was even more demanding: "What is required in feeling is sincerity; in words,
that they be susceptible of proof." These language aesthetics that inherently require
"sincerity" and extrinsically require "proof" are one of the principles of ancient
Chinese aesthetics. Take note that this "proof" does not refer purely to language
techniques, as at its crux is the quality of "sincerity." Confucius's demands of language are even stricter, as he not only demanded beauty but also demanded it to be
poeticized: "If you do not study poetry, you will not be able to converse."

However, our present-day education is nonetheless gradually losing these great
traditions. Many children can sing several popular songs with poor diction and
grammar, yet more and more children cannot "speak"; public speaking becomes
a recitation of one's essay and some are at the point where they do not even know
the basic courtesy involved in calling someone. We hope that through aesthetic
education, children will be able to possess beauty in their language, that is, they
must be able to be amiable, elegant, humble, and appropriate and to avoid foul language and swearing no matter what the circumstances. Beauty in language is also
expressed through one's tone of voice and intonation. When they are speaking to
someone, they must be serious, sincere, clear, generous, and natural and must not
"put on airs" and behave coyly. When listening to someone speaking, they must
also be serious and sincere and must not constantly glance around or interrupt
whenever they please; if they want to present a different opinion, it must be appropriate, disputes have to be well grounded, and finally, they must not insult others
with their words. Even if other persons use impolite language, they must still treat
them with courtesy and use elegant, tactful humor and firm language to show a
high degree of self-cultivation and inner strength. Beauty in one's language is asso-
ciated with beauty in one's actions. Beauty in actions is extremely broad, including
everything from language, the way one treats others, to the way one walks, sits,
and stands, and so on. The Chinese ancients stressed: "Sit like a bell, stand like a
pine, walk like the breeze."

In addition to this, I especially stress that we guide students to learn to interact
with others through the use of aesthetic education and enable children through
their interactions with others to experience the emotional beauty of harmony
and sincerity. Every person lives within society and needs to interact with others.
When interacting with others, one must follow a certain code of conduct, and
conforming to this code of conduct is beauty; doing the contrary is ugliness. We
greatly applaud schools that have proposed the following requirements for their

students: "be particular about one's own appearance, be polite to others, abide by public morals in society, and be filial at home." This not only makes demands of students in terms of beauty but also puts forward the codes of human interaction in society and at home.

China is a country of ceremonies, and the Chinese people have always had the traditional virtues of "following the customary ceremonies" and "being courteous by nature." All primary and secondary school students have everyday codes of conduct, and these codes are an important part of these students' beauty in behavior. School aesthetic education must be combined with the teaching of everyday codes of conduct and place an emphasis on carrying out student guidance in terms of beauty in their behavior, giving prominence to the practicality and effectiveness of aesthetic education in schools.

Literature is an important channel for carrying out "spiritual education." Qin Wenjun, a writer of children's literature, says that literature is like a window—it develops within a child's beautiful soul. Push it open and the soul will become much more bright and spacious, as if one is seeing the flowers of life springing up in front of one's face, drenched in sunlight, moving far away from mediocrity and toward the sublime. However, batch after batch of children are easily infatuated and dazzled by animated films, various commercials that are repeatedly broadcast, and even games that require fighting. How easy it is for people to be caught up in simple amusements; this is exactly human nature's weakness. And so, if we do not push open this window in a child's heart early enough, it will be covered in layers of dust that, with the passage of time, will increasingly harden. Therefore, she believes, "the best type of quality education is to have students understand how to appreciate." Only through understanding how to appreciate a person, art, life, and the world can they go and love, create and pursue, and all these are inseparable from literature. Literature allows people to better themselves, to be happy, and it can also make the world beautiful and plentiful.

Sukhomlinsky once warned educators in *Pavlysh Secondary School*: "Beauty is a powerful source of moral purity, spiritual richness and physical robustness. Aesthetic education's most important mission is to teach children to be able to see the spiritual nobility, benevolence and sincerity within the beauty found in the world that surrounds them (the natural world, the arts and human interactions), and to regard these as the basis for establishing their own beauty." This should also become the goal of our "spiritual education."

8. Cultivate Students' Imagination and Creativity Through the Process of Aesthetic Education

My take on the ideal aesthetic education is that it should be a type of creative aesthetic education. It should place an emphasis on cultivating students' imagination and creativity through the process of aesthetic education, stimulate the impetus and desire to create, and take pleasure in the joy of creation.

In Friedrich Schiller's *On the Aesthetic Education of Man in a Series of Letters*, he believes that within a powerful state, people meet each other using force, and thus people's activities are limited; within an ethical state, people confront each other using the law and people are still limited; it is only in an aesthetic state that people can give freedom through freedom and as a result, they will bring harmony to society and also enable people to become a harmonious whole. This reveals, from one aspect, the intrinsic mechanism of aesthetics and creativity. In other words, through aesthetics education, we can liberate people's perceptions, inspire their spirituality, open up their imaginative space, and thus develop their creativity.

Within the new round of curriculum reform in elementary education, creation, experiences and appreciation, and performances are already viewed together as the content of the main teaching fields. For example, within the music course, creation in music includes two types of content: the first is the use of musical improvisation and creation activities to explore students' hidden potential; the second is the use of musical materials to create music. Examples of the former include doing an impromptu composition with the mood of a song set to the same rhythm and dance, creating an impromptu composition of a musical story, and performing a phrase in life or a line in a poem. Examples of the latter include requiring first- and second-year students to use lines, blocks of colors, and graphics to record voices or music; requiring third- to sixth-year students to be able to correct short melodies; and requiring seventh- to ninth-year students to choose and compose preludes and interludes for songs.

I believe that the biggest breakthrough for the new round of curriculum reform in elementary education is introducing "creation" to the main teaching areas, with it playing a role that cannot be underestimated in cultivating students' creativity. In creative arts education, increasing the use of creative activities will enable aesthetic education to go beyond emulation and technical skills to better reflect aesthetic education's liberation of people's perceptions and creativity's essential requirements.

In actual fact, creativity is a common characteristic of science and the arts. Tsung-Dao Lee devoted many years to the communication and harmonious relationship between the two. Since 1987 he has conducted many international science conferences where artists painted based on scientific themes, with masters in the art world such as Li Keran, Wu Zuoren, Huang Zhou, Hua Junwu, and Wu Guanzhong using artistic brushstrokes to explain their understanding of science. Tsung-Dao Lee said with great feeling: "The common basis of science and art is human creativity, the goal they both chase is the universality of truth. They are like both sides of the same coin and are indivisible." Germany is an advocate of arts and culture and a country that places importance on aesthetic education. Among a crowd in Germany, one would be hard pressed to find someone who does not understand music or musical instruments. This may be one of the reasons why Germans are full of creativity.

Creative aesthetic education needs a relaxed atmosphere. It also needs to allow students to maintain an open and free mentality and to keep having pleasant and happy experiences, as well as to have teachers put their efforts into taking good care of these seeds of creative thinking. This is a true story: There was once a student in the lower grades who had finished drawing a picture of a young person by following the teacher's example but adding a black spot next to the finished picture of the young person. The teacher asked, "What is with this mess?" The student replied, "The young person's shadow." "Who said that you could doodle? Can't you see the picture that your teacher has drawn of a young person?" This student looked again at the model, then looked again at the teacher's serious face, and dumbly nodded his head and obediently used correct fluid to blot out "the young person's shadow." In contrast, in an art class at a Japanese school, while a Japanese teacher was teaching students how to draw an apple, he noticed that one student had drawn a square apple, so he patiently asked, "All apples are round, so why did you draw one that is square in shape?" The student replied, "I saw my dad place an apple on the table at home, which accidentally rolled and dropped to the ground. I thought: if there was such a thing as a square apple, it would be great!" The teacher then encouragingly said, "You really know how to use your brain. I wish you all the best in cultivating a square apple soon." In the two stories cited above, the teachers played different characters with very different roles—to destroy creativity and to induce creativity; thus the same creative behavior in both students met with different fates.

Students nowadays are too bitter, and they sing with grief and indignation: "The most bitter person is me, the most tired person is me, the one who wakes up the earliest is me, the one that sleeps the latest is also me." Under the heavy burden of exam pressure, they cannot experience the happiness of learning and the impetus to create and they cannot revel in the joys of success. With the construction of a series of "standardized" projects, every one of them has become a "standard person" with no personality. This is undoubtedly the sorrow of aesthetic education and the sorry state of education.

The pursuit, discovery, and creation of beauty are the footprints of human civilization's progress and are also the course of a person's flourishing life. Beauty inspires us to seek the truth and guides us toward benevolence. Beauty is a form, and it is also a type of value as well as a spiritual experience; beauty is the source of creation and is also the highest state of life.

If, due to various reasons, Chinese education has ignored, neglected, and even abandoned beauty in the past, then, bathed in the light of the educational ideologies of the twenty-first century, we should start afresh in our search for beauty, revelations of beauty, and our creation of beauty because now is the time.

Dearest friends, let us delight in the first quietly blooming branch of greenery in the early spring; let us cheer as the first rays of sunshine surge forth from the light of dawn; let our thoughts be shaken to their core by Shakespeare, Victor Hugo, Tolstoy, and Romain Rolland; let our emotions soar because of Beethoven, Chopin, Tchaikovsky, Xian Xinghai, and A Bing; let us be equipped with a broad and pure vision, so that we will defy all the turmoil throughout our journey through life; let us possess a beautiful and kind soul so that we can help others set sail on the ocean of life.

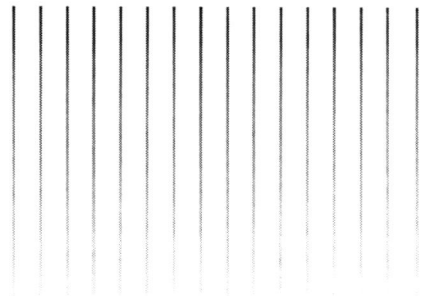

5

My Take on Technical Education

Physical labor is a phrase that once resounded across the heavens.

Physical labor is a term that has a splendid past.

Physical labor enables humans to part ways with apes, creating our own human race.

Physical labor makes the rotten things miraculous, pushing the wheel of history forward.

Throughout the history of humanistic education, there have always been two differing opinions on the treatment of physical labor. One opinion holds that physical labor is magnificent and so education must combine with productive labor to lay the foundations for a person's career and holistic development. Another opinion holds that physical labor is plebian and that the mission of education should be to cultivate people who distance themselves from productive labor and "work using their intellect." Currently, under the tremendous push for exam-oriented education, the discordant cries of the latter opinion appear to be become increasingly rampant. For example: many schools have had their technical classes canceled, and the saying "if you don't study properly, you will end up sweeping the garbage in the future" has become parents' maxim for teaching their children, many of whom have never experienced for themselves the joys and hardships of physical labor. Therefore, it is necessary to reacquaint ourselves with technical education and to call for our "take" on the ideal technical education.

1. Foster Students' Respect for Physical Labor and Cultivate the Attitude of Loving Physical Labor

My take on the ideal technical education is that it should place an emphasis on fostering students' respect for and love of physical labor through their undertaking of physical labor and treating it with pride, enabling students to regularly experience for themselves the hardships and joys of physical labor.

As humanity's most fundamental practical activity, physical labor not only created humanity itself but has also created enormous amounts of material and spiritual wealth, ensuring the continuity and development of human society. Since ancient times, the quality of technical job skills has been the basic quality of people's Lives and work; its importance has long been amply recognized through people's long-term production and living practices. As Soviet educator Anton Makarenko said, physical labor will always be the foundation of human life and the basis for the creation of human life and civilization's happiness. Technical education is a form of education that not only creates future good citizens but raises the future living standards and safeguards the happiness of these citizens. Technical education in primary and secondary schools is an important embodiment of the implementation of quality education and is also an important measure for implementing the mutual integration of education and productive labor. *The Contents of Education: A Worldwide View of Their Development from the Present to the Year 2000*, published by UNESCO in the 1980s, details information "on the design of methodology frameworks for the content of future general education," in which four objectives of technical education are proposed: good job attitudes, technical job skills training, employment training, and adaptability to the world of work. It points out that "technical job skills and technical education are interconnected with every country's needs, resources and prospects and that it mutually coordinates with the 'informationalization' of every aspect of our social lives," fostering students' "analytic attitude and interest in improving their technical job skills," "training students to adapt easily to changes in the labor sector" and thus linking together technical education and the guidance given to students on how to adapt to the future demands of work, reflecting modern society's even more demanding requirements for the quality of people's technical job skills.

Technical education is the generic term for labor education and technical skills education. The fundamental objective of technical education in primary and secondary schools is the multifaceted development of students by having them become accomplished in technical job skills through personally experiencing physical labor. Furthermore, it is a form of education whose distinctive feature is its use of practice-based learning. The objectives of technical education involve three basic areas, namely: the affective domain, whose core comprises the knowledge, attitudes, and emotional factors of physical labor and technical skills; the knowledge and skills domain, whose core comprises the cognition, thinking, and use of physical labor and technical skills; and the practical domain, whose core comprises the application and innovation of technical skills.

Based on a major research project by the Ministry of Education's research task force on the issue of "curriculum reform in labor and technical education," the specific objectives of technical education have been grouped into the following seven aspects:

- To form a proper notion of physical labor, a love of physical labor, of the working people, of life, and a love of the thinking and sentiments of one's hometown
- To cultivate seriousness and responsibility, discipline, unity and cooperation, and respect for public property, and to develop a character that cherishes the fruits of physical labor as well as good work habits
- To preliminarily grasp the basic technical knowledge and skills needed for modern life and modern production
- To preliminarily possess an awareness of safety, quality, aesthetics, efficiency, environmental issues, and vocational and entrepreneurial issues as well as an awareness and concern for the local construction that are linked with technical skills
- To form a vision on economics that links technical skills and economics, as well as a vision on everyday banking and finance
- To possess life skills and a certain level of ability in terms of technical knowledge, technical thinking, technical evaluation, technical application, and technical innovation, as well as the ability to carry out the lifelong learning of technical skills in order to further study and master related technical skills and to lay out the preliminary foundations for meeting the challenges of our future society
- To form an interest and awareness in information technology and to understand and master the fundamental knowledge and skills of information technology

Without a doubt, with the various objectives mentioned above, the formation of the proper concept of physical labor, love of physical labor, love of the working people, love of life, and love for one's homework are the crucial and fundamental objectives.

So how then do we help students to develop corresponding notions and feelings?

The key to forming proper notions of physical labor and cultivating students' respect toward and love of physical labor lies within the practice of physical labor. In primary school, everyone can recite these lines: "At noontide the peasants weed the fields of crops, / Their sweats into the soil fall in endless drops / But from the table bowl, who can ever know, / How all the grains from the peasants' labor grow?" However, the phenomenon of students wasting things is visible everywhere. The main reason is that students have not felt or personally experienced physical labor and so they simply cannot understand the thoughts and feelings expressed in this poem, thus treating the recitation of this poem as just another learning task. However, if we were to have students understand or personally participate in the entire agricultural production process from plowing the ground, sowing the seeds, thinning out the seedlings, applying fertilizer, carrying out pest control and irrigation, to harvesting the crops—enabling them to experience the hard work of agricultural labor—then their attitude toward the working people will definitely undergo a profound change. Again, for example, if we were to have students clean and sweep the streets, then we could inspire students to respect the work of sanitation workers and students would consciously develop habits such as not spitting or throwing fruit peelings and other debris everywhere. Such a result is probably much better than a teacher's repetitive instructions and the society's enforced restrictions.

Of course, we can also see a phenomenon occurring with the implementation of technical education: while students are engaging in physical labor, they are also at the same time cursing it, and so labor education loses sight of its proper role. This is related to our unsuitable teaching methods. In Sukhomlinsky's *On the Issue of Comprehensive Development in Education*, he also analyzes this phenomenon, saying: "You must not expect that physical labor will be appealing to students and that they will suddenly fall in love with physical labor just from their initial first steps into activities involving physical labor. On the contrary, children will feel disappointment much earlier than they will feel exhaustion during the initial period of undertaking genuine physical labor. It is only when students are aware of their own creative efforts and the social significance of physical labor that they are able to truly develop feelings of love for physical labor. Without this element of self-awareness, the teachers' compulsory methods will be met with the students' tenacious resistance and furthermore, the tenacity of the students' actions will increase with the strengthening of compulsory methods."

Fostering students' love of physical labor must not stop at just oral preaching alone and should enable students to get a sense of the joys of physical labor through the practice of it, thus increasing students' love of physical labor.

The power created by that joy and excitement—when students see the crops that they have sown with the utmost care are germinating, when they see the flowers that they have nurtured themselves begin to bud, when they are able to taste the fruits of their harvests that they themselves have achieved through hard work and physical labor—is something that is unmatched by the preaching of teachers and parents, and it is from here that the students' passion for physical labor will burst forth.

The attitude that students possess toward physical labor is closely linked to their parents through verbal instruction and by example. Nowadays, there are some parents who are constantly afraid that physical labor will hold up their children's valuable learning time, and therefore they absolutely do not allow their children to have a hand in household affairs and take charge of everything for their children; seven- or eight-year-old children have to be fed by adults, the majority of high school students and even university students are unable to do their own laundry, and students do not know where to start when faced with eggs cooked in their shell. Some parents even go to the extent of paying money to "redeem" students from having to undertake volunteer physical labor for the school or community. Behind these embarrassing phenomena are flaws in our teaching of technical job skills to our children at home that we should examine.

In schools, the judging for the "three goods" students (who are good at studying, possess a good attitude and character, and have good health) and outstanding student leaders mostly looks at the test results of students' cultural classes, with the results of other subjects being used only as supplementary references, and students' attitudes toward and performance of physical labor is basically ignored. There are some schools that even use physical labor as a means of punishing undisciplined students, such as sweeping the classroom or toilets. The negative consequence of this method of punishment is that students will view physical labor as a shameful activity. These phenomena all severely affect students' proper understanding of physical labor, with fearing and avoiding physical labor becoming a common problem for the majority of students. Therefore, cultivating the proper notion and attitude toward physical labor and strengthening students' awareness of physical labor has already reached a critical point that demands immediate attention.

2. Encourage and Teach Students to Cultivate Good Work Habits

My take on the ideal technical education is that it should encourage and teach students to begin the process of this form of education, from learning how to help oneself to actively participating in all kinds of beneficial physical labor activities practiced in society and cultivating good work habits.

Our country's esteemed educator Ye Shengtao attached particular importance to education that cultivates habits. He thought that education, from a profound point of view, is something that some experts can write large literary works on, but from a simplistic perspective, "education which cultivates good habits" is one phrase that can also explain its meaning. Technical skills education is also no exception, and the cultivation of students' good work habits is not only an important way of developing students' technical skills but also an important objective of technical education.

The formation of work habits is something that needs to be accumulated over a long period of time, and the cultivation of work habits can be carried out in two ways. The first is to have students learn how to help themselves. Sukhomlinsky believed that helping oneself is one of the simplest forms of daily physical labor. Labor education generally starts from learning how to help oneself and, regardless of what form of productive labor each person undertakes, helping oneself will become a duty and habit. Learning to help oneself is an important means of cultivating discipline and the sense of obligation one has toward others. To use one's own hands to satisfy one's individual needs from youth will enable a person to form the work habit of respecting parents, siblings, and classmates. Helping oneself enables physical labor to transform into a general obligation and everyone can equally shoulder the burden. It is only when people have formed a natural aversion toward squalor and untidiness from a young age that this habit becomes the way they view their surrounding environment, and when they possess feelings of aestheticism, it is possible for them to produce a conscious attitude to help themselves.

Due to the fact that the majority of students nowadays are only children, it is very easy for them to form the habit of "living off others" under the doting they receive from their elders. Therefore, labor education that strengthens students' ability to help themselves has important practical significance. Every year when new students enroll at university, surrounding practically every student are a few "accompanying assistants" who follow these students and take care of everything on their behalf, as many students feel that they are incapable of adapting to being away from their parents. Due to individual students' long-term dependence on their parents in all aspects, once they find themselves without this parental care, they find it hard even to exist, and it is no longer uncommon to see examples where ultimately they have no choice but to drop out of school or have their parents move near the school to look after them. Furthermore, instances where students regularly send their dirty laundry to their parents are even more common. In order to change the current dislike of physical labor and inability to perform physical labor among the vast majority of students, parents and teachers must begin with the students' formation of good work habits.

"If a father does not teach his son a means of earning a living, then it is tantamount to teaching him to be a thief." This is an everlasting doctrine that is advocated and used by the Jewish people to help children be self-reliant. Why then not use this doctrine to profoundly enlighten our education system? Parents and teachers who deeply love their children or students should learn how to allow them to carry out their own affairs; what they must learn is how to let go and allow their children or students to undertake the physical labor that is required of them. In a sense, it can be said that depriving children and students of their right to work equates to having them lose the opportunity to grow and mature. Instead, letting go and having children and students participate in appropriate physical labor enables them to possess the most basic skills for living independently. Through undertaking physical labor, they will learn how to respect and understand others, forming good work habits that they will benefit from for their whole lives.

Another important aspect of the formation of good work habits is that it allows students to actively participate in acts of physical labor for the sake of public service on the basis of having first learned how to help themselves. As Sukhomlinsky once said: "What we can strive to do is to enable that desire to do something, which will benefit society, motivate students to undertake physical labor. That is why we allow children to firstly undertake activities which will bring about wealth for the entire nation (such as improving soil fertility; cultivating and protecting agricultural fields, vineyards and orchards; participating in the construction of economic and cultural amenities, building roads and so on). This physical labor which is undertaken for the sake of our society and future becomes a school for educating students. All children who are extremely concerned about what is beneficial to society during their childhood and adolescence will develop a sense of duty and honor. Whenever he encounters any forms of public wealth, his conscience will not allow him to be indifferent."

Acts of physical labor for the sake of public service are activities that one does for others without taking into account any form of remuneration. During the undertaking of these activities, students focus on the needs of society and others and consider what is beneficial to society and others more, thus helping students enhance their sense of social responsibility. Furthermore, students will truly understand the spiritual essence of the motto "one for all and all for one" and will clearly see the role that physical labor plays in society and its meaning, motivating students to consciously develop diligent work habits themselves.

3. Strengthen the Intellectual Content of Physical Labor and Cultivate Students' Innovativeness

My take on the ideal technical education is that it should attach importance to diversity in terms of the practices of physical labor, to enhance its intellectual content, to lead students' hands and minds to be unified, to cultivate their innovativeness, and to enable them to fully put their multifaceted talents to use.

Sukhomlinsky said: "Children's wisdom is at their fingertips." This vividly illustrates the important role that cultivating students' ability to be hands-on plays in terms of developing their intellect. At the same time humankind is transforming the natural world and human society through physical labor, the organs in their bodies are also undergoing a transformation, particularly in terms of the continual coordinating and perfecting of hand and brain functions. Tao Xingzhi also brilliantly expounded on the significance of "the simultaneous usage of one's hands and mind": "At the same time one is using one's mind, one is using their hands to experiment; at the same time one is using their hands, one is using their minds to think and only then is it possible to innovate. Simultaneously using one's hands and mind is the start of innovative education; being fully equipped with the capacity to use one's hands and mind is the goal of innovative education." What should be stated is that among the "five types of education (moral, intellectual, physical, aesthetic, and technical)" that we commonly speak of, technical education is the most effective way to promote the mutual integration between one's hands and mind. In the "Investigative Report on the Current Situation of the Labor and Technical Skills Curriculum" by Chen Ping from the Nanjing Teaching and Research Department, 52.9 percent of primary students, 48.9 percent of junior high students, and 43.4 percent of senior high students believe that the reason why they are interested in labor and technical skills education is mainly because this course "simultaneously uses one's hands and mind."

Due to the fact that the "simultaneous use of one's hands and mind" in technical skills education possesses a distinct practicality and autonomy, it fully expresses the major role that students play in teaching activities, focusing on allowing students to experience, feel, discover, and create, thus enabling them to gain interest and confidence from this and to enjoy the joys of success and the delights of creating. In February 2001, a third-year senior high student named Hua Wei from Jiangsu Xishan Senior High School in Wuxi gained a patent certificate from the national patent department for a "multifunctional laser spirit level" that he developed. The initial reason for Hua Wei's development of his device was the renovations that his family home was undergoing at the time. When the mason was laying the granite tiles, he would repeatedly have to use a spirit level and run string lines to verify that the ground was level, which was very inconvenient. At the time, Hua Wei was struck by inspiration: Wouldn't it be a lot more convenient if projected beams of light replaced the string lines? Under the guidance of the school's technical education teacher, he was finally successful. During the design process, Hua Wei not only learned many technical skills and strengthened his practical competence; he was also able to put his creative thinking to full use.

No matter the time or place, we can easily find many important discoveries and inventions that are made not only because of the extraordinary intelligence of these great scientists but more importantly because they possess relatively high levels of practical competence. They are adept at transforming their thinking into realistic products through their own manual labor. This is most likely closely related to the fact that they paid close attention to their development of technical skills since they were school students.

In regard to the issue of work practices and intellectual development, Sukhomlinsky once wrote this profound statement: "If you wish students to become people who are good at deep thinking, wish for them to be able to express their precise, clear-cut and logically thorough thinking through clear directions and explanations, then you will need to attract them towards physical labor which is rich with ideas, having their knowledge system's various relationships and interconnected systems embodied by means of physical labor. You must bear in mind, physical labor does not only imply actual abilities and skills, but rather, it firstly implies intellectual development, the cultivation of thinking and language." Many research studies also indicate that the more complex and interesting physical labor is, the more distinct its intellectual factors are and the easier it is to stimulate students' enthusiasm toward it. Allowing students to participate in complex skilled physical labor requires them to flexibly use the technical skills and knowledge that they have learned, bringing out their rich imagination and innovativeness, which can powerfully promote students' intellectual development. In short, the key to developing students' intellect by means of physical labor lies in allowing them to learn how to think while undertaking physical labor, stimulating curiosity, thirst for knowledge, and imagination, thus opening up students' intellect for development.

In addition, in technical education we must especially prevent the separation of physical and mental labor that would happen if we allow students to undertake simple mechanical repetitions of labor. Sukhomlinsky also repeatedly emphasized this point through the process of putting technical education into practice at the Pavlysh School. He firmly believed that if physical labor is not a means of honing one's spiritual strength, then this type of labor cannot play a decisive role in people's spiritual lives. Not only that, if physical labor occupied all of one's time and energy, then one's spiritual life would become extremely lacking and dismal.

Furthermore, allowing students to participate in labor encourages them to explore the most optimal work methods, cultivating innovativeness in their thinking and enabling them to continually stimulate their own initiative through the process of undertaking labor. They will become diligent in their studies and dare to put things into practice and, over a long period of time, continually improve their analysis and problem-solving abilities. In addition, this participation in labor will also be greatly beneficial in motivating students to generate passion and bring forth hidden capabilities. In 2001, more than 500 primary and secondary schools from 26 provinces, autonomous regions, and municipalities participated in the National Primary and Secondary School Competition for Creative Works in Technical Education conducted by the Chinese Society of Education's Professional Committee on Technical Education in Primary and Secondary Schools, the Chinese Association of Inventions, and China National Institute for Educational Research, with over 3,000 pieces submitted. Out of all the submitted works, 241 pieces made it to the finals, including pieces that involved various fields such as sound, light, electricity, heat, environmental protection, water conservation, and theft prevention. Some pieces were also awarded national patents or are already in the process of being produced and used.

As the organizer of this competition, Zhu Haozhen, secretary-general of the National Committee for Primary and Secondary Schools Technical Education and Inventions said that in the past, technical education was normally understood as a course where every person would be given a few planks of wood and then, following a set of fixed procedures, churn out something like a chair, with the chairs produced by 50 students being absolutely identical. Nowadays, teachers in these classes hope to give students a real opportunity to not only cultivate students' notion of labor, but to increase their amount of technical skills, leaving space for them to create. Once inventions are assigned as a process of hands-on practice, technical skills education will then become extremely dynamic. This has great inspirational meaning for innovation in our technical education.

4. Take Measures According to Local Conditions to Cultivate Students' Personal Strengths in Terms of Technical Skills

My take on the ideal technical education is that it should take measures according to the local conditions and the local school. On the established basis of classroom teaching in schools, it should allow students to venture out of the school as much as possible to come into contact with society, and furthermore, through the use of a base in technical education that is rich with distinct characteristics, cultivate students' personal strengths in terms of their technical skills.

Our country's land is vast and regional differences are rather large. The differences from the modern industrial cities to the remote, backward mountain areas, such as natural conditions, level of economic development, and schooling conditions, are significant. As a result, carrying out technical education must start by considering the realities facing each region and taking measures according to local conditions and the local school. The content and form of technical education should fully take into account each school's own characteristics, playing to its strengths to fully bring out results that are uniquely its own, reflecting the special characteristics of the technical education offered in different regions and at different schools. For example, our country's first technical teacher of distinction, Zhang Zaichang, is an outstanding teacher who hails from the rural area. He compiled over 200,000 words worth of local teaching materials according to the real-life conditions in the local rural area. He transformed the running of technical classes into "experimental fields" to improve rural technology, extending the school's experimental base to the students' homes and training a large number of technical personnel for the local community. Because he reformed the explorations conducted in technical classes by combining them with the realities facing rural villages and furthermore obtaining clear and effective results, he has been named one of the nation's top 10 young teachers in the first batch of "top 10" outstanding young teachers.

Classroom teaching in schools is the main channel for technical education, with teachers teaching the knowledge of labor skills and giving simple instructions on the use of technical skills in line with the students' usual study habits. Therefore, it is absolutely essential that schools improve the facilities set up for technical education. For example, German schools normally have specialized classrooms for teaching subjects such as metalwork, woodwork, electrical engineering and electronics, nutritional and culinary studies, and plastics processing, with configuration standards that are similar to those for physics, chemistry, and biology laboratories as well as being outfitted with a complete set of safety and technical assistive devices. In Japan, the majority of primary schools have a specialized classroom for home economics that is at least 100 square yards in size, including facilities and resources such as work counters, equipment counters, gas pipelines, electric sewing machines, microwaves, washing machines, and cooking utensils. Secondary schools are equipped with sewing rooms, cooking rooms, metalwork rooms, computer rooms, and so on. In Australia, relatively well-off schools all have workshops for carpentry, metalwork, lathe work, and assembly. Schools that are not so well off are required to have a comprehensive workshop. In every state of Australia, there are also standardized mobile workshops that tour within their allocated states, stopping for four weeks at every technical skills center. Prior to the arrival of these mobile workshops, students must study operating instructions for the various pieces of machinery and view videos and projector slides to understand the functions of the tools and facilities and the safety and operational requirements. When the mobile workshop arrives, the teacher and students can immediately begin the lesson. Before the mobile workshop leaves, the work that students have produced based on what they have been learning will be assessed. Rural schools have very warmly welcomed the establishment of mobile workshops, as it greatly alleviates the challenges of carrying out technical education in rural schools. The use of these kinds of mobile workshops can also be promoted in our country.

Of course, the school is, after all, not a workplace and the extent to which it comes into contact with labor is limited. Therefore, to enhance students' technical skills education, it is necessary to establish a vast base in social education on the foundations of classroom teachings in school and, as much as possible, enable students to be developed and tempered by the "forges of society." Schools should take advantage of the features of technical education and its close ties with production and life; they should allow students to go to the cities' neighborhood factories and the rural villages' open fields so as to gradually come into contact with society, to properly understand society, and to have the courage to participate in society. Schools should also strengthen students' notions of closely linking their own self-improvement to the development of society and turn students' training into a means of producing pillars of society who will be able to use their hands to support and build their own lives.

All levels of government should also actively create requirements that will produce circumstances whereby students engage in social practices in the community. From the perspective of development trends, technical education is in the process of developing toward a curriculum that has comprehensive practical activities. If we were to establish a number of comprehensive social practices for students that blend elements such as leisure, labor, experiences, innovation, and exploration into a single entity to form a base of activities, it would undoubtedly be extremely beneficial.

The social activities base for students established by the Suzhou Experimental Primary School is one such profitable attempt, and the "Oriental Land" built by the Shanghai Municipal Government is an even greater masterpiece. The Oriental Land, an off-campus campsite for Shanghai's youths, is located on the banks of Shanghai's Dianshan Lake and covers an area of about 925 acres (including the surface area of its water). The campsite is made up of eight large park areas: the Knowledge district, Bravery and Wisdom district, National Defense Education district, Survival Challenge district, Scientific Exploration district, Aquatic Sports district, Sports Training district, and Daily Life Practices district. Among these eight districts, the Knowledge Boulevard has 162 sculptures of important historical figures in the development of world civilizations on display and is currently one of the world's largest sculpture parks. The campsite is student focused and is organized around the central theme of innovative educational activities, with a return to the natural world, hands-on activities, and a sense of personally experiencing these activities oneself as its main ideas, enabling a vast number of youths to experience success and joy through partaking in these activities. Various kinds of scientific knowledge constantly emanate from the activities within the eight districts as well as the sculptures, forests, bridges, local houses, footpaths, and rivers, with the campsite fully embodying "rustic charm, childish delight and fun"; every tree, flower, and blade of grass will make youths feel that they are "intimately close to the natural world" and will make them want to be even nearer to the natural world, to feel and personally experience nature for themselves. The campsite extends and expands on classroom teachings, focusing on cross-curricular learning and interdisciplinary integration, making full use of environmental resources to organize learning activities to develop students who are socially and life orientated and are inclined toward the natural world. All the campsite's activities center around the notion of being conducive to the students' healthy growth and are carried out because they are beneficial to the improvement of the students' overall inner qualities. The campsite fully exhibits the major role that youths play and their own initiatives, and it actively creates conditions that allow students to self-manage, self-select, and self-learn, which cultivates their ability to look after themselves, to be independent, and to strive for self-improvement.

On Nanhu Street in Nanjing city, Jiangsu province's first community experiential learning practice base for members of the Young Pioneers has also been set up, a new attempt to encourage students to actively participate in productive labor. Members of the Young Pioneers from six primary schools on Nanhu Street utilize their after-school time to visit 15 local shops, banks, restaurants, photo studios, and newsstands to partake in the work of close to a hundred positions so as to experience for themselves the hardships and joys of the workers. The schools involved have students participate in this activity so that through the process of coming into contact with society, they will learn various technical and interpersonal skills and thus improve their overall inner quality.

What should be noted is that whether within or outside of the school, technical skills education must reduce its lack of objective and intermittency. When Sukhomlinsky criticized schools that had indeed set up many labor activities for students but lacked labor activities that were high in educational value, he was spot-on when he said that their biggest problem was the fact that their labor activities did not carry through from the beginning to the end. Only when these schools felt that they did not have enough manpower were students summoned to partake in labor activities, hurriedly rushing off into battle seemingly as if they were putting out a blaze. Therefore, he strove to reduce emergency response labor activities that were intermittent and lacked prior planning, and advocated performing planned tasks from start to finish through all stages of the labor process to experience the satisfaction of understanding the objective of labor.

As a basic educational course on teaching knowledge of labor and labor skills, technical education should consider vocational and nonvocational practices of labor together, meaning that technical education in schools should also focus on students' undertaking of careers education. Through careers education, we can bridge the gap between students and society, help students analyze and understand various occupations, learn proper ways to seek employment, and enable all students to find their own suitable career paths. Due to the characteristics of careers education, teachers of this subject should not be limited to the school's technical education teachers and should include the participation of people from all industry sectors of society in the teaching process. The format of careers education also should not be purely based on an academic course but instead should adopt a flexible "welcoming the outside in and heading out to meet the outside" format that can be carried out in all sorts of ways such as visiting recruitment agencies (job fairs) and undertaking internships in all sorts of departments.

5. Focus on the Connection Between Technical Education and Morality, Intellectuality, Physical Fitness, and Aesthetics

My take on the ideal technical education is that it should focus on the intrinsic connection between technical education and moral, intellectual, physical, and aesthetic education. Technical education should cultivate morals, increase intelligence, strengthen physical fitness, and have a sense for aesthetics. It should shape students' fine moral character, high personality, and psychological quality and lay out the foundations for students' holistic development.

Technical education not only fulfills the educational objective of developing the quality of students' technical skills but is also capable of bringing about the development of every student's moral character, knowledge, abilities, will, emotions, physical fitness, and ability to appreciate aesthetics through the practice of labor. This is because when students partake in any practices of labor, they must personally experience, operate, understand, and master the entire labor process. Any technical skills that students learn must first pass their own assessment of their actions and go through feedback and adjustments and repeated hands-on training before they gradually form. During this process, students' physical strength and willpower are superbly tested and "put through the mill," their emotions are molded and refined, and their personalities and creativity also acquire a place and a chance to be put to use.

Therefore, the study and mastery of technical skills is the comprehensive use and development of physical strength, intellect, and creativity. Through the implementation of satisfactory technical education, the goals of quality education "to enable those being educated to be mentally and physically healthy and to harmoniously develop their morality, intellect, and physical fitness" are, to a large degree, achieved.

For example, having senior high students learn the craft of technical drawing can strengthen their multilayered thinking and spatial imagination, exercise their ability to be hands-on, regulate the state of their thinking, and improve their learning efficiency. Because technical drawing is in itself a form of art, it can enable students to fully imagine, freely bring out their own abilities, cultivate their ability to appreciate aesthetics, and inspire their passion to create beauty. Therefore, when teaching technical education, teachers should focus on the intrinsic connection between moral education, intellectual education, physical education, and aesthetic education and strengthen the functions of these four types of education within technical education; furthermore, they should link technical education to the whole process of all-round quality education, which cultivates people's holistic development.

Within the technical education curriculum, imparting knowledge and educating people are equally of extreme importance. A technical education teacher once said, "I have taught electronics for many years and remember an incident one year in which a third-year junior high student was often affected by power outages when he himself attended the evening self-learning class at school. However, all of the student's surrounding households were not affected, and it turned out that the student was purposely sabotaging the electricity in order to not have to study by himself in the evenings. Through this incident, it is evident that the student's mastery of the skills related to electronics was quite good and from one point of view it is proof of the effectiveness of his education; however, it also reflects issues in terms of the student's thinking and moral character. It indicates that at the same time as imparting knowledge, teachers must also pay attention to educating students."

At this point, I would like to fervently call out for the construction of a bridge between technical education and other forms of education; for a departure, as quickly as possible, from the narrow scope of technical education being only the teaching of technical skills and for the promotion of technical education everywhere and at all times in our lives. Because technical education is full of the remarkable characteristics of creativity and practicality and is closely connected to production and life, its functions of cultivating morality, increasing intelligence, "strengthening physical fitness, and having a sense of aesthetics are unattainable by other forms of education.

At the same time, an effective means of molding students' good moral character is through technical education. The undertaking of appropriate labor can sharpen students' willpower and is beneficial in shaping students' spirit and mentality to be unafraid of difficulties, to bravely persevere and press ahead and vow to never give up until one's goal is reached. Encouraging students to overcome difficulties while undertaking labor and ultimately succeeding can boost students' self-confidence and strengthen their love of labor and passion for life. Having students accomplish common tasks through cooperation and the division of work while undertaking collective labor can enable them to understand the significance of the individual being subordinate to the demands and interests of the group. It can also cultivate students' sense of the collective and their spirit of solidarity, cooperation, and dedication, allowing them to experience solidarity, mutual help and support, and going through thick and thin together. Following stringent requirements in the use of technical skills can enable students to learn self-adjustment, self-restraint, and self-management while undertaking labor and cultivate students' awareness of quality and work discipline. Guiding students to mutually combine physical and intellectual labor can inspire their own style of pursuing excellence and creativity and of constantly surpassing oneself. Having students deepen their understanding of the working people while undertaking labor can cultivate students' deep feelings toward the motherland, its people, and labor. Through technical education, we can also enable students to personally experience how hard it is to come by material wealth and thus cultivate in them the positive qualities of diligence and thriftiness.

Additionally, research shows that technical education can cultivate some favorable psychological qualities. For example, research conducted by Professor Lu from Tianjin Normal University's Research Institute for Psychological Development shows that teaching handicrafts such as embroidery to boys who are active and absent-minded, have a short attention span, and lack self-control would be most beneficial to the cultivation of their attention spans and self-control.

6. Attach Importance to Differences in Personality and Age and Cultivate Students' Key Competencies

My take on the ideal technical education is that it should attach importance to differences in students' personality and age, establish the idea of student-centeredness, and employ project-based curriculum and behavioral guidance teaching methods, cultivating students' "key competencies" in terms of such areas as planning, work, and social interactions.

Any type of education is carried out on one's own unique self. The implementation of technical education must recognize and respect differences in the students' personalities and attach importance to different students' characteristics such as learning desires, interests, and individual strengths. This is an important safeguard for improvements in the quality of technical education.

Sukhomlinsky believed that it is not possible for the compulsory syllabus to cater to all the students' various individual strengths. Children at an early school age often not only want to complete classroom tasks that everyone else in the class is required to do, such as various sorts of handiwork, but also want to do something of their own choosing. They will not be satisfied with the level of proficiency reached by their class in terms of certain skills and techniques and will also look forward to having a finer mastery over those skills. Furthermore, this desire will gradually grow stronger as they increase in age. Therefore, teachers must fully understand their students' personalities and make the contents of technical education as diversified as possible, allowing all students to find a work task that they themselves like.

Technical education in Japan does precisely that—it attaches great importance to students' different personalities, interests, and hobbies. The syllabus for technical skills/home economics classes offered to Japanese first- to third-year junior high students contains 11 topics to study: woodwork, electrical studies, metalwork, mechanical studies, horticulture, information infrastructure, home living, food, clothing, housing, and childcare. In their third year of junior high school, students can choose 7 of these topics to study, according to their interests and hobbies.

Raising the quality of technical education also requires teachers to fully consider the characteristics of the students' age. The curriculum should be implemented strictly in accordance with the distinctive characteristics of each stage of a student's life, with the teaching content at each stage being taught step by step from the superficial to the profound and from the simple to the complex.

The curriculum of technical education at primary and secondary schools in Japan attaches great importance to students' age levels. Technical education in Japanese primary schools mainly develops students' intuition and feelings; in junior high schools it mainly develops students' abstract thinking abilities and creativity; in senior high schools it mainly develops students' proper judgment and ability to apply what they know. First- and second-grade primary school students are offered life lessons that, through specific activities and experiences, enable students to develop an interest between themselves and their surrounding society and natural relationships; furthermore, allows them to master the habits and skills that are necessary in life. Schools offer fifth- and sixth-grade primary school students "home living" classes in which, through activities related to clothing, food, and living, primary students master necessary basic knowledge and skills for daily living mainly by undertaking activities on the three aspects of clothing, food, and family members.

In Russia, the teaching content of technical education is also strictly differentiated according to the students' age-related characteristics. For primary students, the main learning content includes technology for materials processing, food production, cleaning one's room, gardening, learning how to use a computer, and so on. For junior high students, the main learning content is the processing of equipment materials and spare parts for machinery, domestic arts, sewing, food, handicrafts, maintenance and repair, the use of computers, the completion of one's individual program design, and so on. For senior high students, the main learning content includes home economics; basic knowledge on business management, production, and environmental protection; social labor and occupation choice; introduction to art design; the completion of one's individual program design; and so on. Establishing different educational objectives at different developmental stages of a student's physiology, psychology and social adaptability, formulating different teaching content, and adopting different teaching methods are the important experiences of success that technical education in countries like Germany and Japan have gained.

Presently, technical education in some developed countries such as Germany are making great efforts to promote and use "project-based curriculum and behavioral guidance teaching methods."

What is referred to as project-based curriculum and behavioral guidance teaching methods is the implementation of teaching through the use of projects, that is, the production of a specific product, thereby helping students to master knowledge, develop skills, and cultivate habits. This method of teaching is conducive to the activation of bilateral teaching activities that cultivate students' creativity and practicality and promote the comprehensive improvement of students' knowledge, abilities, and inner quality; thus it changes the problem of "too much of an emphasis on teaching, not enough emphasis on learning; too much emulating, not enough creating" in traditional technical education.

Products for these projects can be concrete and tangible objects such as a carpentry toolbox, an item of clothing, or a plate of some sort of cuisine; they can also be the fruits of some sort of intellectual pursuit such as a special report, film, drawing, and so on. The teaching process is divided into four stages: the decision-making stage, planning and preparation stage, implementation stage, and evaluation stage. The entire process from beginning to end gives prominence to a focus on students and their behavior, having students decide for themselves what product they will create, as well as having them carry out feasibility analyses, formulate a project implementation plan, prepare their tools, procure materials, carry out specific tasks either autonomously or in delegated work as part of a cooperative effort, produce timely feedback, have adjustment strategies, continually test to ensure quality, collate documentation, and finally to display the finished product (either by selling it, giving it to friends and family as a present, or keeping it for one's own use). Teachers, by contrast, play the part of moderators and consultants. They do not issue commands in regard to students' behavior but instead deliberately guide and offer timely reminders and any necessary support. This method is beneficial to the cultivation of students' strong interest in learning and allows the entire learning process for the students to be one in which they "want to learn" rather than one in which they are "required to learn."

Because project-based curriculum and behavioral guidance teaching methods attach great importance to interdisciplinary integration, as well as the close ties between schools and society, their distinct realistic and everyday living-related qualities require technical education to venture beyond the classroom as much as possible and to venture forth into all types of trades and industries such as social management and the service industry. Furthermore, this method of teaching emphasizes teaching students the simultaneous usage of one's hands and mind and guides students to "learn to study, learn to live, and learn to create." This plays an important role in the comprehensive fostering of students' capacities as well as cultivating their "key competencies" in terms of planning, work, and social interactions. The technical education offered in our country's primary and secondary schools would do well to learn from it.

7. Enhance Cooperation Between Schools, Families, and Society and Construct an Educational System for "Great Technical Education"

My take on the ideal technical education is that it should attach importance to grasping the use of cooperation in joint administration between schools, families, and society and construct an educational system for "great technical education."

Makarenko placed great importance on the role that families play in students' technical education. He once cautioned every parent that during the process of educating their children, parents should never forget the principles of work. Children who have received proper labor education at home will be able to smoothly complete specialized education in the future. Despite efforts by the state institutions to educate them, children who have not received any sort of labor education at home will not be able to gain proficient skills, will encounter all sorts of failures, and will not become good workers.

Currently, situations where families do not understand, support, or complement technical education are common. The setbacks that the "DIY" course suffered in Shanghainese families is one such example. The Jing'an Education College Affiliated School in Shanghai, in cooperation with a French education project, began offering a "DIY" course. All elements of this science course, which included content on general knowledge and productive labor, from grand-scale volcanic eruptions to the trivial growth of mung beans, were designed so that they could provide students with hands-on practical experimentations. Because many experimental projects could not be completed in the classroom, the teachers required students to take parts of these experiments home to complete. However, when these students enthusiastically took their experiments home, they encountered opposition from their parents. Some parents believed that having children mix tomato sauce and mashed potatoes together to make a volcano or grow mung beans on a dish not only wasted time originally used for learning but also created a mess at home. Many parents believed that the only form of learning was by doing exercises and that hands-on practice was not learning.

To enhance technical education, it is essential to have the active support and cooperation of society. The influence of society's support for education is mainly evident in terms of the specifications and notions of government policies. The education administrative department must actively determine the status of technical education through formulated educational policies and legislation and actively help members of society to establish proper thoughts and concepts through the dissemination of public opinions. For example, transforming the concept of exam-oriented education by establishing the concept of quality education; transforming the concept of valuing talent and disregarding morality by establishing the concept of holistic development; transforming the concept of evaluating by looking first at results by establishing the concept of all-around scientific quality, and transforming the age-old concept of "those who work with their brains rule and those who work with physical strength are ruled" by establishing the proper concept of labor.

The implementation of technical education requires certain equipment, materials, and sites; therefore, compared to other cultural classes in primary and secondary school, it requires even more funding. If these physical preparations are lacking, then technical education classes will undoubtedly become ornamental. Because the subject areas involved are complex, the aspects of the work involved are broad, and the teaching is not confined to being carried out in the singular classroom, the implementation of the aforementioned project-based curriculum and behavioral guidance teaching methods, for instance, may need to be carried out in school laboratories, computer rooms, and even the "great classroom" of society (such as in shops, administrative authorities, factories, research institutions, and so on).

Therefore, carrying out technical education also requires the guarantee of funding from the education administrative department and funding from the schools. Furthermore, it requires schools to take full advantage of the power of the entire society, actively seeking out the support and cooperation of the community, industrial and commercial enterprises as well as all types of other professions, to establish a variety of practice bases for technical skills. In short, schools must encourage the members of the entire society to be concerned with and support the development of technical education through extensive promotion and mobilization.

To construct the framework for the "great technical education," schools are the core factor. Schools, as specialized educational institutions, must attach a great amount of importance to technical education and be able to constantly carry out reforms and innovations in technical education, such as intensifying appraisals of the quality of technical education, standardizing the teachings of technical education, establishing lateral connections between all subjects, and improving the effectiveness of technical education in schools. Schools should fully exploit their own advantages and forge excellent lines of communication between society, the school, and families, closely linking society and families to the schools' surroundings so as to successfully establish a cooperation and support system for technical education. For example, promoting the importance of technical education to parents through methods such as parenting school, home visits, and parent-teacher associations would enable schools to actively assist technical education that occurs at home, communicate with parents in a timely manner, strengthen correspondence, and avoid the occurrence of contradictions and conflicts between education at school and at home.

8. Assemble an Outstanding Faculty and Use Teaching Materials That Are Practical and Unique

My take on the ideal technical education is that it should have an outstanding teaching cohort for technical education and possess a collection of practical and unique curriculum and teaching materials that provide a fundamental guarantee for the implementation of technical education.

In the vast majority of primary and secondary schools, technical education has already become a forgotten corner of education, and this issue is prominently evident in two aspects: the qualified teachers and the curriculum and teaching materials.

During the development of the five types of education: moral, intellectual, physical, aesthetic, and technical education, moral education has had the use of full-time teachers of politics, class advisors, and various groups and organized institutions; intellectual education has had teachers of specialized subjects in all fields such as literature and language, mathematics, and foreign languages; physical education has had full-time physical education teachers; aesthetic education has had full-time art and music teachers, but technical education very rarely has any full-time teachers. After many years of effort, it was only due to the promotion of the Sino-German Technical Cooperation Program that we began offering the nation's only professional course in technical education at the Suzhou Education College, where the training of students is far from meeting the needs of society.

In contrast, the training of qualified teachers in countries such as Japan and Germany is worth learning from. Japanese primary and secondary school technical education teachers are all university graduates, and these teachers are all required to sit for an employment entrance exam set up by their education administrative department upon graduating from university. Candidates who successfully pass the exam are then put on probation for a year before again undertaking specialized training before taking up a teaching position. All Japanese technical education teachers are full-time teachers. In Germany, the overwhelming majority of technical education teachers are graduates with standard university degrees and furthermore have passed a national teacher qualification exam. Every school has a specialized technical skills teaching and research group, and the workload for technical education teachers is on average 26 to 28 periods a week. Schools that are larger in scale would also allocate two experts, one who is an electrical expert and one who is a machinery expert, to share the work and cooperate with one another to carry out work such as the everyday administration and maintenance of specialized classrooms and equipment. The salary and status of technical education teachers within the schools is the same as that of teachers such as mathematics and German teachers, and their position in society is medium to medium-high in status. It is a profession that is respected and admired by others.

In terms of curriculum and teaching materials, school subjects such as mathematics, literature and language, foreign languages, geography, history, political studies, biology, physical education, fine arts, and so on all have a system of teaching materials and a syllabus. However, the vast majority of technical education classes in schools very rarely have detailed teaching plans, and their teaching syllabus and resources are lacking in terms of being practical and systematic. Many schools never had a syllabus and teaching materials in the first place, and this objectively places technical education in the least important position among the five types of education. With a lack of teachers and teaching materials, these two most basic and core elements, it is hard to imagine establishing and running successful technical education.

The technical aspect of the curriculum for technical education is relatively more intense and is not something that every person will be able to become proficient in. It requires teachers to possess not only fundamental teaching qualities but also expertise in certain technical abilities. Therefore, recruiting a cohort of high-quality technical education teachers is the key to implementing technical education.

In terms of the recruitment of qualified teachers, some schools have implemented a method of "first: through change; second: from schools; third: to offer concurrent posts, and fourth: to hire" that is worth learning from. "First: through change" refers to having teachers of cultural classes who possess certain types of technical expertise become teachers of technical education classes. For example, secondary school teachers of physics, chemistry, and biology can become teachers of handicrafts, manufacturing, appliance repairs, bicycle repairs, and so on. "Second: from schools" refers to recruiting graduates of vocational schools to be full-time technical education teachers at school. "Third: to offer concurrent posts" refers to having teachers who possess some sort of technical expertise also hold a concurrent position as a technical education teacher. "Fourth: to hire" refers to hiring people with expertise from society to teach in schools. In short, it is only through a recruitment method that goes through multiple channels to solve the issue of qualified teachers that the premise and guarantee of development in terms of students' abilities can be offered by schools.

The curriculum is the medium that teachers use to impart knowledge to students and develop students' abilities. Technical education is a subject whose curriculum is strong in terms of practicality; therefore, technical education classes must reflect this distinct practicality in classes such as gardening, planting, crop cultivation, carpentry, simple mechanical repairs, use and maintenance of household appliances, cooking, typing, simulations for driving a car, and so on. In taking these courses, students are able to put skills to practical use through their learning and to learn through putting their skills to practical use. This not only enables students to gain technical knowledge and skills but more importantly allows them to experience the joys of learning and work, which are exactly the important objectives that technical education pursues.

At the same time technical education focuses on practicality, it should also embody its uniqueness. In compiling a technical education curriculum, each school should do so in accordance with the characteristics of their local area, their school, and their students and purposefully offer courses that will nurture students' expertise and abilities in certain areas with their development of a variety of technical skills as a foundation. When learning from teaching resources that are full of local characteristics, students will feel a sense of familiarity, find it very interesting, be able to learn very easily, and have their enthusiasm for learning and creativity greatly stimulated. For example, the city of Suzhou, famous nationwide as the "Garden City," can offer students a course in gardens and flora, allowing them to understand how to produce bonsai, flowers, and plants. Similarly, the ceramics of Yixing in Wuxi enjoy a reputation both at home and abroad, and students can take courses in ceramic crafts, allowing them to understand the production of ceramics. In short, schools must fully tap into all local specialized teaching resources, as this cannot develop students' specialized technical skills but also enable local traditional crafts and skills to spread and be passed down to others.

Dr. Joseph Needham, a British expert on the history of Chinese science, was once quoted as saying that ancient China had brilliant scientific achievements but did not have any technological achievements. One of the important reasons is the neglect of technical education. As people living in the twenty-first century, where science and technology as well as productivity are rapidly developing, we should calmly consider the words of Dr. Needham. We should clearly recognize that we need to first nurture students so that they become qualified workers and then have them become outstanding and talented people. In this new century where education moves with the times, to have students truly become high-quality, talented individuals who are holistically developed in terms of their morality, intellect, physical fitness, aesthetics, and technical skills, we must be collectively concerned with technical education and prop up a new blue sky for the development of education.

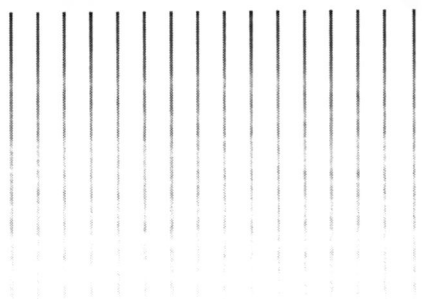

6

My Take on the Ideal School

A quality school is a cradle for human talent; a poor quality school is conversely a tomb for intellect. A quality school is a paradise for children, where they can frequently be joyful and amazed, actively explore, and healthily develop. A poor quality school, however, is a "hell" for children where they are frequently sad and frightened and are passively subjected to a withering away of their personalities.

This sort of quality school is my take on the ideal school.

The director-general of the European Students and Parents Association, at a public hearing on "Quality and Efficiency in Primary and Secondary Schools" organized by the Culture and Education Committee, which was founded by the European Legislative Assembly, put forward these standards for a good primary school:

1. A modern primary school should enable all children within the school to feel that they are not neglected.
2. A modern primary school must participate in educational innovations, with the ultimate goal being the improvement of the quality of teaching.
3. A good primary school will have no "irritating tricks" between the kindergarten and primary school, the primary and secondary school, and the school and students' families.
4. A good primary school must be considerate of the individual differences between students, adopt the use of individual teaching methods as much as possible, and provide special help for slow students.
5. A good primary school must be considerate of children from different cultures.

6. A good primary school must provide children with the opportunity to fully develop. It should not be concerned with only the children's minds but also their hands and hearts; that is, the issue does not lie in only their intellectual education but also their emotional education, social education, physical education and exercise, arts education, and so on.
7. A good primary school must "have its doors and windows wide open," as discoveries begin with investigating things that are in our surroundings.
8. A good school is not an "isolated island," as it must pass through a collaborative network that it has established. This network should lead to teaching being carried out by a veritable teaching team. More broadly speaking, the teaching team should harmoniously cooperate with parental, mental health, medical, and social groups; teaching assistants; and school district supervisors. A good primary school must map out its own actions according to the activity projects of the school.

In Taiwanese scholar You Qiangui's *In Search of a Bucolic Primary School,*[1] he attempts to construct a spiritual, bucolic primary school for children, to build the ideal bucolic academy for society that will be known as the "Utopia" of his grand education dream. What then, would my take on "Utopia" be like? How can we create the ideal campus?

1. Highlight the Distinguishing Features of a School
My take on the ideal school is that it should be a school that has specialties.

The standards used for evaluating a school are manifold and always in a dynamic state of being. However, I believe that what is most important is a school's specialties. The American *Newsweek* magazine once did a large-scale survey of schools from all around the world and finally chose 10 schools that were judged to be the "top 10" best schools in the world. These 10 schools were Lake Tekapo School in New Zealand, Diana School in Italy, Greydamus School in the Netherlands, Shibuya Sixth Elementary School in Japan, Echnaton School in the Netherlands, Pittsburgh's Westinghouse High School in America, Gymnasium Deutz, Thusneldastrasse in Germany, the California Institute of Technology in America, Stockholm's AMU Centre (Vocational Training Centre) in Switzerland, and Cologne's Ministry of Education in Germany.

The education specialty of Lake Tekapo School in New Zealand is a focus on developing students' reading ability, with the reading and writing abilities of students at this school continually ranked at the top in international tests. The important means through which the school is able to raise the students' reading ability is an innovative curriculum, cultivating students' specialized ability in reading and writing through an emphasis on recitation drills and furthermore enabling students to learn according to their own pace. Students with different foundations are also placed in different grades, where the teaching of reading and writing are combined.

The success of Italy's Diana School lies in the results of their teaching in pre-school, which are particularly significant. All four walls of this school are made of glass, and rather than call it a kindergarten, it would be better to call it a happy and boisterous greenhouse. Affixed onto the classroom walls, painted on the windows, hanging from the ceilings, and spread out over the desks are all art works and handicrafts that the children have created. The curriculum at this school is set up by the teachers themselves, and the teaching content revolves around having children learn a variety of skills. Furthermore, it is organized in such a way as to help them to become acquainted with the themes of the world, touching on mathematics, arts, and science. The school designs different "schools" in accordance with students' different ages; for example, the school that students from infancy to three years old enter is called "the nest" and the school for three- to six-year-old students is the "maternal school." The student activities at the different schools are also different. One of the important educational features of the school is its focus on nurturing students' individuality, allowing students to be able to freely carry out various activities in accordance with their own wishes.

At the Greydamus School in the Netherlands, the education specialty lies in its excellence in mathematics. The school has adopted a new, revolutionary teaching system for mathematics: the "realistic mathematics" teaching method. This new course is special because discussions carried out on each problem taught are combined with realistic problems so as to demonstrate that the true meaning of mathematics lies in its being an integral part of normal life.

For Shibuya's Sixth Elementary School in Japan, the specialty is its science education, which places an emphasis on creativity. The educational goals of the school are to train students to be able to raise questions, to form independent ideas, and moreover to develop into students possessing creative intelligence. The school also stresses that students' creative abilities are to be developed through practice, such as having Year 4 students bring their own spare parts and set about repairing toasters when learning basic knowledge about electrical engineering, electrical circuits, and motors and having 10-year-old children use solar-powered batteries and model cars to try to come up with a way of assembling a solar-powered toy car.

At Echnaton School in the Netherlands, success lies in the teaching of foreign languages. Not one of the students has been to such countries as England or America, but their mastery of vocabulary, fluency, and self-confidence is not inferior to and even surpasses that of many American teenagers. Students are able to use English to debate American social issues to improve their presentation skills. The method of success for students learning English at this school is to practice more.

Pittsburgh's Westinghouse High School in America has implemented its "Arts PROPEL" program, which has been hugely successful. The school takes subjects that are usually considered luxury subjects and uses them as major components of education, including music, visual arts, and writing, with students learning how to use arts to express their feelings and to solve problems. This method of education has greatly enriched the students' spiritual lives.

At Gymnasium Deutz, Thusneldastrasse in Germany, success lies in its reverence for trade crafts. Because many students enter vocational and technical schools, this school focuses particularly on the teaching of trade crafts. Not only are specialty courses set up within the curriculum, but students must also work as apprentice engineers for small firms on Mondays, Tuesdays, and Fridays as well as sit for specialized graduation exams. Students are also able to receive remuneration for their time spent learning at these small firms.

The California Institute of Technology in America succeeds by producing a large number of scientific elites. The school is not large, but during the teaching process, students are highly encouraged to conduct research in accordance with their own reasoning so as to produce a completely different way of thinking. Presently, the school has educated more than 20 Nobel Prize laureates, its laboratories have discovered positrons and quarks, and it has opened up new areas of study in many subjects such as seismology, geochemistry, molecular biology, astrophysics, and so on.

At Stockholm's AMU Centre (Vocational Training Centre) in Sweden, educational success lies in creating conditions for student employment. The school attaches great importance to transmitting the necessary knowledge for student employment such as having courses on subjects like modern finance and accounting services, computer technology, and so on. Rates of employment for students of this school are very high.

For Cologne's Ministry of Education in Germany, the educational specialty is attaching great importance to the rigorous selection and training of teachers, as well as the huge increase in teachers' wages, thus allowing some of the best and brightest people to invest in a career in education.

Other media articles report an American university that surpasses Harvard University, that is, Deep Springs College, located in America's barren desert valley. The quality of life at this college scores 99 points, the same as Harvard University; the student-to-teacher ratio at Deep Springs College is 1 to 4, by contrast, Harvard's is 1 to 7; the acceptance rate for Deep Springs College is 7 percent and, compared to Harvard University's acceptance rate of 9 percent, it is even more difficult to enter. However, the rate of enrollment for Deep Springs College reaches 92 percent, far surpassing the rate of enrollment for Harvard University, which is 79 percent.

The founder of Deep Springs College, Lucien Lucius Nunn, an electric-power magnate was once quoted as saying: "The desert has a deep personality; it has a voice. Great leaders in all ages have sought the desert and heard its voice. You can hear it if you listen, but you cannot hear it while in the midst of uproar and strife for material things. 'Gentlemen, for what came ye into the wilderness?' Not for conventional scholastic training; not for ranch life; not to become proficient in commercial or professional pursuits for personal gain. You came to prepare for a life of service, with the understanding that superior ability and generous purpose would be expected of you."

Deep Springs College's motto is: labor, academics, and self-governance. College regulations are extremely strict; students are not allowed to leave the campus without permission, any access to alcohol is strictly prohibited, and watching television is not promoted. Phone and Internet connections are often interrupted due to poor weather, and newspapers are usually two days late because they have to be delivered via the post office.

The college's most distinguishing feature is the students' self-governance. Students themselves are responsible for the complete day-to-day management of the college, with the student board participating and having great authority in all the decision making, including what courses will be offered, the appointment and dismissal of professors, and the admission of new students. It is said that the younger brother of Xiamen University's Professor Liu Haifeng was the college's first Chinese student. When he participated in the college entrance exam, it was the then current students who conducted the process.

At Deep Springs College, classes are held during the morning and students undertake labor tasks during the afternoon. However, students' passion for learning is extremely high. The reading homework for each eight-week semester as prepared by Professor Dave Arndt, a former professor at Yale University, includes over 4,000 pages of reading on the writings of German philosopher Martin Heidegger, as well as a few hundred pages of literary criticism. Having a homework load this large and students this diligent and focused would be hard to come by at any other university.

The reason why these schools are considered the world's successful models of education is actually not because they are extremely formidable in all areas, nor is it because their comprehensive strength surpasses that of regular schools. Rather it is because they are able to stand out in a particular area and display originality; they are able to gain important success in a particular area and enable students to form their own specialties and to succeed in education with these specialties.

In Suzhou, we have advocated for many years for setting up specialty schools and have also formed a batch of schools that have quite a bit of individuality. One example is Suzhou Chengdong Central Primary School, where, although it is relatively unknown, all students are proficient in two traditional folk instruments. The students have performed on stage together with Min Huifen, have added luster and variety to community activities, and have been warmly welcomed by parents and the community. Another example is Wujiang's Tuncun Central Primary School, where they may not have any beautiful school buildings, but every child at this school can write a set of beautiful Chinese characters. Traditional folk instruments and calligraphy are both important parts of our national culture, and allowing students to come into contact with and be trained in the art of calligraphy from a young age will undoubtedly have a profound effect on the formation of their cultural appreciation and state of self-cultivation as well as the enrichment of their future spiritual lives. A further example is Wujiang's Qingyun Middle School, which is special because of its use of emotional education, with some of the students even referring to their teachers as "mother." Finally, Taoyuan Middle School has made a name for itself due to its excellent management. Because they value specialized education, both schools have increased their operational efficiency and enhanced the vitality of the school.

The specialties of a school are extremely important, as specialized education is often the "best point of attack" for changing a school's image. Suzhou City's Sixth Middle School was originally an old school that had a relatively poor foundation, their running of the school was relatively bad and after Xiao Desheng took up his posting as principal, through research and reflection, he resolved to devote his time and efforts to shaping up the school's specialties. He invited university professors from the departments of arts and physical education and set up specialized classes for those subjects and strengthened the teaching of them in the entire school. Soon this specialized education achieved success, and this school has now become an important model middle school for the nation.

In a certain sense it can be said that there is no best, only the most special; to be the most special is to be the best. An outstanding school inevitably has its own specialties, where there is dominance; there is a sense of individual style. If a school does not possess any specialties, then it does not have a strong sense of vitality and will also have no sense of dominance. This is similar to Dalian, which specializes in urban construction; Shenzhen, which specializes in advanced technology; Wenzhou, which specializes in privately owned economics, and Suzhou, which specializes in export-oriented business. They are all famous cities of our country. Of course, the specialties of a school will not be created out of thin air. They are the product of the principal's unique educational philosophy and are gradually formed and established through the long-term development of a school. Of course, these specialties are at the same time established on the basis of the principal's own personal strengths.

2. Display the Quality of a School Clearly
My take on the ideal school is that it should be a quality school.

A "grade" was originally used to explain the percentage of useful components in ore or an ore body. Later on, it was used as a metaphor to describe someone or something that is high or low in value or in standards. The grade, or quality, that we are discussing here is mainly in reference to whether or not the content offered by a school is fulfilling and whether or not it possesses high educational value and standards.

I believe the quality of a school lies first within the quality of its campus; everything, including every detail, every building and every spot of greenery, should be worked at and looked after with extreme care and precision. Details can sometimes better reflect the quality of a school, and the campus should set up a series of decorations that center around the students as well as consider how best to offer students the maximum level of convenience. For example, besides providing students with a good library, every corridor and other areas can also be transformed into places where students can pick up a book at any time. Another example is in terms of computers, which can be deployed to anywhere any student might need one, enabling students to check things online at any time. Management needs to strive to overcome any inconvenience these suggestions cause in order to provide students with the maximum level of convenience.

Second, the quality of a school is reflected in the character of its students. Schools not only transfer knowledge; more importantly, they mold the moral quality of a person's character. Sukhomlinsky once said that when our students leave the school campus, what they should take with them is not only knowledge but also, more importantly, the pursuit of ideals. If schools are able to do this, then students will be able to keep pursuing ideals and keep making progress. We need not worry about these sorts of students. However, at present, when students leave some of our schools they take with them disgust and even hatred for learning.

Therefore, our schools should teach students to passionately love learning and living and teach them to care about society, humankind, and life. If a school makes an effort to develop students' character and moral quality, teaching them to pursue ideals, to care about the fate of our nation, to constantly remind themselves never to be at a standstill, and to never lose hope, then we have given students the true philosopher's stone. This is because people can only receive a high grade if their character and moral quality are perfect, and only then can they become a vaunted member of society and not an outcast.

3. Have a Principal Who Is Full of Charisma and Grand Visions

My take on the ideal school is that it should have a principal who is full of charisma and grand visions.

The principal is the soul of a school. If a school does not possess a soul, then this school also does not possess spirit or vitality and does not possess any of the things that we must have. Principals should first have charisma. They should also have the strength and wisdom to unite all teachers and enable all teachers to discover themselves and unearth their own latent capabilities.

A good-for-nothing principal will constantly complain about the teachers, while an outstanding principal will be able to discover the merits and personal strengths of every teacher and develop the teachers' creativity and enthusiasm to their limits. Principals should understand the needs of teachers and furthermore guide their teachers to recognize what they need. They should create a good atmosphere and at the same time have the best teachers properly rewarded. Principals must be aware of the gap between themselves and great teachers and remind themselves to constantly undertake professional development and improve themselves. Principals must engage in heart-to-heart exchanges with every teacher and win their respect with their sincerity, broadmindedness, and selfless dedication.

Principals should also use their own research and teaching achievements to influence teachers.

It is also extremely important that principals have grand visions. Without grand visions it would be impossible for them to have any achievements. The achievements of a school cannot possibly exceed the goals that the principal hopes to achieve. A soldier who does not want to be a high-ranking officer is not a good soldier, and a principal who does not want to be the best principal in all of the country and even the world is not a good principal.

Of course, setting up the ideal school cannot be completed by just one person or one generation and may require the efforts of several generations. However, we can stand on the shoulders of giants and construct new grades, new realms, and new standards. Every principal, every teacher is pursuing excellence, and so our school will definitely be a good school.

4. Assemble a Cohort of Creative and Vibrant Teachers
My take on the ideal school is that it should have a cohort of creative and vibrant teachers.

The running of the school is predominantly done by the teachers. This dedication and cohesiveness is the key to running a school well. A good school does not lie in its number of beautiful buildings but in its number of great teachers.

Many schoolteachers are very young, and many of the principals at these schools bemoan this fact, complaining that their school lacks older teachers who have extensive teaching experience. In actual fact, although the experiences of older teachers are admittedly important, the passion and creativity of younger teachers is also important. Except for lacking in experience, young people are not lacking in any other aspect, and moreover there are also times when being experienced is not necessarily a good thing. Having no experience frees them of conventions, regulations, and limitations and may make them even more creative. For example, Dou Guimei in the Northeast and Li Zhenxi in Sichuan were both young teachers who attained outstanding achievements, weren't they?

Being young is not a bad thing, as long as you do not repeat the same thing every day but embrace the new sun with each coming day. Zhangjiagang Senior High School, a school that I am familiar with, recruited teachers from all over the nation. In 5 or 10 years, Zhangjiagang Senior High School should have teachers that will appear on the list of the nation's top 10 most outstanding teachers and among the ranks of famous teachers. There is actually nothing all that special about famous people; the key is that they started from scratch, taking it one day at a time.

Success depends not only on wisdom but also on effort. Those who have no impulses or passion will never be successful. Success comes from passion, from the tireless efforts of pursuing excellence. We should give more consideration to what we can leave behind for the world and should establish values in life on how to do this. Someone once asked me: the final destination for all people is the same; why do you bother to try so hard? I replied that it is precisely because our outcome is the same that I hope the process will be different. We cannot require that every teacher is excellent, but we can require that every teacher is able to tackle and pursue excellence.

Greatness is not at all remote and only requires for one to be a person who has the resolve. It requires meticulous accumulation and spending more energy on teaching and thus on the pursuit of one's own career. The most taboo thing for teachers to do is to constantly repeat what someone else has already done (of course, this excludes conscientiously learning from and studying the advanced experiences of others). What is most needed is for teachers to surpass themselves, and in order to do this, they require innovation. Schools should take full advantage of all teaching resources and mobilize all forces that can be mobilized. Schools should do everything possible to invite master educators to come to the school, enabling teachers and students more opportunities to listen to the words of master educators and engage in dialogue with them. This will more or less incite their yearning to be a master educator and become the impetus to be one. It will more or less allow them to feel that master educators are on hand and are not instead all that remote. Throughout the ages, quality schools are bound to be schools where excellent teachers and master educators gather.

5. Have a Cohort of Students Who Are Adept at Exploring and Possess Good Habits

My take on the ideal school is that it has a cohort of students who are adept at exploring and possess good habits.

Students form the main body of the school and are the owners of the learning process. "Today, I am proud of my school; tomorrow, my school will be proud of me" is a saying that many schools use to motivate students to learn. In actual fact, any school at any given moment shares both its glories and disgraces together with its students, and the school and students are bound together by these common interests. Only students can deck out a school with a sense of vitality, as green lawns without figures of students reading, red running tracks without the students' youthful footsteps, and facilities no matter how state-of-the-art will only be still and lifeless. I believe that for students, the two most important issues are for them to be adept at exploring and possess good habits.

Let us first discuss being adept at exploring. Having schools become places where children can independently explore knowledge should be what education pursues. For students, what is most valuable is the spirit of exploration and good habits. If students lose their curiosity toward the world, they will not take the initiative to ask questions and investigate, and that would be tragic for the school, the teachers, and the students. What schools can try to do is have students write papers and academic reports, and when students graduate from senior high school, they should also undertake an oral presentation of their thesis. In America, primary students in years 1 and 2 are already writing papers. When students learn how to explore, their lives will be very fulfilling. Our university students are currently busy whiling away the time with their own forms of entertainment because they lack the spirit of exploration. We must attempt to give our students a variety of problems to solve.

For example, literature and language teaching should break with tradition and have students read a certain number of literary masterpieces, with students being able to graduate only if they are able to complete these readings. If they do not read literary masterpieces, how are we able to develop their finer emotions? How are we able to cultivate their ability to appreciate literature and the arts? How are we able to develop their interpersonal skills? We can also require students to keep a diary and write down the feelings that they experience in their lives. Presently, the political science examinations in Suzhou are already open-book exams, and I advocate that all exams be open-book exams because life itself is an open book. The crux of our education is to have children learn to explore. We believe that changing traditional teaching methods will not affect academic results, as the best and the most outstanding students are not afraid of college entrance exams.

Let us turn once again to good habits. Quality has its origins in habits. Ye Shengtao once said that the true meaning of education is the cultivation of students' good habits. We should form the habit of treating others good-naturedly and being civil and polite. We should also require all children to greet any teacher or guest that they see, on their own initiative, and the teachers themselves should also smile and nod when they catch sight of a student. The mentality that we must enable students to have is the feeling that the campus is a home and that any visitors are guests. This is by no means something superficial but rather something that becomes second nature. We should also have students form the habit of caring for society and the environment. We should require students to refrain from littering everywhere and to be kind to all living creatures and the environment. We should have students form the habit of being diligent with their studies and having a willingness to learn. We should require students to grasp a study method that suits them best and to view learning as a requirement for improving their inner selves, with students learning all the time, learning everywhere, and learning everything. Good habits will provide students with a lifetime of benefits.

6. Use a Curriculum System That Is for All Students

My take on the ideal school is that it should have a curriculum system that is for all students.

Specialized schools should establish a curriculum system that is also specialized. The curriculum system is the space that students depend on for survival and development, and at its core it should be a system that caters to all students. Students are different and so the curriculum should have choices. Just as the quality and standards of a supermarket are determined by its range of commodities, so too should the extensiveness of a school curriculum be an important symbol for measuring a school's quality and standards. Having all students study stipulated courses deprives students of the power to choose, to a considerable extent, and also deprives them of their interests and opportunity to develop in certain areas. Therefore, schools that are financially better off should begin offering elective classes; encourage public figures, experts, and scholars to start elective classes at school; and even encourage the starting of student lectures.

A credit system can be set up so that students can be allowed to advance or postpone their graduation. What we are resolutely against, however, are so-called honors classes and classes where the teaching is either purposefully accelerated or slowed down. As the ancients said, instruction knows no class distinction. Education does not separate people into ranks, which would make children feel as if they have been alienated from when they were young. However, we advocate for stratification in teaching based on the subject area, which would enable students to choose learning content and study methods that are suitable for them, that is, handing over the learning initiative to them. Within the school-based curriculum system, we particularly praise research-based courses. People's ability to discover and their latent capabilities in exploration are enormous, and we must allow students to form the spirit for research and exploration from their youth, to learn to attain knowledge through their own labors, to reorganize information, and to even produce new inventions.

7. Provide Libraries and Computer Rooms That Are Always Open to Students

My take on the ideal school is that it has libraries and computer rooms that are always open to students.

Libraries and computer rooms are the souls of school facilities. Sukhomlinsky once said that a school can have nothing at all except for a library and it can still be called a school. Reading is an important means of enriching a student's spiritual world. Our school education and literature and language education have gone astray, with books at many schools being tools merely for window dressing rather than the spiritual nourishment that children cannot bear to be separated from for even a moment. In view of this, our *Anthology of New Century Educational Works* has a hundred ancient and modern literary masterpieces selected for primary and secondary students. From this we selected a book list of about 20 require readings that we recommend, with the hope that through reading these books, Chinese students of the new century will be able to care more about the humanities and possess a character that is even more noble.

We have already entered a new era, an economic era that deals with a high level of information. Students' learning can no longer be limited to the classroom and the school. The variety of information on the Internet has already become a rich teaching resource. How to enable our students to possess a strong awareness of information and superb information processing capabilities is an urgent task for education.

Therefore, I hope to thoroughly change the traditional layout of a school and transport the school library so that it is inside the classrooms and corridors. By doing this, students can find the books that they want to read, look up the information that they want to check, and surf the Net and contact experts at any time. These places should not be closed due to festivals or holidays. As long as there are students at school, we should make every effort to offer our services and assistance to them and enable them to get the greatest level of convenience.

What exactly is the most ideal school? I would like to summarize by quoting a passage from author Tetsuko Kuroyanagi's *Totto-Chan: The Little Girl at the Window*: "I am quite sure that if there were schools now like Tomoe, there would be less of the violence we hear so much of today and fewer school dropouts. At Tomoe nobody wanted to go home when school was over. And in the morning we could hardly wait to get there. It was that kind of school."[2] This was a school founded by Sosaku Kobayashi in 1937. In 1945 it was destroyed by the war, and although it only existed for eight years, it has been recorded for all of eternity in educational history. Therefore, the ideal school is one that will cause students who come, to not want to leave, and students who leave, to want to come back—that is, to be a school whose memory students will forever cherish.

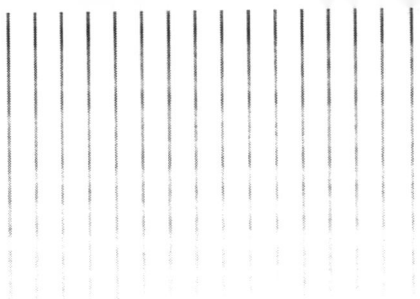

7

My Take on the Ideal Teacher

With the passage of time, what is most profound and sincere, is the teacher's gaze, which can pierce through all the ages and clearly understand the universe;

In the entire world, what is the most extensive, is the teacher's gaze, which can penetrate the astronomy above, and observe the geography below;

In this world, what is most selfless, is the teacher's gaze, which alarmingly watches as fish leap and delightfully follows as birds fly;

The teacher's gaze is a gentle wind, a gentle wind that is their greeting to the young seedlings;

The teacher's gaze is a long piece of silk, a long piece of silk that is their concern for their students;

The teacher's gaze is a deep ocean, a deep ocean that is their love for the world.

This piece of prose is entitled "The Teacher's Gaze" and the connotations sing the praises of teachers. Well then, exactly what sort of teacher is a good teacher? What sort of teacher can be said to be the ideal teacher?

American scholars Zeichner and Joyce once conducted a specialized study on the issue of teachers and believe that historically, all theories on teachers can be divided into five categories:

The first category regards teachers as "good employees." This theory emphasizes that teachers in the classroom teach according to the norm. This type of teacher is based in technical skills and experience.

The second category regards teachers as "junior professors." This model emphasizes that excellent teachers must have a wealth of academic knowledge and good background knowledge. They must also have an extensive academic background.

The third category regards the teacher as a "fully functioning person." This model holds that only a teacher who is able to promote individual development is an excellent teacher and only an education that promotes individual development is the best form of education. This theory fully affirms the value of individual teachers, emphasizing the understanding that teachers have for individual lives, teachers' personalities, and their individual teaching styles. It is concerned with the molding and nurturing of students' personalities.

The fourth category regards the teacher as "the innovator." This model maintains that teachers should be full of dynamism and vitality and that teachers are the source of all educational and social reforms. Teachers should transform society through reforming students and school education.

The fifth model regards teachers as "reflective practitioners." This model holds that teachers are thinkers. During the process of teaching, teachers will not only pay attention to the training of students' cognitive ability but will, more importantly, pay attention to raising students' ability to think.

I believe that of the five teaching models mentioned above, we should support and admire none of these models by itself; instead, an outstanding teacher should be an integration of all these models.

1. Have Broad-minded Ideals and Be Full of Passion and Poetic Sentiments

My take on the ideal teacher is that one should have broadminded ideals and be full of passion and poetic sentiments.

Any teacher, in order to attain high achievements and high standards, must first have "high" ideals. An overseas study once specifically researched the relationship between people's level of ambition and achievements. The conclusion was that the higher people's level of ambition, the greater their achievements. After taking up a teaching post, teachers must set a goal for themselves to struggle and fight for education for the rest of their lives. Only by setting such a goal for themselves can teachers focus all their actions on this target, to continuously enhance their self-awareness and sense of duty and to constantly challenge themselves; otherwise, they will end up taking a roundabout route and waste time and energy.

Teaching has a lot in common with, as well as many differences from, other professions. The complexity and richness in teaching is something that other professions do not possess, requiring teachers to have even higher levels of spirituality and perceptiveness.

Some people say that education is a poem; it can have all kinds of moods and connotations—it can be an idyllic poem, an archaic poem, or even a lyric poem.

What, then, is the prerequisite for teachers to be able to read and understand this poem? It is to set a goal for oneself: I must be able to read and understand this. If you do not possess the desire and urge to decipher this poem, then you will never be able to read and understand it and will also be unable to write your own splendid poem. Makarenko once titled his works as "The Pedagogical Poem," and I believe this makes a lot of sense.

An ideal teacher should be a teacher who is naturally restless and has dreams. In education, every day is a new start and the meanings and themes of each day are all different. Only those who possess strong impulses, desires, a sense of duty, and a sense of responsibility are able to raise questions and seek out "troubles" for themselves as well as live a poetic educational life. Writing a poem requires inspiration, perception, and impulses, and true educators should also possess this sort of character and always look forward to tomorrow. If these impulses were to stop, then education would meet its end.

Outstanding teachers must possess ambitious dreams and must continuously put forward their own goals to pursue while being passionate at the same time. For those who are in the process of growing as teachers, calm thinking is necessary, but what is needed even more is to be full of passion. American scholar Wu Wei once wrote these exciting words in his article "Passion Makes a Successful Teacher": "Teachers who want to teach well are, in most cases, people who have even greater ambitions and unbridled passion. At least a small part of greatness comes from one's innate talent. However, a great teacher is certainly a passionate teacher."

People must be able to dream. Outstanding teachers must always follow their own dreams. When there comes a time where we live without dreams, then the meaning of life will meet its end, as will the meaning of education.

2 Be Self-confident and Self-supporting and Constantly Challenge Oneself

My take on the ideal teacher is that one should be a self-confident, self-supporting teacher who constantly challenges oneself.

Ideal teachers should be adept at understanding themselves and discovering themselves. Why are there some people in life who do not have any passion? This is because they have not discovered their own loveliness and greatness. Understanding oneself is a profound proposition that humankind has faced since ancient times. On the issue of "understanding oneself," we have long held a misunderstanding. Our media and teachers ask us to conduct ourselves properly, so when we are commenting, summing something up, or interacting with others we will always be a little self-deprecating. Of course, during exchanges with others there is no reason why you cannot act this way, but deep down in your innermost being, you must never be self-deprecating. People will never be able to surpass the goals that they pursue. At the same time, people will also never be able to exceed their own assessment of themselves. The assessment one gives oneself is often a sign of whether or not one's career will be a success. Self-confidence enables a person to be self-supporting, and the appropriate "pride" will enable people to be successful. Only self-confidence can enable a person's latent capabilities and talents to be developed to their limits. It is also only self-confidence that will enable people to attain "peak experiences." To foster people is to foster their self-confidence, and to destroy people is to destroy their self-confidence.

The Japanese academic Yasunosuke Sakamoto wrote a book about himself. Within the book is this story: He (Sakamoto) had very poor academic results, and out of the 500 students in the class, he was ranked worse than 470th. However, his father did not lose hope at all and instead constantly went about unearthing the "spark" within him. He would play chess with his son for the purpose of making his mind more agile; he would go hunting in the mountains with his son and praise his keen observations, thus constantly strengthening his self-esteem. Once self-confidence had been established, many things could then be naturally accepted.

Principals should protect teachers' self-confidence, even when it is accompanied by pride. Teachers should also value this self-confidence and not lose it due to momentary setbacks. As long as people's self-confidence is not destroyed, they will definitely succeed. People who have come into this world should have their own value, their own stage, their own role that they play, and their own limits that they can reach. It is only that we often have not discovered the value of our existence and have not established a belief in life. There is a book entitled *No One's Perfect* about a young Japanese person called Hirotada Ototake who was born with no arms and no legs. However, it is precisely this person who managed to enter Japan's Waseda University, by relying on his own tireless efforts, and become a best-selling author in Japan. Therefore, I believe that for a person to achieve success, there are two prerequisites: one is to pursue success and the other is to believe that you are able to succeed.

Any person is able to achieve enormous success, and so is any teacher. It is just that we have yet to find the path.

An ideal teacher should constantly pursue success, design success, and more importantly, make an impact on success. This is because people who have come into this world do not know what sort of people they will become. It is only by tackling every blind spot that has the potential of success that we can reveal the "sparks of success." The fact that teachers have the impulse and the power to impact these sorts of things is remarkable. If teachers were to stop making an impact, then it would mean that they have lost confidence in life and have lost self-confidence in their own existence.

3. Be Adept at Cooperation and Be Full of Charisma

My take on the ideal teacher is that one should be adept at cooperation and possess charisma.

Competition based on cooperation and cooperation based on competition are notable features of modern society. A teacher who is not adept at cooperation will not go far because this society and the teaching profession require cooperation.

The objects of education, that is, our students, reside within an extremely complex social environment where they are constantly influenced from all sides and at all levels. How much influence teachers are able to exert depends on the balance of the force they apply. The extent of success that a teacher's influence is able to achieve depends on the extent and strength of the teacher's coordination with all forces to jointly exert their influence on students. Capable teachers will be able to mobilize an impressive force to achieve their ambitions in education. There are many teachers who personally have great inner qualities, but they lack the spirit of cooperation and quibble about every detail with other teachers. These sorts of teachers will not go far.

Cooperation is multifaceted. It includes cooperation between teachers, between teachers and students, between teachers and parents, between teachers and principals, and between teachers and society.

In regard to cooperation and competition, it is necessary to establish a concept of "win-win." In the past, we often believed that in a competition there is only one winner, and therefore cooperation would have certain difficulties, and would lead to more competition than cooperation. However, in actual fact, only a "win-win" has any real meaning in a competition.

How then can one become a well-loved teacher? In the past, I have always spoken of three essential factors: empathy, respect, and reciprocation.

The first is empathy, to "not do unto others what you would not have them do unto you."

Empathy is the easiest to talk about but the hardest to do. Empathy is a challenge that psychological propositions direct at philosophical propositions. Philosophers tell us that "this existence" can only have "this consciousness"; psychologists, however, refute this and say that "this existence" requires "that consciousness." This is very difficult, as a slip in attention will lead to parochialism and self-centeredness, transforming everything so that it is first focused on oneself. We know that too many standards in life and too much self-centeredness will inevitably lead to conflict. These conflicts can be resolved well through the use of empathy. This is why in work and in life, our teachers must place themselves in someone else's position and consider problems from their perspective more. This does not require teachers to go to the extent of making the time to stand in front of the door to a study room, but rather to be able to understand and sympathize with others. Such teachers will be considered understanding and considerate. So-called understanding and considerate teachers are those who are adept at empathizing. Empathy does not mean that they are unaware of their own existence, but rather that they are aware of what others need; furthermore, they will promptly offer a friendly hand when others need it and will not look on other people's suffering with disregard.

The second factor is respect. Respect is an extremely important psychological need for people. It is also a very high level need and is only created after needs such as a person's survival and physiology are met. Sukhomlinsky once said that self-respect is the most sensitive corner within a person's spirit. People whose self-respect is wounded will contend against you with ten times the madness and a hundred times their strength, as "a gentleman prefers death to humiliation." Therefore teachers must respect others, especially their students' characters.

The third factor is reciprocation. When teachers are interacting with other people, they should be able to learn how to give something to others. When engaging in common activities, everyone is able to share in the results of the activity and acquire an appropriate return from it. A Western theory on social interaction is that one very important point in regard to balance in interactions and relationships between people hinges upon a mental assessment. During this process, every person must make an investment, and this is what we can refer to as the costs. At the same time, every person is able to gain something from the interaction and this is classified as one's profits. If these sorts of interactions allow one to gain some sort of profit, then one will continue with these interactions; if the interactions are a waste of time and energy and not worth it, then one will terminate the interactions. However, when some people regard whether one loses out or benefits at others' expense in the process of education, they are often unable to see what they acquire, and this causes a variety of imbalanced interactions. An excellent communicator and an ideal teacher should also be able to possess the spirit of dedication. We advocate this kind of spirit and state because behind this kind of spirit and state, is the fact that you will be able to be rewarded. All costs will have a return and all investments will be profitable. The process of interaction is actually a process of balancing interests. To quibble over present gains and losses outwardly appears as if one has temporarily gained something, but in reality one has lost long-term benefits and the gains do not make up for the losses.

I feel that teachers who are truly able to practice all of the above three points will definitely win the respect of the teaching community, the principal, the students, and the parents.

4. Be Full of Love and Be Revered by Students
My take on the ideal teacher is that one is full of love and is revered by students.

The education of love is a source of strength for education and the foundation of educational success. As Xia Mianzun says: "Education without emotions, without love, is like a pond without water. Without water, it cannot be called a pond. Without emotions, without love, there is no education." We have many teachers who teach day after day and year after year, but they have never found joy during the course of teaching, nor have their hearts ever burst forth with a surge of love. These teachers will never achieve educational success and will never be able to grasp the true meaning of education.

At the time when I was teaching at university, when students were leaving school and asked me to leave them a message, the sentence that I wrote the most was: unearth the inherent charms in your life and career. For every person, the basis of our survival and development is our careers. Whether you are fed up with it or like your career is crucial to your entire psychological development, your happiness, and your acquiring of a sense of achievement. If you do not like this career, then this career will not like you. If you do not love the teaching profession, then you will not be able to gain any joy from teaching.

In the past, we often said, "As long as there are two buckets of grain at home, do not be a king of children." Dealing with children is indeed an extremely vexing task as teachers come across all sorts of problems and worries every day. However, I say that it is only with great worries that we can have great joy and it is only with major problems that we can have major success. If you carefully unearth the teaching profession, you will discover its actual beauty. It can be said that there is not a profession in the world more beautiful than teaching.

Teachers must be adept at discovering the joys in teaching because every day we embrace a new sun and face children who have extremely different personalities and are all individuals with unlimited future prospects. Among them might be future political leaders, future Nobel Prize laureates, or all sorts of other possibilities. As long as you tend to them with the utmost care, nurture them, help them regain their self-confidence and tap into the hidden potential within them, then their capabilities will be limitless and far surpass what you have imagined. An ounce of work will give you so many times the return!

Teachers are able to take people's creativity, imagination, and all of their capabilities and wisdom and develop them to their limits. It is a profession that is never ending. Is this not worthy of our love? Future educators should invest all their mental and physical strengths into loving students and education. Only love can win love. If you love the teaching profession, then the teaching profession will also love you, and you will then be able to attain the joys of a career. If you love students, then students will also love you and also enable you to forget the outside world and life's troubles when you are interacting with them.

There are also many perks to the teaching profession, such as a few months' worth of vacation a year, which you can use to do many things that you want to do. Engels once said that people's largest realm of development is one in which they are able to use the most leisure time to do things that they want to do. As a teacher, we are able to achieve success and enjoy life to the greatest extent. In this regard, no other profession can surpass that of teaching.

As long as you are able to discover and tap into the sorts of beauty that pervade the teaching profession, then you will be able to generate impulses every day and be able to see that every student is a budding, beautiful flower. It is true that the teaching profession will probably never reach the top of any ranking on careers. However, I believe that outstanding and ideal teachers will most certainly place themselves, within their hearts, at the very top of these rankings! This is why I feel that teachers should make an effort to unearth the hidden beauty in teaching and firmly believe that everything that they do affects a person's life and that it is a profession that is worth a lifetime of struggles. Only by thus doing can you love teaching and be able to invest your whole body and mind into the profession.

In terms of teachers' love for their students, it is important that they believe in every child. Every child possesses enormous hidden capabilities, and each child's hidden capabilities are different. Only by having a discerning eye, discovering each child's hidden capabilities, and encouraging children to be always independently exploring, can we enable their talents to be developed to the fullest potential.

A teacher's love for students is also expressed in the democratic nature of education. The spirit of democracy in our education is still not enough as teachers speak and students listen, teachers issue orders and students obey. Dialogues between teachers and students where they are on equal footing are too few. We often complain that our society still lacks a sense of democracy. However, the foundation of social democracy is democracy in the school. Without democracy in the school, then we would not be able to speak of democracy in society. The cultivation of a democratic spirit must begin at a young age. Democracy is reflected in many ways, including the way teachers speak to students and interact with them. These seem like trivial matters but they all reflect a sort of democracy. Students in China sit upright and still, and when the teacher asks questions, the students all answer in unison. From a foreign educator's point of view, this is inconceivable— how can everyone answer the one problem in unison?

Many of our teachers do not possess compassion. They do not take on the role of teaching and educating others but instead adopt the role of the "teaching police"; they do not recognize achievements but discover shortcomings. When children are very average or very outstanding, these teachers do not recognize and encourage them but instead "magnify" their problems. Therefore, I feel that many of our teachers play the role of the "executioner." Under the hands of our teachers, who knows how many Nobel Prize laureates, literary masters like Lu Xun and Guo Moruo, and other extremely talented individuals have been lost? I have always believed that teaching has a very important prerequisite, and that is love. Only with a foundation in love can teachers be able to invest all their strengths and have no regrets in offering up their youth and wisdom to children and to the teaching profession.

In "Using Love to Create Sentences," the author fondly describes teachers:

I came from ancient nursery rhymes, where the charm that lingers in these nursery rhymes are saturated in notes of love;

I came from the footsteps of the youth, where the footprints created as I walk and recite are bathed with the sunlit rays of love;

I came from the flowerbed of life, where the beautiful flowers are covered in dewdrops of love . . .

In this life, I am destined to busy myself with love, similar to the spring swallow that builds its nest beneath the eaves.[1]

Let us be busy ourselves with love and use love to create sentences!

5. Pursue Excellence and Be Full of Creativity

My take on the ideal teacher is that one should pursue excellence and be full of creativity.

The biggest difference between educators and pedagogues is that educators have the spirit to pursue excellence and be creative. We have many parents who, when choosing teachers and classes for their children, prefer to choose a teacher who is slightly older and is "experienced." What I have to say to them is: you must not do this, as educators are not differentiated by their age.

In recent years, the overwhelming majority of candidates for the national top 10 teachers have been teachers who were born in the 1950s, 1960s or even 1970s, and many were at the same time extremely remarkable and also extremely young. Teachers do not depend on the number of years that they have taught, but on the number of years they have seriously taught. Some people teach for one year and then repeat what they have done for the next 5 or 10 years or even for the rest of their life; other people have seriously taught for 5 years. The achievements of a person who has seriously taught for 5 years and a person who has repeatedly taught the same year for her whole life are not the same.

An outstanding educator should be one who is constantly exploring, constantly innovating, and has determination in teaching. The reason why people are able to achieve success, to a large extent, is because they have determination. We often say that a watched flower never blooms, but an untended willow grows; however, when all is said and done, in most situations, a watched flower blooms and an untended willow will not grow. We must not forget this basic rule. We must not establish success on the basis of unpredictable flukes and chance happenings.

This is why I say that if you do not believe, then start keeping a teaching journal from today onward and be a person who has determination and will seriously sum up the gains and losses of education. I was able to be successful with something today and how did I do it? What did I experience? How do I feel about it? A conflict occurred today. How was it resolved? I encountered setbacks today. Once again, how did I feel about it? You must record all of this without changing one iota. Five years later, make a compilation of the most brilliant sections of the journal and this will become the most wonderful of books; these flickering "sparks" will pierce the soul of the reader.

At present, the problem is that many of us are thrilled and excited but do not commit this to writing, and these "sparks" soon vanish into thin air. To be a person who has determination, anything can become a subject to study and learn from. Only under the premise of one's determination are we able to put together various fragments to create the most beautiful costume. Originally these individual fragments were seemingly worthless when in actual fact it is not that they lack value, but that their value has not been discovered and put to use. If you combine them, they will be dazzling.

Therefore, the ideal teacher should be one who has determination. Primary and secondary teachers conducting educational research should begin with recording educational phenomena and their own thoughts and feelings. By stringing together all these "pearls," you would have a very beautiful necklace. We should encourage this sort of educational research. Of course, this does not exclude the cooperation between teachers and experts in carrying out theoretical discussions; however, when all is said and done, educational research in primary and secondary schools is not the same as educational research for university teachers. I very much appreciate teachers who keep an educational journal, who document their own experiences in notebooks. Perhaps these books can later become "The Collection of Chinese Teachers' Journals."

Our teachers should also create a name for themselves that stands out from the masses and set up their own teaching model. Practically speaking, at present we have many teachers, including many who have been selected as outstanding teachers and teachers of distinction, who often do not have their own distinguishing features. When we select outstanding teachers and teachers of distinction now, we often look at how many articles they have published and rarely inquire about what makes them unique. I believe that only by genuinely establishing one's own style and system can we become educators. "Style maketh man," and only by forming a style and system can one become a great expert.

6. Learn Diligently and Enrich Oneself Constantly

My take on the ideal teacher is that one is a diligent learner and constantly enriches oneself.

To be a diligent learner and constantly enrich oneself are the foundations for becoming an outstanding teacher. An ideal teacher, a teacher who wants to become a great expert, and a teacher who wants to become an educator must start from the basics and slowly but steadily read more books.

In Suzhou, we ran training courses for famous teachers and principals. Apart from various training such as teaching them to "engage in dialogue with masters in their fields," what was very important was to have them read literary masterpieces. If you do not read "The Analects of Confucius" or the works of Tao Xingzhi, Dewey, and Sukhomlinsky, then I'm afraid that it would be very difficult to become an educator. Among the works that we have selected and compiled in our *Anthology of New Century Educational Works* is a teaching series that includes the most classical and outstanding teaching resources on educational science as well as domestic and international educational novels, maxims, talks, essays, stories, and the finest teachings of educational figures as well as a large number of readings on the humanities, nature, and social sciences, which broaden a teacher's horizons. We hope that this compilation can become China's first series of required readings for teachers and become the spiritual food that feeds the growth of outstanding teachers.

Do not view education as something that is very mysterious. Every teacher can become an extremely influential educator in China and set forth to places outside of this country and enjoy a reputation overseas. Everyone is capable of doing this, but the crux lies in whether or not you can be a determined person, whether or not you are dedicated, and whether or not you have the perseverance. Of course, we know that a teacher must possess the appropriate knowledge structures, educational philosophy, cultural literacy, moral literacy, technical accomplishments, and so on.

I think that a teacher's most important duty is to learn. No educator can depart from the educational wealth of the previous generation. In a certain sense it can be said that we use the language of our era and the experiences of our lives to engage in spiritual communications with master educators of the past and to explain our understanding of education.

In reality, many educators merely take someone else's knowledge and apply it to their own teaching practices, which produces many theoretical responses. You must try to seek out and find a theoretical mainstay and response by yourself. Many teachers do not feel anything when they teach and are unable to find their direction. As teachers, you are different from other experts and need to be knowledgeable in various areas. Teachers who do not have a wide range of knowledge would be hard pressed to inspire students in terms of their character. The younger the children, the greater their expectations in their teachers and the more they will regard their teachers as encyclopedias. In their eyes, their teachers are omniscient, and if their teachers are completely ignorant, then they will be extremely disappointed. Therefore, teachers should perfect their own knowledge structure.

Teachers should also strive to understand the world of a child. An adult's world and a child's world are not the same; the children's world has a unique coloring, melody, and connotations. Teachers must experience pleasure, anger, sorrow, and joy together with them; grow together with them; and become a part of their cohort. Teaching requires teachers to be very young of heart in order to be able to communicate with them, to understand them, and to gain their love.

However, we have always advocated the dignity of the teaching profession and encouraged a sense of distance between teachers and students. Traditional Chinese education has many good traits and bad traits. An excessive emphasis on the dignity of the teaching profession is a bad trait.

Teachers should also have three *things*: academic qualifications, personal experiences, and wisdom and insight gained from experiences. These "three things" are intrinsically linked. This does not necessarily require one to travel over famous mountains and great rivers, travel thousands of miles, or read thousands of books, as their value is the same.

We must encourage teachers to be people who explore nature, love nature, love life, and love humanity. We must cultivate this sort of mentality in order to be able to educate children properly.

7. Have Concern for the Fate of Humankind and a Sense of Social Responsibility

My take on the ideal teacher is that one should be concerned with the fate of humankind and possess a sense of social responsibility.

Education is not only about giving children knowledge. What is even more important is fostering a positive attitude in students toward life. Education itself is life. We often complain that society is not like this or not like that. We curse corruption, curse autocracies, curse dictatorships, curse relationships, and curse all sorts of other things. However, we very rarely think that the vast majority of the things we curse are things of our own making. To a certain extent, it can be said that education is the root of a diseased society, so teachers must not shirk their responsibility. Educators, ideal teachers, should be very concerned about society and the fate of humanity and attach great importance to cultivating students' sense of social responsibility. It is also only a teacher's sense of social responsibility that can mold students' sense of social responsibility. Only classroom discussions that a teacher has with students about environment, human population issues, and so on can arouse children's interest in these issues.

If teachers spend the whole day being concerned with rankings and test scores, then how can children become broad-minded? The world within the school and outside of the school should be intimately linked. Furthermore, at present the world outside is indeed very exciting while school life is something that students have no choice in. Therefore, in order to enable students to live better, to have a society that is even more ideal and perfect, we must first cleanse our campuses and also have our school possess a spirit of care for human culture. Sukhomlinsky once said that when children leave school, they do not only take with them their test scores, but more important is that they take with them their pursuit of the ideal future society.

I think that our education and our ideal teachers should do exactly this. In other words, everything that we do is for the sake of preparing for the future. Our education is for the sake of the education of the future and is focused on a lifetime of education for children. Only in this way can we have a strong sense of social responsibility. Therefore, a principal's sense of social responsibility and a teacher's sense of social responsibility affects a student's sense of social responsibility; the democratic style of a campus and teaching methods directly influence a child's way of life. I hope that our teachers will pay serious attention to the world beyond their classroom window.

8. Be Persevering, Tenacious, and Unafraid of Setbacks
My take on the ideal teacher is that one has perseverance and tenacity and will not be bowed by setbacks.

Teachers exist in different environments. Some are in schools for the elite while others are in mainstream schools; some are in urban areas while others are in rural areas. Students also come from different backgrounds and have different foundations. Some people will often complain: how come I have to work in this sort of shoddy school? I always hope that these people can be swapped to a better environment. Such feelings are understandable, but I would like to say that all environments are capable of producing educators; all hardships have the possibility of creating educators. Perhaps leading this school well and enabling these students to achieve the best development is your mission. So it is that whenever Heaven invests a person with great responsibilities, it first tries his resolve, exhausts his muscles and bones, and starves his body.

In reality, whether an environment is good or bad is relative and not absolute. At a school for the elite with a sound reputation, there will be a lot of regulations and the freedom there might be minimal; however, at an unknown school, a person's creativity might be able to emerge even more. I often say to our outstanding principals: you can be proud, but do not get carried away; it is not because the standard of your teaching is particularly high, but because your students have contributed to creating you, your school, and your teachers. To be honest, place these students from schools for the elite anywhere and they will be able to perform very well. This is because through many years of education, they have already developed the habits of self-learning, self-teaching, and self-development. What can truly show your genuine skills is if you teach academically poor students well and manage an inferior school well.

Therefore, I require that our outstanding schools must help or merge with a school that has a weak foundation; otherwise, principals and teachers of those excellent schools will not be able to show their genuine skills. Someone says: "A teacher like me can only teach brilliant students at an excellent school." It cannot be said that there is no logic in his words, but I feel that a teacher who can only teach good students is not a good teacher and a school that can only teach good students is also not necessarily a very good school.

Of course, these are not the universal values of society but the values I have as an educational scholar and educational administrator. What I want is equality in education, to create the opportunity for every child to have an equal education. This is why I exert a lot of energy to transform and assist schools that are relatively disadvantaged. Why has Jiangsu set up so many schools for the elite? One of the purposes of doing this is to put an end to schools for the elite through strengthening them. On the surface we are strengthening them when in fact, we are weakening them. In regard to the development of weak schools, I think that all levels of administrative departments in education should place these schools in a position where they are subject to important consideration. Children are born equal and should have equal educational opportunities. Education should give parents the right to choose and give children the right to freely choose. What the government must do is not to prohibit choice but to exert its best efforts to create a relatively fair environment for children.

I think that in regard to a teacher's growth, an indomitable willpower is extremely important. "The going is the toughest toward the end of a journey," and why is that? It is because when the vast majority of people reach the final 10 miles of their journey, they will feel discouraged and stop. However, people who are truly successful will persevere and finish off the last 10 miles. This requires determination and perseverance, and many people retreat when they are on the verge of success, leading to "failing at the last hurdle."

Of course, it is impossible for us to hope that all teachers will be able to become ideal teachers; that will always be impossible, since people are different and people's values are also different. Some people hope for the spectacular and grand, to be vivid and dazzling and to become educators who are respected and very successful; there are also some people who hope for stability and the calm and quiet. We cannot demand that every teacher have the sorts of ideals and pursuits that I have talked about, but I think that if a society does not have these ideal teachers, if a campus does not have these ideal teachers, then this would be a tragedy—a tragedy for society and also a tragedy for education.

Education needs ideals. Only by igniting the flames of these ideals can we enable our entire nation to become strong and cohesive and to be invincible when competing against other countries of the world.

We should encourage our teachers to never give up at any moment; we should encourage our schools to also never give up at any moment. This is because we are already approaching the verge of success and as we have already pursued it, then we should also get results. Education is an eternal cause for teachers. The pursuit of one generation of teachers, of two generations of teachers, of the entire cohort of teachers will ignite the spark of ideals within school campuses and thus enable our nation to ignite the spark of ideals.

I hope that Chinese education will be full of ideals! I hope that our teachers and principals will be forever full of ideals, passion, and poetic sentiments!

8

My Take on the Ideal Principal

In a sense, a principal is a school. A good principal is a good school. An education department director in Northeast China once wrote a report on principals, using the title "The Soul of a Sacred Garden." The "sacred garden" refers to the school campus and the "soul" refers to the spirit and ideology of the principal. Indeed, a principal should be a school's soul, as it is precisely because of this soul that schools have the opportunity to express the vitality of life. Many studies on being a principal have already done an outstanding job portraying the qualities of excellent principals. What new discoveries can I then have? What should my take on the ideal principal be like?

1 Possess a Dedicated Spirit and Concern for Human Culture

My take on the ideal principal is that one should have a clear understanding of one's own values and mission and possess a dedicated spirit and care for human culture.

The famous Soviet educator Kalinin once said that teachers are the living link between the past and the future, important members of society for overcoming human ignorance and vices and the intermediary between all the noble and great historical figures and a new generation of people. Kalinin refers to teachers here, but I believe that these words can equally be applied to an evaluation of principals. This is because, in a sense, principals are also teachers. They are special teachers, as their special feature lies in the fact that they are teachers of teachers. Schools gather every teacher, but since a principal is a school's soul, the principal is a force that gathers the teachers' minds.

For principals, tenure is limited. Even if some places have set up principal tenures based on a system of objectives and so it is possible for some principals to hold a post for a longer period of time, no matter how long their tenure, in terms of the history of the school it is still very brief and is only a part of the long process of endless development for a school. However, it is precisely these "parts" that come one after another, these principals that come one after another, that create the reputation of our schools and prop up the hopes of Chinese fundamental education. The changes and transitions in a school, the rise and fall of a school, depend to a very large extent on our principal's "soul." It can definitely be said that the quality, standards, and state of a school depend on the principal. It is similar to conducting a battle, in which the principal is the school's highest commander and the teachers are the offices and soldiers. Whether they are able to make a heroic and fearless dash freely across the battlefield, do their best because they are duty bound, and fight a good battle depends upon whether or not the principal is able to bring out and utilize their strengths and unite the goals of the entire school, both teachers and students alike, within the principal's own philosophy for running the school. Therefore, I think that the principal's mission and the responsibility are very great.

For principals to achieve these values and complete this mission requires two preconditions: the first is a dedicated spirit and the second is a concern for human culture.

Let us first talk about a dedicated spirit. The former principal of Shanghai's Jianping Secondary School, Feng Enhong, once said: "Education is a career, a career whose significance lies in one's dedication; education is a science, a science whose significance lies in the pursuit of the truth; education is an art, an art whose significance lies in innovation." I very much agree with these words. He regards education as a science and also as an art, but he first regards it as a career, a career that implies the dedication of oneself. What should be said is that, at present, not every person who works in education regards education as an undertaking and furthermore is willing to devote oneself to education.

Former chairman of the China Association for Promoting Democracy (CAPD), Xu Jialu, once spoke directly about education with well-spoken words that moved me very much. He said:

In regards to the divergent paths in life, despite the fact that the objective world is colorful and unpredictable, there are only two divergent paths, the first is for yourself and the second is for others. There are also only two sorts of things that people pursue, the first is materialistic and the second is spiritual. Ancient Greek philosophers once said that the pursuit of spirituality is the pursuit of the divine; in regards to a pursuit of material things, is the pursuit of the ordinary. Thousands upon thousands of teachers choose to be a candle, a candle that never goes out, as what they pursue is the country, the people and students; they pursue spirituality, the divine. The respect for teacher lies in their choice of an eternally radiant path. Teachers will probably never become millionaires in their lifetime but they have aplenty. To have this group of people in this colorful and unpredictable world, surely they are worthy of us bowing three times to them?[1]

This is the spirit of dedication that teachers have, and a principal, as an organizer and leader of teachers, must possess it even more so.

I have always believed that regarding the position of principal as a way of earning a living is one way of undertaking the post; regarding it as a way of pursuing a career is yet another way. Whether or not principals have any career ambitions is dependent on their mentality. If they treat it merely as a means of earning a living and do things according to professional ethics, discharge their job duties with all of their heart, are never late and never leave meetings early, and complete all the work that is stipulated by their profession, then professionally speaking, they are above reproach. However, this is merely a way of putting food on the table and is only for the sake of solving the issue of one's survival. Undertaking a career is not like this, as there are no limitations in a career. When people regard their profession as their career, their pursuits, ideals, and mentality will be completely different and they will then be dedicated. Of course, this is based on the premise that their basic conditions for living can be guaranteed.

Therefore, I believe that if one does not have a dedicated spirit or even the spirit to devote one's whole self, then that person should not be a principal. This is in the same vein as educators who have said before that one who does not have love should not be a teacher. I believe that the demands of a principal should be even greater than the demands of a teacher. They must place the interests of the school, the development of the school, the students and teachers, in a position that is above all else.

Let us now discuss the concern for human culture. I often extricate myself from education to have a look at education. This is where I am different from my other friends in the education sector. Only by extricating oneself from education can one clearly see what education is like. We know that the quality of society depends on the quality of our schools, and everything that we do, everything our schools teach children, and everything that children experience at school determine what sort of spiritual outlook, moral practices, and state of life they will have in the future. Some principals always complain about society, and their most popular saying is "the arm is no match for the thigh," along with such things as "a few years of success in school come to naught once one watches television." What I would like to ask is: why is it that a few years of success in school will amount to naught once one watches television? This perhaps indicates that your few years' worth of "success" is false success.

When these principals are complaining about society, would they be able to carry out a little reflection on the school itself and their ideology on running the school? The reasons behind the so-called thinking of "the weak cannot contend against the strong" are, of course, multifaceted. However, there is one point that should attract the attention of principals, and that is whether or not our principals possess a concern for human culture and, furthermore, attach importance to developing students' care for human culture. To enable students to internalize education and use it to form their beliefs requires allowing students to absorb the rich nourishment that takes the form of the spirit of human culture. If our students are able to stand at the height of humanity's cultural and ideological progress, are able to possess a broad range of human emotions and be sincerely concerned about our society, country, and world, then after they leave school and enter society, no matter what they encounter, in the depths of their souls the torch of their noble spirit will always burn.

Schools nowadays are relatively closed off, with a "self-loop" being carried out behind closed doors. No communications and further exchanges are being made with society. There are also no in-depth studies and no passing down of the remarkable cultural heritage of humankind. People trained through these means will not have any concern for human culture. In order to possess feelings toward human culture, reading seems to be especially important; if people do not read, it will be impossible for them to have any such feelings. In order to develop this spirit, we must first begin by accepting the finest things in human civilization. Children who read, generally speaking, will have their horizons inevitably broadened, their spirits inevitably enriched, their ambitions inevitably raised, and they will inevitably persevere with their pursuits. When our children leave the school campus, we must have them take with them not only high academic grades to advance in their schooling but, more importantly, a vision of their future ideals and a pursuit of their beliefs in life; most important is that they have truly learned how to be a proper and upright person.

If principals do not possess a concern for and feelings toward human culture, then they will not be able to have their teachers possess these feelings either, and then there is no need to even talk about students' concern for human culture. Once all of our schools possess the spirit of human culture, then our society will have a sense of righteousness and be full of hope.

2. Value the School's Reputation

My take on the ideal principal is that one should value the school's reputation more than one cherishes one's own eyes and life.

I believe that principals who are able to regard the school's reputation and image as being very important will put in their best efforts to safeguard them. Furthermore, a school's reputation is also dependent on a principal's reputation and image. However, in China a principal's reputation and image do not appear to be taken seriously enough yet.

One of the reasons why a principal's reputation has not been taken seriously enough is because the role of a principal has not shifted from the principal as a worker to the principal as a professional. In China, principals are appointed by the higher-ups in the department, and a transfer order on a piece of paper is a "life and death situation" for principals. Therefore, it is not necessary for principals to have their own ideals or their own assertions; not only is it not necessary, it is even something they cannot do! This is because they must take their cue from their superiors, obey the orders of their superiors, and treat the following of orders as their life's mission. This has led the vast majority of school principals to seek short-term benefits and quick relief regardless of the consequences.

In the entire world, principals in China probably have the shortest "lifespan." For example, in the 102 years from 1898 to 2000, Peking University had 27 principals, with an average tenure less than four years. In contrast, from 1869 to 1971, Harvard University had four presidents, with an average tenure of 25.5 years. If the tenure is too short, who would have the inclination to view things broadly and at length? Who would have the inclination to plan ahead? On the contrary, if we were to take the road of professionalization, then principals would be like entrepreneurs who accept options on the market. The relationship between the school and the principal is a contractual one, and the principal's duty is to run the school properly according to the requirements of their agreement. It is not necessary for principals to look around too much but rather to do the opposite of freely and creatively realizing their own educational assertions.

As I have mentioned earlier, any principal is a part of the history and the long process of development of a school. The history of a school is precisely dependent on the efforts of generations upon generations of the principals who maintain it. However, our country has yet to form this sort of common practice, that is, to establish the image of a principal. When I was overseas, I saw that many schools attached great importance to this point. For example, in Japan, many schools have photos of generations of principals hung up in their conference rooms or in their auditoriums, with the status of any one of these principals in their school's history not being affected by any changes caused by the glories and the disgraces that the school may face. This is because for the Japanese, as long as a person has been a principal at this school, one should leave traces behind in the school's history. When I was in Japan, I visited no less than 50 schools, and all the schools had photos of principals who had served at the school in the past.

However, in the schools in our country, at most, the period of time that each principal has served at the school will be clearly indicated in the photo album for the school's anniversary. This is obviously not enough. Please note that the Japanese practice is not merely to promote each principal, but to give principals a reminder: what will you leave behind in the school's history? At the same time, it also allows all the people in the school—all the students and teachers—to see what their principals have done in the position, what new chapters have they added to the school, what improvements have been made under their leadership, and if any development has been made. I think that if the principals can see images of themselves and their predecessors, then their sense of responsibility will increase greatly.

If all principals were to make an effort to add luster and color to their school, then despite the fact that their work will be very difficult, it will be very noble. People often say that love for one's students is the inexhaustible driving force for a teacher. Principals must not only love their students but also love the teachers and the school. Therefore, a principal's love is even more extensive and even richer in meaning.

The long history and tradition of excellence of a prestigious school is formed from the struggles of several generations of principals who spared no efforts and did their utmost for the school, and like the baton of our Olympic long-distance relay, it has been passed down from one to another. When principals step down from their position, when they look back, if they are able to be like Pavel Korchagin and write an answer for a life with no regrets, then I think that they are extremely remarkable teachers.

Tianjin's principal Wei Li can be said to be such a principal. When Wei Li was in the process of writing for a book that I edited, *Recordings of the Thoughts of Famous Chinese Principals in Regards to Running a School*, he wrote this incredibly moving passage:

> [Forty-one] years have passed. In the blink of an eye, everything that I have done during my time as a principal is still vivid in my mind as if it was just yesterday. The experiences that I have had in my life have been experienced while serving as a principal and not only do I not have any regrets, I feel proud. The alumni of our school are innumerable. Many of them have contributed in their posts to the construction of socialism and have become the backbone of all sorts of battle-fronts. They have used their own practices to prove that they are successors of the revolutionary cause. From them, I can see my ideals and the relay baton of my revolutionary cause has already been passed on to them and is in their hands and thus my life's worth has achieved embodiment. My life's worth is education and it is being principal. If there is an afterlife, then in my afterlife I will still want to be a principal.

I feel that Principal Wei's heartfelt words are indeed a review of his lifetime of work as a principal and are a satisfactory answer. Therefore, I believe that for an ideal principal, words and deeds should place the interests of the school and the school's reputation in a position above all others.

3. Pursue One's Ideals of Life and One's Philosophy and Unique Style for Running a School

My take on the ideal principal is that one should constantly pursue one's own ideals of life and philosophy on running a school and should be a principal who possesses a unique style for running a school.

Here there are three key points: The first is one's ideals of life, the second is one's philosophy on running a school, and the third is a style for the running of a school. These three points are integrated in a single entity.

Principals should pursue their own ideals of life. When we talk about ideal teachers, we talk quite a lot about the ideals of a teacher. In reality, we know that whether or not a teacher has any ideals depends to a great extent on whether or not the principal has any ideals. A principal who is full of ideals will mobilize the teachers' passion, tap into their latent potential, and raise the sails on the ship that is the teachers' ideals.

I often say that a life without ideals is bound to be a mediocre life and a life that makes very little contribution to humanity and to society. Similarly, a principal without ideals is also bound to be a mediocre principal and a principal who accomplishes nothing in regard to the development of the school. All the things that one does will never surpass all the things that one pursues.

Ideals are the source of producing miracles. The experiences of many famous scientists' growth can attest to this point. Within our lives, we can also cite many such examples. For all the brilliant people who have achieved success in their careers, every one of them set very high goals for their own struggles. I think that principals should also be like this. Napoleon once said: "Those soldiers who are not willing to be a general are not good soldiers." By the same token, principals who are not willing to be good principals are also not good principals, and this is even more the case for those who are not willing to surpass themselves.

In taking up the principal's post, one must benefit everyone related to the school campus. During your term of office, you must be better than your predecessor and even more outstanding; you must lay a solid foundation for your successor and only by doing so can you become an outstanding point in the long process of a school's development.

The Song Dynasty's Zhang Zai said: "If your ambition is great then your talents and career will be great; if your ambition endures, then your strength and moral character will endure." Only if one's ambitions are far-reaching can one's moral character be perfected. Ambitions must not only be big, they must also be long lasting. These are all spoken from an idealistic perspective. The principal's ideals are not only personal ideals. Principals must also treat their ideals as the ideals of the teachers and treat their ambitions as the ambitions of the teachers. In management studies, there is a term called "shared vision." There is a very popular book called *The Fifth Discipline*. One of the disciplines is building a shared vision, which is the objective that schools pursue and the state that they want to achieve. Principals must allow all teachers and students to clearly know this and to realistically pursue this. It is in fact an action that transforms a principal's ideals into the ideals of all the teachers and students. This has great significance in terms of the management of objectives.

Western psychologists conducted a very interesting experiment. They had three groups of people do the same thing; one group used an objectives-based model, another model was based on having no objectives, and the third used a model based on short-term goals. They compared the groups' efficiency in undertaking these activities, and the results of those with and without objectives were very different. Therefore, there is a significant difference in regard to whether one has or doesn't have any goals in life and whether a principal has or doesn't have any ideals.

Sukhomlinsky said: "For principals to lead a school, they must first be leaders of educational ideology and then they can be administrative leaders. They must be adept at carrying out analyses and summaries and to flexibly put to use the conclusions of these summaries. This is where the essence to implementing educational ideals lies. What we always strive to do is to have the entire staff, from the principal to the workers who guard the entrances, to realize educational ideology and to have the entire staff to be completely absorbed with putting educational ideology into practice." These words summarize a principal's philosophy on running a school and ideology on running a school very incisively. To judge whether principals are simple administrators or educators, one just has to see whether or not they have their own philosophy on running a school and whether or not they have their own educational ideology.

Where does educational ideology and educational philosophy come from? One of the important sources is from the understanding, study, and mastery of past and present educational masterpieces, both Chinese and foreign, and the philosophy of educational masters. Philosophies on thinking are not created out of thin air. I place great emphasis on reading, as in recent years there are very few Chinese principals who can truly and systematically grasp the context of educational ideology. However, once one is able to enter this state, one's growth will be extremely fast. Systematically accepting the influence of educational philosophy is very important. The professional teacher-training courses at university for the past few decades have always taught the same three disciplines. We do not have a setup whereby teachers have a list of required readings. I believe that drawing up this book list is very necessary. We should have our educators systematically read a few educational masterpieces; it does not have to be all that many, even just 20 books. If you do not read these 20 books, then you cannot possibly be a teacher, and it would be even more impossible to be a principal. This is because a person who does not have a system for accepting the wealth of educational ideology found in the history of humankind will not have extensive feelings on education or ambitious educational ideals. Ideologies are not things that are created from thin air. Similar to the production process, raw materials are required for processing. A blank space is impossible to process, and no matter how much you let your imagination run off, it is still wishful thinking.

Therefore, I advocate that China launch a reading project for teachers, and even more importantly, a reading project for principals so that they will honestly, realistically, and conscientiously read one book after another. Without a source, one cannot go very far. The ideologies of a principal also have one very important source, and that is interacting and communicating with people. A principal who is not adept at interacting and communicating is not a good principal. Frequent interactions will bring about purity and honesty and the concept of change for teachers and principals. To accept all the brilliant things that others have to offer within a short period of time and to explore and put them to use in one's work is very effective. I very much advocate for our principals to engage in more interactions, to work hard at these interactions, and furthermore to interact with top-quality masters in their fields. Principals should also be adept at reflecting on their own educational practices. Reflection means to review and consider everything that one has done on that day. Keeping a teaching journal is an excellent form of reflection. Our actions in education may perhaps appear ordinary and bland, but in actual fact, the educational situations that we face every day are actually different; it is just that you have not attentively discerned and carried out careful reflections on this. Upon reflecting and observing, you will discover that there is actually such beauty in life, in education, and in schools. If you were to go and watch educators, you would find that their daily work is also very ordinary; it is just that they put a little more dedication into their work, spend a little more time documenting their educational careers, spend a little more time reading, and compared to us, reflect on their actions in education a little more. Becoming an educator is not all that remote. Every principal is capable of becoming an excellent educator, and so our principals must learn to reflect on their educational practices.

I believe that the so-called style for running a school is the embodiment of a principal's teaching ideology, which is full of individuality. So how do we form our own style for running a school? A principal must of course carry this out in a thorough and practical manner. However, merely doing this is not enough. History will not remember hard work; history remembers praiseworthy achievements, and these "praiseworthy achievements" are your innovations and your style. First is to be unique, second is to be unique, and third is also to be unique. Only by being unique will you stand out from the masses. It is the only means of surpassing other principals and being a giant among dwarves. Students with no personal strengths, teachers without personalities, and schools without distinguishing characteristics are the greatest tragedies in education. Do not dwell on those with devious abilities and maverick geniuses. We should tolerate children and teachers and enable schools to set up unique features and their own style. Only with uniqueness and style can one have a graceful bearing and status. Setting up a school that is unique and full of individuality is precisely the glory in life that one should achieve as a principal.

4. Be Broad-minded and Full of the Power to Inspire and Create Cohesiveness

My take on the ideal principal is that one should possess broadmindedness and be accommodating and tolerant of diversity. One should also be a principal who strongly possesses the power to inspire and create cohesiveness.

My take on the ideal principal is one who should possess a sort of charisma. There are, of course, many factors that constitute a principal's charisma, but one of the most important is the principal's accommodating and tolerant broadmindedness. As a principal, broadmindedness is extremely important because a principal's tolerance and generosity will determine whether or not she is able to accommodate the best talents.

A principal's broadmindedness is first reflected in being able to accept different educational ideologies. When Cai Yuanpei was running Peking University, he put forward these principles: "academic freedom and an embracing of universal values." He introduced very Western and very Shanghai-style professors to Peking University and also retained very traditional and conservative professors on campus, allowing them to bring out the best in each other and vie against each other. This not only enabled Peking University to become a truly prestigious university, but it became the birthplace of the Chinese New Culture Movement, thus giving birth to first-rate thinkers of the twentieth century. Principals must have their own educational ideology, but they cannot possess only their own educational ideology; rather, they should respect the various viewpoints and notions of other teachers at the school. They must respect the individuality of teachers' ideologies and encourage teachers to be teachers who have ideologies. Only a campus with an atmosphere that is brimming with ideas can train a new generation of people who are full of ideas. If a school has only one voice, which is the principal's voice, then it would be difficult for this school to say that it is a school with life and vitality.

Principals' broadmindedness is also reflected in whether or not they are able to be tolerant toward individuality in other teachers' teaching. In a certain sense, quality education is precisely personalized education. However, individuality can only depend on individuality to develop it. Without a teacher's individuality, students absolutely won't have any sense of individuality. In schools, a teacher's individuality is reflected in the individuality of their teaching and is often a reflection of their creativity. What we should be able to see is that in schools nowadays, a uniform teaching model is ubiquitous. Some principals are used to unifying everything: teaching styles, teaching programs, teaching methods, teaching strategies, even the way lesson plans are written, and so on. All of these require so-called standards. At these sorts of schools, teachers with individuality will not be able to gain the principal's recognition.

I believe that, from a macro point of view, the head of a school should of course put forward some uniform goals and guiding opinions. However, for a macro blueprint to become a concrete reality precisely requires every teacher's creative work, not to mention that different subjects, grades, and student targets should have different teaching methods. Even if the subject, grade, and student targets are the same, they can still use different teaching methods because teachers are not the same! Therefore, principals must be tolerant of individuality in teaching. Stifling individuality in teaching is to stifle creativity. Teachers who lack creativity absolutely cannot cultivate students who are full of creativity.

Truly broadminded principals are also people who are good at humbly learning from other teachers. As much as possible, we hope that a principal's knowledge structure can be more comprehensive. However, a principal cannot possibly surpass other teachers in every aspect. So what can be done? The best way to solve this is to honestly learn from other teachers. This also involves the issue of a principal's relationship with the teachers. The relationship between a principal and a teacher is that of a manager and one who is being managed, but this is only one aspect of their relationship. An important aspect of this relationship is that principals and teachers are both engaged in the practice of education and are both seeking out like-minded individuals in educational regularity. In other words, it is an equal relationship between colleagues. Since this is the case, for principals and teachers to mutually learn from one another is only natural. Learning from teachers, and even from students, absolutely will not reduce a principal's prestige. Many practices of outstanding principals have already proven this. Principals must be good not only at studying but also at studying people's minds. Only a principal who is good at studying the minds of surrounding teachers can be a truly brilliant principal.

5. Be Adept at Coordinating Relations and Mobilizing All Forces to Develop the School

My take on the ideal principal is that one should be adept at coordinating all sorts of relations and able to mobilize all forces that can be mobilized to boost a school's development.

In this day and age, the role of a principal is indeed not easy. This is because they have many roles to play in society. For the majority of the time, it is as educators, but sometimes they are also entrepreneurs (as they need to consider the necessary funds for developing the school), and at other times they may also be social activists (needing to have dealings with society for the sake of the school's development), and so on. Therefore, an excellent principal should be one who is adept at handling various relationships. This is particularly important.

First, principals need to properly handle relationships with the leaders in charge of higher authorities and win their support. The development of any school is inseparable from the support it receives from those in charge of the departments of higher authorities. Therefore, principals need to take the initiative to listen to the opinions of these higher authorities and actively accept their guidance. They must not only respect the instructions of their superiors but also obey them. Even if they do not share the same ideological view for the time being, they must obey these instructions. Of course, principals might sometimes have a few of their own unique ideas for running a school. This requires principals to strengthen interactions and communications with their superiors and to win their understanding and support.

Second, principals need to handle relationships with corporations properly. At present, Chinese corporations have not formed a perfect system to support education. This will often require principals to actively establish connections with related corporations and to win their support. In regard to the support of corporations, some people may only be able to think of financial assistance for the school. This is also a very important aspect, as attracting funding assistance from society and corporations for running a school is something that is advocated by the government. However, corporate support is not merely financial assistance. It should also include allowing entrepreneurs to put forward suggestions in regard to educational development from the perspective of society and economic development. This will frequently broaden our own horizons. In addition, it is also very important that through linking up with corporations, we can strengthen communications between the education in schools and society, and this can even include the means of broadening students' social practices.

Third, principals must be good at handling relationships with the community. They must learn how to take the initiative to care about the community and to care about the development and fate of the community. They must enable the school and community to grow together and for students and community residents to share the joys of educational success together. Principals who do their job well will attach great importance to the relationship between the school and the community and be very adept at making use of the resources of the community where the school campus is located. In actual fact, community resources are very abundant. School resources such as libraries and sporting facilities must also be opened up to the community as much as possible. On the one hand, libraries and sporting facilities, for example, have been unreasonably allocated, and on the other hand, their rate of use is low. Why not open these resources up to the society? Doing so will enable the library and sporting facilities to be more fully utilized. Therefore I feel that some of a school's resources, such as its computers, can be shared with the community. If principals do not have a sense of social responsibility, how can they possibly expect society to care for them? Schools must have a sense of social responsibility.

Fourth, principals must be adept at handling relationships with other schools. Within the context of an examination-oriented education, the relationships between schools are very strained. In fact, competition does not hinder cooperation, instead, cooperation is the basis of competition and competition is the basis of cooperation. Whether it be competition or cooperation, there is not only the one winner and one loser. The proper relationship between schools should be one in which they are both opponents and friends. Prestigious schools should have even more of a sense of responsibility and duty to assist disadvantaged schools, to transform them, to improve their running, and to head down the path of development together.

6. Attach Importance to Educational Research

My take on the ideal principal is that one should attach great importance to educational research and be a principal who becomes an excellent organizer and practitioner of educational research work.

Recall Sukhomlinsky's point above about the principal's important role in leading the entire staff to implement educational ideology. I understand this to say that a principal's leadership of a school is first a leadership of educational research and then a leadership of administration. The success or failure of educational research in a school is, to a very large extent, dependent on whether or not it is supported, encouraged, organized, and led by the principal. The importance of educational research to a school goes without saying. Educational research is a school's first productive force and is an important condition for a school's advancement to a new level. The better the setup and implementation of educational research in a school, the more a principal's own distinctiveness can be reflected in the unique running of the school. Educational research is also an important factor in strengthening a school's cohesiveness, as it can allow all teachers to truly put their time and energy into research and reflection on their own work. At the same time, educational research is an important means of training young teachers, especially great teachers. Therefore, an investment in educational research is a principal's most visionary investment, and principals who do not value educational research are clearly principals who lack foresight.

How then should a principal organize educational research?

First, principals should be good at arranging for teachers to read masterpieces and study theories. The vitality of educational research comes from its practice, managing these practices, to a large extent, is dependent on a solid background in theory. For a principal to organize teachers to carry out educational research requires arranging for these teachers to conscientiously study educational masterpieces.

Second, principals must strive to invite famous experts to come to the school to talk about their experiences and act as guides. Connecting with experts and engaging in dialogue with them often allows us to reap unexpected profits. Many famous experts have their own unique views and are able to give us insightful ideas. By listening to their experiences and accepting their guidance, we are able to shorten the process of grasping new ideas and concepts and to reach the stage where we can engage in dialogue with them. Famous experts also have extensive social influence and social connections. They can promptly tell us the most recent educational information, which helps us in communicating with the outside world and takes us out of the classroom into the world beyond our classroom window. Therefore, I advocate that to engage in educational research properly, principals must get hold of master educators and engage in dialogue with them.

Third, principals can contact colleges and universities and have them come to set up a research base and conduct experiments. Some tasks require primary and secondary students to design and carry out work by themselves, and they may have a certain amount of difficulty with this. In these sorts of situations, principals can invite colleges and universities to engage in these tasks together with the students. By working with colleges and universities, primary and secondary school principals and teachers will naturally understand and truly grasp the aspects and methods of educational research such as task design, sampling, testing, taking measurements, and so on. This is a shortcut for schools to train in educational research and to improve their level of educational research, and is much more effective than attempting to grasp concepts on one's own or merely reading books.

The fourth condition is that principals should actively hold academic discussion forums and research seminars. Primary and secondary schools, especially those that have comparatively better conditions, can integrate the special features of their schools and host a few academic discussion forums and research seminars. We can also take the initiative and try to win contracts to host a few national academic conferences. For schools, although these activities do require some investment, the benefits that they bring are often multifaceted, long term, and hard to estimate. Through these activities, the level of educational research, the abilities and reputations of teachers and the principal, and the quality and state of the school will gain improvement.

The fifth condition is that principals must be adept at mobilizing teachers' enthusiasm and creativity. The subject of educational research is the teacher, and in order to properly implement educational research in one's school, it is most important to rely on the school's teachers. Principals must adopt various methods to establish a powerful mechanism for guiding and encouraging teachers and to fully mobilize the entire teaching staff's enthusiasm and creativity for taking part in educational research. Furthermore, they must actively construct an educational research institution within their school, establish a cohort of teachers to be the backbone of educational research, and enable both these elements to play an important role. Only in so doing can we ensure that the educational research in a school is extensive, thorough, and persistent and ensure that we will achieve genuine results, produce talented individuals, and achieve benefits.

Of course, the most effective way for principals to organize educational research is to take the lead themselves. Confucius said: "When a ruler's personal conduct is correct, he will be obeyed without the issuing of order." Only by practicing what they preach and absorbing themselves with research can principals call on the vast range of like-minded master educators to wholeheartedly carry out research together. Only principals who achieve their own success in research can have the power to persuade and inspire teachers and allow them to possess character that stems from the academic, which will make its way into teachers' hearts. It can be said that all genuinely outstanding principals will also, at the same time, be people who pursue and are successful in educational research.

7. Emphasize Teachers' Development and Tap into Their Latent Capabilities

My take on the ideal principal is that one should be able to produce a glorious stage for teachers and should be adept at enabling every teacher to head toward success.

The school is not only a place where principals can realize their dreams. It is also a stage for teachers to display their capabilities. Principals have to be particularly adept at producing a glorious stage for teachers. A prerequisite for the development of a school is precisely that teachers have such a glorious stage. A principal's mission is to set up this stage and enable every role to be played. A principal must push teachers forward to the front of the stage and allow teachers to play the leading role. In a sense, there is no differentiation between leading and supporting roles in a school as every person plays the leading role in his position. A principal helps teachers to have even better growth.

When are principals the most proud and the most spirited? It should be when each and every teacher is full of life and energy. The art of your leadership as a principal is reflected precisely in enabling all teachers to be able to tap into their latent capabilities and to put all their might into working for you. In actual fact, every teacher has considerable latent capabilities, and whether or not these latent capabilities can be tapped depends to a large extent upon your attitude toward every teacher and whether you give them the opportunity to put their talents to use. In short, it depends on whether principals are able to bring people together.

In Tao Xingzhi's *Create Manifesto* he wrote: "Creating people who are worthy of their admiration is a teacher's success. Creating students who are worthy of their admiration is a teacher's greatest happiness." In his opinion, teachers' greatest success and greatest happiness lies in having students surpass them and be worthy of their admiration. Well then, by the same token, the success of a principal lies in the success of a teacher. If principals want to achieve success in their own career, then they should put their efforts into creating conditions that will allow every teacher to have a sense of success.

Wise principals are not at all afraid that teachers will "steal their thunder." On the contrary, they always encourage teachers to tackle brilliance head-on, to pursue excellence, to carry out educational exploration, to write and propound ideas, and to make a name for themselves and become experts. Furthermore, these principals are willing to pave the way for the growth of their teachers and always put all their efforts into allowing teachers to stand on their shoulders so that they can see even further, jump even higher, and do even better! Sukhomlinsky once proudly said that at his Pavlysh Secondary School, there were a group of teachers who deserved to be called "educators." Additionally, I believe that if a school produces a large group of expert teachers, or even educators, then this school is definitely a first-rate school and, of course, the principal of this school is definitely a first-rate principal.

To enable teachers to be successful, the prerequisite is that the principal must truly understand the characteristics of every teacher's personality. This requires principals to regularly carry out heart-to-heart interactions with teachers on an equal footing and to carry out candid communications with teachers, also on an equal footing. Teachers who work under such a principal will have a sense of happiness, and they will produce a passion for work from the bottom of their hearts, as a saying describes: "A gentleman will die for one who appreciates his worth." Furthermore, this passion will allow them to ultimately head toward success in their career. Having a large cohort of teachers who are successful in their careers marks the success of a principal.

8. Focus on Creating a Beautiful Campus Environment and a Strong Cultural Atmosphere

My take on the ideal principal is that one should enable a school to possess a beautiful natural environment and a strong cultural atmosphere.

Outstanding principals can enable the environment to become a silent educator. They can enable students from the moment they enter the school campus to be subtly influenced by a sort of truth, goodness, and beauty. The campus environment is not something that is separate from education. It is an integral part of education to the extent of even being education itself. A famous educator once proposed: "Let all the walls in the school speak." This is the educational effect that a focus on the environment has on people.

Schools are always linked to lively and adorable children. Therefore, a school campus should first be what children consider the ideal garden and paradise. When Sukhomlinsky was first establishing Pavlysh Secondary School, he personally designed the construction blueprint for the school. The first thing he considered was that the school must have the beauty of nature and have fresh flowers and trees. The constructed Pavlysh Secondary School is often referred to in Sukhomlinsky's works as "my most beautiful school under the blue sky." With some schools, at present, the more they build on their campuses the more luxurious their constructions become, but they are increasingly distancing themselves from nature and from children's hearts. These schools might have fountains but not soccer fields; they might have synthetic tracks but not lawns where students can roll about when they are excited, and they might have stainless steel sculptures but no places provided for students to randomly write graffiti. A truly beautiful campus environment should be a "people-focused" environment: it should hold nature in high regard while at the same time being people oriented. Having everything focused on students' development will enable every blade of grass and every tree, every brick and every tile, to reflect a caring attitude toward people.

Apart from the natural environment, the cultural atmosphere of a school also plays an essential role in the growth of students. Teachers are the propagators of humanity's cultural and ideological progress, and schools should be the hallowed halls of cultural and ideological progress. Every corner of a school should exude an air of cultural excellence. All first-rate schools place great importance on creating a cultural atmosphere within the campus.

The so-called cultural atmosphere within the school campus, I think, can at least be reflected in the following aspects.

First, have students understand their own school's history. Schools must let students know about the journey that the school has taken in the past and the number of illustrious people who have graduated from the school, thus producing within them the enterprising spirit of "Today, I am proud of my alma mater; tomorrow, my alma mater will be proud of me."

Second, install a "solid" symbol of the campus culture, such as specially setting aside space to use as an "art wall," "biology corner," "literary garden," and so on. We must allow students to be able to see the sparks of wisdom twinkling in every part of the campus and then to ignite the light of their own wisdom.

Third, organize various activities in conjunction with various special days. Take note that this does not only refer to days such as National Day and Teachers' Day, but also includes anniversaries of important historical events and historical figures, for example, "Anniversary of the First Human Landing on the Moon," "918 National Humiliation Day," "Zhu Ziqing's Centenary Anniversary," and so on.

Fourth launch some activities for students' self-presentation and self-invention, such as a student television station, student radio station, science and technology week, and art festivals.

Fifth organize more student clubs and allow students' talents to be brought out more, such as through book clubs, calligraphy associations, dance associations, and so on.

Principals are the chief architects of a school and the designers and administrators of the environment of a school. The principal's mentality can be seen in the spirit of the finer details, because every detail in a school is able to reflect a principal's spirit. The school environment is most capable of embodying the unique qualities of a school and reflecting the mental outlook of the teachers and students. Of course, it is also most capable of reflecting the principal's cultural quality and pursuits in education.

Chinese education is currently in the new century and this Chinese education calls out for a large number of educators. From whence are these educators born? I believe that the future Chinese educators will not be born in the study, nor in an ivory tower; they can only be born from the front lines of education and from among the numerous outstanding education practitioners, but first, they will be born from among the numerous outstanding principals! My take on the ideal principal is in fact the archetype of the numerous outstanding principals by my side. I have written down my sincere respect for them and also my fervent longing for the emerging Chinese educators of the new century.

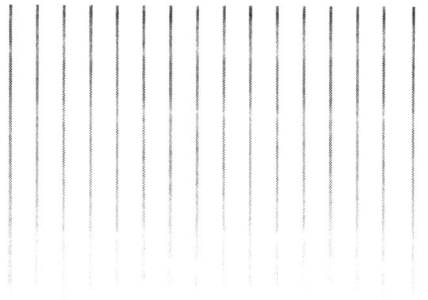

9

My Take on the Ideal Student

The competition in today's society is a competition of comprehensive national strength that centers on the economy and science and technology. However, ultimately, it is a competition of education, which is ultimately dependent on the quality of the students it develops. Within the entire education system, students are the main subjects, and all education that is carried out revolves around the students. Without students, education would not exist. The real meaning of education is to mold students into the future pillars of society. Then what sort of outstanding qualities should our future pillars of society be equipped with?

1. Possess Good Moral Character, Love Life, and Be Full of Ideals and Youthful Energy

My take on the ideal student is that one should have good moral character, be fair and considerate, ardently love life, and be full of ideals and youthful energy.

The same principle is applied to becoming an upright person and becoming a capable person. Without becoming upright, one cannot become capable. Outstanding students place the perfection of their moral character in the highest position of importance and strive to achieve a harmonious unity between truth, goodness, and beauty. Among them, love and compassion are two important expressions of good moral character.

It can be said that a person without love and compassion is an "unhealthy" person. Love should begin from the things around oneself, from a love of every blade of grass, tree, flower, small animal, one's parents, grandparents, uncles and aunts, to a love of one's own studies and life (to be industrious and hard working), and finally, to a love of the collective, the motherland, and the people. Sukhomlinsky once wrote on the front entrance of his school: "love your mother" to educate students and to stimulate students' inherent love. Some people do not agree with this, and Sukhomlinsky refutes these criticisms by saying that if people do not even love their mothers, then what can they love?

Love is priceless. To cultivate a love is very important, and no matter what one does, one must have a love for it, since other qualities are all extensions of love. Only with love can one experience the joys of life; only with love can one create harmonious interpersonal relationships; only with love can one enjoy the beauties of life; and only with love can one feel the greatness of the human race. In this world, the sky and the oceans are the vastest things in the world; however, what is even vaster than the sky and the oceans is a person's heart. A person full of love will never feel lonely. Only love can win love. May all the students in this world begin with a love of their parents and come to love all the fine things in life.

Compassion is also an important manifestation of good moral character. When students without compassion treat other people "coldly," they will also be "isolated" by society. Only by possessing compassion can one help the weak and have one's own value embodied; only by possessing compassion can we enable society to burst forth with waves of love, and only with compassion can we enable our society to truly possess a sense of equality. "Treat with the reverence the elders in your own family and the families of others. Treat with the kindness the young in your own family and the families of others." Outstanding students should learn to take pleasure in helping the classmates by their side, who may have difficulties with their learning or in their life, and to help them to grow together. This is an important way of developing students' compassion.

Another expression of good moral character is to have a sense of fairness. In regard to fairness, there are usually four states: one that places the common good above all else, one that places public interests before private ones, one that places private interests before public ones, and one that takes account of both public and private interests. Requiring a person to be completely selfless and to completely place the common good above all else is indeed a little harsh. However, being able to deal with various issues in a fair manner is something that everyone is capable of doing and something that we should do. Social fairness is an important prerequisite for healthy social development. If a society does not have even the most basic sense of fairness, then the society's benign development has also lost its most basic prerequisite. Outstanding students should begin developing the quality of fairness from a young age. Whether or not students possess the quality of fairness can be expressed in many different forms. For example, cheating during a test at school is one of the forms of unfairness. Cheaters attempt to invest the least amount of effort, to the extent that they rely purely on opportunism for the purpose of achieving their own ends. For the students who have achieved results through their own painstaking hard work, the success of the cheater is a form of unfairness. If cheaters take this sort of unfair quality, formed during their student days, into society, it will expand to many unsavory elements in their moral character, such as selfishness, favoritism, corruption, and so on, which are extremely detrimental to the development of society.

In addition, far-reaching ambitions and ideals are also among the important prerequisites for a student's success. In ancient China, establishing far-reaching ideals was called "establishing aspirations." Since the time of Confucius, successive generations of scholars have recorded "establishing aspirations" to be a requirement of learning. Confucius said: "Any army may be deprived of its commanding officer, yet a man cannot be deprived of his will." Ming Dynasty scholar Wang Shouren wrote: "Whenever and wherever, a gentleman must put aspirations in the first important place." He also wrote: "If one's aspirations are not clearly established, there is nothing in this world that one will be able be to accomplish, if one's aspirations are not clearly established, then one is like a ship without a rudder, a horse without reins, drifting indulgently, exactly where is one heading?" Additionally, Wang Yangming believed: "If one's aspirations are not clearly established, there is nothing in this world that one will be able to accomplish. Even if they possess a hundred skills, there is nothing that does not rely on one to have aspirations." For students, the meaning behind establishing far-reaching ideals and life goals from the time when they are students is even more significant.

Ideals are the wings for a student's rapid development. For a student who is full of ideals, life will definitely be very fulfilling. Only by having ideals can one have a way forward and only by having ideals can we have the power to move forward. If students do not have clear and far-reaching ideals, then they have no hopes in and pursuits of beauty and their actions will lose direction and power. These students will be depressed by the slightest of setbacks in learning and in life and will be unable to recover after a minor hitch. On the other hand, if students possess far-reaching ideals and ambitions, they will clearly recognize the significance of their actions, consciously adjust their actions in accordance with their aims, and not rest until their aims have been reached. Marx had a famous saying: "My goals remain the same from start to finish." This is the reason why his resolve was unshaken and he was able to fight courageously and with determination under difficult conditions in which he was poor and destitute, with a wife sick and a child dead. Students must not establish ideals that are too ambitious or separate themselves from actual conditions and a basis in reality. The journey of a thousand miles begins with a single step, and the loftiest towers rise from the ground. Realizations of any ideals should be realistic and begin from the work that is in front of one's eyes. However, the ideals that students establish cannot only view what is in front of their eyes, as they will lack the sense of a challenge. If one were to take a passive attitude toward one's work, then the incentives of these ideals will lose their significance.

Ideals are the visions that students have for better prospects in the future and are beautiful as well as magical. To fight for one's ideals, no matter how hard or tiring, is something that one can take pleasure in doing. On the contrary, a lack of ideals means the termination of a way forward and an end to the meaning of life. Students are full of ideals, and this is where their hopes for success lie. So let every student enthusiastically embrace ideals and head toward tomorrow!

2. Actively Forge Ahead, Dare to Innovate, and Be Full of Unique Insights and Ideas

My take on the ideal student is that one should actively forge ahead, dare to innovate, and display originality. Ideal students should also be students who are full of personality and their own unique insights and ideas.

Innovation education is the core of quality education and is becoming one of the hot topics of discussion in educational exploration. To accompany humanity's steps into the knowledge economy of the twenty-first century, the talented people that the new century needs are not "reading machines" but rather innovative talents who are full of personality. Cultivating students' innovative qualities has been regarded as one of the important goals of education and is receiving increasingly more attention. Early on in the 1930s, the famous Chinese educator Tao Xingzhi strongly advocated for innovation education, as did his teacher, American educator John Dewey, who criticized the drawbacks of traditional education as lacking innovativeness and advocated for innovation education to develop students' innovative thinking and abilities. However, due to the characteristics of economic development in an industrial society, innovation education did not receive any genuine attention. Even in this present era, due to the influences of various factors, the development of students' innovative qualities has not been given due attention. This, to a great extent, has restricted the development of the overall quality of students.

Traditional learning is a sort of learning that is inherited and sustained. Through learning, students gain access to concepts, methods, and principles that have already been established to cope with situations that one already has prior knowledge about and has already encountered. This sort of learning is still capable of solving problems in an agrarian and industrial society. However, in the era of the knowledge economy, cultural knowledge, science, and technology as well as economic development are rapidly changing, and the way we consider problems is very different from the way we did so in the past. People not only have to adapt to the social patterns of life that are already present, but what they require more is to create new living conditions and to constantly improve themselves. This requires an emphasis on the formation of students' innovative spirit, innovative ideas, and innovative behavior. Only students who have received innovative education and carried out innovative learning are able to swiftly accept new knowledge in a knowledge economy and society and to create a new world and a new life. Harvard University's president Neil L. Rudenstine spoke these thought-provoking words from the lectern at Peking University: "In the course of stepping into the new century, one of the best sorts of education is one that is beneficial to people who possess innovativeness, one that allows people to become even better at thinking, have even more ideals and insights to pursue and become people who are even better and more successful."

It can be said that excellence in innovativeness fully reflects a person's sensitivities toward finding problems, the psychology of active exploration, and adeptness at seizing opportunities. Innovativeness is not just an intellectual characteristic but also a characteristic of one's personality and a reflection of one's mental state as well as one's overall quality. On the basis of innovation education being extremely significant to a person's development, in 1996 the International Commission on Education for the Twenty-first Century's report *Learning: The Treasure Within* regarded it as the highest goal in education: "The duty of education, without exception, is to enable every person's innovative talents and innovative potential to bear fruit. . . . This goal is more important than any other goal."[1] In short, no matter if it is from the perspective of the development of the country and its people, or it is from the perspective of a person's individual development, the cultivation of students' innovative quality can be seen to be extremely urgent.

The cultivation of students' quality cannot be separated from the education at school, in society, and at home. However, to have students themselves consciously put their efforts into attaining this goal is also an important factor of the development of innovative qualities. In our country's traditional educational ideology, there is a sort of "herd" thinking, with many students having also formed "yesman" habits, not daring to express their own views and opinions and not daring to deny authority. In regard to innovativeness awareness and innovative thinking, these students are obviously lacking and do not have an innovative personality. In contrast, outstanding students consciously cultivate a "pioneering" personality from the school and dare to put forward their views on difficult problems, dare to "split hairs," refuse to blindly follow so-called authority, step out of their comfort zone so as to set off from a realistic point for the sake of truth, and dare to challenge any sort of authority. These students will constantly produce innovative views and ideas, not only at school but also in their future work. They will make even more prominent contributions to society and become the true pillars of society.

The characteristics of an innovative personality are not characteristics that one is born with, they are gradually formed under the influence of one's school, family, and society. So long as students are determined, most of them will definitely be able to form the characteristics of an innovative personality.

3. Have Self-confidence, Strive for Self-improvement, and Never Bow Down to Difficulties and Setbacks

My take on the ideal student is that one should have self-confidence and strive for self-improvement. Ideal students will never give up and never bow down to difficulties and setbacks. They are students who are full of a strong fighting spirit and optimism.

Self-confidence is one of the essential qualities of an outstanding student. American thinker Ralph Waldo Emerson said, "Self-trust is the first secret of success."

Napoleon Hill also said, "Confidence is life and strength, confidence is the root of establishing a career, confidence is miraculous." The ideas and views of these scholars fully express the important role that self-confidence plays in the development of one's life. Self-confidence is an important spiritual pillar in one's life and is the guide to success.

Psychological studies illustrate that people's needs and expectations are continuously developing and are never ending; however, new goals are always based on existing goals. The more experiences people have with success, the higher their expectations and the stronger their self-confidence will be. When students study, self-confidence is particularly important.

Through conducting a survey, Japanese educator Shinobu Tazaki discovered that a lack of self-confidence led to underachievement in a third of students. Within our nation's schools are many students who possess a fear of learning, and the more they learn, the more confidence they lack; the more they learn, the more they feel that they are not learning material and always think that they are dumber than other people. With an inferiority complex that is caused by a lack of self-confidence, not only will their regular learning be affected, but even their individual mental and physical activities and interactions will be affected. Even if they originally possessed excellent innate talents, it may be difficult to bring out these talents.

Therefore, during our life of learning, cultivating students' self-confidence is an extremely important task. Only with self-confidence can one dare to face difficulties; only with self-confidence can one fully bring out one's own abilities; only with self-confidence can one forever maintain an optimistic attitude; and only with self-confidence can one be adept at handling various relationships. In facing the complicated world and the bumpy road of life, a moment of confusion, loss, a moment where one is at a loss as to what to do, is hard to avoid. However, no matter what situations we encounter, we are not to doubt our own abilities. If people do not have confidence in themselves, then who can they still expect to believe in them? Students must reach a state where they are self-confident and strive for self-improvement. In addition to the attention that teachers and parents pay to the use of appropriate teaching methods, what is more important is for students to give their own life a precise positioning and to be adept at finding role models in life and goals to struggle toward from those by their side, allowing them to constantly improve by following their role models and to always feel the role that incentives play.

An indomitable will and a spirit of self-improvement are also basic qualities that students of today must possess. There is an ancient saying: "The will is the leader of the passion-nature." The will is the commander of the spirit and the center of one's character. The quality of a strong will is an important guarantee of success in one's studies and work and is the basis for achieving success in one's career. *The Book of Documents, Hounds of Lu* writes: "in raising a mound of nine fathoms, the work may be unfinished for want of one basket of earth," referring to quitting before one's work is finished when constructing a large mound of earth and being unable to complete the task before one is short one basket of dirt. This idiom expresses both a regret when one fails to finish something due to the lack of just one thing and the philosophy that we should persevere when doing something, as we can only achieve success when we do something to its end.

In *On Learning* our country's ancient educator Xun Zi preaches: "The finest thoroughbred cannot travel ten paces in one leap, but the sorriest nag can go a ten days' journey. Achievement consists of never giving up. If you start carving and then give up, you cannot even cut through a piece of rotten wood; but if you persist without stopping, you can carve and inlay metal or stone." This profoundly reveals the importance of perseverance in everything that we do. If students possess such a quality, then no matter if they are in a favorable situation or are facing adversity, they will not sink into despair. If students possess such a quality, then after they graduate and start to work, no matter where they are placed, they will flourish and thrive. Only students who possess this quality can be full of competitiveness in the future society.

Of course, a strong will is not something that one is born with and is also not something that develops overnight. An indomitable will and spirit of self-improvement are developed from the little details in one's everyday life. The process that occurs each time one overcomes difficulties is the process whereby one's will is strengthened. Marx once said, "There is no royal road to science, and only those who do not dread the fatiguing climb of its steep paths have a chance of gaining its luminous summits." Life is the same. When faced with the ups and downs in life, only those who possess a strong will can live a colorful life. When students solve a difficult problem and put their efforts into learning how to do something, these are processes for cultivating one's will. As the ancient saying goes: "Do not think any virtue trivial, and so neglect it; do not think any vice trivial, and so practice it." The saying embodies this argument.

Using a motto to motivate yourself is an effective means of developing willpower. When Xu Teli, one of the predecessors of revolutionaries, was learning French in his forties, he once used the following words as a motto: "Learn a word a day and achieve success in five years." Under this force and support, he mastered French in three years with a willpower that average people will find difficult to imagine and a persevering spirit of learning. Peking Opera performer Yuan Shihai hung up three handwritten characters on his wall, "practice every day," in order to improve his own performance skills, and at 70 years old he still persevered with this. In his youth, Mao Zedong had this motto: "Perseverance favored, there is no need to rise at midnight and retire at dawn; the most unprofitable of all is to work by fits and starts." From these examples we can discover that possession of a strong will is one of the important factors for the success of famous people. Students should also select a suitable motto for themselves in accordance with their interests and hobbies and use it to motivate themselves to continually put effort into everything they do.

A person who has a strong will is usually an optimistic person. People who are optimistic in life regard difficulties with common sense. "Difficulties are like a spring. If you are strong, it will be weak; if you are weak, then it will be strong." However, pessimistic people will often artificially exaggerate difficulties and be frightened by them. Only optimistic people are able to meet external obstacles and inner conflicts head-on, to bravely confront difficulties and endure the testing of adversities. The English novelist Thackeray writes in *Vanity Fair*, "Life is a mirror: if you frown at it, it frowns back; if you smile, it returns the greeting." An outstanding student should always smile at life. As Pushkin writes, "If by life you were deceived, / Don't be dismal, don't be wild! / In the day of grief, be mild / Merry days will come, believe." The difficulties in our studies and life are like the ocean sprays in the sea. Only by regarding the setbacks and difficulties in our life of learning with a normal state of mind can we enable our students to develop a strong will and create a good life in the future.

4. Have a Rich Spiritual Life, Extensive Interests and Hobbies, and Certain Personal Strengths

My take on the ideal student is that one should have a rich spiritual life, extensive interests and hobbies and a certain number of personal strengths.

Life in the modern-day society is richly colorful and provides a very good environment and conditions for the enrichment of our spiritual lives. These should be enjoyed and made use of as much as we like, especially by our young students. Therefore, we often refer figuratively to a student who resides in modern society but does not know how to enjoy music, has no self-cultivation in the literary arts, is completely ignorant about any ball games, has no understanding of the natural sciences, and cannot manipulate a computer properly, as a "studying machine." Possession of a rich spiritual life, extensive interests and hobbies, as well as a certain number of personal strengths has already become an important part of the cultivation of a student's overall quality. A student who has a rich spiritual life and a student who lacks spirituality differ in their meaning for living in this world, their degree of satisfaction in their lives, and the degree to which they are healthily developed psychologically. In Sukhomlinsky's *100 Pieces of Advice for Teachers* as well as in *To Children I Give My Heart*, he greatly emphasizes the need to enrich students' spiritual lives. He believed that if children possess very healthy feelings of joy and fun for life and their own personal strengths, then we need not worry about these students. This is because they neither have the interest nor the time and energy to engage in unhealthy activities, as their activities have already been enriched with and surrounded by healthy feelings of joy and fun.

Many parents worry that their children will do bad things. The main reason for this is because their children have not developed healthy interests and hobbies and they most likely place their energy and time into unhealthy activities under the lure of unsavory environments in the outside world. Because people's needs are a unification of the materialistic and spiritual, once basic materialistic needs have been satisfied, they will urgently pursue fulfillment in the spiritual realm. Students are in a phase of their lives where they have an abundance of energy and will often have a sense of unease (youthful restlessness). At this time, providing them with a life that is healthy and spiritually rich will shift their attention. As the saying goes, "Make trouble out of nothing." Many students become corrupted by bad examples because their spirits are empty and they have nothing to do so they become drawn toward a divergent path. Therefore, developing interests for students that are healthy and possess positive meanings is extremely important.

Students must be adept at actively finding meaningful content from interesting elements and thus gradually cultivating good inclinations. To cultivate good interests, one must pay attention to three aspects. The first is to promptly overcome difficulties. When we first come into contact with something, we often have a relatively stronger interest due to curiosity; however, when we encounter difficulties that are hard to overcome during the process of learning, our interest will greatly decrease. Once we have prevailed over these difficulties, our interest will once again greatly increase. The second is that we must choose problems that have a certain degree of difficulty. Cognitive psychologist Jean Piaget believed that people's interest levels are at their highest when conflict occurs between external stimuli and one's existing knowledge structures and one is able to resolve this. The third is to have made positive psychological preparations and furthermore to actively engage in activities, to be humble in victory, to lose with grace, and to regard activities with wholehearted enthusiasm.

Expertise is the strongest impression that individuals can have. Presently, many schools fly the banner of holistic development to cover up drawbacks of holistic nondevelopment in education. Both a person's energy and time are limited; therefore, in a certain sense, cultivating students who are holistically developed in all senses of the term is very difficult to accomplish and is a "purely ideal state." In a sense, holistic development is holistic nondevelopment (namely, mediocrity). Quality cannot possibly be the average of one's combined qualities in all areas and also cannot demand that a person have both the mathematical qualities of Hua Luogeng as well as the literary accomplishments of Qian Zhongshu. A person's formation and development of favorable qualities should only occur after the person is equipped with the basic qualities that a modern-day person needs. It should be carried out in accordance with one's interests and hobbies and also submit to the demands of society and strive to develop one's personal strengths.

What is truly feasible in education is to display students' personalities and to cultivate students' personal strengths. The model for cultivation, "basic qualities plus personal strengths," is the direction that the development of students' qualities should take. Students should clearly put forward challenges for and requirements of themselves. What are my personal strengths? When I have grown up, what can I rely on to have a foothold in society and to survive? What grounds do I have for adding my own individual touch to society? How can I make society listen to my voice? What must I do in order to find my own footprints in the course of history? These all depend on one's individual characteristics.

A person who does not have any individual characteristics will probably be very quickly forgotten by history. Personal strengths are very important for a person's individual development, the progress of society, and the times. This is especially the case when one enters a society of lifelong learning, a society where those who have leisurely lives are increased. Only those who have individual characteristics and personality can make even greater contributions to history.

5. Be Adept at Cooperating and Associating with Others

My take on the ideal student is that one should be adept at cooperating with others and associating with others. Ideal students should have harmonious interpersonal relationships and be popular, "likable" characters.

We exist in an extremely competitive era, where competitions for knowledge, talented people, energy resources, products, and so on are ubiquitous. However, we also exist in an era that demands extensive cooperation. The era where "people do not visit each other all their lives, though the crowing of their cocks and the barking of their dogs are within hearing of each other" is gone forever. Large-scale socialized production requires that the overwhelming majority of jobs be completed through cooperation with many people. The era that is dependent on an individual's struggles to achieve success is basically gone. Cooperation and competition coexist. The cooperation based on competition and competition based on cooperation that characterizes this era is becoming more and more obvious. We should establish a sense of competition and furthermore channel competition into our normal state of affairs and the atmosphere of friendly cooperation.

As Chapter 3 noted, over the years Nobel laureates have increasingly moved toward collaborative research, which accounted for 41 percent of the Nobel Prize laureates; in the second 25-year period, this proportion was 65 percent; in the third 25-year period, this proportion rose to 79 percent. From a macro perspective, the future society requires large-scale tactics, interdisciplinary cooperation, adeptness at concentrating manpower and popular feeling, and the power to unite people to struggle and fight even more. From a micro perspective, being adept at cooperation is also the basis for the development of psychological healthiness and individual personalities. Since people live in the world, their own feelings are often dependent on other people's feelings for them, and their happiness is often dependent on whether the people around them are happy. Being adept at cooperation not only means that people will be able to find joy in their work, but that they will also be able to find joy in their lives.

There is always happiness everywhere in life. When you help someone when they are troubled or worried by extending a friendly hand at the critical moment, then when you encounter difficulties, other people will also help you, and thus everyone will be able to experience the boundless joys of being an upright person in this world. A person who treats others with a happy heart will usually also be able to receive this same kind of joy. Those who are reclusive and narcissistic and do not associate with others will not be able to enjoy this happiness. Therefore, having students learn how to associate and cooperate with others from primary school is an extremely important task.

The small world that students live within is actually a microcosm of society. There, they learn how to deal with others, experience life, and form preliminary norms for interpersonal relationships. When they graduate and head out into society, how they associate with others, to a very large extent, is dependent on the experience they gained during their time as a student. Normally, a student who had a lot of friends at school and was popular with teachers and classmates will, upon graduating from school and starting work, most definitely be adept at dealing with the various interpersonal relationships in society and be skilled at interpersonal exchanges. Conversely, those who were antisocial and reclusive and did not like dealing with other students will become people who, when associating with others after graduating, will be thwarted at every turn and become a "strange person" that people will fear meeting.

Well, then, how can we form good collaborative relationships with others in our studies and in our lives?

- *Learn to understand others and to make allowances for others.* The ancients spoke of being "a gentleman who will die for one who appreciates his worth." Today, we speak of "long live understanding"; both these sayings emphasize the importance of understanding. When conflicts and differences of opinion happen between classmates, they must learn to "empathize," to consider the problem from the perspective of others more, and thus be able to more easily understand the actions of others.
- *Be adept at discovering the shining points of others.* Confucius said: "When I walk along with two others, from at least one I will be able to learn." Every person has strong points and we must learn to appreciate the worth of other classmates, as "gold can't be pure and man can't be perfect." Our goal in cooperation is to avoid weaknesses and to learn from other people's strong points; only in interpersonal associations can classmates mutually accept one another.
- *Maintain a suitable distance in interpersonal exchanges.* There is an invisible distance between people, and if one were to not achieve this distance or to exceed it, then it would cause discord in one's interpersonal relationships. In real life, many friendships are strained because they became too close.

Good interpersonal relationships are not only conducive to the healthy growth of students but can create a harmonious environment for one's learning, as the mutual assistance and learning among classmates will promote everyone's progress. Confucius said: "Studying alone without companions, one is bound to be limited in one's horizons." One aspect of character is something people are born with, but what is more important is the cultivation of one's character after one's birth.

All outstanding students should strive to expand their interests and hobbies in accordance with the unique characteristics of their personalities. They should take the initiative to interact, come into contact with others, and form character traits of being lively, cheerful, vivacious, and positive.

6. Be Diligent in Thinking, Have a Rich Imagination, and Grasp the Systematic Method of Learning

My take on the ideal student is that one should have a solid foundation in knowledge, be adept at learning, be diligent in thinking, and have a rich imagination. Ideal students should also grasp the scientific method of learning and use the least amount of time to achieve the highest level of learning efficiency.

We have continuously advocated for new models of education such as quality education and innovative education, the purpose being to promote the improvement of the different abilities of a student. However, no matter what abilities are to be improved on, the key lies in using a solid foundation in knowledge to pave the way for improvement. Otherwise, the improvement of these abilities will be totally unrealistic and will have no practical significance. Therefore, students must pay attention to learning how to have a foundation in knowledge and must not "put the cart before the horse."

Imagination is an important dimension of a student's ability to think and has great significance in a student's learning. Einstein said, "Imagination is more important than knowledge. For knowledge is limited, whereas imagination embraces the entire world, stimulating progress, giving birth to evolution." British physicist John Tyndall also believed: "With accurate experiments and observations as the basis of research, imagination becomes the designer of theories for the natural sciences." Students who have a rich imagination will definitely work hard and produce solid work in their learning. When Einstein was 16 years of age, he had this sort of "strange imaginative thought": If I were to ride a beam of light to pursue another beam of light, what phenomenon would be produced by this? It was the start of his theory of relativity that he later proposed.

Imagination is a valuable quality and is the source of invention and innovation. A person without imagination cannot possess an innovative spirit, which constantly explores. Imagination can enhance a student's learning initiative, foresight, and creativity and allow students to find unexpected inspiration and shortcuts in their learning. Therefore, students must pay attention to the development of a rich imagination in their learning.

To grasp the scientific method of learning by using the shortest amount of time to attain the highest level of learning efficiency, is one of the secrets behind the success of numerous "smart" students. An outstanding student will always treat the classroom as the focus and strive to prepare for future lessons and to review past lessons. This is the core of the scientific method of learning. Classroom lectures are the most important. The focus that outstanding students have in class is extremely concentrated, as their train of thought is always revolving around the teacher's activities. Normally they are able to solve the problems put forward during class; thus, they do not need to spend too much time after class to understand the problems.

In order to increase the efficiency of their learning within the classroom, students must properly carry out the various preparations for class, such as intellectual preparations, physical preparations, mental preparations, material preparations and so on. During class they should be proactive, bravely make vocal statements, actively think, and conscientiously take notes. "A beard well lathered is half shaved," and thus, preparations before a lesson can save time and raise one's learning efficiency and level of attentiveness to class lectures. It can also cultivate the ability to self-learn and form a virtuous cycle in one's learning. Review can consolidate all the knowledge that one has learned, deepen understanding, and allow students to "gain new insights from reviewing old material." It can also allow them to check their knowledge, see if there are any gaps in their learning, and grasp how to make their knowledge complete and organized.

Of course, the scientific method of learning is not fixed, and students should choose different learning methods in accordance with their own foundations and personality traits. One's most appropriate learning method is one's best learning method. Students who have mastered a set of scientific learning methods that are suitable for them will inevitably save effort and lead to better results in their learning.

Learning cannot be separated from one's memory recall. Having an effective memory capacity is one of the foundations of success in learning. Scientists have carried out in-depth research on the human brain's memory capacity and have revealed many valuable rules about memory recall such as the Ebbinghaus For-getting Curve. These scientific discoveries are extremely beneficial to raising the efficiency of students' memory recall. All students should work at coming up with a memory recall method that is suitable for them based on their own unique characteristics, such as trying to recite, using memory charts, and so on.

Students are the future of our country, the hope of the nation, and the builders of the future society. Students' development and the nation's future and destiny are closely related and intrinsically linked. Mao Zedong once put forward this ardent hope to the next generation: "The world is yours, as well as ours, but in the last analysis, it is yours." I sincerely hope that every student will not fail to live up to the great trust that this era has placed on them and that they will strive to improve their own qualities and to struggle for the sake of carrying out the rapid development of China!

10

My Take on the Ideal Parent

"Parents are a child's first teacher" and "the hand that pushes the world forward is the hand that pushes the cradle." Since ancient times, people have been well aware of the vital importance of a child's education at home. From the point of view of the education that a person receives, the education at home is received the earliest and longest, and most deeply affects the person. People are not able to separate themselves from the influences of the education they receive at home from the time they are born till they become adults. Every word and every deed of parents has a didactic, influential, and subtle impact on their sons and daughters.

The healthy development of the future society is dependent on the mental outlook of the future generation. The formation of a favorable mental outlook comes from education, and the contents of education largely depend on the education one receives at home from one's parents. Parents are the entire source of education at home and are indispensable in the formation of children's healthy personalities. Usually, behind outstanding children who become outstanding human talents, one will find the shadow of a warm and harmonious family; similarly, for a person who has formed an unhealthy personality, one can most likely find conflicts and contradictions within the family. The focus of modern-day society is school education, and what parents consider more is also school education. However, they neglect the fact that they themselves are the real educational foundation. They are key to determining the fate of their children. This has formed a misunderstanding about the education one receives at home.

Faced with an increasingly complex and hard-to-regulate social environment and the reality of declining effectiveness in moral education, the education one receives at home has shown an unprecedented role. Families must take the initiative on the important task of educating their children. In order to educate children even better we must be better at improving the quality of their parents. What sorts of characteristics do high-quality parents have then?

1. Make Children's Personalities Healthy and Sound and Give Precedence to Attaining Moral Perfection

My take on the ideal parent is that one should give precedence to making children's personalities healthy and sound and to attaining moral perfection. Ideal parents should also strive to cultivate in children personal qualities and good habits such as a pursuit of excellence, independence, autonomy, perseverance, diligence, thriftiness, and so on.

At all times and in all places, many educators believe that in regards to a child's development, personality and morality come first, as the significance of the development of one's personality and moral perfection far surpasses the development of one's intelligence. A healthy society first requires a stable foundation for social order. People follow basic laws, have a grasp of basic civilization, and have relatively good behavioral habits. These are the basic conditions for a normally functioning society. One important function of education is to cultivate members of society (especially starting from the time they are students) with healthy and sound personalities and moral perfection to maintain social stability and to promote social development. If education cannot realize this objective, then no matter how smart, how competent, and how great the intelligence of the people they cultivate, they will only be able to become destroyers of society and obstacles for social development.

The ancient scholar Sima Guang once divided people into four categories: those with virtue but not talents, those with talents but no virtue, those with no virtue and no talents, and those who have both virtue and talents. He believed that people who had no virtue but did have talents were vile characters. In actual fact, these people are not only vile characters but also will have great negative impact on society. Our society must do its utmost to decrease the number of these types of people. Among other methods, parents at home must assume an important duty and within their education of their child must pay attention to the establishment of scientific education objectives in regard to family health.

Good personality traits are a basic requirement of modern people, and in regard to the cultivation of children's good personality traits, education at home should include the following five aspects:

- *The pursuit of excellence.* Ideals are symbols that determine how far a person can go. Behind people's actions there are sure to be a variety of factors that drive them. However, without a doubt, the highest state that one can reach is sure to be one's ideals. If people always feel that they have not yet attained the state that they want to reach, then this power will become their constant progressive force. They can never surpass the state that they want to surpass. We often give ourselves a position, and once we have done so, it is very difficult to surpass this point. Only by cultivating excellence and constantly facing toward those who climb toward even higher states can we reach the splendid summit. For children, ideals are the most sacred, and allowing students to consciously pursue the sacred is the perfect sort of home education. In reality, parents can do absolutely nothing, as long as their children know of never-ending pursuits, then they are at least halfway toward success.

■ *Independence and autonomy.* Developing a child's independent personality is extremely important to the child's growth. A baby's first cries in the world, although they cannot be called exquisite poetry, are still referred to as a stately declaration of independence. When people leave their mother's body and enter the world, an important mission is for them to rid themselves of attachments, pursue independence, and form their own personal symbol so that they can leave their own individual mark on the world. In the course of a person's development, there are generally two instances where one has to be weaned. The first is the weaning that occurs during one's childhood, whereby students rid themselves of their physical attachment toward their parents; the second is during their adolescence, whereby children not only physically but psychologically begin to rid themselves of their parents' control. This trend, from the very start of one's growth, is never ending. From the time when they have just learned to walk, children often push away their parents' hands and demand to walk on their own. During their adolescence, children often lock their things up and do not allow their parents to look at them. In finding work, children begin to rid themselves financially of their parents. To demand independence is human nature. Parents cannot treat children as their vassals, they cannot demand that children act in accordance with their will, they cannot mold children according to their own designs and limit their children. A parent's primary duty lies in discovering the child's individual strengths and then cultivating, strengthening, and improving these strengths. In actual fact, before children enter school they already have a relatively complete individual nature and take this sense of nature with them when they enter school. Afterward, their achievements at school, their free handling of various relationships, and the formation of their independent and autonomous consciousness depend, to a large extent, upon the home education that they have received from their parents before they enter school. To respect children, letting go and allowing them to grow and to cultivate their independent and autonomous consciousness is a basic requirement of all parents.

■ *Perseverance.* One's will is an important symbol determining one's success. Parents should teach children to be aware that whether or not one is able to grasp success largely depends on whether one perseveres. Both the tenacious struggles of Olympic athletes in the stadium to snatch gold and the significant achievements that occur during the process of scientific research are the results of efforts and struggles. The saying that "the going is toughest toward the end of a journey" illustrates that many people who have already tenaciously striven toward a goal and are on the verge of success lack the final amount of patience and, in the end, have nothing to show for their efforts. The biggest difference between people who have achievements and ordinary people lies not only in the fact that the former put in more work, but more importantly, that they are able to use an indomitable will to overcome one difficulty after another and reach the shores of success. Therefore, parents must pay attention to the cultivation of their children's willpower.

▓ *Diligence and thriftiness.* "Do not financially pamper a child" is a warning that many visionary educators direct at parents. The sort of concept of money that children have is quite important to their future growth. Diligence is one of the most basic principles for being an upright person. Children are to be trained to cherish food, toys, and utensils from a young age, to empathize with the toils of labor, as "a bowl of porridge and one grain of rice should be considered the hardship of their harvest"; thus we will cultivate in children the good qualities, which will become second nature: to cherish everything and not to waste products of nature. The cultivation of these good qualities will give children a lifetime of benefits. Of course, a proper concept of money is not merely an issue of diligence and thriftiness; it should also be how one is able to scientifically organize one's life, to reasonably spend money, to distribute one's allowance, to grasp a few basics in terms of knowledge about modern-day economics, and so on.

▓ *Good habits.* Ye Shengtao once said education can be summed up as the cultivation of habits. Good habits come from cultivation in the small things in one's everyday life. For parents, cultivating good habits in children from a young age will mean that these habits will become natural and a regular tendency. Later on, these children will then naturally engage in some sort of behavior formation. Good habits will allow people to have a lifetime of benefits. Keeping a diary is precisely one such good habit. Through keeping a diary, children can engage in summing up and deeply reflecting on their studies and life; they can exercise their abilities to observe life and master language and thus improve their level of writing; they can express their emotions and regulate their feelings; they can cultivate their independent personalities and ability to independently handle situations; and they can exercise their willpower, open up their hearts, and cleanse their souls. Children's habits can be molded additionally from the three aspects: living habits, study habits, and thinking habits. Among these, living habits are the foundation and they have a great impact on the cultivation of good study habits and thinking habits. It is hard for us to imagine that a child who is careless and vague in life and constantly forgetful can be very structured in learning. Normally, children who are well organized in life are definitely also tidy and orderly children. Therefore, parents can begin by cultivating living habits from all the small things in a child's life, thus gradually developing the child's good study and thinking habits.

2. Let Children Grow in a Relaxed Manner, Freely and Happily

My take on the ideal parent is that one will forever maintain a youthful attitude and understand how to give children their own childhood and childlike innocence. Ideal parents also let children grow in a relaxed manner, freely and happily.

In Ming Dynasty philosopher Li Zhi's *Theory on Childlike Innocence*, he believes that the innocence and whims of a child are the most precious. Childlike innocence has no hypocrisy, no mutual deception, and no intrigue. A child's smile is the most innocent, the most natural, and the most dazzling. A child's innocence is something that no riches in one's life can replicate, the most real and most beautiful flower of humanity, and the most genuine and purest breeding ground for humanity's future. Only children who fully enjoy innocent fun can have a healthy disposition, a perfect personality, and developed thinking. Parents must treasure their child's innocence just as they treasure their own eyes. Childlike innocence is the truest mirror of childhood; innocence is pure, immaculate, and uncontaminated. Only with a childlike innocence can one open oneself up to accept love; only with childlike innocence can one be filled with an interest to explore; only with childlike innocence can one expose one's inner world; and only with childlike innocence can one expose one's all without glossing over anything. The key to educating people is to educate their hearts. Parents must not teach the profane and vulgar to children. Parents who teach children to be good at pretending, covering up, and currying favor will undoubtedly stifle children's pure nature.

When parents are teaching children, they must maintain a youthful attitude themselves. Parents must return to their childhood days and strive to play together and grow together with their child and to become one of the children. Parents should respect a child's interests and hobbies as much as possible, allow children to go down the path that they have chosen, and appropriately guide them, to truly "give their childhood to their child." The children of today, especially children living in the city, no longer have any childhood joys. The games of yesteryear are all but gone, and so unearthing traditional games and helping children to recover the childhood that truly belongs to them has already become an urgent task for parents.

Presently, when a child has just been born, or even before he has been born, many parents have already envisioned a future for him and expect him to become a music maestro, a great painter, and so on. Prematurely having children learn passively and master various skills is actually not a proper and reasonable approach. Many parents believe that games are merely games and playing is merely playing. They believe that games and play are only a waste of time and energy. This view is completely wrong. Parents should recognize that games and play are an important source of a child's cognitive and creative world. While playing games, children's imagination and creativity can be fully developed. They will consciously create rules, follow rules, learn how to be an upright person, keep promises, and embody the various roles in society. Therefore, games are a child's spiritual world and kingdom. The cultivation of a child's many abilities and habits is reflected in play.

In order to let children have a happy childhood life, parents must understand the psychology of a child and respect childhood. As the saying goes, "Children say what they think without fear." A child's candid nature often gives parents a lot of embarrassment in life; at these times, parents have to respect children even more. A young child's heart is precisely the same as tender sprouts and is very vulnerable. If children receive criticism when they have said or done something wrong, then in the future, they will not dare to speak or act. All of this will hinder their ability to freely express their own opinion and to do the things that they want to do. Parents should not be afraid that their children will do something wrong and should have children learn to grow by learning from their mistakes. One example is having children keep a journal from the time they are young. Parents should not busy themselves too much with correcting their spelling mistakes and thus neglect developing the mood of the entire article. Children's spelling mistakes can be slowly corrected later on, but no one is able to help them create this mood. Too much interference and criticism of children will cause them to be at a loss as to what to do, to be constrained, and to become people who have no initiative or drive.

3. Be Adept at Tapping into a Child's Latent Capabilities and Developing Their Personal Strengths

My take on the ideal parent is that one should be adept at discovering the children's gifts, tapping into their latent capabilities, and developing their personal strengths.

As the saying goes, "There is no bad child in this world, only bad parents." Parents often complain and criticize children, but they often do not know that they are the ones who should receive complaints. I often say that our education has stifled many geniuses; however, among the ranks of "executioners," the ones who truly begin passing this baton are the child's parents. During a child's formative education, many parents have already begun to stifle the child's gifts and latent capabilities.

For parents to discover and also cultivate children's gifts and latent capabilities, the most important condition is that they encourage children's expressions of themselves. They must be good at observing the child's bearing that reveals itself in a child's various expressions. Parents who force children to progress in the direction that they have already planned out for them will often cause "a watched flower that never blooms." The domains that parents choose for their child are often not the ones where the child's best gifts and latent capabilities lie.

For parents to discover and also cultivate children's gifts and latent capabilities, they should also firmly believe in their children. All children have their own gifts and latent capabilities; for them to come to this world, they inevitably have value in their existence and possess the possibility of limitless development. The road of life appears to be very long, but there are only a few times when one plays a decisive role and is allowed to choose at a critical juncture in life. The greatest responsibility in being someone's parent is to fully believe in a child who is facing hardships and to say, "You can do it!" The sound of these words, surging with passion, will undoubtedly be a powerful force in propelling a child to overcome hardships and to continue moving forward. This will often produce unexpected miracles. Many parents are impatient for results in terms of a child's development, and if the child fails to meet their expectations, they will feel resentful toward the child. In actual fact, there are many examples of "late bloomers." For example, the young Hegel did very poorly in school, was often mocked by other students, and gained the nickname of "old man" (meaning that his actions were slow). His classmate Friedrich Schelling held the post of associate professor at Jena University at the age of 23. Hegel was 35 years old when he took up the post of associate professor, but Hegel was not impatient and quietly devoted his energy to his thoughts. Later on, Hegel became the principal of Berlin University and became a great philosopher of his generation.

Parents must be patient toward their children and never lose faith in their children, no matter what. At present, in education there are not many people who are tolerant of the "Han Han Phenomenon." He wrote two books during high school, but his homework in six subjects was "red-flagged." Fortunately, his parents did not hurt his feelings but rather encouraged him and gave him confidence and motivation. I think that this was also the most important support for Han Han's constant efforts and his continuous progress forward. Of course, temptations in life are constantly increasing, under the context of the varying attitudes that people have toward Han Han's reputation. Whether he is able to know himself and to grow healthily also depends on whether or not his parents' minds are clear and their teaching appropriate.

For parents to discover and cultivate their child's gifts and latent capabilities, they must focus on their child's early development. There are critical periods in a person's learning. For example, it is best to begin learning languages before the age of 12; if one misses this opportunity, then it would be very difficult to learn. Children in urban areas have stronger language skills when compared to children in rural areas. This is because cities are a multilingual environment and at any time the environment is changed by various languages; however, rural villages are a closed off, monolingual environment that hinders students' language development. Psychological studies have shown that during a person's early development, there is a certain "critical period" for the attainment of many behaviors and abilities. During this critical period, if one possesses good stimuli from the environment and appropriate opportunities to practice, then certain behaviors and abilities will be better developed; language skills are such a case, as are skills in art and sports. If one were to engage in sports for the first time at 50 years old, it would be impossible to achieve an Olympic gold medal.

For parents to discover and cultivate a child's gifts and latent capabilities, they must respect a child's interests and choices and encourage their child to discover things that suit her through the process of constantly trying things. This sort of discovery can only occur when a child is in the process of creating her own interests; otherwise, it will have the opposite effect. In real life, when parents forced a child to learn the piano it ultimately led to the tragedy in which the child cut his or her own fingers. Parents have no choice but to ponder on this.

4. Treat Children as Equals and Friends

My take on the ideal parent is that one should treat children as equals and friends. Ideal parents should not act as elders who suppress children and use the rod as a way of teaching children.

We often complain about class distinctions and hierarchy in society. In reality, the source of this still lies in schools and in the home. In schools, teachers and students are not equals; take the universal form of teachers speaking and students practicing what they have learned from listening. If students were to oppose their teacher, then this would be disrespectful to the teacher. At home, the relationship between parents and children is also unequal. Parents have the supreme authority, and children must be submissive and obey them unconditionally. If we do not regard children as equals, then they will never be able to form independent personalities.

Survey research has discovered that the way parents educate children at home as well as the attitude parents have toward their children is the greatest factor in influencing children's character development and formation of their personalities. Parents of a democratic-style family will often appear in the family like an older friend that children can rely on. They will give children the freedom to develop their own interests and hobbies, are able to often exchange opinions on various things with children, often demonstrate their trust in their children, and even if their children fail on a test, they will still encourage them enthusiastically.

A democratic family educates children under the premise of understanding, respect, and encouragement. In a harmonious family atmosphere, children are able to easily tap into their latent capabilities and, as a result, it is a scientific teaching method. Normally, children who are creative, lively, innocent, and cheerful will have tolerant parents with whom they are on relatively equal status. In regard to this relationship with children, people often hold the negative attitude toward these parents, that they are "not being aware of everyone's proper place." In reality, this sort of relationship should be advocated. As the saying goes, "A great man is great because you have to kneel to look at him." Children are the same. If they do not kneel to look at their parents and the authority of their teachers, then their creativity, imagination, and independent character will gradually be established.

In foreign countries (such as the United States), parents place a lot of emphasis on treating children as equals. Before entering a child's room, they will normally knock and also ask, "May I come in?" However, in China, parents have no qualms about charging into a child's world, nor do they have qualms about making their child's secrets public. Children do not have their own place in the world nor their own freedom of choice. Of course, an emphasis on equality does not mean that parents do not give their children any help or any criticisms or suggestions.

The crux of the issue is that parents teach their children with a more democratic method, giving them the chance to choose and the right to explain themselves. When children feel that their parents are not teaching them as elders and from a position of authority, they more easily accept the opinions of parents.

In regard to the issue of corporal punishment, the theory of home education and the reality that exists are very different. The theoretical world has always called out for an end to the corporal punishment of children, as various sorts of problems occur due to corporal punishment. However, in reality, many parents still place a lot of emphasis on using corporal punishment methods. As the sayings go, "under the rod a faithful son will grow," "spare the rod and spoil the child," and "one hit and the test scores will come." Many parents believe that only by hitting and scolding a child can a child become a talented person, but they are not aware that this will bring about many adverse consequences. If the brawls between children are learned from their parents, then we are using one kind of violence to subdue another kind of violence. One reason behind an increase in youth violence is television and movies. In reality, it is even easier to find the root cause of this at home, because many families regularly stage thrilling "fighting scenes."

5. Set a Good Example and Keep One's Promises

My take on the ideal parent is that one should have harmonious family relationships, be able to set a good example, and keep one's promises.

Parents are a whole entity in education and the education of children requires the cooperation of both parents; only their joint efforts can educate a child properly. This is the best guarantee of success in education. Parents must reach a basic consensus on their important values and education methods. Harmonious family relationships are very important to a child's education, and parents should pay close attention to what they say and how they act in front of their child. If parents are always quarreling and going to war over their children, then they can very easily bring trauma to the tender hearts of children from a young age, as it is not conducive to a child's healthy growth.

From a psychological perspective, the development of human behavior is, to a large extent, through imitation. This is one of the fundamental ways that children learn. When parents make a slight slip, it will have a negative impact on their child. Imagine a family where a child's parents gamble and "play mahjong" all day. How could a child be expected to "grow up from the filth and not be corrupted," be strongly motivated, and also constantly strive forward? The example parents set strongly stimulates the process of growth for a child. Parents' good and bad habits will directly influence children.

The famous educator Anton Makarenko once said this to parents:

> Your own conduct is decisive. You are constantly educating your child—even when you are not with him. Your manner of dress, how you treat your friends or enemies, even what you laugh at—read in the paper—all this has great meaning

for the child. You may not even be aware that your thoughts are affecting him in unseen ways—a change in your voice. . . . If you are coarse or boastful at home or—much worse—if you are insulting to mother, there is no use thinking about bringing up your children. You are already bringing them up badly and no advice will help you. The parent's own self-discipline—control at every step—this is the most important method of bringing up children correctly.

Therefore, parents who truly know education should know how to make some sacrifices for their children and give up any unsavory personal hobbies. Parents should avoid taboos and getting into disputes over education when they are in front of children. This is because if they were to do so, children would understand intuitively, immediately seize the opportunity, and side with one party to attack the other party. In doing so, they would further exacerbate family conflicts and deepen the tension between parent and child.

Having children learn how to respect people is one of the basic qualities of humans and is also an important objective of home education. Only by respecting others can one win the respect of others; only respect can create harmonious interpersonal relationships. Maslow's hierarchy of needs theory places winning the respect of others as second only in importance to the actualization of one's self-worth. In order to cultivate children's habits in this aspect, parents should make strict demands of themselves to respect the elderly, their neighbors, and colleagues; establish the most direct example for children; and enable children to subtly be subject to various good values and behaviors. In addition, self-esteem is a child's second life. Sukhomlinsky regarded self-esteem as a person's most sensitive corner, and parents must cherish a child's self-esteem in the same way they would cherish a flower.

Keeping a promise is a traditional virtue of the Chinese nation. As the ancient saying goes, "A word spoken goes faster than a swift horse." At home, parents must treat their children in accordance with the sayings "every word carries weight" and "a promise is a promise." In ancient China, the widely circulated "Zeng Zi Kills a Pig" story profoundly tells parents that keeping a promise is not just a sort of behavior that one honors, but what is even more important is that it cultivates children's awareness of trust in keeping promises. This is an extremely important quality and can be said to be invaluable. In a market economy society, trustworthiness has already become a business's biggest trademark and is a huge, intangible asset. Keeping promises has already become important capital for an individual to live life in peace. Therefore, parents must practice what they preach and cultivate their children's awareness of trust.

6. Give Children More Praise and Encouragement and Never Carry Out Humiliating Criticisms

My take on the ideal parent is that one will never lose hope in one's child and will never be stingy with praise and encouragement. Ideal parents will also never use humiliating criticisms.

As the saying goes, "There is nothing sadder than a withered heart." For parents, to lose hope in their child signifies the end of education. Furthermore, for children, to lose hope in themselves signifies the end of progress. Belief and self-confidence is the source of power for a person to continuously forge ahead. People's development of their latent capabilities appears as a normal distribution curve. Geniuses and idiots are both in the minority and when added together are no more than 5 percent of people. However, the level of intellectual development of the vast majority of people (more than 95 percent) is pretty much the same. In regard to these people, everyone has a hope of success and opportunities will appear for every person. The crux lies in whether everyone grasps these opportunities and whether or not they have lost hope in themselves. Only with hope can we have pursuits and the power to move forward. In life it is also the same. Only when people believe that they can still be themselves and still have signs of hope will they continuously put their efforts into doing something.

When we cultivate people, we are cultivating their self-confidence. When we destroy people, we also destroy their self-confidence. In our present-day education, no matter if it is the education at school or the education at home, there are sometimes processes that constantly destroy a person's self-confidence. Presently there are many parents who play the role of the "executioner," doing bad things with good intentions, doing wrong things with good intentions, and using a gentle hand to do some extremely cruel things. There is a phrase that criticizes these unhealthy tendencies very clearly: "If someone says that you're capable of doing something, then you can do it, even if you could not; if someone says that you're incapable of doing something, then you will not be able to do it, even if you could." This phrase is very thought provoking when used in regard to education. I once jokingly referred to this as "Zhu Yongxin's law on education." Indeed, in educational practice, if someone were to say that you are capable of doing something, then people who are incapable will slowly become capable. Many people constantly strive toward doing something under the encouragement of their parents, teachers, and leaders, and ultimately they are able to achieve success. If someone were to say that you are incapable of doing something and do not give you the chance to use your talents or to exercise your growth, then you will not strive to overcome various difficulties, nor will you exercise your growth or practice your talents, and slowly your talents will dry up and degenerate, and then you will not be able to do something, even if you could.

In the process of educating their children, many parents are extremely stingy with their praise and encouragement. They do not know how big an incentive their praises and encouragement are for children. In actual fact, every child is very concerned about praise. To them, a parent's every smile, every word of praise, every confirmation will arouse strong emotions within them and raise their hopes. When children lose hope, a parent's one phrase of encouragement, "you can do it, you can definitely do it," will enable children to once again get back on their feet. Only by enabling children to be full of self-confidence can we enable them not to fear setbacks in life. Every child has a stage that is most suitable to perform on, and so-called academically poor students are fundamentally students who lack confidence in themselves and in whom parents and teachers do not have confidence. Once these students find their self-confidence, they will be like a bird who recovers from having its wings broken and will be able to once again take flight.

Even if children have intellectual disabilities, they also will be able to find their own value. Zhou Zhou, who has an intellectual disability, has an IQ of only 30, which is barely equivalent to the intelligence of a three- or four-year-old child. However, in September 2000 the 22-year-old Zhou Zhou jointly performed with the world-renowned Boston Symphony Orchestra and showed an amazing talent for conducting, causing Americans to exclaim with astonishment. From the moment he was born, his parents believed firmly in one principle: the child is innocent, and since we have given birth to him, then we have a responsibility to him; since God was unfair to him, then as parents we should use two times the amount of love to compensate for him. Zhou Zhou's IQ is comparatively lower, but his ability to imitate is incredibly strong and he has an amazing perception for music. In his mind is a type of latent ability that we are still incapable of understanding and recognizing. Only through his parents' focused cultivation and constant encouragement and praise was Zhou Zhou's unique talent able to be developed to superior levels. When faced with the success of a child who has an intellectual disability, what reasons do parents of children possessing normal mental faculties still have for not believing in their own child?

"Recognition leads to success, complaints lead to failure." This is the understanding that a father named Zhou Hong has on education. His daughter Zhou Tingting became deaf and mute at a young age, and with the help of her parents and many well-meaning people, not only is she able to speak very well, but to also fully develop her various latent capabilities. In 1993, she was chosen as one of the National Top Ten Young Pioneers. Later, she also became a university student. Faced with this sort of example, what impressions do those who are parents have?

7. Make Use of Various Educational Scenarios and Be Full of Educational Resourcefulness

My take on the ideal parent is that one should be adept at learning and possess educational reasoning and awareness. Ideal parents are also able to make use of various educational scenarios and possess educational resourcefulness.

In Sukhomlinsky's *The Pedagogy of Parents*, he proposed that all people who apply for a marriage certificate must study parenting education; otherwise, they will not have a marriage certificate issued to them. Parents who have not received scientific training in systematic education are the same as a driver who has not received a driver's license. If they hurriedly set off, they are bound to cause adverse results. Therefore, a robust and perfect society should have parents attain the necessary scientific knowledge on education through various means.

At present, many schools have set up "parenting schools," but for parents this sort of education is, in reality, already a little late. This is because before children enter school, parents have already engaged in education at home. If they are already able to understand educational theory from the time their child is born, then they will have educational reasoning and an educational awareness and will be able to handle a child's education at home properly and achieve favorable results. Conversely, if parents unconsciously try to understand, seek out and make attempts in education at home, by the time they are able to master the unique characteristics and principles of education at home and realize that they have to educate children, their children have already grown up. India's hero Mahatma Gandhi had a son when he was very young. He was busy with his own personal struggles, and by the time he realized he had to teach his child properly, his son had already grown up. Furthermore, his son had been thoroughly corrupted by learning from bad examples, and no matter how he tried to change him, he was unable to do so and regretted it for the rest of his life. From this it can be seen that parents' initiative in mastering a comprehensive system of educational theory in regards to home education as early as possible and developing self-cultivation is extremely important.

Everything in life is educational. Every moment in life is educational. Parents should take the initiative to enrich their own literacy in educational science, to grasp all educational opportunities, to enable children to be subtly educated in an enriched environment. This is the most comprehensive education. When compared with school education, home education is able to occur anywhere and at any time and is pervasive. Parents cannot be like schools and set up their own classroom at home and have children sit and listen to lectures. They can only carry out their education of their children at all times and in all places through coming into contact with nature, playing games, having meals, shopping, and other daily processes in life. Parents must always remember their duty, restrict their own words and deeds, and give children an education that is holistic and constant, one that is carried out rain, hail, or shine.

In order to cultivate parents' educational literacy, society should provide parents with some suitable reading material that is rich in educational rationality. In numerous richly colorful ancient texts on family education in ancient China, the contents involved various aspects of home education, such as ideological morality, how to be an upstanding person, skills and abilities, tempering of one's will, national integrity, and so on. These rare educational materials contain many things that we can learn from in regard to raising the literacy of modern parents in scientific education. We should further organize, summarize, and bring the content of these materials to the height of their development.

8. Cooperate with the School and Community to Carry Out an All-Around Education for Children

My take on the ideal parent is that one should strive to cooperate with the school and community to carry out an all-around, multilayered education for children, thus contributing to a child's healthy and happy growth.

At present, the contact and communication between parents and schools are becoming increasingly less. Traditional home visits are basically no more, and this causes fewer and fewer opportunities and means for parents to understand their child's performance at school. This, to a large extent, affects students' educational results. Parents should be adept at taking the initiative to communicate and connect with schools. They cannot only listen and comply completely with teachers, and neither can they only persist in their own views. Parents should strive to become the "intermediary coordinator" between the school, teachers, and children. For example, with some students who have strong personalities and are often subjected to unfair treatment at school, parents must pay attention to adopting the appropriate methods to overcome two tendencies: namely, excessively blaming teachers and being partial toward the child, or being partial to the teacher and excessively blaming the child. Parents should persevere in encouraging and helping their children to face the unfair treatment according to the truth and facts. Parents must strive to become good helpers for the school and teachers in regard to assisting children's healthy growth and with the school and teachers jointly undertake the responsibility of educating children properly.

Children are a group of people in society who are in the process of growing. They are very malleable, very easily influenced by their social environment, and vulnerable. Therefore, parents should use various means to cooperate with schools and communities to educate their children and to protect them. Parents can use various ways such as by telephone, letters, and parent contact cards as well as school visits to actively participate in school-organized activities. In particular, they need to regularly take the initiative to keep in contact with the teacher in charge of their child's class and other subject teachers, to promptly understand their child's performance in school, to cooperate with teachers, and to assist in their work of teaching children to properly study, live, and think. Parents should also promptly reflect on children's behavior at home and thus enable a strong, cohesive force to form between the school, the family, teachers, and parents. In addition, the community is the place where children live, and whether the social order in the community is good or bad, whether work is carried out well or not, directly influences a child's growth. Parents must adopt a leading role to actively participate in the construction of the community and create a fine place for their children to grow in.

Children are the "sun" within their parents' hearts, and their parents' hope in life. Parents will feel the continuation of their own lives as they watch their children grow healthily. To hope for the success of their children is the common aspiration of all parents in this world. However, becoming qualified parents is the critical factor for their child's success. I request that all parents in the world remember these words: "You do not have to be a genius, but you can be the parents of a genius." Let all of our parents strive toward raising the level of their own attainments in self-cultivation and affixing wings for flight to the growth of geniuses!

PART 2

Three chapters in this part discuss the modernization of education and the issues of innovation education and national cohesion. After being published as articles in *Guangming Daily* and *Educational Research*, they caused considerably large social repercussions. Many primary and secondary schools have reprinted the article on innovative education and distributed one copy per member of their teaching staff. These issues are essentially issues that belong to the realm of educational policy and are issues that educational policy makers and educational operators should be keen to discover and to reflect on. I have treated research on educational policies as an important meeting point between theory and practice, between education researchers and education administrative managers. The significance of the former to the latter goes without saying. There are also many contemplations within the chapters in this part on various major issues related to educational activities. Education admittedly requires ideals, passion, poetic sentiments, and vitality. However, education also requires cool-headed analyses and in-depth thinking, especially during the decision-making process. It all the more requires collection and selection, thorough analysis, using different means to tackle the same problem, and pooling wisdom together for mutual benefits. In this way, rational thinking will enable the spark of ideals to become even more brilliant. This part also include analyses and outlooks on the future trends in education. Research on future education essentially is an activity in the exploration of educational ideals; only with a clear grasp on the future general trends in educational development can we enable our educational activities to be even more rational and our educational ideals to be even more goal oriented.

11

The Modernization of Education and Humankind

Modernization is a huge transformation experienced by humankind in the twentieth century, especially after the Second World War. It has its foundation in industrialization, its objectives in transforming the face of economic backwardness and social sustainable development, and is a movement that has swept the globe. The modernization of education is an important component of modernization. In the twentieth century, particularly since the 1990s, it has received an unprecedented amount of attention and has been considered "the driving force behind modern civilization and social progress." The reason why modernization of education has fully experienced this interest is its inherent logical connection with the modernization of humankind and of society.

1. Modernization of People as a Prerequisite of the Modernization of Society and the Ultimate Goal
The fundamental objective of modernization is to create a warm and wonderful home for humankind and to improve people's quality of life and their standards; the modernization of people is not only the prerequisite of the modernization of society but is also the ultimate goal of modernization.

The issue of modernization had already started receiving attention before the Second World War began and in recent years has become a systematic discipline. Western modernization theory is a derivative of mainstream social science; its research subject is the process of major change in third world countries, that is, the developing China. China's modernization has experienced long-term exploration. From the Hundred Days Reform (1898) led by Kang Youwei and Liang Qichao a century ago, Chinese intellectuals began explicit discussions on exploring the road to modernization for China. Hu Shi in the 1930s pointed out: "The people who advocated for 'reform' 30 years ago are the people who advocated for modernization at the time." In 1933, Shanghai's *Shenbao Monthly* published a special edition on "The Issue of Modernization in China." In 1964, Professor Cole from Tufts University in America held a lecture on "a comparison between modernization in China and Japan" at the Chinese University of Hong Kong, which garnered a lot of attention at the time. Cole used the concept of modernization to illustrate the economic changes in Japan and China in the past century. He believed that modernization is technological and economic change, as well as the changes to culture, the social system, and psychology that are driven by these. At the time, most discussions revolved around comparisons between Chinese and Western cultures, and few included economics, especially the human factor. It was not until the late 1970s that our country had an overall shift in its development toward a route that focused on the realization of socialist modernization. Under the new circumstances due to the reform and opening up of China, "modernization" became one of the most resounding terms and the strongest voice during that era. People also began to focus on the implementers of modernization—the issue of the modernization of people. The progress and deepening of understanding that modern people have toward the connotations and process of modernization is one that progresses from material modernization to system modernization and then to the modernization of people.

The connotations of social modernization are incredibly rich. They include aspects such as the economy, politics, life, and people's concepts. Measuring social modernization is generally done by examining both its quantitative and qualitative aspects. From a quantitative perspective, it is mainly examined by developing a comprehensive index system for screening, such as the American Social Health Association's (ASHA) comprehensive evaluation system, the Physical Quality of Life Index (PQLI), the United Nations Human Development Index (HDI), the United Nations measurement system for living and welfare standards, France's economic welfare index system, as well as Inkeles's 10 standards for modernization, and so on. Among these, we can carry out an examination by using of Alex Inkeles's 10 standards on modernization: (1) GNP per capita exceeds US$3,000; (2) the value added to agriculture in the country's GNP accounts for less than 12 to 15 percent; (3) the total value added to the tertiary sector of industry is more than 45 percent; (4) the number of people employed in nonagricultural labor accounts for more than 70 percent of the total employed population; (5) the number of literate people accounts for more than 80 percent of the total population; (6) the proportion of school-aged youths in higher education accounts for more than 10 to 15 percent of the population; (7) the urban population accounts for more than 50 percent of the total population; (8) the average number of patients per doctor is less than 1,000; (9) the average life expectancy is more than 70 years; and (10) the natural population growth rate is less than 1 to 1,000.

Some researchers believe that, although Inkeles's list of 10 standards on modernization grasps the main features and key variables in social modernization, with the development of the times it has been revealed to be relatively simple and outdated. For example, in regard to the GNP per capita, the World Bank's *1995 World Development Report* uses the three GNP per capita standards of US$695, US$696 to US$8,626, and exceeding US$8,626 per capita to divide countries or regions into three categories: low income, middle income, and high income. US$3,000 per capita is relatively low. Other than this, other factors that should be included in the index system include the contribution rate of scientific and technological progress in economic growth, the Engel coefficient, social security coverage, the gap between the rich and poor, the crime rate, and so on.[1]

An analysis of modernization from a qualitative perspective is mainly the rationalization of a quantitative index system and a summary of many dimensions. There are two typical classification approaches.

The first is proposed by the Jiangsu Provincial Academy of Social Sciences. Using southern Jiangsu as their subject, they summarized the connotations of the objectives of modernization into four areas: (1) to be driven by national sustained economic growth and to carry out economic modernization with industrialization as its core; (2) to organize hierarchies based on management science and with systematic innovation as its central point, and to pursue efficiency, order, and democracy as its symbol of political modernization; (3) to establish the acceleration of social mobility and universal social relationships as its connotations, and to modernize the social structure by urbanizing the features of the social landscape; (4) to treat the changes to people's lifestyles and system of values as its main theme, and to use the spread of modern mass communication as the vehicle for the modernization of culture and people.

Another classification was proposed by historians and sociologists. They divided modernization into three layers: material, institutions, and people. The modernization of the material is represented by a nation's GNP and uses economic indicators as its core; the modernization of institutions uses political changes and reforms in management systems as its core; the modernization of people uses the enhancement of people's quality as its core. The inner core of modernization is the people, the middle layer is the system, and the outer shell is the material. Generally speaking, what people are most concerned about and will first pay attention to is often the modernization of the material, then from the external to the internal they will gradually begin to concern themselves with the modernization of institutions and people. This is the normal thought process of modernization. With England as a representative of old capitalist countries and China as a representative of developing countries, what both will often choose is this model for modernization. With Japan as a representative of emerging capitalist countries and South Korea as a representative of a developed country, they will often choose the exact opposite and adopt the modernization of people as a foundation as well as carrying out the strategy of synchronized modernization of institutions and materials. This is the conscious thought process of modernization.

The biggest difference between natural thinking and conscious thinking is whether or not it regards the modernization of people as the result of social modernization or the cause. Facts prove that the natural thinking of using the primitive accumulation of resources as a starting point for modernization is perhaps an appropriate method for old capitalist countries; however, for modern developing countries, it is not the best method. In regard to this, Inkeles had this insightful explanation: "Many developing countries who are committed to modernization, slowly become aware through experiencing the long-term pains and tribulations that give birth to modernization, that the mentality and spirit of their nation's people are still firmly locked on a traditional consciousness which forms serious obstacles for economic and social development." He believed that countries can introduce science and technology from abroad to act as the most notable symbols of modernization and transplant the highly effective industrial management methods, government organization structures, and education systems with all of their course content from highly developed countries to their own country. They believe that by bringing advanced technology from abroad to their own country, they will be able to stand among the ranks of modernized countries. However, what they achieve is often failure and frustration.

If a country's people lack an extensive modern psychological basis of genuine vitality that they can give to these systems and technologies, then no matter how perfect their modern system and management methods are, or how advanced their technical and industrial skills are, these factors will become a pile of rubbish in the hands of a group of traditional people. Therefore, Inkeles came up with this conclusion: "The modernization of people is an essential factor in the modernization of a country. It is not a by-product of the process of modernization, but rather a prerequisite for the success of the modernization institutions and economy reliant on long-term development."[2]

In actual fact, the modernization of people is not just a prerequisite of social modernization; more importantly, it is the ultimate goal of social modernization. The fundamental objective of modernization is to create a warm and wonderful place for people and to raise the people's quality of life and living standards. People are the main subject of modernization. The process of social modernization is also the process of gradually realizing the modernization of people, which is what drives the modernization of institutions and materials.

2. Perfecting Modern Education and Developing the Modernization of People

Modern education activates the self-consciousness of people; it shapes the cultural quality, behavior, and attitudes of modern people and plays a key role in the development of people's modernity.

The first person to directly research the modernization of people was the German sociologist Max Weber. In the wake of the emergence of modern capitalism, not only is there a need for a new economic system, but also the need for a new social order and new lifestyles. Because the modern life started up by the Industrial Revolution is in many ways different from life in the Middle Ages, new social conditions and social living urgently needed the creation of a generation of social newcomers, namely, new capitalists. The emergence of this new generation is an important condition for the creation and maintenance of new social living. French economist Jean Monnet believed that modernization has to first modernize people and then modernize materials. This mechanical division of priorities may not necessarily be desirable, but the emphasis on the thinking of modernizing people is certainly visionary.

Former director of the United Nations Development Programme (UNDP) Paul G. Hoffman once said that the belief of developing countries that they can achieve modernization by establishing factories is simply an illusion. Industrialization first means to establish markets and market information systems. He criticized simple understandings of modernization and pointed out that the modernization of materials cannot be undertaken by itself. American sociologist Alex Inkeles did an in-depth study of this issue. From 1962 to 1964, he organized a group of sociologists to undertake a long-term study of six countries from Asia, Africa, and Latin America (Argentina, Chile, India, Israel, Nigeria, and Pakistan). They interviewed over 6,000 people and published *Towards Modernization* and *Investigation on Individual Modernization*, which put forward many modern insights into the issue of the modernization of people.

Inkeles believed that the modernization of people is an essential factor in the modernization of a country. It is not a by-product of the end process of modernization but rather a prerequisite for the success of the modernization system and the economy's reliance on long-term development. He proposed 12 qualities and characteristics that modern people should possess and explained that the differences between modern people and traditional people can be generally summarized in three aspects: being open and receptive to new things; being autonomous, and having initiative and creativity; and being compatible, having a sense of trust in society, and being able to properly treat others and themselves.

Our country's exploration into modernization began quite early on. Yan Fu, who advocated for "Inspiring the People's Power, Illuminating the People's Wisdom, Promoting the People's Morality" in the late nineteenth century and Liang Qichao who advocated "New People" in the early twentieth century can be said to be the first to have researched modernization in our country. Earlier articles related to the issue of modernizing people; there were also Lin Yutang's "Machine and Spirit" published in December 1919 and later on, Pan Guangdan's "Industrialization and Personality." They criticized the national character's weaknesses and based themselves as the ones to rouse the entire nation to become aware of their own responsibilities, to straighten the nation's spine, to inspire national spirit, and to recast the "national soul." Although many ideas have their limitations, as a kind of exploration they still have relatively high theoretical value. During the New Democratic Revolution, although the Chinese Communists did not directly research the modernization of people, they wrote brilliant expositions around the subject of "people" as their key factor, or from the perspectives of cultivating one's moral character or one's code of conduct. Many of these articles are still considered classics today, such as Mao Zedong's "Serve the People" and Liu Shaoqi's "How to Be a Good Communist."

After the founding of the New China, the problems on which researchers theorized began to become enriched. However, still no systematic elaboration was carried out on the issue of the modernization of people. Following the acceleration of the process of world modernization, human factors became more and more important, and in the 1970s and 1980s many academics began to truly turn their attention to the issue of the modernization of people. In regard to the modernization of Chinese people, Yang Guoshu and his followers carried out in-depth studies. In his works such as "Chinese People and Modernization" he put forward and also expounded the specific details on people's modernity.

Inkeles, Yang Guoshu, and others had their own specific historical contexts in regard to their surveys and research on the modernization of people. This means that their discussions on the characteristics of the modernization of people and the analyses of contemporaries on the characteristics of the modern person will undoubtedly be different.

The modernization of people is an issue that is much more complex and much more difficult to define when compared with social modernization. Research on the modernization of people often starts from an analysis of the differences between traditional and modern people. Through research on countries such as Chile, Argentina, India, Israel, Nigeria, and Pakistan, Inkeles revealed 10 characteristics of traditional people:

- Has a fear or dread of innovation and social reform
- Is distrustful or even hostile toward new methods of production and new ideas
- Has a passive acceptance of fate
- Has blind obedience and trust in traditional authority
- Lacks efficiency and personal efficacy
- Has the virtues of obedience and humility and lacks the creative imagination and behavior to break obsolete ways
- Is narrow-minded, guards oneself, and persecutes different ideas and views
- Measures and judges everything against ancient people, sages, and traditional thinking
- Is completely indifferent to public affairs in society, is isolated and disconnected from the world, and is arrogant
- Does not place importance on the practical, immediate benefits of nor have a significant relationship with education, academic research, and so on

On this basis, Inkeles proposed 12 characteristics for the modern person:

- Is ready and willing to accept new life experiences, new thinking, and new behaviors that one has never experienced before
- Is prepared to accept social reform and change

- Is open-minded, respects and furthermore is willing to consider all aspects of different opinions and ideas
- Is concerned about the present and the future, is punctual, and has a good grasp on timing
- Has a strong sense of personal efficacy, is confident in the abilities of people and society, and is focused on efficiency when they do things
- Can plan one's own present and future
- Seeks out new knowledge and is respectful of knowledge
- Trusts the power of human reasoning and a society governed by rationality, and trusts others
- Values technical expertise and has an underlying mentality of being willing to receive different compensation in accordance with the level of technical skill
- Is happy to allow oneself or descendants to choose to leave an occupation that is traditionally respected and dares to challenge the contents of education and conventional wisdom
- Has mutual understanding, respect, and self-esteem
- Understands the process of production

In order to effectively measure these characteristics, Inkeles also compiled a scale for overall modernity.[3]

Through surveys and empirical research in Brazil and Mexico, Kahl, another sociologist, also put forward numerous characteristics of the modern person:

- Is positive and takes the initiative in terms of the way one conducts oneself rather than being negative and passive, believes in planning in advance on important issues in life, and has a sense of security that one can consciously implement these plans
- Relies on one's own strength when implementing plans and objectives rather than relatives and other people
- Has a tendency toward individualism, is not willing to overly endorse others in one's own work group
- Welcomes the excitement and opportunities of a city life and has adequate skills to make friends in the city
- Places emphasis on the variability of the social structure in the city and advocates that any person is capable of influencing society; Believes that opportunities in life and in one's career are not fixed; even if a person has humble beginnings, one can still realize dreams and aspirations
- Maximizes the possible uses of mass media[4]

Taiwanese scholar Yang Guoshu also carried out an extensive amount of research on the issue of the modernization of the Chinese people. On the basis of the five characteristics of traditional Chinese people (complying with authority, having filial piety, abiding by the laws and maintaining the accomplishments of one's predecessors, accepting one's fate, and protecting oneself and male superiority), he proposed five characteristics for individual modernity: equal authority and openness, independence and doing as one wishes, optimism and being one who strives forward, respect for emotions, and gender equality. Equal authority and openness emphasizes an equality of power, namely, that the common people can criticize officials, students can debate with teachers, children can argue with their parents, and so on. It harbors an attitude of openness and tolerance. Independence and doing as one wishes refers to being independent and autonomous in one's life and one's actions and minimizing the influence that others have on one as much as possible. Optimism and being one who strives forward refers to having an optimistic attitude toward social development and a trusting attitude toward the people and affairs around oneself. Respect for emotions refers to an emphasis on the fact that all interpersonal relationships should be based primarily on genuine feelings and does not necessitate a focus on other factors. Gender equality refers to the fact that in terms of educational opportunities, job postings, social status, and so on, males and females should be equals. In terms of independence in personalities, work outside of the home, socializing, and making friends, husbands and wives should also be equal.[5]

In Chinese academia, there are also some people who sum up the modernization of people as the modernization of cultural quality, the modernization of behavior, and the modernization of attitudes toward life.[6]

The process of modernizing people is carried out alongside the socialization of people. It is restricted by factors such as family, school, and society and is influenced by factors such as the legal system, mass media, education levels, and so on. At the same time, it is also subject to the process of implementing the selections and adjustments of these constraints and influences. During the process of modernizing people, the law and education have important significance. The ancient Chinese long had the saying: "School education first, law control second." In taking a step toward modernization, people will always go through a process whereby they move from heteronomy to self-discipline and from negatively coping to positively adapting oneself.

The role that the legal system plays in regulating human behavior and shaping people's level of civilization is not to be underestimated. In fact, the relationship between the modernization of the legal system and the modernization of people is in itself a complementary relationship. The forcefulness and authoritativeness of the legal system inhibits the natural impulses of human nature and inhibits behavior that goes against modern civilized culture. In this sense, the legal system creates civilized culture. However, the agents who implement and supervise the legal system are also people. Only people of high quality can protect the system's seriousness and authoritativeness, ensure that all are equal before the system, and produce truly meaningful awareness of the legal system. These high-quality people cannot separate themselves from the role of education, and so the legal system itself must also use education as its basis.

Education has an even more direct role to play in the modernization of people. The research of Inkeles et al. shows that there is a significant positive correlation between education and modernity. Among their research subjects, of those who had received relatively less education only about 13 percent possessed the qualities of modernity, while of those who received relatively more education 49 percent possessed the qualities of modernity. This shows that education has a "direct and independent contribution" to the modernization of people.[7]

The enormous role that education, especially modern education, plays in the modernization of people is determined by the nature and characteristics of modern education.

First, modern education possesses a great amount of human interference and clear purposefulness. It comes up with social norms in accordance with society's basic requirements of individuals and the direction of individual development and regards the development of modernized people to be its fundamental duty. The greatest feature of modern school education is that it fills everything with a sense of science, culture, and ethics. All activities and environments are carefully organized and put through special processing, they are carried out under the guidance of experienced educators, and the results of activities also undergo a check to make sure they meet objectives. In this way, education can rule out and control the influence of adverse factors and allow the younger generation to healthily develop in accordance with the requirements of social norms.

Second, modern education is relatively strong in terms of its planning and systematic nature. The content of modern education revolves around the development and expansion of the aforementioned social norms. It not only considers the specific requirements that sociopolitical systems, economic systems, and the development of productive forces have for talented people, it also considers the logical order of knowledge and the characteristics of students and their receptivity, thereby ensuring the cultivation of talented people who are high in quality and efficiency. Therefore, people who have received a modern education tend to show a certain advantage, not only in terms of the quantity and quality of their knowledge but also in terms of their attitude toward accepting knowledge and receptivity to knowledge. Compared with people who have not received a systematic education, they also tend to be a notch above the rest in terms of aspects such as social awareness and a sense of social responsibility.

Again, modern education possesses a certain lifelong nature and openness. Modern education emphasizes that "the process of education must continue throughout one's life," stressing the integration between education at school and education in society. This provides the modernization of people with context wherein they have a vast amount of learning time and space.

In short, modern education not only plays an important role in regard to social norms by cultivating and shaping modern people's cultural quality, behaviors, and attitude toward life; to a large extent, it also activates people's self-awareness, improving the level of requirements of modern people and their ability to self-learn, enabling modern people to constantly improve and develop themselves in an atmosphere that is open and conducive to lifelong learning. In this sense, we can say that without a modernized education, there would be no modernization of education, nor would there be any truly meaningful modernization of people.

3. Grasping the Connotations and Trends of Modernization and Propelling the Modernization of Education Forward

The modernization of education uses the modernization of educational thought as its logical starting point for expansion. It involves many aspects such as educational content, educational facilities, teaching methods, educational staff, educational management, community education, and so on.

As with the modernization of society and people, opinions differ on the definition of the connotations of the modernization of education. According to different classification criteria, there are mainly the three-factor theory, four-factor theory, six-factor theory, and seven-factor theory. The three-factor theory is modeled on the three levels of social modernization, and it classifies the modernization of education into the modernization of materials, the institution, and ideology. As Yang Dongping proposes in "The Modernization of Education: The Great Duty that Transcends Centuries," the modernization of education can be classified into three aspects:

1. The development of education in terms of its quantity and scale as well as the degree of sophistication refers to aspects such as the conditions for the running of the school, school buildings, equipment, technical methods, educational expenditures, and so on. This is often used as an indication of social modernization in education, such as the literacy rate in proportion to the entire population, the proportion of university students who are school-aged youths, the ratio of GNP to educational expenditures, and so on.
2. The modernization of education on an institutional level refers to the establishment of an education system that is politically, economically, scientifically, and culturally compatible with modern society, including the national education system, the school's education system and the system of running a school, and so on.
3. The modernization of educational values, ideas, concepts, and so on refers to the establishment of new educational concepts, content, and methods that are in tune with modern life and world civilization and the cultivation of modern social citizens who are full of a sense of responsibility and creativity.

This three-factor theory holds that the core of modernization in education lies in the modernization of educational values, ideas, and concepts, which is the real connotation and the underlying objective of modernization in education.[8]

The four-factor theory has two types. The first adds to the three-factor theory the level of modernization of knowledge, which refers to the modernization of the teaching setup in education, the curriculum, teaching materials, teaching methods, learning methods, and so on. The other type defines the connotation of modernization in education as being the modernization of educational ideas, educational content, teaching methods, and the education system. As Gu Ming-yuan believed: "the modernization of ideas is the forerunner, the modernization of content is the main subject and the system and means are its safeguards."[9]

The six-factor theory was proposed by the Jiangsu Education Committee at the end of 1993. It mainly includes the modernization of educational thinking, the level of educational development, conditions in regard to the running of the school, qualified teaching staff, and educational management.

The seven-factor theory was proposed by Zhou Defan, deputy director of the Jiangsu Education Committee. On the basis of the aforementioned six theories, he also put forward the modernization of community education. He believed that the modernization of community education is not only the proper meaning of modernization in education but that it also complements the modernization of other aspects of education and that they mutually promote each other. He also believed that the modernization of community education is indispensable to the modernization of education as well as the cultivation of modernized people. Only by attaching importance to researching home education and researching the development and expansion, construction, and use of modern social educational resources can a more complete modernized education system be built.[10]

In my opinion, in terms of operational convenience and feasibility, there is no harm in being more specific with classifications and more detailed; however, in terms of the depth and systematic nature of theoretical research, classifications can be more generic and broad. Below, we will focus on discussing the connotations of the modernization of education from an operational perspective.

The first aspect is the modernization of educational thinking. Educational thinking mainly involves the views people have on many basic issues in education, for example, issues related to educational ideals and the ideal education, what sort of people should be developed through education, how to develop people, and so on. The modernization of educational thinking refers to being able to grasp the rules of educational development and the characteristics of the times and to establish a proper outlook on education and human talent, such as the concept of holistic education, lifelong education, democratic equality, multicultural education, quality education, and so on. The modernization of educational thinking is the precondition for the modernization of education. If we do not modernize the educational thinking of educational leaders at all levels and in all classifications and of the extensive number of teachers, then we cannot implement truly meaningful modernization in education.

The second aspect is the modernization of educational content, also known as the modernization of the educational system. It includes the modernization of the curriculum system and the content of teaching materials as well as other similarly adaptable teaching methods. Generally speaking, the level of the curriculum determines the students' level of quality, the structure of the curriculum determines the structure of students' quality, and the modernization of educational content determines the modernization of students' quality. Presently, apart from optimizing subject courses, strengthening course activities, and developing environmental courses, it is very important to establish a set of curricula and a system of teaching materials that are in accordance with modern educational concepts and a union between internationalization and localization. The modernization of educational content lies at the core of the modernization of education.

The third aspect is the modernization of educational facilities, also known as the modernization of the conditions for the running of the school. It refers to possessing school building facilities and equipment that are more advanced; being able to use modern information technology, physical training equipment, artistic teaching methods, and sophisticated scientific laboratory equipment; and equipping the school with an adequately resourced library. The modernization of educational facilities is the foundation for the modernization of education. Library resources are an important aspect of the modernization of educational facilities that cannot be ignored.

The fourth aspect is the modernization of the teaching staff. This refers to having teachers who possess relatively high levels of academic qualifications and cultural knowledge, are equipped with a spirit of dedication, are "insatiable in learning, tireless in teaching," pursue excellence, are paragons of virtue and civilized culture, and possess good basic skills and techniques in teaching. The modernization of the teaching staff is the root of the modernization of education. A sign of the modernized teaching staff is transforming teachers with craft knowledge to scholarly teachers and educators. Establishing a set of systems for the training, selection, professional development, and promotion of teachers as well as fundamentally improving the status of teachers and their wages is the key to modernizing the teaching staff.

The fifth aspect is the modernization of educational management, which refers to the modernization of the three aspects of management staff, management system, and management methods. That is, to be armed with modernized educational thinking, to have a high-quality cohort of management staff who possess modernized management knowledge, to have a complete educational management system that has been modernized, and to be equipped with modernized management methods, thus enabling educational management to become scientific. The modernization of educational management ensures the modernization of education. Presently establishing an educational evaluation and incentives mechanism in line with the current conditions of China is imperative to the modernization of educational management.

The modernization of educational development levels can be regarded as one aspect of the modernization of educational management, as it is also known as the modernization of the educational structure. This refers to being able to form various types of educational structures, hierarchical institutions, professional structures, and a complete range of subjects and to possess a distinctive educational system. The modernization of educational development levels is in fact a result of macro educational management and at the same time, it is also a sign of modernization in education.

The sixth aspect is the modernization of community education, the establishment of a mutual system between the school and the community to form a holistic structure that is "school-based, coordinates with the community, planned overall by the government to jointly educate and train talented people" and will reach the state where "students care for the community and the community cares for students and schools open up to society and society's facilities are opened up to the school."

The content of these six aspects is an integrated whole that uses the modernization of educational thinking as its logical starting point for expansion and development. The top priority is the modernization of the teaching staff. Harvard University's president James B. Conant once said that a school's reputation does not lie in its school buildings or its number of people, but rather, in the quality of its generations upon generations of teachers. Therefore, the modernization of the teaching staff should become the first strategic focus that leaders at every level consider when pushing for the modernization of education. As the point of attack for the modernization of education, these leaders can discriminate according to specific situations: put their efforts into the improvement of educational facilities, make an issue out of educational management, and ponder over the issue of educational content and community education. However, no matter what is chosen as the point of attack, they should place an emphasis on the principles of overall advancement and the optimization of the institution, ensuring that the modernization of education is an overall development of the entire entity.

These trends in the modernization of education have important implications for our push for modernization at all levels of education. We should become fully acquainted with the historical mission that is within the progress of modernizing education so as to cross into the new century. We should learn from the various experiences of modernization both at home and abroad, grasp the current background for our country's modernization of education, actively and steadily push for the modernization of education, and enable education—this "key that leads to the new century"—to be able to smoothly switch on the light of the new century and open its glorious door.

12

Educational Innovation and Innovative Education

The knowledge economy has started to take shape. The development of a knowledge economy mainly relies on new discoveries, inventions, research, and innovations. Its core lies in innovation and includes knowledge and technical innovation, and the basis for knowledge innovation, technical innovation, and the cultivation of innovative talent is education. Presently, there are many factors in our education that are not compatible with the demands of innovation in a knowledge economy. Therefore, carrying out innovative education has already become a requirement of the times.

1. Innovative Education and the Developmental Requirements of a Knowledge Economy Era

Innovation is the soul of national progress, the enduring force for national prosperity and development. Innovative education is a requirement of the times that the knowledge economy puts forward to education.

Science and technology have never had so much power and such unimaginable speed in profoundly influencing the economic and social development of humanity. As we look ahead toward the bright future of the twenty-first century, a completely new economy is in the process of forming and developing; it is explosively expanding across the entire globe and is bringing humanity into a brand-new era—the era of the knowledge economy.

This type of economy uses the continuous innovation of knowledge as its main basis for development. It relies on new discoveries, inventions, research, and innovations. It is a knowledge-intensive, intelligent economy and at its core is innovation. It emphasizes that the innovative quality of workers is the main growth factor in economic development, and it also emphasizes that creative and intelligent factors such as new inventions and designs as well as creative concepts and theories are able to bring sustainability and stability to the development of the economy and, furthermore, bring huge material wealth.

Presently, in an era when a knowledge economy is starting to take shape, the unique status and value of innovativeness has become increasingly apparent. This is determined by the modes of economic growth of the special features of a knowledge economy. It can be said that without innovation, the main body of a knowledge economy will lose its vitality.

From a macro perspective, in the era of a knowledge economy, innovation determines a country and nation's comprehensive strength and competitiveness. Jiang Zemin once pointed out that innovation is the soul of a nation's progress and the enduring force for national prosperity and development. A nation without innovation will find it hard to stand among the other nations of the world. In world history, China had once created a splendid civilization and culture; in particular, the Four Great Inventions of ancient China powerfully show the Chinese people's brilliant wisdom and excellent talents in innovation.

However, in modern times, China's innovativeness is significantly inferior to that of some other countries. For instance, the Nobel Prize is the highest accolade in the world of science and a prize that, to a great extent, reflects the scientific and innovative strength of a country and its people. From the establishment of the Nobel Prize to the present, there have been more than a hundred selections for the prize, but among the winners of these hundred-odd selections, who number over a thousand, Chinese national citizens—who belong to a major country that accounts for one-fifth of the world population—do not account for even one of them. In stark contrast to this, Chen Ning Yang, Yuan T. Lee, Tsung-Dao Lee, Steven Chu, and many other Chinese-Americans have achieved this glory within the territory of other countries. This presents us with a grim and realistic problem: why is it that intelligent Chinese people can only demonstrate their superior innovative talents in a foreign environment? Furthermore, Qian Xuesen's question of "why can we not cultivate talented people" is a problem that is even more worthy of our serious discussions and careful considerations. However, there is one thing that is certain: a serious problem exists in our system for cultivating innovative talents. We still lack the appropriate soil for the cultivation of innovative talents and have still not formed a systematically efficient and functioning mechanism for the development and training of innovative talents.

The significance of innovation in terms of the development of a country and nation of course does not merely lie in whether or not scientists have won a Nobel Prize; its real significance lies in the fact that it has a decisive influence on the promotion of economic development and the enhancement of overall national strength. Therefore, at present, many countries regard the establishment of a national system of innovation to be an important strategic task. One example is Japan, whose main feature has always been "imitation." In the past, the Japanese actively advocated using large investments to buy the production lines of high-tech products in America and thus based themselves in the use of the innovative knowledge of other countries to develop and manufacture products. Although the Japanese existed in a period when they had an agricultural and industrial economy, they miraculously and rapidly rose up all at once and had the potential to dominate the world. However, faced with the knowledge economy era, whose main features are its knowledge and technological innovations, due to the fact that their economic development lacked its own system of innovation they therefore lost their basis in stability, resulting in their suffering huge losses during the Asian financial crisis. Therefore, to greet the arrival of the knowledge economy, the Japanese government has begun to vigorously adjust their educational and research policies and institutions. They have decided to bid farewell to the "imitation era" and to vigorously promote "establishing a country on scientific and technological innovations." In recent years, there is a clear upward trend in Japan's investment of funding for research and innovation.

The measures that Japan took to welcome the knowledge economy era should be a source of enlightenment for our country. Various factors such as inadequate investments and unreasonable systems of innovation and operating mechanisms have caused a huge gap between our country's innovative abilities and its national needs, as well as international levels of advancement. Therefore, only by establishing a national system for innovation that is in line with a socialist market economy and comprehensively improving the nation's innovative abilities can we improve our nation's international competitiveness and position in the world structure. People have already reached a consensus on this point.

We know that innovations are not pure fabrications but are built on the basis of the dissemination, transformation, and application of knowledge. Furthermore, innovation is deeply rooted in education; whether it be knowledge innovation or technological innovation, it cannot separate itself from the support given to it by education. Therefore, comprehensively improving the nation's innovative awareness and ability should first begin with the innovation of education and with vigorous advocacy and implementation of innovative education. This should highlight the cultivation of contemporary students' innovative spirit and truly cultivate high-quality talents who have an innovative awareness and innovative abilities that adapt to trends and thereby improve the entire nation's level of innovation. Only in this way can we enable our country's smooth move into the knowledge economy era and to reduce the gap with developed countries in regard to the development of knowledge economies.

From a micro perspective, innovation in education also helps individuals develop their good qualities and personalities. Traditional learning is a type of learning that is inherited and maintained; students learn already-established concepts, methods, and principles and so cope with situations that have already been encountered. This type of learning is still able to solve problems in an agrarian and industrial society. However, in the upcoming knowledge economy era, cultural knowledge, science, and technology, as well as economic development, will undergo rapid, substantial changes, and the way we ponder problems will also be very different from the way we did in the past. People must not only adapt to the social patterns of life that are already present; they also need to change the living conditions that are already present, create new living conditions, and constantly improve themselves. This requires an emphasis on innovative spirit, innovative concepts, and innovative behavior.[1] Only by also accepting innovative education and carrying out innovative learning can people be able to rapidly accept new knowledge in the society of a knowledge economy and create a new world and a new life.

Harvard University's president Neil L. Rudenstine once spoke these thought-provoking words from a lectern at Peking University: "In the course of stepping into the new century, one of the best sorts of education is one that is beneficial to people who possess innovativeness, one that allows people to become even better at thinking, have even more ideals and insights to pursue and become people who are even better and more successful."[2] It can be said that superior innovative abilities can fully reflect a person's psychological orientation in regard to discovering problems and actively exploring and whether or not one is adept at being sensitive toward seizing opportunities. Innovative abilities are definitely not only an intellectual characteristic but even more a reflection of the characteristics of one's personality, state of mind, and overall quality.

The significance of a basis in innovative education is extremely important to a person's development. In the 1996 report published by the International Commission on Education for the *Twenty-first Century, Learning: The Treasure Within*, it was regarded as one of the greatest objectives of education, as "the duty of education, without exception, is to enable every person's innovative talents and innovative potential to bear fruit. . . . This goal is more important than any other goal."

No matter if it is from the point of view of the development of the country or its people or from the perspective of individual development, the implementation of innovative education has become very urgent. Although historically there have long been calls for innovative education, such as in the 1930s when our country's famous educator Tao Xingzhi strongly advocated for innovative education or when American educator John Dewey once criticized the drawbacks of a traditional education that lacks innovativeness and advocated for creative education that develops students' creative thinking and abilities. However, due to the characteristics of economic development in an industrial society, innovation education did not receive any genuine attention.

Today we are faced with a third human civilization—the arrival of the knowledge economy. The demand for innovative education in economic and social development has become increasingly urgent. It requires reform in the education system, educational modes, educational structure, teaching methods, and teaching content to carry out innovation in education in order to improve the innovative abilities of educators and to cultivate a large cohort of talented people who meet the demands of the times and the arrival of the knowledge economy.

2. Innovative Education Focused on the Cultivation of the Ability to Innovate

Innovative education, based on the principle of innovation, cultivates students who possess innovative awareness, innovative thinking, innovative skills, creative feelings, and an innovative personality.

Early on in the twentieth century there were already people who put forward the concept of "innovation." At the time, these people were mainly economists who raised this concept from the perspective of technical application. With the continuous development and changes in society, the meaning of innovation has also continuously been extended and deepened. Literally speaking, innovation includes all new things such as the process of developing things, the results of developing things, new discoveries and inventions, new ideas and concepts, new doctrines and techniques, as well as new methods. Furthermore, students' ability to innovate is cultivated through innovative education and teaching activities, thus achieving education in all the abovementioned new things. This is precisely what innovative education is. Among these, the cultivation of the ability to innovate is the core of innovative education. Or it could be said that innovative education is based on the principle of innovation and treats the cultivation of students who possess a certain innovative awareness, innovative thinking, ability to innovate, and an innovative personality as the main objective of its educational theory and methods, enabling students to firmly and systematically grasp subject knowledge and at the same time develop their ability to innovate.

The first aspect of innovative education is the cultivation of an innovative awareness, that is, the cultivation of the concept and awareness of a respect for innovation, a pursuit of innovation, and pride in innovation.

Only under the guidance of a strong awareness of innovation can people produce a strong motivation for innovation, establish goals in innovation, fully bring out their innovative potential and ingenuity, and release their passion for innovation. In the 1950s and 1960s, many scientists treated "Goldbach's conjecture" as a crucial goal. Our country's esteemed mathematician Chen Jingrun at the time also treated Goldbach's conjecture, known as "the pearl on the mathematical crown of laurels," as his own task. Under the encouragement and motivation of a strong innovative awareness, he was able to put in an unimaginable amount of energy and passion and achieved fruitful results. Innovation arises from passion driven by conscious thinking, and innovative thinking is the highly concentrated mental state that is formed from love, pursuits, struggles, and dedication; it is immersed in the sort of environment that produces conscious thinking. This is the "devotion to one's work and pioneering spirit" in UNESCO's "three passports" and Peter Senge's realm of "self-transcendence" in his "fifth discipline."

The second aspect of innovative education is the cultivation of innovative thinking. It refers to the thought process of inventing or discovering new ways of dealing with something. It requires the reorganization of concepts in order to produce some sort of new product.

The so-called improving mental models refers to the cultivation of innovative thinking. Innovative thinking has five distinct features: active search for differences in nature, keen powers of observation, creative imagination, unique knowledge structures, and active inspirations. This sort of innovative thinking ensures that students are able to successfully solve problems new to them and to profoundly grasp knowledge with a high level of mastery. Furthermore, they are able to extensively transport this knowledge into the process of learning new knowledge, allowing them to smoothly complete learning activities. It can be said that innovative thinking is the key to the entire intellectual structure of innovative activities and the core of an ability to innovate. Innovative education and teaching must strive to cultivate this type of valuable thinking quality.

The third aspect of innovative education is the cultivation of innovation skills. It reflects the motor abilities of the main behavioral skills in innovation. It is formed under the control and limitations of innovative intelligence and belongs to working mechanisms of innovative activities.

Innovation skills mainly include the information processing ability of the main subject of innovation, a general ability to work, practical abilities, operational capabilities as well as the ability to proficiently grasp and put innovation skills to use, an ability to express the results of innovation, performance abilities, an ability to objectify, and so on. The cultivation of innovation skills should be placed in a position of extreme importance. In our country's school education, we need to strengthen the training of scientific abilities and scientific methods that are centered on basic skills.

The fourth aspect of innovative education is the cultivation of creative feelings and an innovative personality. The process of innovation is not merely a process of intellectual activity. It also requires the motivation of creative feelings, factors like far-reaching ideals, a strong belief as well as an intense passion for innovation, and so on.

Innovation "contains: objectives for innovating which have both the nobility of selection for the purpose of promoting the evolution of human civilization and uniqueness; noble sentiments of throwing oneself into the process of innovation for the sake of improving humanity's aesthetic value; a pioneering manner of fully tapping into one's abilities in order to promote the spirit of altruism; a passion for seriously grasping innovation skills for the sake of optimizing an individual's creative social function; an honesty and open-mindedness to transform one's own brief life into the sequence of human civilization for the sake of the pursuit of everlasting value objectives."[3] Only under the role of the dual factors of intelligence and creative feelings can people's ability to innovate achieve a combined effect. Apart from creative feelings, personality also plays an important role in the formation of innovative strength and innovative activities. To a certain extent, differences in personality traits also determine the size of innovative achievements. An innovative personality, generally speaking includes good personality traits such as courage, a sense of humor, a strong sense of independence, perseverance, meticulousness, and so on. It can be said that for those who are subjects of education, possessing superior creative feelings and good personality traits are the ins and outs of forming and fully developing the ability to innovate.

3. Stimulation of Latent Capabilities and Formation of an Innovative Environment

Innovative education requires the three aspects of society, school, and the home to form environments and atmospheres that are conducive to innovation.

Every person possesses the potential to innovate. However, to transform a potential innovativeness into innovativeness in reality must require stimulation of these hidden capabilities and an environment and atmosphere for the formation of innovativeness. Only within a concentrated innovative social atmosphere and an environment that is conducive to innovation can the cultivation of innovative talents be realized. This environment and atmosphere mainly includes the three aspects of society, school, and home.

Society and Innovative Education

A social ethos and support system that is conducive to innovation and encourages innovation should be set up in the entire country. It should include an education-oriented holistic guidance, funding for research and innovation, and a public opinion–oriented view on talented people who conform to the characteristics of the times. Of course, it also requires the establishment of a national innovation system based on educational research and technological innovation at its core.

First, the relationship between the education administrative department and the school needs to be properly handled. Within our educational management system, the education administrative department's management of schools is too broad and too rigid. Schools lack a certain degree of autonomy and can only operate and develop within a unified educational model; this somewhat hinders the schools in tapping into and developing their own innovativeness and is not conducive to having schools develop innovative talents according to their own characteristics.

Second, an increase is needed in the intensity of cultivating innovative talents. The government also needs to increase its funding of educational innovation. Cultivating an ability to innovate that is merely cleverness and wisdom is not enough; it also requires a huge amount of research funding, well-equipped facilities, and favorable environmental conditions as support, such as the famous Bell Labs, whose annual funding for basic research is US$500 million to US$600 million and funding for development research is US\$5 billion to US\$6 billion. It is precisely because of strong financial backing that the Bell Labs were able to produce six or seven Nobel Prize laureates.

Again, the government should make use of public opinion methods to guide the whole society to form a proper understanding of and respect for talented people and knowledge, especially a social ethos that values knowledge innovation, technological innovation, and innovative talents. It is only within this kind of social ethos that the development of people's desire for knowledge will be promoted, people's interest in innovation will be stimulated, and the development of new ideas will be encouraged.

At the same time, there is also a need to promote and protect people's passion for innovation and the results of innovation through drawing up policies, laws, and regulations such as to further improve intellectual property laws, train talented people in innovation, and create incentives for innovations, thus comprehensively pushing the formation of a national innovative atmosphere forward.

The establishment of a national system for innovation that is geared toward the knowledge economy era is an extremely urgent task for the government and is also the soil in which our country's intellectual education can smoothly develop. A national system for innovation is a network composed of relevant structures and organizations for knowledge innovation and technological innovation. It is mainly made up of research institutions, institutions of higher education, and some other educational training institutions; its main function lies in promoting knowledge innovations, technological innovations, and the dissemination and application of knowledge. Its specific details include the allocation of resources for innovation, the carrying out of innovative activities, the establishment of a system for innovation, the construction of related infrastructure, and so on. With the great importance the country attaches to innovative projects and its proper guidance, inevitably, under the influence and support of this sort of social environment, school education will place the training of educated people's innovativeness at the top of their list. Educated people themselves will also actively take the initiative to become immersed in the activities of innovative education, promoting the smooth and effective implementation of innovative education.

Schools and Innovative Education

Schools are the place where students directly receive an education, and they should all the more set up a favorable environment and atmosphere for innovative education. A school's training objectives, style of study, learning atmosphere, and management system play a very important role in the formation of students' innovative awareness and the improvement of innovative abilities. Traditional school education had always treated knowledge transferral as the school's training objective; under the domination of values that made being able to sit for exams their goal, teachers and students found it very difficult to form an innovative awareness. Exam-oriented education emphasizes school advancement as the one and only objective that education is to pursue. It caused teachers and students to exist in an atmosphere of high tension and mechanical transfer of knowledge and seriously _mpeded students' cultivation of innovative abilities. Studies have shown that "psychological safety" and "psychological freedom" are two important conditions _or forming innovative abilities. Therefore, only by setting up educational objectives _hat are compatible with the trends of the times and forming a school spirit for _he entire school that is relaxed and lively and has interpersonal relationships can an appropriate climate and soil that is conducive to the cultivation of students' _nnovative abilities be formed. Some scholars have suggested that schools treat the guarantee of students' psychological safety and psychological freedom as the core of setting up an innovative educational environment and atmosphere.

Changing the traditional exam-oriented form of education is the key to _mplementing innovative education in schools. Many aspects of exam-oriented education such as its educational philosophy, purpose, methods, and content are _ncompatible with the innovative education that we advocate today. Due to the _nfluence and dominance of the old ideology of "he who excels at learning can be an official," in terms of its relationship with knowledge, ability, and quality, exam-oriented education overly emphasizes the transferral of knowledge and neglects the cultivation of students' abilities, especially the cultivation of innovative abilities. Students trained under these sorts of educational ideas and concepts will only focus on committing knowledge to memory and will not attach importance to the cultivation of their overall quality and innovative abilities. In terms of the relationship between teaching and learning, exam-oriented education overly emphasizes the teacher's leadership and neglects students' subjectivity. During the teaching process, teachers carry out a one-way transferral of knowledge to students; students learn passively and their subjectivity and enthusiasm is greatly inhibited.

Without initiative and enthusiasm, innovativeness will lose its foundation. In addition, in regard to the demands made of students, exam-oriented education overly emphasizes uniformity, ignores individual differences, does not attach importance to students' individual development, and implements a standardized curriculum, standardized teaching resources, and standardized tests. The knowledge structures and thinking of students cultivated under these standardized regulations will likely be identical, lacking in personality and originality.

In short, this old teaching model which emphasizes committing things to memory and taking exams but neglects innovative exploration has already seriously influenced students' holistic development, which should be active, lively, and free, and have a distinctive personality. Thus it is far from meeting the demands that the future society will make of innovative talents. Faced with the arrival of the knowledge economy, the teaching world has spent the last few years constantly calling out for the establishment of a quality education model to liberate students from the midst of exams and grade advancements. It treats the improvement of students' overall quality and abilities as its educational objective. In quality education, innovative education becomes the entire education model's soul and is treated as central to the educational objective of cultivating innovative personalities, innovative thinking, and creative abilities. The gradual improvement of quality education is bound to play a significant role in promoting the development of education.

The Home and Innovative Education

The home is a place that students cannot choose and cannot avoid. It has an even more profound and pervasive influence on the cultivation of students' innovativeness. An appropriate home environment is the foundation and an important condition for the cultivation of children's innovativeness. A home atmosphere that is conducive to innovation is mainly expressed in such aspects as the objectives of home education, interpersonal relationships at home, and so on.

The German scholar Gottfried Heinelt pointed out that the most important factor in triggering innovativeness is one's parents. A relaxed, unfettered, and lively atmosphere assists in the launching of innovative activities. If children actively interact with their parents, role models will play an enormous part. From a young age, children will try to think up new and original ideas and will make their own behavioral patterns unique. This is especially displayed in their inquisitive attitudes. This sort of inquisitive attitude is guided by a curiosity in certain things and a pursuit of knowledge. The former gives rise to questions only in terms of its significance for pseudo-creativeness; furthermore, it is advantageous for knowledge, the deepening of knowledge, an interest in information, and genuine innovativeness.

From Gottfried Heinelt's analysis of the relationship between the home and the cultivation of innovativeness, we can see that the role of a favorable home environment in the cultivation of children's innovativeness cannot be easily ignored.

4. Open and Democratic Principles of Practice in Innovative Education

A promotion of innovative education must persevere in principles of practice that are stratified, foundational, demonstrative, open, democratic, and inspirational.

Innovative education has already become the main theme of school education in the knowledge economy era. How then are we to successfully promote and implement innovative education? I believe that we must proceed from the following principles.

The Stratification of Innovative Education

The stratification of innovative education refers to targeting people at different levels in education. It requires the establishment of different educational objectives and different educational means and content for innovative education. Specifically speaking, it is targeting the features of students at different stages of their education (primary, secondary, and tertiary) to carry out innovative education that is adaptable.

The cultivation of an innovative awareness and innovative abilities does not happen overnight. It requires laying out a solid foundation during early childhood and primary school. Carrying out early innovative education for children assists in the cultivation of their innovative awareness and innovative spirit and promotes their early proficiency and accomplishments. In regard to the cultivation of children's innovativeness, we should proceed from the following few aspects

First, place an emphasis on cultivating children's powers of observation. From a young age, children possess a strong instinct and need to come into contact with and explore objectives. This instinct and need is the basis for innovative thinking, and it should be taken advantage of to improve their powers of observation. Children can have new discoveries only with a basis in observations.

Second, place an emphasis on protecting children's curiosity. Curiosity is a huge driving force for scientific inventions. Without curiosity and a thirst for knowledge, we would not be able to create inventions and innovations that are immensely valuable to society and humanity. Because children are limited in terms of their knowledge, they very easily demonstrate a passionate curiosity toward things, and they will explore things and discover problems using their own methods. As educators, we should pay attention to protecting children's curiosity and spirit of exploration and stimulate their desire for knowledge. This is the basis for the development of innovativeness.

Third, emphasize developing students' imaginations. One's childhood is the period of time in which the imagination is expressed most actively. A child's imagination is the basis for the child's activities in exploration and innovation. All activities in innovation begin with an innovative imagination.

Fourth, place an emphasis on cultivating children's practical abilities. Professor Chen Ning Yang once pointed out: "In terms of practical interests and abilities, Chinese children are distinctly not as adept as European and American children. This is mainly due to the fact that they do not have the opportunity to be hands-on." It is only through some realistic hands-on activities that the results of innovative thinking can become substantial while at the same time enabling their innovative thinking to be even more in line with reality and to possess actual results. Additionally, it can allow them to see the results of their own innovations, to experience for themselves the joys of innovation, and to further stimulate their awareness of innovative exploration.

Fifth, stress the educational function of the use of games. Games are the main ways of training children to innovate. Through the use of games, we can develop children's knowledge and improve their ability to adapt. For example, when children are playing games such as "play house" and "building blocks," it is very easy to put innovative thinking to use. However, many parents and teachers do not truly value or take advantage of the role that games play in cultivating innovativeness. Our country's famous cartoonist Bi Keguan pointed out that "children's games contain too much creativity. It is unfortunate that many parents spoil the fun of this and obliterate most of a child's creativity!"

Carrying out the proper innovative education for students during their secondary schooling is a crucial period for the cultivation of students' innovative abilities. Secondary school the best time for the development of an adolescent's intellectual ability and is also the main period for mental and physical development and the formation of worldviews. In this period we should place the cultivation of their innovative spirit in a prominent position. At this stage, the focus and methods of innovative education should be consistent with the characteristics of secondary school students.

First, we must stimulate their desire for knowledge and innovation. Extensive knowledge is the basis for the formation of innovativeness, and adolescents in secondary school already possess the ability to accept large amounts of knowledge. Therefore, we must stimulate their desire to seek out knowledge through various methods. This desire is an important motivator for promoting people to carry out innovative activities. At the same time, we must also increase the training of their innovative awareness.

Second, we must attach importance to the training of secondary students' study habits and learning abilities, which are an important guarantee for the development of innovativeness. Only with the establishment of good study habits and abilities as a basis can secondary school students efficiently accept knowledge. Furthermore, it lays the foundations for advancing into higher levels of schooling and entering society. Good study habits and learning abilities mainly include the ability to self-study, powers of observation, the ability to ponder and reflect, the ability to imagine, the ability to be creative, and the habit of using all these abilities.

Third, attach importance to the cultivation of creative feelings. The feelings of secondary school students, such as love, their sense of beauty, envy, and so on are extremely abundant, and these can all be used as sources of motivation for innovation. Tolstoy repeatedly spoke from an artistic perspective about the role that passion plays in the creative process. He said: "Without passion, creation would be impossible. For any literary work to be written well, it should be sung from the writer's soul." Many teachers place great emphasis on enabling students to be intensely influenced by emotions, leading them to fully realize their potential, develop their intelligence and wisdom, and liberate their passion for learning and innovation.

Fourth, attach value to the cultivation of the special talents and interests of secondary school students. During the period of their secondary schooling, the characteristics of students' personalities have already been developed relatively distinctly and prominently. Teachers should pay attention to educating "students with special or irregular talents" according to the students' circumstances, give advice appropriate to their situation, teach in line with the students' abilities to enable these students' special abilities and interests to be fully tapped into and developed, and provide good educational conditions for the cultivation of innovative talents. Many historical examples of producing great innovative talents can prove this point. Holistic development does not mean balanced development. Offering students with particular talents, especially "students with special or irregular talents," a relaxed educational environment and special policies is an integral part of cultivating students with innovative abilities.

Fifth, develop various forms of extracurricular activities that are conducive to the cultivation of innovative abilities. Organizing science and technology groups, launching small invention contests, and so on will enable students to combine rational knowledge and perceptual practices, and undoubtedly these will be greatly beneficial to expanding innovative thinking. In 1954, Japan founded many "Sunday Invention Schools" and later on they also founded organizations such as "invention clubs for boys and girls." After students went through the learning and training process, the efficiency rate of inventions and innovations was increased manifold.

Colleges and universities are the main forces for the promotion of knowledge and technological innovations in our country. The importance of carrying out innovative education in colleges and universities is self-evident. The innovative education in colleges and universities must also form their own characteristics in accordance with their own features. One important means is to enhance the combined efforts of teaching and research and to focus on the cultivation of students' innovative abilities.

For a long time, we thought more highly of "lectures, teachings, and explanations" that "only elaborated on the theories of predecessors without offering any original ideas of one's own" and involved "sitting and prattling about general principles" and by contrast, students' creative and innovative spirits were relatively ignored. This is obviously incompatible with the educational function of contemporary colleges and universities. From a global point of view, the large majority of countries place great emphasis in colleges and universities on the integration of education and society and the integration of colleges and universities and industries. The high-tech industrial parks in many countries and regions such as America's Silicon Valley, Japan's Tsukuba, and Taiwan's Xinzhu City have several or even dozens of universities to act as technical support.

Therefore, we must increase the combined efforts of colleges, universities, and enterprises and colleges, universities, and research institutions, enabling students in the practice of research and production to cultivate practical innovative abilities. This is not only conducive to the development of our country's research work, but at the same time it is also a new way of cultivating innovative talents to face the knowledge economy era. Of course, apart from focusing on students' direct participation in innovative activities for research and production, there is also a need to focus on the cultivation of university students' overall quality as well as the training of innovative thinking and methods.

The Foundational Nature of Innovative Education

Innovativeness is not created out of thin air. Its emergence and development requires a solid foundation. This can be understood from two perspectives: a physiological basis and a knowledge basis. In human physiology, the structure of the brain can be divided into the left brain and the right brain. The left brain is related to abstract thinking, symbolic relationships, and logical analyses of details. It carries out the functions of abstract thinking and summarizations. On the other hand, the right brain has the advantage of perceptual awareness and carries out the function of visual thinking. Scientific research has shown that people's innovative abilities are closely related to the right brain and can only attain a balanced development with the functions of both the left and right hemispheres of the brain. Only with the two sides of the brain closely coordinating with each other can people's innovative abilities gain a high degree of development.

However, current educational theory and educational practices are basically all to do with the left brain. From primary school education to postgraduate education, no matter if it is in terms of educational content or teaching methods, verbal thinking is emphasized and nonverbal thinking is taken lightly; abstract thinking is emphasized and visual thinking is taken lightly. However, these forms of thinking that are taken lightly or ignored are precisely the factors that are extremely important in innovativeness and are important functions of the right brain.

Therefore, innovative education must set forth from people's physiological potential by continuously developing the left brain's functions at the same time as it pays attention to developing the potential of the right brain, such as attaching importance to music, art, sport, and so on. More use of intuitive teaching and a variety of extracurricular activities, especially extracurricular science and technology activities, allows the two hemispheres of a student's brain to healthily and harmoniously develop. By proceeding from a basis in physiology, it lays the foundation for the development of students' innovative abilities. This is the reason why 37 states in the United States gave children free tapes for playing music and Israel allows kindergarten children to play computer games.

The formation and development of innovativeness still relies on a solid basis in deep knowledge. Without knowledge, it would be difficult for people to form correct views, and analyses of problems would have no basis. Even if people were to have some inventions and innovations, they would have lost their foundations. Knowledge can be divided into the two aspects of general knowledge and expert knowledge. Innovative education raises high demands for both.

America once carried out an analytic survey of 1,131 scientists on aspects such as their theses, results, promotions, and so on. They discovered that the majority of these talented people gained success due to their broad range of knowledge and that very few of them were proficient in just one specialty. Therefore, America advocated for simultaneously strengthening foundational professional learning and promoting an "encyclopedia-style" education. Because of the influence of the former Soviet Union's strict subject classification for arts and sciences, students' learning in our country (especially in higher education) is increasingly specialized and narrow, which produces a very negative impact on the broadening of one's horizons in terms of knowledge.

Of course, at the same time we emphasize the knowledge aspect, we must also place an emphasis on the deepening of expert knowledge so as to cultivate new kinds of talents who possess both specialized and broad knowledge and skills and properly handle the relationship between "broad" and "restricted" knowledge, to use restrictions to control broad knowledge and to have "one specialty and many abilities." This is the basis for cultivating innovative thinking and abilities.

The Demonstrative Nature of Innovative Education

The so-called demonstrative nature refers educators' own innovative awareness, thinking, and other factors that they should use to influence and drive the formation and development of innovativeness for those being educated. In a certain sense it can be said that only innovative teachers can implement innovative education and cultivate innovative students.

Research results show that teachers with a relatively strong degree of innovativeness are, to a much greater degree, able to cultivate students with innovativeness when compared with teachers with relatively lower degrees of innovativeness. This is because in order to have teachers be even better at cultivating students' innovativeness than they are now requires teachers' methods to be even more flexible, more innovative, and more experimental than current practices. Teachers with relatively higher degrees of innovativeness will take the initiative to explore and innovate in this area and cultivate students with relatively high degrees of innovativeness by using good innovative teaching methods.

In addition, the innovative spirit that teachers themselves possess can also greatly boost students' passion for innovation. Teachers are likely to discover the principles for forming and developing innovativeness through their own innovative practices to provide innovative education with the most direct and most profound experiences and to establish innovative education on the basis of science. Thus, they will be consciously combining knowledge transferral with innovative thinking during the teaching process, discovering students' innovative potential, seizing the crucial points in students' innovative thinking, and carrying out a multi-layered, multiangled cultivation of students' innovative abilities and innovative personalities.

The Openness of Innovative Education

Traditional education has demonstrated a closed-off nature in many aspects. This, to a certain degree, has hindered the cultivation of students' innovativeness. The openness in innovative education referred to here can be understood from the following few aspects.

First, the openness of innovative education is reflected in its teaching content. Currently, the contents of many courses are obviously outdated and are not conducive to having students accept new information. Teaching content also needs to reflect the "Three Orientations" as proposed by Deng Xiaoping; it has to reflect a relevance of the times and inventiveness, have teaching materials on new scientific research results and new scientific concepts promptly compiled, and have a fundamental concept of the objective material world as being one in which teachers help students to establish developments and changes and rather than make them isolated and silent, and thus lead students to explore even newer knowledge and cultivate their innovative spirit.

Second the openness of innovative education should also be reflected in terms of its international context. The two major traits of a knowledge economy are that it is knowledge based and globalized. During the process of our country's implementation of innovative education, we must emphasize exchange and cooperation between countries; fully digest and absorb every country's advanced science and technology, education, and culture; and lay out the foundations for our country's innovative education. In addition, we must also establish an international innovative awareness, actively participate in international activities for innovation, and thus have our own innovative achievements.

In addition, the openness of innovative education is also expressed in the openness of modern educators as well as in aspects such as the openness of teaching methods and means and so on.

The Democratic Nature of Innovative Education

The principle of innovative education's democratic nature is that it emphasizes the formation of a democratic atmosphere that is conducive to innovation through the process of education, in terms of aspects such as teacher-student relationships, the teaching environment, the degree of freedom in student development, and so on. Among the abovementioned content on an innovative environment and atmosphere, this point was also raised. Here, we will mainly discuss this point from the micro perspective of the detailed teaching process.

Traditional education emphasizes "the dignity of the teacher" and "the teacher's authority." It is precisely these concepts and ideas that have produced great obstacles for the development of students' innovativeness. German Gottfried Heinelt proposed: "Teachers who want to promote the innovativeness of their students must advocate a cooperative socially integrated style. This is also the development of a collective innovativeness." In innovative education, in the process of classroom teaching, teachers should mainly take on the role of organizing, guiding, controlling, and explaining. They have to change the bad teaching practices—the teacher alone having all the say in the classroom, and rote learning—and form a lively student-centered learning situation. Doing so will easily arouse the students' passion for innovation. Torrance proposed several requirements of teachers for cultivating students' innovativeness, namely, five democratic suggestions such as to respect questions that are different, respect concepts that are different, give students opportunities to learn in which marks are not counted, and so on. Stanford University's president Professor Gerhard Casper, speaking about the success of Stanford University and Silicon Valley, said he believed that a relaxed and free learning environment is one of the important reasons for the cultivation of students' innovativeness.

In addition, the democratic nature should be reflected in the teachers themselves. In educational management, the image of teachers who are too centralized and too rigidly controlled needs to change, enabling teachers' teaching activities to become innovative activities, not just in name only. Only by doing this can the abovementioned demonstrative principles be realized.

The Inspirational Nature of Innovative Education

The principle of this inspirational nature is mainly in regard to targeting the teaching methods in innovative education. Innovation itself is an independent activity. A teacher's main role in the process of innovative education lies in inspiring and guiding students.

Among traditional teaching methods, the one-sided emphasis on tedious exercises, blindly copying notes, and excessive reciting, as well as the particular bias toward exams based on rote learning, attaches importance only to the memorization of knowledge and neglects the understanding and digestion of knowledge. It hinders the development of students' initiative as well as their thinking, resulting in a great reduction in their ability to shift knowledge, let alone develop their innovative thinking and innovative abilities. Very early on in our country, in *The Book of Rites, On Learning* the following was written: "Thus in his teaching, he leads and does not drag; he strengthens and does not discourage; he opens the way but does not conduct to the end without the learner's own efforts. Leading and not dragging produces harmony. Strengthening and not discouraging makes attainment easy. Opening the way and not conducting to the end makes the learner thoughtful. He who produces such harmony, easy attainment, and thoughtfulness may be pronounced a skillful teacher." This emphasizes focusing on the important significance of enlightening students and cultivating their independence, and for the present day cultivation of innovative talents, these words still act as an important reference. Only through heuristic teaching can we mobilize students' initiative and self-consciousness, arouse their active thinking, and cultivate their ability to analyze and solve problems. Under the teacher's guidance and inspiration, students will seek out rules for themselves and make new discoveries and innovations.

The different aspects discussed above on the implementation of innovative education are the principles that innovative education should comply with. Apart from the above points, there are also some aspects that need to be focused on such as reforming the present assessment system that is centered around exams, adopting modernized teaching methods that are conducive to the development of innovative thinking, and so on. The implementation of innovative education is a long-term and complex task; only by further deepening educational theory and constantly improving in our practice of education can our country's innovative education become increasingly more mature.

In short, innovation is the force that pushes humanity to constantly grow and always move forward and an inexhaustible source of national prosperity. The key to whether or not we are able to stand among the other countries of the world, stand at the forefront of history, and place ourselves at the height of science and technology lies in the level of our ability to innovate. Furthermore, all of this deeply relies on whether the country and nation's innovative education can be smoothly implemented. In meeting the challenges of the knowledge economy, innovative education historically takes up the great mission of knowledge and technological innovation and the cultivation of innovative talents!

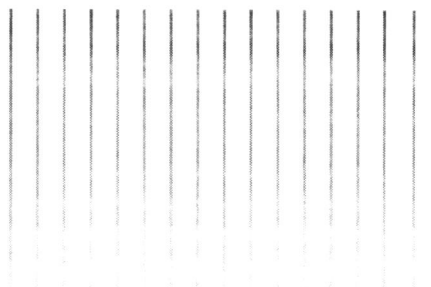

13

The Cohesiveness of Education and the Chinese People

During a time of increasingly fierce world competition in a country's comprehensive national strength, national cohesiveness is gradually beginning to be regarded as an important condition for the formation and development of comprehensive national strength and is an important guarantee of a country's political stability, economic development, and social progress. Enhancing national cohesiveness has its foundations in education. Education plays an important role in raising the level of the entire nation's thinking and understanding, forming a new era of common national values and a group consciousness as well as possessing a rich contemporary national spirit. Improving the entire nation's scientific and cultural quality and social productivity through education, especially undertaking the development of education for ethnic minority groups, has prominent significance for the formation of national cohesiveness for the present-day Chinese people.

1. Enhancement of National Cohesiveness to Improve Comprehensive National Strength

National cohesiveness is an important part of comprehensive national strength. It is a great force that drives a country to live and multiply, to resist aggression, and to prosper; it is also an important symbol of national prosperity

The strength or weakness of national cohesiveness to a great extent influences all aspects of development such as a country's political, economic, and cultural development. As a U.S. representative of the realist school of thought, Hans Joachim Morgenthau, believes, essential factors of national strength include not only geographical conditions, natural resources, industrial capacity, armament status, population, and diplomatic and government qualities, but also national characteristics including such aspects as national traditions, national cohesiveness, and so on. In terms of the issue of comprehensive national strength, Professor Cheng Chaoze of Shanghai University of Finance and Economics proposed that comprehensive national strength is an open and dynamic system; it includes both the internal "hard" parameters of national land, population, resources, economy, science and technology, and national defense as well as the internal "soft" parameters of strategic objectives, national cohesiveness, and so on, as well as the "collaborative" parameters of the social system, elements of the government, and levels of government policy.[1] In addition, there are many other scholars who in their analyses of comprehensive national strength also mention the essential factor of national cohesiveness and furthermore place this essential factor of national cohesiveness in a position of importance among the developmental indicators of comprehensive national strength. Reality and numerous historical facts are eloquent testimony that national cohesiveness indeed has an important, fundamental position in the development of comprehensive national strength. The present competition among the nations of the world, to a great extent, is expressed in the strength or weakness of their national cohesiveness. Therefore, in Jiang Zemin's speech at the Third National Education Work Conference, he first proposed the idea of treating national cohesiveness as an important part of comprehensive national strength. He also proposed the important role of developing elevated national spirits in promoting the country's economic development and social progress. Furthermore, we must treat national cohesiveness as a great force for driving a country to live and multiply, resist aggression, and prosper, as well as a symbol of national prosperity.

The Chinese nation is a great nation that possesses a long history. The history of the development of the Chinese nation is actually also one of the continuous integration of all ethnic groups, a nation united to work toward creating a new era of history for the Chinese nation. It is precisely because the Chinese nation possesses a strong national cohesiveness that it can carry out new processes in the history of the development of the Chinese people. Whether it be in the past or the present, the cohesiveness of the Chinese nation is a source of life and spiritual power for the continuous prosperity of the Chinese nation.

The reason why the Chinese nation has been able to work hard and endure hardships during various stages of history, to possess a dauntless national spirit, to constantly enrich and develop the wealth of material and spiritual culture of the Chinese nation, thus promote the progress of civilization; the reason why the Chinese nation is always able to be united during various stages of history to oppose ethnic separatism and national division, to rise up and resist foreign aggression, to firmly safeguard the sovereignty and independence of the Chinese nation, to dare to carry out brave and tenacious struggles against reactionary classes, reactionary forces, and reactionary social systems that oppose historical development and social progress, even at the expense of the lives of countless outstanding sons and daughters to promote the advance of the motherland toward prosperity and strength . . . is the fact that the Chinese nation possesses a profound and strong national cohesiveness and great national spirit that supports the ideas and behaviors of the Chinese people. This type of powerful national cohesiveness is gradually formed, developed, and thoroughly tempered by the history of the Chinese people. This great national cohesiveness exhibits a special status and importance even more in the present.

Our country is a multiethnic country. To realize that the modernization of socialism is the common goal and common task of the people of all ethnic groups and to accomplish this great cause, we must have unity and cooperation among all the people of all ethnic groups and have a stable and united environment.

It can be said that national unity is the basis for the unity and stability of a country. A strong cohesiveness between all ethnic groups is the driving force and source of a country's development. It is precisely because the Chinese people have always had these types of unparalleled advantages and spiritual wealth, which includes a love of the motherland, a firm belief and glorious tradition in safeguarding unity, a powerful team spirit and national cohesiveness, that the Chinese nation is still able to maintain social stability and to carry out rectification of errors, reforms, and opening up in the world's ever-changing international environment. This is the fundamental reason why our country is able to gradually improve and develop its comprehensive national strength in the world.

As long as the people of all ethnic groups consciously safeguard and constantly enhance the national cohesiveness of the Chinese nation, no matter what turmoils and upheavals are in the world, they will not be able to shake the Chinese nation's great wall of steel. Therefore, our country's continuous strengthening and enhancing of the cohesiveness of the Chinese nation in the new century is not only a trend of the times and one of the tides of history but also a necessary condition for the great prosperity and revival of the Chinese nation in the twenty-first century.

2. Promotion of Consensus and Identity Between All Ethnic Groups to Enhance National Cohesiveness

The formation and development of the Chinese nation's cohesiveness hinges upon the consensual feeling the Chinese people of all ethnic groups have toward the national values and national spirit, their sense of identity toward developmental goals of the Chinese people, a sense of destiny that is closely related to the Chinese people, and a sense of belonging in sharing their joys and woes with people of all ethnic groups, as well as a sense of responsibility and a sense of duty toward devoting themselves to the interests of the nation.

From the connotations of national cohesiveness, according to the definition of group cohesiveness given by American psychologist Leon Festinger, national cohesiveness should enable members of the nation to maintain cooperation within the national group or enable people to gather the feelings within the national group. Precisely speaking, it is a kind of feeling that enables its members to feel emotionally closer to some people in comparison to other people.[2] From this sense, we believe that the formation and expression of Chinese national cohesiveness should include the following four aspects.

First is the consensual feeling Chinese people have toward Chinese national values and national spirit. The national spirit is a sort of pursuit of values and spiritual support that is accumulated through the nation's history, handed down from generation to generation, and is constantly developing. By pursuing the attributes of their common values, people will always use designated methods to achieve the goal of a pursuit of values. When these "designated methods" form nationalized and relatively stable traits, they will constitute value-oriented national culture.[3] The formation of national cohesiveness, ultimately, is established on the basis of common values. Without common values, the entire nation would have no common direction, goals, and pursuits and would not have a common ideal of uniting all the ethnic groups in China. When the nation forms common values, then the cohesiveness of the Chinese nation will have a basis; under the guidance and norms of common values, a collective consciousness will be formed; the stronger the collective consciousness, the stronger a nation's cohesiveness will be.

Second is the sense of identity that all Chinese ethnic groups treat as a developmental goal for the Chinese nation. A sense of identity, the same goal for the formation of national members and the development of a nation, is an indispensable condition for enhancing national cohesiveness. To have common national development goals is a banner that calls out for the formation of national cohesiveness. It will greatly stimulate the high morale of the members of the nation and be part of the enthusiasm related to the process of realizing its objectives.

During the Anti-Japanese War, the national common objective of "defeating Japanese imperialism, achieving independence of the Chinese nation" had once called out and rallied people of all ethnic groups in the country. It formed a great wall of steel for the Chinese nation, crushed the ambitions of the Japanese imperialist occupation of Chinese territory, and achieved sovereignty and independence for the Chinese nation. Currently, our Party proposes to establish socialism with Chinese characteristics, treating our country's construction and transformation into a prosperous, democratic, culturally advanced, modernized, socialist country as a common objective and ideal of all ethnic groups in our country. It is precisely under the guidance and call for common national development objectives and ideals that all members of the Chinese nation are able to actively throw themselves into the modernization of socialism, to form a strongly cohesive army for the construction of socialism, and to continuously open up new phases for the construction of socialism.

The Chinese nation has a strong sense of pride. This national pride, in practice, allows every member to express a strong sense of destiny that is closely related to the nation as well as a sense of belonging, to share their woes and joys with all of the nation's ethnic groups. It enables every member of the Chinese nation through the practice of national pride to know that the nation's rise and fall and development will inevitably influence the happiness and development of every individual within all ethnic groups. Furthermore, it is the need to fuse ethnic individuals and their affiliated ethnic groups into one single entity in the subconscious mind, to emotionally experience expressions of pride or the appropriate feelings of joy, pain, grief, and indignation for the rises and falls of the Chinese nation. As individuals live together for a long period of time with other members of their same ethnic groups, they will gradually form a suitable and particular ethnic language for their lifestyles, values, and ethics, as well as behaviors that they are mutually familiar with and able to calmly express. There will be no suspicions and no discrimination between people and they will be able to gain self-esteem.

On the contrary, if they were to go and live with other ethnic groups, especially in the initial stage, because they have not become accustomed to the ethnic group in terms of their physiology and psychology, it will cause frustrations in love.[4] At this time, the expression of a sense of belonging to one's ethnicity and a shared sense of destiny is particularly strongly. This is one of the important reasons why many Chinese expats fervently hope for the prosperity and success of the Chinese nation. Each member of the Chinese nation possesses a sense of destiny that is closely related to the Chinese nation as well as a sense of belonging to all of the nation's ethnic groups. These should be the important conditions and symbols of the formation of Chinese national cohesiveness.

Finally, the cohesiveness of the Chinese nation is also expressed in its members' sense of responsibility and duty to devote themselves to the causes of the Chinese nation and furthermore, to put this sense of duty to the nation's development into practical actions. One important reason why the Chinese nation has stretched uninterrupted over several millennia and has been able to develop into one of the most dynamic and most promising nations in the world today lies in the fact that every member of the nation is able to relate one's own life to the rise and fall of the nation and express this sense of responsibility and duty through practical actions. Fan Zhongyan once put forward these words: "Be the first to feel concern about the State affairs and the last to enjoy oneself." Gu Yanwu advocated: "The rise and fall of the nation is the concern of every citizen." Both reflect that the outstanding sons and daughters and people with noble ideals relate their lives to the life and death of the nation. In the Chinese nation's history of development, there have been many people who devoted themselves to the nation and performed heroic feats—these feats are inseparable from their sense of responsibility and duty to the nation. This is a direct driving force for the formation of national cohesiveness and is also the most realistic manifestation of national cohesiveness.

3. The Role and Impact of Education on Enhancing National Cohesiveness

For the promotion of national cohesiveness, education plays a fundamental role of dissemination, infiltration, and integration. It plays a crucial role in influencing the formation of a nation's awareness of self-improvement, a sense of duty to the nation's revival and development, and expression of national pride.

The formation and development of the Chinese nation's cohesiveness has important significance and plays a role in improving our country's comprehensive strength and achieving the great revival of the Chinese nation. What, then, is the basis for promoting the formation and development of national cohesiveness? It is education. Jiang Zemin, in his speech for the Third National Work Conference, noted with great foresight: "In today's world, the competition of comprehensive national strength is increasingly reflected in competitions of economic strength, the strength of a country's national defence and national cohesiveness. Regardless of which aspect of strength is being enhanced, education still has a fundamental status." Jiang Zemin's claims, no matter whether in history or in the construction of present-day socialism, have had their validity and scientific nature proven. In the developmental process of the Chinese nation's history, in the formation and development of national cohesiveness, education has always played a role in dissemination, infiltration, and integration. Our country's feudal society lasted for several thousand years and formed a complete feudal education system. Fundamentally speaking, the feudal education system served to maintain the rule of feudal emperors and the landowning class. Therefore, feudal educational ideology and theory, which represented Confucian education, advocated the feudal ethics and moral education that taught the Three Cardinal Guides and Five Constant Virtues, loyalty to the sovereign and nation and no rebellion against the emperor. This mainly started out as a maintenance of the feudal rule, a way of cultivating the talents that they needed and to impart the art of "governance."

However, from another perspective, we can see that these educational systems and ideologies advocated by Confucianism at the same time also have a positive affect on national unity and stability and play a definite role in promoting the formation of national cohesiveness. For example, as early as more than 2,000 years ago, our country's great educator Confucius focused on expounding the unification of educational ideologies:

When good government prevails in the empire, ceremonies, music, and punitive military expeditions proceed from the son of Heaven. When bad government prevails in the empire, ceremonies, music, and punitive military expeditions proceed from the princes. When these things proceed from the princes, as a rule, the cases will be few in which they do not lose their power in ten generations. When they proceed from the great officers of the princes, as a rule, the cases will be few in which they do not lose their power in five generations. When the subsidiary ministers of the great officers hold in their grasp the orders of the state, as a rule the cases will be few in which they do not lose their power in three generations.

When right principles prevail in the kingdom, government will not be in the hands of the great officers. When right principles prevail in the kingdom, there will be no discussions among the common people.[5]

This idea of Confucius greatly inspired and influenced the thoughts on national unity of Mencius's "settled by one," "the whole world as one" strongly advocated by Xun Zi, as well as "one rule is a government, two is disorder" put forward by Lu Buwei, and had a positive effect on safeguarding national independence and promoting national unification in ancient China.

On Learning, our country's earliest educational classic, also made its intentions clear from the outset when it proposed the educational ideological stance of "when establishing states and governing the people, make instruction and schools a primary object." Furthermore, in *The Great Learning*, among the "eight steps" of education in great learning that are proposed, "First free yourself of wrong-doings and evil thoughts, then bring order to your family, after which govern your people well and the land is yours" can be treated as an objective of Confucian education. This targeted the strife that engulfed the lands after the end of the Qin Dynasty and it attempted to solve the issue through education. This reflected demands of some of the landowning class for an end to the social unrest and their desire for the lands to be governed justly as well as for national integration and unity. Through the long-term influence of ancient China's education, a large cohort of outstanding patriots emerged in China's history and left behind many poems that were full of patriotic feelings, such as Yue Fei's "To recover our mountains and rivers / Then report to the emperor" and Wen Tianxiang's "None since the advent of time have escaped death, may my loyalty forever illuminate the annals of history," and so on. Their great patriotic feats at the same time influence and educate generations after generations of outstanding sons and daughters of the Chinese nation, directly propelling the formation and development of national cohesiveness.

With the start of the Opium War in 1840, the big powers of the West invaded and occupied Chinese territory by military force, and after they caused China to be reduced to a semicolonial, semifeudal society, the Chinese nation was subjected to being looted countless times by the big powers of the West and was on the verge of complete destruction. Internally, the Chinese nation had no democracy, and externally it had no background of sovereign rights. Out of a strong sense of duty to the Chinese nation and concern for the fate and future outlook of the country and its people, some people with advanced learning began exploring ways to save the country and its people in these new conditions. They aroused the awakening and cohesiveness of the entire nation to save China from a perilous situation. Among these ideas, "education for national salvation" had mainstream status at the time.

Looking broadly at the developmental course of modern Chinese education, whether it be trends in thinking such as pragmatic education, reform education, democratic revolutionary education, Westernization education, or scientific education, most of the educational theories and perspectives were focused on the macro aspects and explored how to reform China's preexisting education system, eliminate the ignorance of the nation's people, cultivate genuine talented people, unite all the Chinese nation's sons and daughters to rebel against the oppression and humiliation of the Western powers, and achieve a Chinese nation that strives to become stronger and become self-supporting.

For example, Kang Youwei and Liang Qichao, the famous representatives of the reforming movement, attached great importance to the social role that education plays and treated engaging in educational tasks to be an important means of undertaking political activities and saving as well revitalizing the Chinese nation. They strove to awaken the country through education, to reform the country, and to cultivate new talents who would politically reform and strengthen the country so that it could become self-supporting. This is again similar to the ideas put forward by Yan Fu, famous representative of the "education for national salvation" school of thought who proposed that the root of the Chinese people's "cumulative weakness and poverty" lay in the fact that "the people's wisdom is already low, their morals are already weak." If this situation was not changed, then according to the law of "natural selection," the Chinese people were bound to become slaves of imperialism.

In Yan Fu's educational thinking, the development of education is the basis and the first condition for the recovery of a country and nation. He strove to "strengthen people's power, to enlighten people's minds, and to refresh people's virtues" through education in order to improve the overall quality of the Chinese nation and furthermore to inspire patriotic fervor, a sense of national pride, a sense of national duty, and a sense of national responsibility in the members of the Chinese nation. Practice has proven that Yan Fu's thoughts on education for national salvation did indeed play a significant role in encouraging the process of forming Chinese national cohesiveness.

In addition, many thinkers who are part of the school of thought for bourgeois revolutionaries, such as Sun Yat-sen, Zou Rong, and Chen Tianhua, clearly expressed the ideological orientation of education for national salvation, such as Zou Rong's *Revolution Army* and Chen Tianhua's *A Sudden Look Back* and *An Alarm to Awaken the Age*, which are all very influential works. They strove to use the strengthening of education concerning the national crisis of their country to stimulate in the entire Chinese nation the sense of urgency needed to save itself and thus promote the formation of the cohesiveness of the Chinese nation.

Education during the "May Fourth Movement" also played a key role in the process of promoting national cohesiveness. The May Fourth Movement was a huge turning point in ideological and cultural education and the reform movement. Its slogans on "democracy and science" awakened the Chinese nation from a deep sleep and reshaped the Chinese people's national spirit, causing the nation's self-awareness to gradually mature. Especially influential were a cohort of vanguard fighters for ideological and cultural education with Lu Xun as their representative, who with sharp strokes of their pens denounced the darkness of the old China and clearly showed the direction of development for the Chinese nation.

These people greatly inspired the Chinese people's sense of responsibility toward the development of the Chinese nation and furthermore started a new upsurge in national cohesiveness.

Under the influence of the May Fourth Movement's cultural spirit, many educational campaign thoughts and ideological trends emerged in China, designed to rouse a national awakening and to achieve national self-reliance. For example, China's modern representative of rural education, Y. C. James Yen, believed that the root cause of the Chinese nation's poverty and backwardness was the fact that the majority of civilians lacked knowledge and did not have the consciousness of cooperation. Therefore, Yen proposed "four major educations" and "three major methods" and strove to achieve cohesion and revitalization of the Chinese nation through improving the ideological and cultural qualities of Chinese farmers. Although his theory was exploited by the Kuomintang (KMT), from an objective point of view it still has a certain positive significance for the raising of the national consciousness and the overall quality of the Chinese people.

One important reason why the Chinese nation in modern times has had unprecedented national cohesiveness and unity lies in the fact that through advanced ideas on dissemination and education, the national consciousness, sense of national crisis, national pride, and sense of responsibility of the Chinese nation was raised, enabling the Chinese nation to awaken from a deep slumber. It greatly inspired the patriotic enthusiasm of members of the Chinese nation; thus they consciously join in on the extent of amalgamation and integration of the nation's people, truly realizing a social mental state with a high degree of cohesiveness in which the entire nation draw breath as one and have a common destiny. It can be said that without the education and dissemination for the Chinese nation, as well as improving the entire nation's quality through education, this consciousness of national self-reliance and the sense of responsibility toward national revival would be difficult to form, let alone an unprecedented upsurge in national cohesiveness.

Practice has proven that the current process of establishing socialist modernization cannot be separated from the unity and cooperation of the people of all ethnic groups and levels of education, which, just as before, plays an important role in promoting national cohesiveness. The history of the development of the Chinese nation is the continuous integration of all ethnic groups, with the use of unparalleled national cohesiveness to overcome all difficulties and to create a better future for the nation. Education is the essential basic condition and catalyst for the cohesiveness of the entire nation.

4. Strengthening Ideological Education to Enhance National Cohesiveness

To enhance national cohesiveness, there is a need to strengthen ideological education, to improve the levels of thinking and understanding of the people of all ethnic groups and to form a national spirit for the new era that has shared national values and a collective consciousness, as well as being rich in the flavor of the times.

The formation of national cohesiveness needs shared national values, national spirit, and common national development goals, as well as a sense of duty and responsibility toward the nation. Only through the special means of education can these psychological factors be successful in pervading the consciousness of people's thinking, especially with regard to ideological and political education.

At present, the common ideals of the people of all ethnic groups are to build our country into a prosperous, democratic, culturally advanced, modern, socialist country and to achieve the great rejuvenation of the Chinese nation. These common ideals and beliefs gradually managed to penetrate the consciousness of every member of the Chinese nation through the channel of education, thereby enabling the entire nation, under the guidance of common ideals, to overcome all difficulties, find strength in the unity of their wills, and create miracles for the Chinese nation in the new era.

Jiang Zemin said when fully affirming the significant role of education in the promotion of national cohesiveness in contemporary socialist construction that, after the severe floods of 1998, it was precisely because of Party leadership and the organization of hundreds and thousands of soldiers and civilians to collaboratively fight and tenaciously struggle that they were able to achieve great victory over the floods, furthermore forming a great spirit to fight against floods. This was not only a test of combat effectiveness for the whole country but also a test of national cohesiveness. In the face of such huge national cohesiveness, any difficulties, obstacles, and enemies can be overcome. Jiang Zemin believed that those heart-stirring, mighty, and majestic flood rescue scenes would be impossible to find in Western countries, and furthermore, that this huge national cohesiveness comes from the Chinese nation's fine traditions and from the noble ideals of the Communist Party of China, the superiority of the socialist system, and from a patriotic, collectivist, socialist, and Marxist education. A correct world outlook, an outlook on life, the establishment of values, the carrying forward of fine national traditions, the formation and consolidation of common ideals and spiritual pillars of support, and the continuous improvements of scientific and cultural levels are all inseparable from the work of education. These are also important foundations and content for our national cohesiveness. Therefore, Jiang Zemin required that all levels and types of educational institutions and all educators should assume the solemn duty of enhancing China's comprehensive national strength, including the strength of national cohesiveness. According to the spirit of Jiang Zemin's speech, in the process of promoting national cohesiveness and enhancing ideological and political educational work, we must concentrate on the following four aspects of ideological education.

Strengthening Patriotic, Collectivist, and Socialist Education

There is a need to strengthen patriotic, collectivist, and socialist education. This is the core of ideological and political education and is also a guarantee of the formation of national cohesiveness. The motherland, in the meaning of nationality, is the unity of various natural and sociocultural environments where the people of the nation exist and develop. The psychological occurrence of patriotism has it as its solid foundation and source of uniqueness; it is deeply rooted in the cultivation of natural human emotions and national psychology. Through patriotic education, we can evoke people's sense of belonging toward and pride in a nation, form national cohesiveness, and stimulate their sense of responsibility and spirit of dedication toward their own nation. The Chinese nation has a long history of civilization and the Chinese people have lived and multiplied in the land of China for many generations, creating a brilliant material and spiritual civilization and forming unique historical and cultural traditions; these provide our implementation of patriotic education with some rare teaching materials. Furthermore, the Chinese nation has a long history of patriotic ideology, which has popular support and possesses great cohesiveness and vitality. In the past, we have relied on the patriotic spirit of education to enable the Chinese nation to get through many crises. In the present age, patriotic education is still a major way to promote national cohesiveness. Advocating the spirit of patriotism to all members of the Chinese nation plays an important role in casting the soul of the nation, revitalizing the national spirit and the cohesion of national strength, and establishing national exploits. Patriotic education is the great banner of all the ethnic groups of the Chinese nation under which they unite in the great cause of socialist construction. It also transforms the patriotic spirit of people of all ethnic groups and their cohesive strength into a tremendous material force for the construction of the motherland and actions for defending the motherland.

As early as 1990, Jiang Zemin proposed in his report at a meeting for Beijing youths to commemorate the May Fourth Movement: "In the history of our country, patriotism has always been a banner to mobilize and encourage people to unite their efforts in their struggles, it is the common spiritual pillar for people of all ethnicities and it plays a major role in maintaining the unification of the motherland and national unity, resisting foreign aggression and promoting social progress. Under the incentive of the patriotic spirit, our country and nation's ceaseless self-improvement possesses great cohesiveness and vitality." Therefore in our work in education, we should be fully aware that patriotism is the important ideological basis and powerful spiritual motivation of a country and a nation of united people. In the process of implementing ideological quality education in the present day, a proper grasp of patriotic education should be carried out first.

At the same time as strengthening patriotic education, we need to also strengthen collectivist education and socialist education; these three are a unified entity. The Chinese nation is world renowned for attaching importance to the whole entity, and under the influence of traditional collectivist national spirit and notions on national culture, it plays a considerable role in promoting the enhancement of national cohesiveness and solidarity, constituting one of the ideological origins of the Chinese national cohesiveness. In modern times, we have to continue to attach importance to collectivist education and enable the nation's people of all ethnic groups, under the conditions of a market economy, to unswervingly safeguard the collective interests and interests of the nation, to cultivate a sense of collective responsibility and honor, and to enable each member of the collective entity of the Chinese nation to become interdependent in a united and cohesive entity. Under the banner of collectivist education, the morale and dedication of every member of the collective entity will be inspired, forming an even more unbreakable cohesiveness for the Chinese nation.

In addition, patriotic and socialist education is also uniform in nature. History has repeatedly shown that socialism is both the fruits of refining Chinese people's patriotism and also the concentrated expression of the Chinese national spirit of patriotism in reality.[6] Therefore, in socialist education we need to establish the firm belief of the people in socialism, to allow socialist and communist beliefs and ideals to become the common pursuits of the entire people of all ethnic groups and to have all members of the Chinese nation united under the banner of socialism. This is the source of strength for the smooth development of socialist modernization.

Strengthening Education on the Fine Traditions and National Spirit of the Chinese Nation

There is a need to strengthen education on the fine traditions and national spirit of the Chinese nation and to enable the cohesiveness that has long been formed in China's national history to become even more consolidated and powerful in the new era. Fine national traditions and national spirit, compared to social psychology and concepts, are more concrete and able to retain their original form. The Chinese nation has a long history of splendid culture and is world renowned for its hardworking reputation while at the same time also being a nation that is passionate about freedom and rich in revolutionary traditions. These outstanding national traditions and national spirit have written brilliant chapters in the history of the Chinese nation. Chinese history, especially its modern history, has been a history of heroic struggles and entrepreneurship for the Chinese nation; these are the best teaching materials for education, which promotes national cohesiveness. Through education, the vast majority of young people have come to understand the 170 years since the Opium War, the more than 90 years since the May Fourth Movement in Chinese history of indomitable resistance to foreign aggression. Through a progressive approach to history, from distant events to recent events, from shallow concepts to the profound, they will come to be well acquainted with China's long history of national traditions and spirit, and this will greatly stimulate their sense of national pride and sense of belonging, as well as their sense of duty to the nation.

At the same time, through education in the nation's traditions, we can enable all members of the Chinese nation to understand the struggles, sacrifices, and wave after wave of heroic feats of the Chinese Communist Party for the revitalization of the Chinese nation as well as the realization of humanity's noble ideals. We will promote the unity of wills and inspiring heroic feats and thus, we will powerfully enhance the self-esteem and solidarity of the members of the Chinese nation and affirm the path of development and the common beliefs of the Chinese nation.

The fine traditions of the Chinese nation and their national spirit not only inspired the Chinese nation to create brilliant civilizations; henceforth it will also become the deepest cultural motivation for rousing the Chinese nation to advance, unite, and progress.

Enhancing the Cultural Psychology of the Nation, National Values, and Common National Developmental Objectives

There is a need to enhance the cultural psychology of the nation, national values, and education with common national developmental objectives, which are conducive to the formation of the Chinese nation's cohesiveness. The national psychology, class psychology, and social mass psychology are all the same; they are all made up of needs, interests, views, feelings, emotions, public opinions, traditions and other social psychology phenomena. These aspects jointly form the psychological mannerisms of a nation, becoming the overall psychological characteristics of a nation. The psychological mannerisms of a country include national character, the self-awareness of the nation, national pride, and national traditions, habits, and stereotypes.[7] Moreover, all ethnic groups, "in the long interactive process between the culture of humanity and the natural world, form ethnic cultural characteristics, furthermore, they will ultimately settle and accumulate in cultural psychology, forming specific ethnic psychological structures."[8] Period-specific cultural and psychological structures of a nation are formed from specific social psychology, cultural views, and the national spirit of revitalization; therefore, all countries emphasize the sense of belonging in the psychology of their national culture. National psychology and national culture are the concrete details and important conditions of the formation of national cohesiveness. Furthermore, all these must basically go through the channel of education to achieve the transmission and permeation of national culture and psychology. For example, Japanese classrooms are imbued with the cultural consciousness of "Yamato damashii" or "Japanese spirit"; teachers make efforts to express the national character's traits of cooperation and coexistence. In American classrooms, the proud spirit of the citizens of the United States of America is especially emphasized, thus giving students a strong identity as citizens of the world or masters of the world. The Chinese nation is a great nation that holds an important position among the other nations in the world; its cultural psychology goes even further back to the dim and distant past, and it is also precisely under the nation's firm national culture and psychology that all ethnic groups of the Chinese nation have been able to extremely easily form common values and beliefs. In the new period of socialist construction, we must continue to fully use education as a form of dissemination and permeation in the formation of national cultural psychology and to enable the development of Chinese national cohesiveness with even more solid content and foundations.

Japanese thinker Nakamura Hajime, in *An Essay on Comparative Thinking*, proposed: "The Chinese people are a great nation of people, its culture has been handed down as the Chinese spirit, if they had abandoned their historic and cultural foundations, then China would have long come to a standstill and would have also lost their own culture forever. China's reforms must be based on their own culture and this type of culture is a part of world civilization. China cannot carry out reform by slavishly following Western Civilizations. If they were to put aside their own cultural foundations to carry out Westernization, then China would inevitably collapse and perish."⁹ This is an argument that is worth our serious attention.

The logical starting point for our country's traditional culture is the standards of value of its "social standards," while the logical starting point of modern Western culture is the standards of value of the "individual standards" of one's innate human rights. It should be said that the purposes and nature of national psychology and culture advocated by feudal bureaucracies are fundamentally different from the present-day view of social standards. However, from another point of view, this sort of national culture and psychology that was formed in China's national history has an extremely important effect on present-day national integration and cohesive psychology. Therefore, in order to fully bring into play the use of national culture and national psychology in the process of national cohesion, we should adopt various forms of education through various types and levels of educational institutions and put our efforts into the organized, large-scale, sustained creation and transmission of a specific national culture and psychology. This is the fundamental condition of survival for a nation and is the precondition for its development.

Enhancing the National Education of the Chinese Nation

There is a need to enhance the national education of the Chinese nation. This is a key link in the formation of a national consensus and the promotion of national cohesiveness. In the contents of national education, there is a particular need to emphasize an awareness of resources, the environment, and the population, to enable young people to have a clear awareness of basic national conditions in these areas. In addition, through the dissemination of knowledge on national conditions to enable every member to understand their own nation's history and its current situation, we also need to understand the national sense of responsibility and duty that we should all possess as descendants of the Chinese nation. We should enhance their national consciousness, raise their national spirit, and enable every member of the Chinese nation to unite and manifest within themselves the aspects of national self-esteem, self-confidence, awareness of self-empowerment, and a sense of national pride, thus forming a strong national cohesiveness. We must also motivate every member to work together for the sustainable development of the Chinese nation. It can be said that the success of national education is to a certain extent related to whether or not the Chinese nation has the ability to stand among the world powers of the twenty-first century.

What needs to be pointed out is that when we are carrying out the aforementioned aspects of ideological education, this educational content should permeate social education, school education, and home education. Furthermore, we should target different people to educate and take care that we are using appropriate teaching methods for them. For example, within the school education system, the teaching resources, methods, and so on of ideological education in primary, secondary, and tertiary education should be differentiated. The contents of ideological education are not confined to the ideological and political classes. Any school subject or activity can be permeated by the abovementioned educational content.

In addition, when we implement the education of the Chinese nation's patriotism, national values, national spirit, and national situations, we are not denying the international principles of education; our promotion of national cohesiveness through education does not mean that the educational content is limited to source material that introduces our country. Rather, the promotion of the Chinese nation's sense of national responsibility and urgency must be through an awareness of the social development of other countries and nationalities and through learning the advanced experiences of developed countries and the national spirits of other nations. In the process of promoting national cohesiveness, these methods can achieve a similar effect.

5. The Role of Education in Improving the Quality of All the People to Enhance National Cohesiveness

To enhance national cohesiveness, we must strive to fully bring out the role that education plays in improving the overall scientific and cultural qualities of the entire nation as well as the role it plays in cultivating talents. We have to promote good social habits and the formation of social morals. We need to also push the all-around progress of spiritual civilization forward and create good human infrastructures and a good social environment for the enhancement of national cohesiveness.

The formation of national cohesiveness is a conscious action of the Chinese people. Whether national cohesiveness is able to form and whether this cohesiveness is strong or weak is to a large degree dependent on the overall quality of all the members of the Chinese nation. Within this overall quality, scientific and cultural quality form the basis for all other qualities. Lenin once pointed out that a country full of illiterate people is incapable of establishing socialism. Similarly, a nation with numerous illiterate people and low levels of science and culture would also find it difficult for its members to consciously form a sense of responsibility and duty to the nation.

Scientific and cultural education has an important influence on forming and updating people's ideology and notions. In modern society, people's level of education directly determines the formation of their values as well as their lifestyle choices and so on, thereby influencing the national culture, the national spirit, and the degree of development of the nation as a whole civilization. Therefore, we must pay attention to the important role that education plays in terms of improving the scientific and cultural quality of the entire nation. It is necessary to use a variety of educational means to spread certain knowledge on natural science and social science to all of the members of the nation, allowing the entire nation to acquire a certain basis in science and culture. Only by gaining a deeper understanding of the relationship between themselves and the development of the nation can they consciously choose to develop themselves, improve themselves, and link themselves to the path of national progress. In this sense, the formation of national cohesiveness is all the more persistent, sturdy, and widespread.

At the same time, enriching people's minds through civilized, scientific, and healthy knowledge enables people to receive a subtle education in regard to the optimization of the mannerisms of social morality, the creation of an active and high-spirited cultural atmosphere, and the dissemination and spread of modern civilization. It has a direct effect on the promotion of a good social environment and will enable an entire society to demonstrate a high degree of development in its civilization. In this sort of civilized and harmonious social atmosphere, all the members of the nation will be able to spontaneously generate a strong sense of national belonging and national pride, thereby greatly enhancing the development of national cohesiveness.

In addition, not only can the overall cultural quality of the nation be improved through education, but it can also cultivate a cohort of sophisticated and innovative talents, thus improving the Chinese nation's status in the world and its influence. This will also enhance the national confidence and national pride of all members of the Chinese nation and play a direct or indirect role in propelling the formation of national cohesiveness forward. However, although present-day China has a large population, which accounts for a quarter of the world's population, the number of outstanding talents who have made a first-rate contribution in terms of science and technology and make an impact on the world is relatively small. This, to a certain degree, influences a nation's self-confidence and pride and also has a certain influence on the formation and development of national cohesiveness. This is why Deng Xiaoping once pointed out: "When China, a vast country with a billion people, has developed its education, it will enjoy an enormous superiority in intellectual resources that no other country can match. There is no doubt that when we have that superiority, together with an advanced socialist system, we shall be able to attain our goals."[10] Deng Xiaoping's brilliant exposition should have great significance as a source of guidance and inspiration on the issue of how we should make use of education in the present day to promote national cohesiveness.

6. Using Education in the Development of Productive Forces to Enhance National Cohesiveness

To enhance national cohesiveness, we must further increase the important use of education in promoting the development of productivity and improving the comprehensive strength and the standard of living for the entire country; we must vigorously develop the education of ethnic minorities and improve the overall quality of ethnic minorities as a whole.

National cohesiveness is the result of the dual factors of material and spiritual accumulation. The quality of a country's economic development is directly related to the personal interests of its members. When a country's economy is strong, the quality of life and standard of living of its members can be guaranteed and improved. This is the first essential factor for the promotion of national identity and national sense of belonging that members of a nation have toward their country.

In the context of extraordinary times, a nation's backwardness and poverty might be able to inspire an active entrepreneurial spirit and cohesiveness in the members of its nation. However, in the peaceful present-day social environment, it is very difficult to imagine that a nation's backwardness and poverty will be a strong cohesive force among the members of its nation. By contrast, education plays an enormous role in socioeconomic development by propelling it forward, thus producing an indirect impact on the promotion of national cohesiveness

Deng Xiaoping once pointed out that "education is a nation's most fundamental cause; the realization of the Four Modernizations relies on knowledge and on human talents," emphasizing that science and technology are the primary productive forces and education is the ideology of its basis. The American economist Edward Denison once carried out specialized calculations on the role that education plays in America's economic growth. According to his calculations, the 21 percent national economic growth in America from 1929 to 1957 should be attributed to education. From 1909 to 1929, the contribution of material capital to economic growth was still almost double that of school education; however, from 1929 to 1957, the contribution of school education had already surpassed that of material capital.[11] Former Soviet Academy of Sciences scholar Stanislav Strumilin also carried out calculations on this issue. He suggested that out of the Soviet Union's increase in national income, 30 percent was from education.

These examples all fully illustrate that education possesses enormous economic benefits and is the basis for promoting the development of productive forces and improving overall national strength. Especially with the arrival of the era of the knowledge economy in the twenty-first century, the nation's economic growth is even more dependent on the development of education.

Therefore, education plays an extremely distinct and large role in using the means of enhancing a nation's economic strength to promote national cohesiveness. British education economist John Sheehan believes that the economic benefits of education are sometimes direct, sometimes indirect, sometimes tangible, and sometimes intangible. Among these, he pointed out that education does not only bring with it an increase in productivity; furthermore, "education will also bring many social and economic benefits, promote social solidarity and stability and thus promote production efficiency."[12] Therefore, it is necessary to further increase investments into education and implement the strategy of "revitalizing the country through science and technology."

Our country is a unified multiethnic country with 55 ethnic minority groups, ethnic autonomous regions with an area that accounts for 64 percent of the entire country and a population of approximately 90 million. Due to complex social and historical reasons, most ethnic minority people live at the borders of our country where national defense hubs are located. According to statistics, China's land border is 21,000 km long, bordering 136 counties and 14 countries. The vast majority of ethnic minorities live together or in colonies and some even live across the borders. Additionally, the ethnic origins, language, customs, habits, and religious beliefs of some ethnic minority groups are similar to some ethnic groups in neighboring countries, and so they have had a complex history of long-term social contact with these neighboring countries. This has enabled many ethnic minority groups in our country to shoulder the dual task of developing friendly relationships with neighboring countries as well as resisting foreign aggression and defending the frontier of the motherland.[13]

Therefore, ethnic minorities occupy a very important position in the Chinese nation. Whether or not national cohesiveness is able to form between ethnic minorities, and ethnic minorities and the Han people, has a crucial impact on the development of the Chinese nation. Since education plays a very important fundamental role in the formation of national cohesiveness, rapidly developing the education of ethnic minorities should be an inevitable requirement and trend to achieve national integration and cohesiveness.

In the education of ethnic minorities, we must first strengthen the patriotic education that will enable them to gradually establish a Marxist national outlook, to have a proper understanding and properly regard the formation and development of all ethnic groups in our country and the Chinese nation as a whole, and to profoundly understand that our country is an ancient civilization with a long history and that our country is one big family that unites and loves all ethnicities in the nation. We must enable ethnic minorities to achieve what Fei Xiaotong proposed as the mentality of "a united nation where everyone feels that they belong to one common shared entity" within their ideological awareness, to firmly establish a unified sense of the Chinese nation as a large family and a strong national awareness, national self-confidence, national pride, and a national sense of responsibility and duty, eliminating the influence of parochial nationalism. To develop the educational cause of ethnic minorities, we must make efforts to spread the cultural education within national education, enhance the quality of education in ethnic minority areas, improve the overall quality of ethnic minorities as a whole, and then spur the economic development and social progress of ethnic minority areas.

The education of ethnic minorities is an important part of the education of the country as a whole. Its relationship with the education in other regions in the country is one of interdependence and mutual restraint. The development of the country as a whole is inseparable from the development of national education, and agreement and coordination between the development of both is a necessary requirement of the promotion of national cohesiveness.

Looking around the world and ahead into the future, at a time when the competition between countries of the world in terms of comprehensive national strength is becoming increasingly fierce, the position and role of national cohesiveness in international competition is becoming increasingly apparent. In Jiang Zemin's speech at the Third National Education Conference on education and national cohesiveness, he spoke on how to promote national cohesiveness toward the twenty-first century. We must lift up the great banner of "revitalizing the country through science and technology," carry forward the Chinese nation's long tradition of education, make full use of all kinds and forms of education, unite all members of the Chinese nation and condense them into a force in this era that cannot be stopped by any other force, and work together to achieve the great revitalization of the Chinese nation in the twenty-first century!

14

The Scientific Outlook on Development and Chinese Educational Reform

Scientific development without education, is scientific development without people, which is scientific development without society, which is incapable of achieving the ultimate development goal of realizing a people-centered and comprehensive development of society. The significance of a scientific outlook on development does not only lie in correcting the tendency in socioeconomic development to have growth only in their GDP. As a train of thought and strategy for the analysis and solving of issues, the concept of scientific development also has great significance as a form of guidance for the reform and development of Chinese education.

1. Scientific Development of Education as a Requirement for Socioeconomic Development

The realization of the scientific outlook on development depends on education, education's establishment, and realization of the concept that scientific development is the precondition and basis for realizing the scientific development of the society as a whole.

At the third plenary session of the Sixteenth Central Committee of the Communist Party of China, the following goals were proposed: "Adhering to being people-oriented, establishing a comprehensive, coordinated, sustainable view of scientific development and to promote socio-economic development and the comprehensive development of people" and adhering to the "overall plan for urban and rural development, regional development, socio-economic development, harmonious development between people and nature, domestic development and opening up to the outside world." The Seventeenth Chinese Communist Party Congress report also clearly pointed out: "The Scientific Outlook on Development is a scientific theory that is both in keeping with Marxism-Leninism, Mao Zedong Thought, Deng Xiaoping Theory and the important thought of Three Represents and is in step with the times. It fully embodies the Marxist worldview on and methodology for development and represents the latest achievement in adapting Marxism to China's conditions. It is the crystallization of the collective wisdom of the Communist Party of China (CPC) and a guiding ideology that must be upheld and applied in developing socialism with Chinese characteristics."[1]

The relationship between education and a scientific outlook on development is very intimate. First, the state of development of a country's education, such as the degree to which compulsory education is universal, the years of education per capita, the ratio of funding for public education, the developmental state of regional education, and so on are most capable of reflecting the degree of a society's comprehensive, coordinated, and sustainable development. Education is a social and public undertaking and the basis of the harmonious development of society and sustainable development. In fact, an important aspect of implementing a scientific outlook on development is to coordinate and plan the entire development of the economy and education as a whole. Since the Sixteenth National Congress, the country has officially launched a series of policies such as free urban and rural compulsory education and free teacher education, which are the efforts to put a scientific outlook on development into practice.

Second, the focus and difficulty of the scientific outlook on development lies in education. The contribution rate of our country's human capital (technological progress) to economic growth is only about 35 percent, far below the 75 percent level of developed countries. In 2003, for example, we consumed 26 percent of the world's steel, 30 percent of its oil, 60 percent of its cement, and produced only 4 percent of the entire world's GDP. This is closely related to the state of our education's development, especially vocational education, which is lagging behind. When all is said and done, is education "people-oriented" or "exam-oriented"? Is it a comprehensive, coordinated, and sustainable form of development, or is it a one-sided, imbalanced, unsustainable form of development? Is it an overall plan that takes all factors into consideration, or a trade-off? The urgently needed scientific outlook on development is clear on these fundamental thoughts and conceptual questions in regard to educational development.

Third, many of the problems that exist in China's education can be truly resolved only under the necessary guidance of a scientific outlook on education. In terms of the current situation, we must not only solve the nonscientific developmental problems that exist in education itself; at the same time we must also promote overall realization of a scientific outlook on education for the entire society through education. As the pioneering and fundamental department for the whole society, education must provide intellectual support for all branches and systems in society, train professionals, spread advanced social philosophy, and fundamentally guarantee people's comprehensive development.

Therefore, from this perspective, the implementation of a scientific outlook on development depends first and foremost on education. Nobel Prize laureate and economist Amartya Sen believes that development cannot be understood simply as industrialization or the increase of a resident's income, but should be regarded as a process of expanding freedom. Furthermore, education has important significance in expanding humanity's freedom and improving the quality of life. One's educational situation affects one's essential freedom to depend on the enjoyment of a better life. The development of education, especially the development of basic education, is conducive to the eradication of poverty and the gap between the rich and the poor.[2] From a certain perspective, the establishment of education and the implementation of a scientific outlook on development are preconditions and the basis for the implementation of scientific development in society as a whole. We believe that saying this is not excessive at all, because after education went through its few years of great development (such as the increase in higher education enrollments and the spread of compulsory education), indeed Chinese education requires rethinking on the idea of a scientific outlook on development so as to guide the direction of the future of China's education reform and development as well as the development of the society as a whole.

2. Imbalance in Educational Development and Its Effect on Social Development

The prominent problems in present-day educational development are mainly expressed as imbalances in the regional development of education, urban and rural development, and group development.

Since the reform and opening up to the outside world, our country's education has made great achievements that have received worldwide attention. In 2000, as scheduled, the goal of the "two basics" was achieved, higher education developed at an unconventionally rapid speed; education provided the country's economic and social development with a large cohort of talented people and provided the reform and opening up of the country and various undertakings with strong support. However, "in recent years, our country's great developments and great reforms in education have caused new and old conflicts to be relatively concentrated, new situations and new problems are constantly emerging and behind these achievements are some hidden damages."[3] Compared to a scientific outlook on development, the nonscientific educational phenomena and tendencies are still very serious and these signs can be seen whether at a macro level or at a micro level. These are prominently displayed in the development of education.

Considering the subsystems of education from the perspective of a sociomacro system, the degree of imbalance in educational development is far greater than the degree of imbalance in socioeconomic development. Furthermore, it limits holistic, coordinated, and sustainable socioeconomic development. This is mainly reflected in three aspects.

The first is the regional imbalances in educational development. The education in the central and western regions lags behind when compared to the education in the eastern regions. The research group survey of Professor Yuan Zhenguo showed that there was a difference between the average educational spending budget for students in the eastern and western regions. In primary education, the difference in the budget in eastern regions and in western regions expanded from 3.5 times in 1996 to 3.85 times in 2002; the budget difference in normal junior high education expanded from 3 times in 1996 to 3.39 times in 2002; and in senior high education it expanded from 2.8 times in 1996 to 2.92 times in 2002.[4] Due to inadequate investments, the level of educational development in the central and western regions—aspects such as the popularization of the "two basics," the strength of qualified teachers, school buildings, and the support of home education—are all lagging behind the eastern region. For example, in 2003 the average educational funding for primary school students in Shanghai was RMB3,715, which is 8.89 times the RMB418 spent on students in Guizhou. Regional differences in economic development lead to differences in the quality of the labor force between regions and furthermore exacerbate the regional imbalances in socioeconomic development.

The second aspect is imbalances in urban and rural educational development. In terms of the urban-rural contrast, for a long time 60 percent of the national educational budget is used for compulsory education, and of this funding, only 35 percent is invested in rural compulsory education.[5] An obvious urban-rural "dual structure" exists in education: some urban schools have broadband sockets fitted to each classroom desk; some rural schools are forced to have children use sand instead of paper, twigs instead of pens. Some urban schools have more than one sports field covered with a synthetic athletic track; some rural schools do not even have one basketball provided for them to play with. Some urban schools easily invest tens of billions of yuan; some rural schools have to count the use of each stick of chalk. Some urban schools, even if placed in Europe or America, would be considered first-rate; some rural schools, even if taken to African countries, would still be considered poor.[6] The differences in urban and rural education is particularly the imbalance of basic education. It directly damages educational equality—causing a portion of the children in rural villages to lose at the starting line. At the same time, it leads to conflicts in the internal structure of the education system. For example, village children from relatively better off families will rush toward urban schools where excellent teachers are assigned, resulting in the impoverished scene of "people being deprived of a means of living" as well as a lack of rural culture emerging in rural schools and education. In the process of constructing a new socialist countryside, society is concerned about this issue, has placed rural education cultural development within the overall plan for social development, and regards these as the targets for key support; however, this has only just begun and there are developmental problems left over from the past and thus rural schools are in urgent need of more appeals and concern during their process of development. Some deep-seated problems, such as whether or not we have truly grasped the essence of rural education and to what degree have we truly approached rural education itself, are still worth pondering.[7]

The third aspect is the imbalance in the development of group education. There is an obvious gap between the educational resources of different groups in society. Relatively speaking, disadvantaged groups have less opportunities to receive a quality education, especially children of migrant workers in urban areas, the children of the urban poor, rural girls, people with disabilities and mental disabilities in the special education system, and so on; all exist in a relatively disadvantaged position in education. British philosopher John Rawls wrote that social welfare is determined by the people in the worst conditions in society; only when conditions of those people in society have improved can social welfare increase. Alternatively, we could say that the decisive criterion of a just society is the position of those people who are in the worst conditions in society. In fact, the development of social civilization is not in how many social gains are enjoyed by minority groups, especially the gains of educational development, but more importantly, it is in whether or not the vast majority of social groups, especially disadvantaged groups, are able to enjoy their well-being. The "people-centered" and "education is to serve people" thinking proposed by a scientific outlook on education is to enable education to benefit the wider masses.

In terms of the internal situation of educational subsystems, imbalances in educational development are reflected in the education structure, goals, subject classifications, and the orientation of its values.

First, the internal structure of education is unreasonable and its development imbalanced. The development of public and private education, formal and informal education, and nondiploma education is not coordinated enough, and the ratio of all kinds of education from secondary education and up is unreasonable. According to the latest statistics released by the Ministry of Education in 2009, various types of private schools (educational institutions) in the entire country number 106,500 (excluding 19,300 private training institutions), and the number of students in degree courses has reached 30,653,900. Among them, there are 89,304 private kindergartens with 11,341,700 students; 5,496 private primary schools with 5,028,800 students; 4,331 private normal junior high schools with 4,338,900 students; 2,670 private normal senior high schools with 2,301,300 students; 3,198 private secondary vocational schools with 3,181,000 students, and 658 private universities and colleges (including 322 independent colleges) with 4,461,400 students.[8] Private education plays an increasingly large role in the development of education as a whole, but in actual fact, private education has not achieved the same legal status as public education. After the official launch of "regulations on the promotion of private education," although in legal texts private education and public education have equal legal status, the government's policies in practice are far from seriously implementing provisions on the equal legal status of teachers and students of private and public education who are, as a matter of fact, unequal. A considerable portion of the government's policy-making departments still regard private education as being supplementary to public education, a stop-gap measure to solve conflicts caused by educational supply and demand in times when the government's financial resources are inadequate; thus the development of private education still faces all sorts of obstacles and unequal treatment. In addition, the academic forms of education that our country's higher education seeks to rely on—university research, combined university research and teaching, and university teaching, as well as training institutions—also lack a reasonable hierarchical structure. At the same time, there are relatively prominent situations where our country emphasizes higher education and does not take basic education seriously, emphasizes normal education and does not take vocational education seriously, and emphasizes formal academic education and does not take informal nondiploma education seriously. Furthermore, secondary vocational education, including vocational schools, technical schools, and so on, is subjected to all kinds of prejudice; in reality, it is difficult for it to keep pace with normal secondary education.

Second, there is an imbalance in the development of educational objectives, with an emphasis on training skilled personnel but not on educating people on how to be upright. Our education is only concerned that students make a name for themselves, become experts, and specialize in certain fields while neglecting to teach them how to behave as an upright person; our education is concerned about exam scores and neglects the cultivation of the comprehensive qualities of moral character and one's psychology. In terms of science and humanities, knowledge and morality, intelligence and emotions, and so on, students are unable to achieve comprehensive and coordinated development; profit making becomes an important goal of a school, causing the educational activities for training people to be alienated, becoming a type of utilitarian economic activity. In terms of the means of education, classroom teaching becomes the only means of education and teaching; students are isolated from richly colorful social lives and social activities by rigorous class times. In regard to those being educated, "good students" who look forward to advancing to the next grade will receive full attention at school, while students with mediocre test scores become "tagalong students," and students with poor test scores are discriminated against. Therefore, how to enable our education to be open to all people and students of all aptitudes; how to enable people to access comprehensive development in regard to their rational and irrational thoughts, science and humanities, knowledge and moral character, intelligence and character, personality and potential, spiritual and cultural aspects, and so on, are problems that should be seriously considered in the establishment and implementation of a scientific outlook on the development of education.

Third is the imbalance in the development of the humanities and science. An emphasis on science and contempt—even discrimination—toward the humanities has already become a direct cause of influences on the development of the human spirit. Secondary schools prematurely separate science and the humanities and cause most of the outstanding students to choose science; a relative proportion of the students who pick the humanities are students who are not good at science and do so involuntarily. Therefore, from the start of high school, students who study science basically no longer study history and geography and no longer read classical literary masterpieces. This directly influences improvement in their appreciation of humanities. At the same time, students who study humanities also bid farewell to natural science and no longer study physics, chemistry, and biology. The formation of their scientific attitude and scientific spirit is of course directly affected. This is a devastating blow to the development of the humanities and social sciences in China.

In addition, the orientation of the entire education system toward exam-centered education to a large extent causes education to lose its need to satisfy people's development and its essence as a promoter of people's holistic development, making it hard for the people-centered scientific outlook on development to be implemented in education. Education now tends to be exam focused and arrogant, it does not regard people as people, and it has already become a prominent feature of the modern examination system. The selection function of examinations causes Chinese education to become increasingly difficult and the learning content increasingly complicated. Most students feel that they have difficulties with their learning. Many rural students and their parents believe that the learning content is of absolutely no use to their current and future lives, and many urban students and their parents also believe that the things the child learns will never be of use in the child's life. One test determines one's entire life. For the sake of good test scores, people can use unscrupulous means to compete, and schools are also ranked according to their test scores. The problem is that the internal functions and focus of education are narrow, resulting in education not being able to meet the needs of the people and also resulting in education finding it hard to meet the needs of social development.

3. Developing Educational Science for Running Education That Satisfies the People

Running an education system that satisfies the people is an important task for the entire society and also a commitment that a government has to its people.

The report for the Seventeenth CPC National Congress put forward new requirements for education: "The modern system of national education will be further improved, a basic system for lifelong education will be in place, the educational attainment of the whole nation will rise to a much higher level, and the training of innovative personnel will be improved markedly." Furthermore, in regard to accelerating the promotion of improving people's lives and social construction, it proposed: "Giving priority to education and turning China into a country rich in human resources," requiring that we "run education to the satisfaction of the people."[9] In Wen Jiabao's Report on Work of the Government (2008), he clearly proposed that "China cannot modernize if education is not made universally available and if its quality is not improved. We must ensure that our children receive a good education, provide education that satisfies the needs of the people and improve the overall quality of the population," regarding "the running of an education that satisfies the needs of the people" as an important task for all of society and also as the current government's commitment to the people.

Running education to the satisfaction of the people is a concentrated reflection of the urgent longing that the broad masses have for the improvement of the quality of education, the improvement of the educational structure, the adjustment of the layout of education, and the expansion of access to quality educational resources. It cannot evade two basic questions: the first is what kind of education is an education that satisfies the people; the second is how to run education that satisfies the people. The important thinking of scientific outlook on development provides a set of core standards and core principles of choice for determining the basic characteristics of such an education. An education that satisfies the needs of the people is not a static concept, but rather something that constantly grows, develops, and improves itself in practice. Perhaps there is no such thing as the best education, only an education that is better and more satisfactory; however, under the guidance of a scientific outlook on development we can describe the basic characteristics and basic requirements of an education that satisfies the people. In this regard, I very much endorse the description that Fu Weili has put together, namely, that an education that satisfies the people should be fully able to meet the growing educational needs of the broad masses of people; to make an overall plan that relates to people's long-term and immediate benefits; to fully embody the spirit of fairness and public participation, and to guarantee the comprehensive, coordinated, and sustainable development of all levels and all types of education.[10] At the same time, an embodiment of an education that satisfies the people should also be the implementation and promotion of quality education.

First of all, an education that satisfies the people should increasingly fully meet the growing educational needs of the broad masses of people. In today's era, education has already become the fundamental driving force for enhancing national strength and achieving the comprehensive development of people's individual qualities. The demands that the countries of the world, especially developing countries, make of education has always maintained a trend toward rapid growth. Within the 30 years of China's reform and opening up to the world, we have clearly felt this trend. For example, since the late 1990s people have urgently demanded that we force the higher education in our country to enter a period of rapid development; people are increasingly raising strong demands that basic education enjoy equal access to quality educational resources, and a learning-oriented society and lifelong education have already become hot issues of social concern. These all raise new demands for new educational reforms and development for the new century. Therefore, to run education that satisfies the people, we must be extremely concerned about these changing trends in the educational needs of the masses and regard the expansion of high-quality educational resources, the increase of personalized educational resources, and the development of a learning-oriented society and the promotion of lifelong education as the basic strategic goals of promoting educational development.

Second, an education that satisfies the people should have an overall plan that takes into account the relationship between people's long-term benefits and immediate interests. On one hand this requires earnest concern for the educational demands of the masses and meeting the educational needs of people at present. On the other hand, there is a need to also guide the masses to have the right educational demands and not to blindly cater to all the needs of students and parents. This precisely requires education to have an overall plan that takes people's long-term benefits and immediate interests into consideration. This is because individual requirements are generally more likely to reflect the personal pursuit of immediate interests while ignoring the realization of the country's benefits and long-term benefits. In fact, the grasp of the vast majority of students and parents on educational objectives and regulations is intuitive or even superficial; simply complying with the demands of students and parents cannot guarantee that education will advance in accordance with its own conventions and stipulated path. If one succumbs to the unreasonable educational demands of students and parents, then one could easily cause education to deviate from its path of healthy progress and ultimately cause great damage to a student's mental and physical development and the long-term and fundamental benefits of the masses. For a long time, school education found it difficult to go beyond the demands and "oppression" of test scores and exam-oriented learning, which actually caused students and parents to be trapped in the immediate benefits of a "one-sided pursuit of enrollment quotas" and pursuit of exam-oriented results. Education should make considerations from the perspective of the long-term benefits of the country, children, and adolescents; meeting the immediate educational needs of students and parents does not mean that there is no bottom line. It must be controlled in terms of whether it meets the needs of the country as a whole and people's long-term benefits, as well as whether it complies with the students' learning and is within the premise and scope of objective laws on mental and physical development.

Third, education that satisfies the people should fully embody the spirit of fairness and public participation. The Seventeenth CPC National Congress report points out: "Education is the cornerstone of national rejuvenation, and equal access to education provides an important underpinning for social equity" and "To realize social equity and justice is a major task of developing socialism with Chinese characteristics." From the point of view of the value and basic functions of education, the biggest difference between education and other social structures is that it must nurture talented people for the future society. Education is aimed at the future; it does not merely copy the existing society but must also guide the younger generation to create a more progressive and healthy society. The balanced development of education, especially compulsory education, is the basis for establishing a more democratic, more equal, more harmonious, and more civilized society.

Therefore, for education to change from being elitist to being for the masses and to pursue the coordinated and balanced development of basic education should be an important and essential aspect of education's implementation of a people-focused, scientific outlook on development and an education that satisfies the people. Only by having more and more people experience and enjoy the opportunity and right to access quality educational resources can the entire society's degree of satisfaction toward education achieve an upgrade as a whole. In regard to the current basic education, the gap between the eastern and western regions, rural and urban areas, quality schools and disadvantaged schools is still relatively distinct. The issues of students in remote rural areas having difficulty attending school, of having the children of migrant workers attending school near where they live, of making improvements to the accommodation conditions of rural boarding schools, as well as of urban schools charging fees for school choice are all still very prominent. These are all important aspects in regard to the need to implement a scientific outlook on development, an embodiment of fairness in education, and the running of education that satisfies the people.

Furthermore, an education that satisfies the people should also allow people to participate in the management of the school. Because public schools use taxpayers' money for setting up and running a school, taxpayers enjoy the right to participate in the management of the school. Doing so will allow parents and others to show a willingness for education, to participate in the management of the school and to provide educational resources, building a more extensive and realistic path and platform for education, thereby reflecting, at an even higher level and in terms of its implications the fundamental objective of socialist education: "People's education run by the people, to run education properly for the people." At the same time, people's spirit of participation in education is also reflected in the school's internal management and in the relationship between teachers and students. This is why we must provide conditions and opportunities for students to actively participate in the management of the school and set up equal relationships between students and teachers. Through allowing a vast number of teachers and students to participate in the management of the school and building a new school culture and new teacher-student relationships, a basis is established step by step for a democratic and equal future society.

Fourth, an education that satisfies the people should be able to ensure the comprehensive, coordinated, and sustainable development of all levels and all types of education. The Seventeenth CPC National Congress report repeatedly mentioned the important ideas of "comprehensive, coordinated and sustainable"; implemented specifically in education it is to "optimize the educational structure, promote balanced development of compulsory education, move faster toward universal access to senior secondary education, vigorously develop vocational education, and improve the quality of higher education and also attach importance to preschool education and care about special education." People's educational benefits are not empty; they are actually a collection of the educational benefits of people from all aspects and all walks of life.

Education's distinct public nature determines that it must go through comprehensive and coordinated development and structuring so as to have the greatest possibility of implementing and protecting the educational benefits and needs of as many people as possible, including both high-income groups and low-income groups, both secondary school students and preschoolers, and both the parental groups who want their children to achieve academic development and parental groups who want their children to achieve vocational development. If education is only concerned with or only satisfies the educational interests and needs of a certain group and is unable to satisfy the educational interests and needs of the overwhelming majority of people, then it will certainly not be able to satisfy the vast majority of people.

Again, from the perspective of systems theory, the national education system itself is an organic whole; to develop only a single aspect of education will not only bring harm to the development of other aspects of education but will also bring hidden harm to its own long-term development. For example, at the end of the twentieth century, in order to meet the urgent needs of the broad masses of people to receive higher education, through increasing enrollments our country's higher education was able to develop at an incredibly high speed. Through 2009, the gross enrollment rate for our country's higher education has already reached 24.2 percent with the number of current students reaching 29,790,000. The rapid development of higher education has spurred the development of normal senior high schools, but in the process of branching out in secondary education, the healthy development of secondary vocational education has simultaneously been affected, causing vocational education to suffer difficulties in terms of a decrease in student enrollments, and higher education itself has also entered a crisis in regard to how best to ensure the quality of education. Therefore, an education that satisfies the people must have a scientific overall plan that considers all levels and all types of education to ensure the comprehensive, coordinated, and sustainable development of education subsystems.

Fifth, the embodiment of an education that satisfies the people should be an implementation and promotion of quality education. To properly run education that satisfies the people requires the continuous implementation of quality education. On August 29, 2006, at the collective study for the thirty-fourth Political Bureau of the CPC Central Committee, General Secretary Hu Jintao pointed out that quality education is to solve issues on what sort of people we are to cultivate and how to cultivate these people. This is the theme of educational reform. This requires education from beginning to end to persevere in focusing on educating people and giving top priority to cultivating people's moral integrity, treating the cultivating of people as the fundamental duty of school education, and integrating the core value system of socialism into the entire process of national education. This is not to say, however, that the transfer of knowledge is not important, but rather it clarifies the issue of the priority of various objectives and the orientation of educational values at the ultimate level of education; it is also not the case that education only has a purpose and a result and does not pay attention to the methods and means, but rather that it must follow the scientific laws of education and teaching itself to achieve reasonable educational objectives.

The current problems that are especially prominent in education are the orientation of educational values toward utilitarianism, the instrumentalist approach to teaching methods, and the orientation toward antiscientific teaching styles; these are due to the dilution of the fundamental purpose education, that of educating people, or alternatively, the orientation of education's priority goals that thereby hinders the healthy, coordinated, and sustainable development of education and the healthy and harmonious development of students. Without a comprehensive implementation of quality education, there would be no comprehensive development of students, no self-coordinated and harmonious development of the students themselves, and no sustained development of students would be even more the case.

Quality education in the new era should be able to reflect the harmonious development of people, concern itself with students' fundamental interests and their lifelong development, and encourage students' ability to have a happy life for the rest of their lives. To implement quality education, education's fundamental purpose and a scientific approach is to also strive to properly run education that satisfies the people.

Perhaps there is no such thing as the best education or the most satisfactory education, but the construction of a better education that is able to make people even more satisfied is a fundamental requirement of the development of socialist education under the guidance of a scientific outlook on development.

4. Comprehensive, Coordinated, and Sustainable Development of Education

Only by implementing the comprehensive, coordinated, and sustainable development of education can the current prominent problems in education be fundamentally solved and an education that truly satisfies the people be properly run.

Under the new circumstances of socialist construction, characteristics of new stages have already emerged from our country's education. For example, having a school to attend has already been fundamentally resolved, but having a good school to go to has become a prominent contradiction; quantity and scope have already been fundamentally resolved, but quality and structure are problems that have become major contradictions. Along with the continuous improvements in the degree of the popularization of education at all stages, the orientation of the important points, core, and values of our country's development of education is also changing. Examples are the increasing shift from the educational expansion of quantity and scale to the enhancement of the quality of education and its connotations; the shift from more concern about "hardware" such as facilities and school buildings to more concern about "software" such as qualified teachers, management of standards, the campus culture, and so on; the shift from more concern about general standards and uniform levels to more concern about personality traits and the development of creative abilities; and the shift from more concern about development that has a key focus to more concern about development that is balanced.

In short, the development of our country's education is facing new situations, problems, and challenges such as those previously described. On the one hand are problems that are especially prominent due to imbalanced development in education. On the other hand are people's increasing demands and expectations of education and the cries for implementing high levels of equality in education, which are becoming increasingly vocal.

In this kind of new historical period, the comprehensive implementation and practice of a scientific outlook on development has important significance in terms of guidance for promoting the scientific development of education. Henceforth, within a period of time, ideas on the reform and development of our country's education should promote the comprehensive, coordinated, and sustainable development of education, reflecting a people-centered developmental purpose and developmental methods that take into account all factors when planning. Only by implementing the comprehensive, coordinated, and sustainable development of education can we fundamentally solve present prominent problems in education and properly run education that truly satisfies the people.

Promote the Comprehensive Development of Education

The comprehensive development of education is embodied in the three dimensions of global development, development as a whole, and omnidirectional development.[11] The global development of education first requires placing educational development within the elevated understanding of rejuvenating a country through science and education and making the country stronger by producing more outstanding personnel. Science and technology are primary productive forces, human resources are primary resources, and education is the most important and most fundamental way to develop human resources. Only by placing education within the overall situation of the country's development and the overall situation of the developments of this era can we consciously persevere in placing education in a strategic position by prioritizing its development. Second, the development of education is not just the development of one aspect or one field. It must be completely and simultaneously grasped from many aspects; it includes all levels, types;, and aspects of education; and it is also the establishment of a perfect national education system and a lifelong education system. Finally, to grasp the overall situation requires simultaneously attending to all sides and giving prominence to its key points. Comprehensive development does not at all mean balanced development; it is not a type of load shifting but takes stock of the situation and combines general development with focused development on key points, mutually promoting work in all areas by drawing on the experiences gained on key points. Over the past decade, we have regarded rural education as the top priority of education all along and treated the task of promoting balanced development in compulsory education as our top priority. At the same time, we have regarded the construction of key universities as the developmental focus of higher education, thus sustaining both ends of development in order to bring the vast majority forward to guarantee the overall advancement of education.

The comprehensive development of education refers to the fact that education is an undertaking of the entire nation. Orientation toward the entire nation's people is a public welfare requirement of education and is also an outcome of the reform and opening up of China, with people sharing its requirements. How to handle the relationship between mass education and gifted education is an unavoidable conflict in the selection of educational policies and also a focus regarding how to implement the comprehensive development of education. Since the reform and opening up of China, our country's government has attached great importance to mass education. The Compulsory Education Law issued in 1986 was our country's first education law, and in 2006 the Compulsory Education Law was amended, further emphasizing the public welfare and equality of compulsory education. Of course, emphasizing mass education does not at all mean that high-quality and high-standard education is neglected, nor does it mean that the cultivation of innovative talents is neglected. What is important is the more reasonable allocation of educational resources and sharing of educational costs, allowing all sorts of talents to be suitably placed and "enjoy their rights to an education."

Omnidirectional educational development refers to the overall implementation of the Party's education policies to adhere to the comprehensive development of the aims of education—moral education, intellectual education, physical education, and aesthetics education—and not to narrow the scope of educational activities to book reading or intellectual activities. Second, education must insist on teaching in line with students' individual abilities and provide alternative developmental space for students with different characteristics or ability structures, ensuring that each person is able to achieve appropriate development and allowing every student's personality to become even more distinct, unique, and advantageous through receiving an education. Third, through the process of education, there is a need to attach importance to the mutual development of both students and teachers, as teachers and students are interdependent; the development of teachers is the key to improving the quality of education and also guarantees the improvement of the teacher's quality of life and happiness. Without the development of teachers, there would be no student development or progress.

Promote the Coordinated Development of Education
The coordinated development of education includes coordination between education and external relations and coordination of the internal relations in education.[12]

First, in terms of the coordination between education and external relations, education must adapt to the requirements of socioeconomic development and train sufficient applicable, diverse, brilliant, and talented people for our country's socioeconomic development. At the same time, in the rapid development of the knowledge economy and increasingly fierce international competition of today, education must also play a pioneering role, being appropriately more advanced in its development and providing a talent pool for the future development of society. This requires our concepts of education, the education system, educational content, methods, and so on to be closely linked to the realities of our country's political, economic, and social construction, fully reflecting the requirements of a socialist market economy and actively taking the initiative to satisfy and push forward China's construction of modernized socialism. In May 1985, the CPC Central Committee's Decision on Educational System Reform proposed: "Education must serve the construction of socialism and the construction of socialism must depend on education." The Sixteenth CPC National Congress report also emphasizes: "We must carry out the Party's education policy that education should serve socialist modernization and the people and integrate itself with productive labor and social practice." This is the simple truth that we have reacquainted ourselves with through the lessons of history and the requirement of the times to change from "class struggles as the key link" toward economic construction as our focus.

Second, because internal relations in education can have different classifications from different perspectives at different stages of social development—for example, the coordinated development of the scale, structure quality, and benefits of education; the coordinated development of urban-rural education and regional education; and the coordinated development of all levels and all types of education—the key areas, aspects, and targets of coordinated educational development are also not the same.

The Seventeenth CPC Congress report proposes to "optimize the educational structure, promote balanced development of compulsory education, move faster toward universal access to senior secondary education, vigorously develop vocational education, and improve the quality of higher education, and to also attach importance to pre-school education and care about special education,"and to "support the development of education in poverty-stricken and ethnic autonomous areas, improve the system of financial aid to students, and ensure that children from poor families and of rural migrant workers in cities enjoy equal access to compulsory education as other children." This clearly suggests the key areas, aspects, and targets of the present coordinated development of education.

The key areas of the present coordinated development of education are mainly the following:

Compulsory education and its balanced development. This includes balance in urban-rural, regional, and interschool development. Presently, our country's educational development is already gradually showing the characteristics of a "post-compulsory schooling era" and is shifting from being more concerned about the quantity and scale in education to being more concerned about the quality and connotations of education. Therefore, narrowing the gap between urban and rural areas, regional areas, and schools which were caused by long-term historical reasons; putting funds into aspects such as the allocation of qualified teachers, school facilities, policy permits, and so on; developing standards; setting a bottom line; strengthening weaknesses; and significantly lessening the gap in compulsory education are all, without a doubt, the actual requirements of a coordinated development of education.

The development of preschool education and special education. Preschool education is the basis for cultivating the quality of the citizens and involves millions and millions of families. Professor Pang Lijun, an expert in early childhood education, proposed the establishment of the new notion that "for social development, education must be prioritised; for the cultivation of talented people, pre-school education must occur first." Although in recent years all parts of the country have continuously improved the degree of attention that they place on preschool education, when compared with school education an obvious gap still exists; for example, the admission rate is low, management responsibilities are relatively obscure, large discrepancies in quality exist in terms of the running of the campus, and so on. This does not match the achievements of our country's development of compulsory education. For the millions of children with special needs, special education is a major affair that has a lifelong impact. In recent years, special education in all parts of the country has significantly improved, but there is still much room for expanding the strength and improving the level of special education.

The important aspects of the present coordinated development of education are mainly the following:

The coordination between quantity and quality. Over the past decade, our country's compulsory education has achieved universal coverage; high school education has had substantial growth, with gross enrollment rates reaching 60 percent; higher education has developed by leaps and bounds, with gross enrollment rates in 2009 already reaching 24.2 percent. The important tasks for the next stage, especially in terms of higher education, are to improve the quality of education, teacher quality, and the teaching model for education, as well as have education achieve its own characteristics and its own standards.

The coordination between vocational education and general education. The proper development of vocational education has great significance in terms of reasonably using human resources and meeting the various demands of social development. The key to properly handling the relationship between the needs of the country and individual needs lies in vocational education. However, the demands for the development of vocational education are high, the investments are large, and the classifications are numerous, and thus difficulties far surpass those of general education. At present, the appeal of vocational education is distinctly not as great as that of general education and needs the continued attention and strong input of all levels of government.

The important targets of the present coordinated development of education are mainly the following:

The poverty-stricken regions and the ethnic minority regions. Our country's lands are vast, its people are numerous, and its development is imbalanced. The level of educational development in poverty-stricken regions and ethnic minority regions needs to be raised as a whole. In the past few years, our government has introduced a series of measures to support development in poverty-stricken regions and ethnic minority regions, to increase the central government's transfer payments, and to significantly lessen the gap between the education in poverty-stricken regions and developed regions and between the education in ethnic minority regions and Han regions. However, due to the limitations of historical patterns formed over a long period of time and natural conditions, there is still a long way to go in thoroughly lessening these gaps.

Students from economically disadvantaged families and the children of migrant workers. For the majority of people, these are the important targets of coordinated development in education. In recent years, our country's government has adopted the use of a series of preferential policies in regard to students from economically disadvantaged families. In the wake of advancements in our country's industrialization and urbanization, the number of migrant workers' children attending school continues to grow; furthermore, the second generation of migrant workers' children are already starting to be born in the cities. In terms of the large cities where the children of migrant workers are presently relatively concentrated, the proportion of migrant workers' children who are new students at primary school has already surpassed the proportion of students who are the descendants of the original residents of the city. The country attaches great importance to the issue of education for the children of migrant workers and, in 2001, the State Council explicitly resolved the issue of the "Two Priorities" policy for the education of migrant workers' children by prioritizing district government management of migrant workers and prioritizing the full-time work of public primary and secondary schools. However, the circumstances in each region in terms of the resolution of this problem are not at all balanced. From a strategic level, our country is even more concerned with the education of students from needy families and migrant workers' children. This is both a requirement for the construction of modernization in our country and a requirement for enabling all people in the nation to share in the fruits of reform by having practical concern for disadvantaged groups in society.

Promote the Sustainable Development of Education

To achieve sustainable development in education, it is necessary to persist in prioritizing the development of education, to persist in conducting affairs in accordance with educational regulations, to mobilize enthusiasm to the greatest extent in the running of education at all levels of government and among all social forces, to mobilize the enthusiasm of the vast majority of educators, and to provide those being educated with a richly colorful developmental space that is full of creativity.[13]

First, persistence in managing educational affairs according to the law is the fundamental guarantee for achieving sustainable development in education. Our country has already established the basic framework for a system of educational laws and regulations, managing educational affairs according to the law has become a social consensus, and the development of education has entered a path of standardization. The National People's Congress and its Standing Committee have drawn up and issued a number of specific education laws one after another, such as the Regulations Concerning Academic Degrees, Compulsory Education Law, Teachers Law, Education Law, Vocational Education Law, Higher Education Law, The Regulations on the Implementation of the Non-State Education Promotion Law, and so on. The State Council has formulated a number of administrative regulations in education such as Regulations on the Eradication of Illiteracy, Regulations on the Management Kindergartens, Regulations on the Running of Educational Institutions with Social Resources, and so on. Education has developed from having no legal basis to preliminarily forming a socialist educational legal system with Chinese characteristics, and the important aspects of major issues in education and the work of education now has a legal basis and guarantee. Henceforth, we must fully understand the basic status and important role of legislative work in education; we must also constantly improve the quality and efficiency of educational legislation, treat ensuring the realization of people's right to receive an education as its core, promote people's comprehensive development, and be even more concerned about balancing the rights and benefits of all sides. To solve prominent conflicts in practice, we must strengthen the relationship between specific educational legislation and the regulations for micromanaging activities in education and place an emphasis on improving the focus and operability of legal regulations. At the same time, there is a need to perfect the form and methods of legal regulation in all aspects of running education and for the government to shift from direct educational administrative management to mainly implementing macro management and providing public education services.

Second, persistence in deepening the reform of the educational system is the key to sustainable development in education. The reform and opening up of our country is one of the main themes of contemporary China. Reform is a powerful driving force for the sustainable development of the educational cause and its key is a reform of the system. In 1985 the CPC Central Committee's Decision on Educational System Reform established a completely new stage for the reform and development of China's education with the running of compulsory education by local authorities and the establishment of a three-tier school system laying the foundations for setting our compulsory education on the fast track. The decentralization of authority in higher education has formed a diverse model for the running and development of the school and opened up a broad path for the training of more talented people and better talented people. After 1998 our country's reform of the higher education system has provided higher education with favorable conditions to leap forward in its development. Presently, our country's education system is already shifting from a centralized, authoritarian model under a planned economic system to one that has been adapted for socialist market economy system. With economic development and improvements in people's living standards, our society bears an even stronger demand for learning than other countries with the same income level; however, both the overall level and financial support of education in our country are still lower than the world average. Society's strong demand for education and the lack of high-quality educational resources form a great contrast. There are still institutional barriers in education that restrict further development of effectiveness in education. In the face of these new problems, we must continue the spirit of reform and innovation, to liberate the mind, seek the truth from facts, and explore new thinking and new models to reform the educational system.

Third, persistence in scientific and democratic policy making is a necessary condition for the sustainable development of education. At present, the development of our country is currently in a crucial period of reform and opening up, and it is facing profound changes in the international environment. At this critical stage of development of risks and opportunities, whether decision making is good or bad is crucial to the success or failure of educational development. We must use a scientific outlook on development as a form of guidance to improve the scientific and democratic nature of decision making in education and the effectiveness of educational decision making. To introduce major reform measures in the decision-making process requires going through in-depth research, scientific proofs, and careful planning, to first carry out trials and then promotion. Its concrete steps should be incremental and constantly summarized and perfected. In the decision-making process, it is necessary to continually improve openness and transparency, to raise its level of participation, to extensively gather the wisdom of many, and to pool their talents together. In terms of the decision-making methods, in the face of the common phenomenon in modern society of information asymmetry, we must extensively collect information, carry out detailed analyses and summaries on the different aspirations and points of view of different groups of people, and reflect the fundamental interests of the most extensive number of people to the greatest extent. In the evaluation of the resulting decisions, we must establish an awareness of evaluation and a mechanism for evaluation criteria and information feedback and ensure the continual improvement of the decision-making process.

Within a scientific outlook, comprehensive development, coordinated development, and sustainable development are complementary; comprehensive and coordinated development are the basis for sustainable development. Sustainable development maintains the continuity, momentum, and vitality of development and keeps it abreast of the times. To construct a socialist education with Chinese characteristics and to properly run education that satisfies the people requires us to accurately grasp the scientific connotations, spiritual essence, and fundamental requirements of a scientific outlook on development. We must persist in the comprehensive, coordinated, and sustainable development of education and strive to transform the requirements of a scientific outlook on education into the right ideas, policy measures, and practical actions for promoting the development of the educational cause. This has important significance in guiding the promotion of the scientific development of the educational cause.

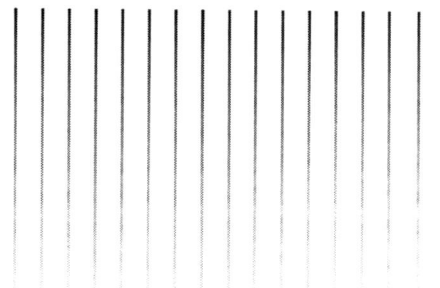

15

Trends in the Reform of China's Basic Education

Since 1900, basic education has been through approximately three major reforms.

The first time was from the start of the twentieth century to approximately the 1930s and was marked by John Dewey's pragmatism philosophy of education. His famous educational ideology was that "school is society" and "education is life"; he advocated regarding children as the focus in advancing educational activities as a whole. This pragmatism philosophy of education changed the educational state of affairs, which, before the twentieth century, separated itself from social life and was far removed from the practices of society. It had a fundamental impact on the education system, educational content, the form of education, and educational methods within America and even the entire world.

The second time was in the late 1950s when Dewey's educational ideology encountered new challenges. Dewey's philosophy of pragmatism emphasized being child centered and did not emphasize the rigorousness, logic, and scientific nature of a curriculum system, allowing children to learn whatever they like doing and have them learn through playing games. It gave more attention to the revolutionary aspect of education. In 1958, the Soviet Union's artificial satellite was launched, all levels of American society were shaken, and its leading positions in education and science were challenged. American scientific communities and the public began to blame American education for focusing on life and not paying attention to knowledge systems and the nature of science, resulting in a decline in the country's level of science and technology. Therefore, with Jerome Bruner's curriculum theory centered on the structure of knowledge as a symbol, a new reform began. This reform emphasized the structure and logic of knowledge systems and attached importance to making curriculum structures scientific.

After the 1980s, education faced its third reform. This time the reform had two important contexts. The first was represented by Bruner's structuralism and cognitivism. It emphasized making courses structured and making education scientific, but it relatively neglected the connotations of human culture of education itself and also neglected education's concern for the whole society. The decline of the humanistic spirit in the West has aroused people's concern; with problems related to the environment, resources, and population emerging one after another, people began to look for their causes in education. Dewey's subtext was again put forward and people believed that we must not only teach students scientific knowledge, but what is more important is to teach them how to be an upright person, to care about the development of all of humanity, and to care about the development of the entire society. In the 1980s, education, which revolved around this theme, was further deepened. The second context was the challenge of the new century. Humanity once again faced the moment of crossover into the new century. The sort of manner that humanity would adopt as it stepped toward the twenty-first century was also the starting point and entry point for the third reform of education.

With this context, the trends in the reform of basic education are expressed in the following 10 aspects.

1. The Trend in Making Education Scientific, for Quality in Science

The trend in making education scientific requires the scientific background of enhancing education and educational reform, a strengthening of the position and role of research on educational science, and the promotion of turning to science for quality and to methodology for efficiency.

Making education scientific is a trend that has endured since the second time education was reformed. Its characteristics can mainly be expressed in three aspects.

The first aspect is that it attaches great importance to the organization and arrangement of science education and scientific educational content. In the 1980s, in order to improve the quality of teaching, America drew in a large number of the best scientists, primary and secondary school principals, and teachers to research the problem of teaching materials in primary and secondary schools. In 1985, the American Association for the Advancement of Science officially launched Project 2061, on which the scientific community and technology community spent five years between 1985 and 1989 researching the issue of improving the teaching content in primary and secondary schools. Project 2061 was named after the next time Halley's Comet and Earth will meet. Its aim is to use the most detailed organizational arrangements to teach the most important knowledge to students in the most reasonable way so as to lay the foundation for the future of twenty-first-century education for the citizens of the United States. Apart from the United

States, Japan, Germany, and our country also attach great importance to the arrangement of scientific educational content. China's new planned curriculum is an attempt at doing thus.

The second aspect is that it attaches great important to research on educational science, strengthening the scientific background of educational reform. Research on educational science has received unprecedented attention. Educational theorists are coming out of their studies one after another to find the meeting point between theory and practice and to focus on using a scientific spirit and attitude to carry out educational reform. The new experiments in basic education and education in China in the early twenty-first century are all educational reforms carried out by the people under the leadership of university professors.

The third aspect is that it attaches importance to the use of scientific methods to carry out educational activities. It does not only teach the best educational content to students but also uses the most optimal methods to instruct students. People have begun to universally recognize the necessity of turning to science for quality and to methodology for efficiency.

America's Project 2061 proposes clear requirements as to how to teach science, mathematics, and technical knowledge, such as advocating that teaching should begin with problems or phenomena that students are interested in or are familiar with, as students will feel perplexed, ask questions, carry out discussions, and then try to find the answer. It advocates allowing students to actively participate, including activities such as collecting, screening, classifying, observing, sketching, interviewing, surveying, and carrying out opinion polls; the project also advocates focusing on gathering and using evidence, enabling the students themselves to determine what evidence is related to the problem and to explain the meaning of the evidence. Last, it advocates that the teaching of science should reflect the values of science, as science is not just the cohesion of a large amount of knowledge; it is also a sort of social activity that integrates the values of humanity. Therefore, teachers should welcome curiosity, reward creativity, encourage healthy skepticism, and avoid dogmatism.

2. The Humanization Trend, for Cultivating a Humanistic Spirit

The humanization trend in education requires education to teach students to care about humanity, society, and the future and to cultivate students' spirit of humanistic care.

Scientific development is a double-edged sword. On the one hand, it has brought glad tidings to humanity and provided favorable conditions for raising our quality of life and improving our lifestyles; on the other hand, the negative effects that science has brought on humanity cannot be ignored, such as environmental pollution, deforestation, the consumption of resources, and so on. Thus, "sustainable development" has become an important banner in the third reform of education. The so-called theory of sustainable development, simply put, has three aspects:

first, that the development of some people cannot affect or be at the expense of the benefits and development of other people; second, that the development of one generation cannot be at the expense of the benefits and development of the next generation; and third, that the development of humanity itself cannot be at the expense of the benefits and development of other species.

To explicitly raise the issue of humanity's life and death and to explicitly teach how to attend to this sort of development was a very important context for educational reform in the late 1980s and early 1990s. Against this sort of backdrop, UNESCO, after an emphasis on "learning to study," also placed great emphasis on "learning to care," demanding that education must teach people to become concerned about people themselves and the environment they exist in. This included eight specific aspects: (1) to care about oneself, including caring about one's own health; (2) to care about one's family, friends, and colleagues; (3) to care about others; (4) to care about society and the country's government, economy, and ecological interests; (5) to care about human rights; (6) to care about other species; (7) to care about earth's living conditions; (8) to care about the truth, knowledge, and learning.

Learning: The Treasure Within is a report submitted to UNESCO by the International Commission on Education for the Twenty-first Century. The report proposes The Four Pillars of Education, which are learning to know, learning to do, learning to live together, and learning to be. These four aspects are the new requirements of the aims of twenty-first-century education and are also the pillars for each person's life. This shows that in the twenty-first century, basic education's trend toward humanization goes without saying. Our country's proposal for the implementation of quality education in primary and secondary schools. and for importance to be attached to the issue of university students' cultural quality education, are all closely related to this context. In short, humanity has increasingly come to clearly recognize that the main duty of today's education should be to educate students to learn to care about humanity, learn to care about society, and learn how to conduct themselves.

3. The Trend in Making Education Comprehensive, for Optimizing Education

The trend in making education comprehensive requires the school system, educational content, and methods to better reflect synthesis and to achieve the effect of optimizing education.

Making education comprehensive is a distinct feature of the third reform of education. It is expressed in the following four aspects.

The first aspect is the comprehensiveness of the system. More and more schools are taking on the three functions of providing education on general cultural knowledge, education to academically prepare students for the next grade, and vocational and technical education. For example, in America, 85 percent of schools fall into this category and 90 percent of students study at these sorts of schools. The National Association of Secondary School Principals in America believes that this is the best structure for secondary schools in which everyone can learn something useful.

The second aspect is the comprehensiveness of the content. This includes two characteristics. The first is the redivision of the field of scientific knowledge. For example, the curriculum reform program drawn up by America proceeded from the point that is most capable of improving the efficiency and practical application of learning, dividing existing scientific knowledge into six categories: the empathic domain, which includes psychology and literature; the aesthetics domain, which includes music and the arts; the symbolic domain, which includes languages and mathematics; the experiential domain, which includes natural science and social science; the ethical domain, which includes morals and ethics; and the review and survey domain, which includes history, philosophy, religion, and so on. The second characteristic is the offering of integrated disciplines. For example, in Japanese primary schools, "society" and "science" are merged to form "life classes"; in senior high schools, comprehensive classes on "mathematical sciences" are offered with content that includes comprehensive mathematics, computational mathematics, comprehensive physics, comprehensive biology, comprehensive geoscience, and so on.

The third aspect is the comprehensiveness of educational methods. This refers to the effective coordination, assemblage, and integration of all sorts of educational methods to optimize the effects of education.

The fourth aspect is the comprehensiveness of the school and society. The reform of basic education increasingly attaches importance to bonding with the entire community. Schools and communities must establish an interactive mechanism and form a complete educational structure that "gives priorities to schools, coordinates with communities, is planned overall by the government and has the society participate in educating talented people together," thus achieving the win-win state of "students caring for the community and the community caring for students; schools being opened up to society and social resources being opened up to schools."

4. The Trend in Making Education Psychological, for Cultivating Healthy Personalities

The trend in making education psychological requires education to focus on the cultivation of psychological quality with a healthy personality as its core, enabling educational activities to penetrate deeply into a student's psychological world.

More and more people are beginning to recognize that the fundamental issue of education is the issue of people; the issue of students, fundamentally speaking, is a psychological issue. Rather than say that the best students have a high IQ, it would be better to say that they have strong psychological qualities. Educational practice also tells us that self-confidence and good study habits are important factors that affect our level of learning. Therefore, attaching importance to psychological education that cultivates psychological qualities has already become an important feature of reform in basic education. The trend in making education psychological can be expressed in the following three aspects.

The first aspect is that in terms of the aims of cultivation; highlight psychological qualities that have the cultivation of healthy personalities as its core. "America's Potential," a report published in September 1988 in America, points out: "To develop people's talents for the 21st century, means cultivating people who have clear goals in life and a sense of social responsibility, who have high a degree of adaptability in applying knowledge and skills that they have learnt in a changing environment, who have a creative awareness, who are also able to constantly acquire new knowledge and overcome their own limitations."

The second aspect is to make the main points of research on educational theory psychological. Educational theory has begun to treat knowledge, intellectual and nonintellectual factors, and quality education as the main themes for research.

The third aspect is making experiments in education psychological. A number of well-known experiments in education, such as the experiment on improving the quality of mathematical teaching over a large area conducted by our country's Gu Lengyuan, Qiu Xuehua's teaching experiment attempts, and Li Jilin's situational teaching experiments, all contain important psychological principles.

5. The Trend of Informatization, for Training Students to Use Information to Access Knowledge

The trend of informatization requires the further training of students' information awareness and ability to process information so as to better make use of online educational resources.

Informatization is one of the fundamental characteristics of the future society. In 2010 the global number of Internet users had already exceeded two billion; this number fully expanded nearly 700 times the three million users in 1994. In 2009 alone, the number of web pages in our country reached 33.6 billion, with an annual growth rate that exceeds 100 percent. With the developments in information technology and the information industry, under the driving force of the informatization wave, a series of new changes have appeared in education.

The function of computers in modernizing education has been greatly enhanced. In the wake of the entry of computers into every classroom and home, computers are being more widely used in schools, and the educational software for every school subject is being widely developed and put to use. It is also possible to link the three systems of school education, home education, and social education through a computer network. An open style of teaching will emerge, with students not needing to go to schools to attend school, as they will be able to receive an education at home.

To adapt to this, education on information processing has been strengthened at all stages of learning; teachers are actively and flexibly putting all kinds of machines and teaching materials related to information media to use, such as developing and using computer compatible e-books, electronic libraries, educational software, and so on. The role of the teacher has also undergone some changes. The main duty of the teacher is not to use "chalk plus talk" in the classroom but to provide consulting services. Teaching methods based on classroom teaching have become a method where the teacher assists as a tutor and students use various kinds of information to take the initiative to attain knowledge. The use of the information network can break the shackles of classrooms, school campuses, and even national boundaries that are still in the midst of traditional concepts; information can be mutually exchanged, software shared, files transferred, and so on. Sharing online information resources has gradually become a new landscape for education.

6. The Trend of Internationalization, for Using Education in International Relations

The internationalization trend requires further strengthening foreign languages education and education on international understanding, developing the role that education plays in international economics and cultural exchanges.

An information society is bound to be an international society. In the wake of the high level of development of modern transport and communications technology and the increasing frequency and expansion of economic, scientific, technological, cultural, and educational exchanges, the world has become smaller and the ties between countries are also becoming increasingly closer. At the same time as continuously developing collaborations and friendships, conflicts and friction are also being increasingly exacerbated; the issue of war and peace, global environmental issues, cultural misunderstandings, and issues of cultural friction are also starting to flourish. These issues raise a new challenge, for education and educational objectives, content, methods, means, and so on are currently undergoing vigorous reform to meet this requirement.

The internationalization of education can be mainly expressed in the following three aspects: the first is to generally strengthen foreign languages education; the second is to open up educational institutions to the international community; and the third is to attach importance to the education of international understanding, which is characterized by an understanding of the international community and concern and tolerance for different cultures. Of course, how to maintain and carry forward the fine tradition of Chinese cultural education in this internationalization trend is also a task that should be given great importance.

7. The Individualization Trend, for Running a Distinctive and Unique Education

The individualization trend requires schools to have their own special characteristics and personal strengths and for their teachers to have their own teaching style. It also requires schools to discover the uniqueness of every student and to respect students' ingenuity.

Individuality is the soul of education. The true mission of education is to fully tap into the potential of every student so that students form their own unique personality. An education that has individuality is the best form of education. The individualization trend has the following two features. The first feature is that different regions and different schools are beginning to abandon the views and practices of standardization and normalization and are focusing on pursuing their own unique running of the school and educational style. Weaker schools in particular are regarding the individualization of education as an opportunity for change.

The second feature is a focus on the development of students' personalities during the educational process. Many teachers are increasingly coming to deeply understand that discovering students' uniqueness and respecting their ingenuity is the secret to success in education.

In recent years, the unique education of many of our country's urban secondary schools has achieved initial success, such as Shanghai's Jianping Secondary School's "choice education." They proposed "creating an atmosphere of choice, providing opportunities for choice, expanding the range of choices and developing the ability to choose." The entire school's courses have changed from only knowledge-based courses to three types of courses: compulsory knowledge-based courses, elective cources, and leisure courses, which are run equally on a par with each other. More than a hundred elective courses have been opened up already. For each course, students can choose the teacher and also the pace of the lessons.

8. The Democratization Trend, for Cultivating Civic Awareness and Democratic Spirit

The democratization trend requires education to properly handle the relationship between fairness and efficiency, to cultivate the civic awareness and democratic spirit in teachers and students, and to allow citizens to participate in educational decision making and teachers to participate in school management.

The democratization of education is also one of the global trends of the reform process of basic education. Along with continuously pushing forward social democratization, the maturation and development of people's awareness of democracy and democratic spirit and the democratization of education are also increasingly seen as being important. The democratization of education is mainly expressed in the following three aspects. The first aspect is the equality of education opportunities, the basis of equality in education. *Learning to Be* points out that "equal access to education is only a necessary—not a sufficient condition for justice. . . . This must comprise equal chance of success." With the implementation of compulsory education systems in various countries, the main conflict in many countries is no longer the issue of whether or not people have the right to an education, but rather whether or not people can have a better education. The "school selection craze" is an important issue that is receiving attention from society in these countries and in our own country. Therefore, improving the quality of all types of schools, especially weaker schools, through a variety of measures has already become an important part of the reform of basic education in every country.

The second aspect is democratic teacher-student relationships. In the reform of basic education, countries have come to generally be aware that democratic teacher-student relationships will enable the education process to be lively and active and safeguard the full development of students' creative spirit and creativity. Only within a democratic atmosphere can people with a democratic spirit be cultivated.

The third aspect is the mutual participation of teachers and students in the management of the school. School management is no longer to be monopolized by the school principal and a small number of people. Teachers and students have a say in the policy decisions for the development of the school as well as the day-to-day running of the school.

9. The Legalization Trend, for Regulation and Improvement of Educational Actions

The legalization trend requires that the development of the entire country's educational cause be effectively pushed forward and guaranteed through educational legislation, enabling educational actions to be even more regulated and improved.

In the process of reforming basic education, all countries in the world attach great importance to the construction of a legal system, which enables educational actions and educational administrative actions to be carried out in strict accordance with relevant educational legislation. Furthermore, educational legislation can effectively push forward and guarantee the development of the entire country's educational cause. The legalization of education has the following two basic characteristics.

The first characteristic is the increasing improvement, rigor, and systematization of educational laws. Take America, for instance, which successively issued the Regional Development Act, the Manpower Development and Training Act, the Vocational Education Act, the Equal Employment Opportunity Act, the National Vocational Student Loan Insurance Act, the Vocational Education Amendment Act, Job Training Partnership Act, and so on, just for vocational and technical education. In Japan, Sanseido published "Interpretations of the Six Education Laws," which included 187 educational legal documents separated into 11 categories; among these were 41 documents that related to school education and 12 on school health care.

The second characteristic is the emphasis on the legalization of curriculum standards. Although Japan's "Primary Schools' Learning Guidelines," the "Junior High Schools' Learning Guidelines," and the "Senior High Schools' Learning Guidelines," for instance, have not been included within the legal documents for education, in a certain sense they play a quasi-legal role in education.

10. The Trend in Lifelong Education, Connected to the Entire Course of Life

The trend in making education lifelong requires connecting education to the entire course of people's lives, from the cradle to the grave, and to further increasing the flexibility and openness of education.

Since Paul Lengrand proposed the concept of lifelong learning, social knowledge has rapidly been updated and people's leisure time has rapidly increased, promoting the accelerated progress of lifelong learning. In the early 1970s, the UNESCO report *Learning to Be* clearly requires "lifelong education as the master concept for educational policies in the years to come for both developed and developing countries." Immediately following this, first America and then many other developed countries developed a Lifelong Learning Act.

The implementation of lifelong learning does away with the concept of dividing a person's life into school, work, and retirement. Schools are no longer the place for preparing a student for everything in their lives, as education is connected to the entire course of people's lives—from the cradle to the grave.

In the field of basic education, making education into a lifelong process is expressed in the following three aspects.

The first aspect is an increase in the flexibility of school education. In Japan, for instance, a credit system for senior high schools was established in 1988, enabling people with different academic backgrounds to access a senior high school education according to their needs. Schools offer diverse subjects, the amount of teaching time is flexible, and a system for accumulating course credits is implemented, with senior high schools and specialist schools mutually recognizing these course credits. Some countries even allow students to learn at home.

The second characteristic is that schools will open up to society and become the front for lifelong education. For example, schools will open their sports venues, gymnasiums, libraries, and classrooms to the public and also organize all sorts of lectures for the public, thus serving the lifelong education of the community. Schools are not only a place for young students to learn but should become a place of learning that can be used by every person for one's entire life.

The third characteristic is the unprecedented amount of attention placed on the continuing education of teachers. Advanced study and training systems and regular training systems for new teachers have already been formally written into every country's Teachers Law.

16

The Direction of Reform in Chinese Higher Education

In the past two decades, China has made great progress in terms of the development of its higher education as a whole, and the most significant of its achievements is its shift from being elitist to catering to the masses. In 2007 China's mass enrollment rate in higher education reached about 23 percent; in 2011, it reached 26.5 percent. Quantitatively speaking, our country's higher education has already made an enormous leap forward. Through Project 211, Project 985, and so on, scientific research in colleges and universities has also made great progress; through teaching evaluations and the construction of disciplines, teaching management in higher education institutions has gradually become more and more regulated and the level of teaching has steadily risen. Higher education institutions have also put in a great amount of work in regard to helping disadvantaged social groups. At present, China has already become the country with the largest number of people who are accessing higher education.

At the same time, in these past few years, doubts about China's higher education have also been prevalent. Exactly where are these issues manifesting themselves? How should they be solved?

1. The Urgent Need to Officially Recognize Problems in Higher Education

The main problems that exist in higher education are the trend toward making higher education more administrative, insufficient management of distinctions among universities, the lack of outstanding talents entering the ranks of university teachers, the need for further improvement in the quality of teaching, the faking of achievements by a small number of higher education institutions, the serious problem of university debts, and so on.

First, the trend toward making higher education more administrative is relatively prominent. Higher education institutions are divided into vice-ministerial level and bureau level institutions, and so on. The administrative levels and the internal administrative department on campus each have rather strong characteristics of their own. The academic focus, the school atmosphere, and the academic interests of scholars at higher education institutions have been affected.

Second, relatively speaking, the management of classifications of higher education as a whole is not enough. The trend of assimilation at every university is serious, with all universities heading toward developing into comprehensive universities. The special characteristics of schools are not distinct, and the boundaries between schools are becoming more and more blurred.

Third, a large number of the most outstanding talents have still not entered the teaching ranks at university. Currently, all levels of science academy, social science academy, and writing and art academy institutions are separate from the universities, which also means that nonuniversity organizations have gathered a large number of intellectuals. I believe that we can set aside the funding for these organizations, allocate the money to the universities, and have the intellectuals gathered by these organizations also be allocated to the universities. The scholars, writers, poets, artists, and so on from the research organizations mentioned above should all be professors at university. Overseas universities have writers in residence, poets in residence, artists in residence, and so on. Even more of the social elite are gathered at university, and only these sorts of universities can have a cultural atmosphere and academic ambience. In regard to the specialists and scholars themselves who work at the organizations, the university environment would be even more conducive to their development. Furthermore, this can also enable the government to save a lot of administrative costs.

Fourth, the quality of teaching at university needs to be further improved. China's higher education progressed from being elitist to catering to the masses too quickly, using only the short span of 20 years to complete this process, whereas Western countries go through more than a century of development to make this change. The rapid expansion of higher education has led to a few problems, such as the fact that there is a distinctly insufficient number of qualified teachers, causing a portion of the university and college teaching staff to be quite a mixed bag, and thus the quality of teaching cannot be guaranteed; the universities' ability to independently innovate is relatively not strong enough, and so on. Our universities still basically extend and continue secondary school teaching methods, and the traditional "chalk plus talk" situation is very serious. It can be said that our universities still treat knowledge as a starting point. A survey once discovered that Chinese university students read less than one book per month; furthermore, not even 20 percent of students truly read books in a specialty field, and a mere 9 percent read foreign books. In contrast, American university students read from 500 to 800 pages every week.

Fifth, a small number of higher education institutions appear to be faking their accomplishments. At present, there are some professors who hold a teaching post at two or three schools at the same time, leading to the achievements of one professor being counted by three universities, and this type of repetitive counting exaggerates their academic achievements. Professors can hold more than one teaching post and teach classes, but academic achievements should not be used by the schools where they are holding these concurrent posts. In my opinion, the number of professors who teach at more than one school should not exceed a certain percentage. In addition, there are specific issues, such as the issue of assessments of institutions of higher education. Some of the current assessment policies do not match actual practice and are not conducive to genuine competition. Furthermore, the various kinds of educational assessments, especially an assessment of academic degrees and so on, often become a public relations competition between schools. Having "favorable conditions" is not as good as having "favorable relationships," with the assessors and many schools' main focus is not on its construction, but on its "tackling of relationships."

Sixth, the problem of university debt is serious. In the process of a new round of development, in order to adapt to the needs of an increase in enrollments, a considerable number of schools constructed new campuses and a very large portion of the efforts of these schools has been put into borrowing money and paying it back. In contrast, the efforts used for developing the school's content and meaning has not been enough. In 2006 and 2007, I successively put forward "Proposal on the Strict Control of University Constructions of New Campuses" and "Proposal on Solving the Issue of Large Loans and Debts of Universities and Colleges as Quickly as Possible." The potential risk for colleges and universities is that the fees at many schools go completely toward paying the banks, and so they do not have the necessary funding to invest in teaching and research. Principals also have quite the headache over paying back these debts and are not in the mood for teaching and research.

2. The Need to Cure the Disease of Making Universities More Administrative

The university administrative leadership should be a post held by a professor who is elected via a democratic election, then appointed by the principal, and puts the tenure system into practice.

China's cadre (similar to civil service) system has always been a serialized system. Generally, people are promoted level by level from staff members to assisting roles of divisions, leading roles of divisions, assisting roles of departments, and leading roles of departments. It would be very difficult for the majority of people to be promoted through a breach of this set process. Therefore, if university professors and management personnel want to carry out exchanges of personnel with government, then colleges and universities must have rankings for comparison with government levels.

All along, the leaders of public universities and colleges in China have all had administrative rankings. Originally, the Party secretaries and principals of undergraduate colleges were of departmental rank. In the past decade, universities ranked as the "985 universities and colleges" became "assistant ministerial level universities" and their Party secretaries and principals became assistant ministerial level cadres appointed by the Chinese Central Government. In 1999, only 9 colleges and universities entered the first phase of Project 985, whereas by 2007 the number increased to 43. To a certain extent, the emergence of assistant ministerial level universities has also enhanced the positioning of officials and the awareness of officials for university and college leaders. The university principals also basically appoint the abovementioned positions, and this also strengthens the government's administrative management and control of colleges and universities. It can be said that the current university and college rating system and administrative system are both administratively guided. The strong administrative feel of universities and colleges has caused unavoidable problems of school corruption and corruption in education to appear on the school campus, which originally had a strong academic atmosphere.

In a certain sense, the principals of colleges and universities are actually promoted and appointed as officials; some college deans, department heads, and professors are also transferred between colleges and universities and government institutions. If the university's administrative rankings are canceled, it may cause scholars and professors not to have the chance to enter the cadre system and to participate in management of public affairs. I believe that there is an alternative approach: academic institutions should be given privileges so that they do not have to enter a serialized process and are able to carry out a process that is not that of the public services process. However, university professors should be able to become section heads, division heads, and heads of provincial departments. As long as there is a complete evaluation mechanism for employees and job requirements and evaluation methods are clear-cut, then this is an operable system. A government administrative sequence for promotion in universities is something that is not found overseas. To have administrative rankings actually restricts a lot of professors from having the opportunity to enter the government administrative sequence for promotion.

Under these existing circumstances, how do we start in order to weaken or even rid universities of these administrative characteristics? I believe that the key is to amend the Higher Education Act and establish a staff system for universities. Universities should have only a small number of office workers, who are the management staff. These staff members are part of a lifelong tenure system. These people should consult the system of government management as a reference, which has many levels of management and a lot of room for promotion. However, these types of promotions are salary based and are not linked to the position. Other staff should all be on duty rosters. In universities, a rather large problem is that the boundaries between administrative staff and specialist staff are relatively distinct. I believe that the administrative staff and specialist staff of universities and colleges should not be clearly separated, but instead a rotation roster should be implemented. Administrative leadership positions, such as the position of dean, should be undertaken by a professor, a tenure system should be implemented, and after their term is finished these deans should return to being professors who lecture. The deans and other administrative staff should be chosen through a democratic election and appointed by the principal. All other similar positions should be undertaken by professors using a rotation system. This can greatly reduce the number of administrative staff for university and colleges and improve the quality of work of the administrative staff. At present, there are too many administrative staff members in colleges and universities. Furthermore, administrative staff are under less pressure than professors in regard to being appraised. Therefore, in colleges and universities, being an administrative staff member, to a certain extent, seems much more appealing than being a professor.

In actual fact, at universities at the moment, to truly solve the problem of higher education becoming administrative requires a furthering broadening of our thinking; that is, to have the management of schools become administrative but also have the management staff of universities and colleges become academic. At the moment, many leaders and administrative staff members of colleges and universities still want to write articles and have academic titles conferred on them. In actual fact, it would be fine if they were just to do their job properly in providing leadership and administrative services. They should not participate in the process of gaining an academic title, as it is quite absurd for government administrative staff to want to have academic titles conferred on them. Administrative staff should have a channel for promotion in their own positions so as not to reenter the process of gaining an academic title.

I suggest that a firewall be put up between administrative resources and academic resources so as not to allow administrative authority to monopolize academic authority, nor to allow administrative resources to carve up academic resources. If universities do not solve these problems, or are unable to solve them, then there is no need to mention what will happen after 50 years' time, because even after another 100 years, we will still not be able to enter the ranks of the world's first-rate universities. The problem of the system is a very large problem and we must truly pass the academic authority of universities to the professors. At present, the power of the administration is too strong and affects the development of academic strength.

3. The Need to Explore Managing the Classification of Universities

Universities should be divided into national, provincial, municipal, and private universities. Private universities should also be further divided into for-profit universities and not-for-profit universities.

I advocate that we implement the classification management of universities. Universities should not superficially speak about whether or not to industrialize higher education. This is because the requirements of each school are different and thus they cannot be lumped together. At present, the classifications of Chinese universities are very indistinct. Universities should be divided into national, provincial, municipal, and private universities, with private universities further divided into for-profit universities and not-for-profit universities.

Public universities are government institutions and provide the people with public goods, governments should provide financial support for their expenditures, and they should be a completely nonindustry institution. Private universities that are not for profit also should not become industrialized. For-profit universities can, of course, head down the path of becoming industrialized. Therefore, discussions on whether or not universities should be industrialized should first define and classify universities. Not-for-profit universities cannot become industrialized, while for-profit universities such as America's University of Phoenix must become industrialized. The problem that is now raised is that at these public universities, financial allocations are not enough to pay for all the schools' expenses. It is precisely as a result of this that colleges and universities have no choice but to try every means to acquire additional revenue. Take, for instance, college and university admissions; although they do not have autonomy in the full sense in regard to making decisions on school admissions, they are able to gain a certain degree of freedom in terms of methods such as making use of their right to send 120 percent of candidates' files to related enrollment units for selection if the candidates achieve the enrollment standard, policies to add bonus marks, recruiting students with particular personal strengths, a flexibility index of 2 percent, and so on. Some universities and colleges now have a 5 to 10 percent quota for students who specifically want to select a particular university or college, and as long as students have enough funds for the processing fee, they can be admitted. Generally, each one of these students who selects a particular university or college has to pay a fee between RMB50,000 to RMB100,000. This has already become an integral part of the school's funds.

In other countries, universities can take full advantage of social capital—for example, the donations of various foundations and so on. But the base budget of our universities cannot rely on this, and the allocated funds for public universities cannot make up for this difference. However, at the moment, all levels of government cannot completely guarantee these allocated funds, one of the reasons being that there are many universities and so the government's financial burden is quite heavy. If the number of public universities were halved, then government funding would not be so scarce. I advocate that universities be restructured: 10 to 20 national universities would be retained, with each province retaining about 2 public universities and each city retaining 1 to 2 municipal universities. The remaining public universities can be "sold off" and handed over to enterprises so that the spirit of enterprise is used to transform these universities. Policies such as tax exemptions for famous Chinese enterprises that run a university should also be launched. In so doing, truly meaningful competition will exist between universities.

4. The Need to Explore Subject Paths for Establishing a World-Class University

To establish a world-class university, the method of "slimming down" should be fully put to use in terms of the construction of subjects; at the same time, we should develop subject evaluation criteria and, furthermore, strongly support basic subjects that do not have a close relationship with the commercial market.

In the past decade, the amount of State funding that is used for higher education has greatly increased; for example, schools that have entered Project 211 and Project 985 have all acquired a huge amount of funding. However, is the target that we have put forward, of establishing 100 world-famous schools, too high? Presently, the number of schools that can be truly referred to as world-famous does not even number 100. If we were to focus our funding on only a few schools, would the results be even better? The Hong Kong University of Science and Technology used more than a decade to become a world-famous university. If China were to give some domestic elite schools a lot of funding, it is entirely possible to establish world-class schools. However, many schools have put their money into the construction of the "hardware" of the school. I believe that for universities, the key lies in its subjects. By aiming at a position in the world in accordance with the subjects they offer, universities are more able to attract talented people, and so universities should invest in accordance with the subjects they offer. Project 211 grants support according to the school; if its support were granted according to the subjects offered, perhaps the results would be even better.

Presently, many graduate advisors at colleges and universities, especially academic advisors belonging to the engineering faculty, have the task of applying for research grants, creating an enormous amount of pressure for teachers who are absorbed in the academic cause; furthermore, it causes some scholars to become business oriented. In actual fact, this type of situation also exists abroad. Many colleges and universities abroad also call their professors "boss." The emergence of this type of situation in China is related to China's current mechanism for research evaluation, as it is a mechanism that is too eager to seek short-term benefits. The time taken to conduct scientific research is often relatively long, with results often taking 5 or even 10 years, but at present they are evaluated every year. This causes some professors to focus on the "packaging" and not on intrinsic and lasting features related to their research. In universities, the evaluation of the scholars themselves places too much of an emphasis on the achievements that they publish, their research funding, research topics, and so on and neglects the approval given to them by the academic circles themselves. In other countries, people place great emphasis on scholars' influence within their subject area, their academic status, and their academic prestige. Some subject areas have short research cycles while others have long research cycles, some have a close relationship with the commercial market and some do not; therefore, different subject areas should have different evaluation criteria and be treated differently.

How can we enable basic subjects without a close relationship with the commercial market to have sufficient funds for development, yet not rely on scholars to frantically run about applying for research grants? First, the government must change its investment system for research and have different policies for different subjects. The government should include basic theoretical and long-term development and invest more in research. It cannot allow these teachers to orient themselves toward the commercial market, as doing so will not generate any revenue for it. Second, the private funds for supporting universities are very insufficient. One way for university professors to obtain funding is from the government, mainly for basic subjects and subjects that are closely related to the country's long-term development. Another way is for professors to directly orient their subjects toward the commercial market; this task can be handed over to entrepreneurs to undertake. There are also some subjects that are in between these two groups, not basic subjects but also not directly oriented toward the commercial market. There are many people in society who are particularly interested in these subjects, such as a few particular local art type specialty subjects. These types of subjects depend on foundations. They cannot get any funding from the government or from commercial enterprises but they can get funding from foundations. In other words, allow different types of professors to get funding from different avenues. Currently, China's not-for-profit organizations are still not developed enough and the scope of these foundations is still small; it is perhaps still not realistic to obtain a large amount of funding from foundations. Therefore, there is an urgent need for support from all sectors of society to be developed. At present, some external conditions might still need to be met, but this is just one aspect. The government can also introduce tax exemptions and other incentives.

The key to building a first-rate university lies in the cultivation of great masters in the true sense of word. What are great masters? From an academic perspective, they should be internationally recognized leaders in their subject areas; for example, those who have mastered the key global techniques are creators of some of the world's cutting-edge technology and proponents of crucial theories. It would be incredible if Chinese universities were to have some of these sorts of scholars. This requires that our universities recruit first-rate teachers from all around the world.

Another standard of world-class universities is that they must recruit world-class students. Without world-class students they would also not become a world-class university. At present, there are problems in regard to our recruitment of students. First, the standards of the foreign students recruited are relatively low. The students who go to attend Harvard and Yale are the best students in the whole of China. For Tsinghua University to enhance its quality it must recruit the best students from around the world and have them attend Tsinghua University, so that at last the students in some subjects should be the best in the world. Second is that Chinese universities have not managed to recruit the best students from within the country; many of the best senior high students choose to go overseas to attend university.

Therefore, without first-rate teaching staff and first-rate students, we will never be able to establish a world-class university.

5. The Need to Encourage the Input of Private Capital

The running of colleges and universities should be changed from an examination and approval system to an admission system. At the same time, reforms should be implemented for independent colleges and to enable public colleges and universities and private colleges and universities to competitively develop under the same standards.

China's private capital has not yet truly entered the field of education. First, there is no good mechanism to attract private capital to enter higher education. Because public schools account for the vast majority of schools, there is not much space left over for private capital; a lot of the private capital that has previously entered higher education is now painfully struggling. Second, China's procedures for setting up a private college still uses an examination and approval system and not an admission system; a series of thresholds cause private capital to have great risks after entering higher education, development is slow, and it is very difficult for universities to achieve the goal of establishing first-rate universities in a short period of time. They must first begin dealing with junior college degrees, which are generally two years; once the first batch of students have graduated, they are entitled to move on to undergraduate courses that run for four years; once the first batch of those students graduate, they are entitled to move on to applying themselves to the master's courses. This cycle is too long; a good university cannot be established without 20 years' worth of time. The country should formulate a standard that includes what conditions are to be used for recruiting doctorates and what conditions are to be used for recruiting university undergraduates. As long as students meet these conditions, they should be able to settle the matter of recruitment in one go. Just like running an enterprise, it is not necessary to first set up a small factory and run it well before once again setting up a larger factory. The country should focus on the establishment of standards and not on the establishment of thresholds. Fraudulent schools can be blacklisted and never allowed to enter these standards. Third, at present public universities have established a considerable number of independent colleges. These independent colleges are actually privately run, their fees are about the same as private schools, but they present themselves under the glittery signboard of a public school. This is very unfair to other private schools, and so the development of genuine private universities is more difficult. The government should relax its restrictions and encourage even more private capital to enter the field of higher education.

The existing policies for independent colleges are also one of the most important reasons why private capital has had limited entry into higher education. Many independent colleges have to "pay rent" to their parent schools and find it very difficult to properly handle the relationship between themselves and their parent school. Independent colleges are often weak and their profits are not large.

There are also some stipulations that are not reasonable, for example that independent colleges must have 500 mu of land (approximately 33.35 hectares). This requirement is not rational. Many famous universities overseas only have 200 mu or 300 mu of land. The City University of Hong Kong has just 100 mu or so of land and has recruited nearly 20,000 students. Universities are mainly regarded for their quality, not for how much land they take up. If private capital enters the field of higher education and furthermore competes with public schools under the same standards, then this would also be a kind of boost for public schools. Public schools lack sensitivity to changes in society, as no matter if they run well or not, the government would still give them funding. Public schools lack an inner drive and a force to push them to improve themselves. Private universities would not be like this, because private universities have only two routes—brilliance or death; there is no middle road. Schools should talk using the employment rates of their graduates and rely on their own credibility to enable society to recognize them and to enable the commercial market to recognize them. The model case is the China Europe International Business School. It offered its own diplomas to students without first going through the process of obtaining permission from the education authorities. The Education Department did not give its recognition and so the early graduates of the China Europe International Business School do not have diplomas issued by the Education Department. However, later on, both America and Europe recognized the school, believing that it is one of the best business schools in China, and the school was also recognized by the Chinese Education Department. I have visited Beijing Geely University, which is also presently issuing its own undergraduate and graduate diplomas. We should encourage them to explore and allow society to choose. As long as there is a market for their graduates, the schools can continue to run.

6. The Need to Accommodate People with Unusual Talents and "Geeks"

Universities should accommodate people with unusual talents and "geeks." They should encourage students to participate in scientific research as early as possible. These students should also have genuine academic freedom.

Many real master scientists are people with unusual talents and "geeks"; only such people are able to produce great results that are different. However, in reality, people with unusual talents and "geeks" in the true sense of these terms are not eligible to enter the higher education system in China. For example, these days when famous schools such as Tsinghua University come to Jiangsu to recruit students, they require students to achieve nothing lower than a B grade in every school subject, and independent enrollment candidates cannot have an admission test score that is lower than the first (of five) batch of admission scores. Thus, geniuses such as Qian Zhongshu and Wu Han would not be able to even set foot inside a university.

We now tend to fly the "banner" of comprehensive development while undertaking the compromising act of nondevelopment. By requiring that students be good at all subjects, they will have no aspirations of their own, no direction for their efforts, and none of the dedication of a scientific spirit. We cannot encourage egalitarianism, nor can we encourage equal development; otherwise it will lead to mediocrity. This is the case at all universities in China, not just Tsinghua University. However, Tsinghua needs to keep this in its mind: Give all of the world's people with unusual talents and "geeks" to me.

Universities should encourage undergraduate students to participate in scientific research as early as possible. The moment students enter university, they should be both learners and researchers; from the start they should have a research spirit and ability, as only this can allow them to grow and mature. Liberal arts students should read and have discussions together. Science and engineering students should participate in experiments. However, at many universities, laboratories are basically not open to students and students need to go through numerous obstacles in order to enter the laboratories, which is very troublesome. The consumption of materials used in experiments is also controlled very strictly. A student who wanted to independently conduct experiments might be able to do so only after graduation. Therefore, we must pay attention to the construction of public laboratories and allow students to regard laboratories as another classroom. Libraries and laboratories are extremely important to the growth of university students.

In terms of the training of talented people, I particularly emphasize the academic freedom of universities. In regard to this point, we have still not done enough. We need academic freedom and an atmosphere of academic democracy. Universities, in the first place, are places where various kinds of ideas and various kinds of creativity can freely grow, requiring that we listen to and accommodate different voices. Under the precondition of not violating any legal or academic regulations, our universities should allow ideas to have ample room for exchange and allow learning to have room to freely grow. This is something about which all our universities need to show particular concern. Without it, we would also not get very far.

Reform is not bold and decisive but must be taken one step at a time; the key is in finding a direction. Exactly how the path of higher education should proceed and what is the direction of reform are questions that require genuine research. As far as I know, relevant departments have already started to consider amendments to the Higher Education Act. We all expect that these amendments will solve the problems that exist at present in higher education. However, reform is a long process, and for higher education to reach its desired state might require the efforts of several generations.

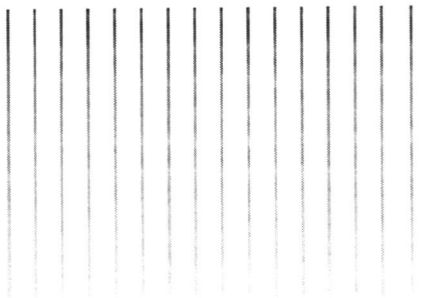

17

Trends in the Development of Chinese Curriculum Reform

Faced with the informatization of the future society and the new impact of internationalization, countries around the world are beginning to be aware of the position and value of education in the twenty-first century. This sort of "end of the century thinking" has caused many countries to consciously carry out an all-around reform of education to orient it toward the twenty-first century, and curriculum reform is often at the center of educational reform in every country.

Looking ahead to our country's curriculum reform for the twenty-first century, I believe that development trends will appear in which learning to care is the main theme, internationalization is the focus, localization is the trait, and diversification is the direction.

1. Learning How to Care as the Main Theme of Curriculum Reform

The trend in curriculum reform, which uses learning how to care as its main theme, will guide the younger generation to extract themselves from their small circle in which they only care about themselves. It will guide them to go beyond themselves and care about society.

Trends around the world in reforming curricula to orient them more toward the future have roughly the basic characteristics of modernization, internationalization, localization, making education comprehensive, making education more activities based, and so on. However, "learning how to care" tends to be the hidden theme in every country's curriculum reform. In the twenty-first century, this theme will move from being hidden to being prominent and become one of the main contents for our country's future curriculum reform.

As we all know, in 1972 a report entitled *Learning to Be* was published by an international committee headed by former French prime minister Edgar Faure and convened by UNESCO. It pointed out that "education is overreaching the frontiers which confined it in centuries-old tradition. Little by little, it is spreading, in time and space, to enter its true domain—that of the entire human being in all his dimensions"; as education greatly extends through time and space, it requires "a sweeping reorganization of the structure of educational procedures on the lines of lifelong education"; "it can be said that for a country to use the goals of lifelong education as the direction for its educational subsystems, then it has a unique and appropriate answer to the challenges of the modern era." The report puts forward circumstances for the purpose of adapting to the acceleration of the rate that knowledge becomes outdated and the rapid development of science and technology, thereby giving rise to adjustments in the industrial structure, rapid changes in the labor market, and so on. Relying only on the knowledge and skills one learned at school can no longer meet the needs of economic and social development. Therefore, a person must "learn to be," that is, one must arrange one's life in accordance with the theory of lifelong education.

The twenty-first century will be an era in which the development of science and technology will move toward being even higher, even newer, even sharper, and even more refined. Humanity will further understand nature, set up new sources of energy, and conquer illnesses that troubled the twentieth century such as cancer and AIDS. The scientific and technological society will bring more material wealth to humanity and an even greater amount of convenience in people's lives. At the same time people are enjoying the bounties of advanced technology, people will also be faced with unprecedented challenges. Therefore, in the late 1980s, at the Twenty-first Century Education Seminar hosted by UNESCO, the Education assistant director-general of the organization, Colin N. Power, put forward this new point of view: lifelong education refers to the challenges that the development of the economy and of science and technology, industrial restructuring, and labor market fluctuations have on the individual. At present, the challenges facing humanity are far beyond the scope of the individual, such as changes in the atmosphere, the destruction of the ozone layer, acid rain, radioactive pollution from nuclear power plants, water pollution, the decrease of arable land, the extinction of species of plants and animals, deforestation, the dramatic growth of the world's population, and so on. These are all serious threats to the survival of humanity. To solve the abovementioned problems requires the implementation of "the spirit of global cooperation" and for the younger generation to be taught to extract themselves from their small circles and to learn to care about the world that is beyond themselves. This will lead to the transformation of educational concepts from "learning to be" to "learning to care."

The report *Learning to Care: Education for the 21st Century*, which was put together through a roundtable discussion at the International Seminar on 21st

Century Education jointly hosted by UNESCO and the National Centre for Education Development Research, points out: "We need a newer and higher overall formula for the thirst for knowledge. We should focus on concentrating the thirst for knowledge on finding solutions to solve the problems facing us at all levels, from local to global, which may the best way to implement such a holistic approach." This will inevitably involve the future overall reform of educational content and the curriculum. From the point of view of the reasoning for reform in many countries, reform is mainly implemented to break the subject-centered structure of the curriculum and its content and to implement interdisciplinary synthesis, the synthesis of basic knowledge and abilities, and the synthesis of the breadth and depth of knowledge.

A representative among these implementations is America's Project 2061. It reflects the entirely new framework of a reformed primary and secondary school curriculum for the twenty-first century. Within the design of various types of curriculum reform, the strict boundaries between every subject are to be broken and are replaced with a new overall combination of courses. Courses that were neglected in the past, such as physical education, aesthetics education, moral education, labor education, and so on, will become important elements of the new curriculum system; at the same time as emphasizing the "visible" curriculum, it will also place great importance on the "hidden" curriculum. The "visible" curriculum focuses on knowledge, skills, and understanding, while the "hidden" curriculum focuses on care, motivation, and attitude. Despite the fact that country-specific curriculum reform measures are not completely the same, a common line of thinking is that they all proceed in designing their reforms from the overall quality of the new people of the twenty-first century as their starting point. The current trend in curriculum development is that increasingly more emphasis is placed on the "hidden" curriculum.

In the high-tech twenty-first century, education will focus more on the theme of humanity's survival and development; moral education and environmental education courses will be universally offered and strengthened in order to cultivate the humanistic, moral, and international spirit of the younger generation. Along with the high degree of synthesis and integration of science and technology, a number of peripheral subjects, related subjects, and interdisciplinary subjects will appear one after another, and the trend of making school curricula comprehensive will also emerge.

Our country is currently devoting its efforts to the construction of modernization. How to avoid the problems that have emerged during the process of industrialization in other countries, such as the end of traditional families, the breeding of individualism, or selfish motives that harm others for one's own personal gains, as well as a weakening of the sense of responsibility toward serving one's society and so on, is something that our country's educational reforms for the twenty-first century must first solve. Curriculum reform will also unfold with this issue at its central content.

2. Internationalization as the Central Core of Curriculum Reform

The trend of Chinese curriculum reform, which has internationalization as its central core, will further strengthen the education of foreign languages and international understanding and cultivate talented people who possess an international awareness, an international perspective, and the ability to carry out intercultural exchanges.

The future society is a society that will have extremely frequent international exchanges. Along with the high degree of development in modern transport and communications technology and expansion of economic, technological, cultural, and educational exchanges, the earth is rapidly "shrinking" and the concept of the "global village" indicates that the future society will be an international society.

In an international society, no country can survive and make long-term development completely isolated from the international community. Economic dealings are increasingly breaking national boundaries, and the opening up to the international community of various countries has already become a developmental trend of modern society. The enterprises of many countries no longer carry out production only for their own country but rather orient themselves toward the world and furthermore rely on the world to carry out production. At the same time, multinational consortia are increasing every day, regional economic cooperation is constantly strengthening, and a trend toward internationalization emerges.

In an international society, the solutions to many issues, such as war and peace, global environmental issues, cultural misunderstandings and cultural friction, and so on, are beyond the abilities of one or a few countries but await the combined efforts of all of the countries to solve them. Therefore, only by proceeding from the point of view of the whole of humanity and actively contributing to solving the various problems in the world for the sake of humanity's peace and prosperity—participating in creating humanity's culture that will enable nature, people, and machines to jointly survive—can the international community develop healthily and steadily.

In this context, adapting to the international community has already become an important part of future educational and curriculum reform for every country in the world. For example, at Nihon University in 1990, the majors labeled "international"—international relations, international politics, international economics, international culture, and so on—reached 48 subjects, having grown four times in quantity in a decade.

Modern education itself is an international phenomenon and is the result of mutual exchanges, mutual learning, and mutually learning from each other's strong points to offset each country's own weaknesses. Presently, anything that happens at a certain country's major educational symposium is spread widely throughout the world within a very short time. At the convening of many international academic conferences on education, the close relations between the educational institutions of various countries, the frequent exchanges between specialists and scholars, the rapid transfer and extensive spread of educational information, and so on greatly promote the exchange of education and culture between countries. In order for education to adapt to this continuous increase of international exchanges, it needs to vigorously promote the internationalization of the educational courses, thereby cultivating talented and internationalized people who are necessary for adapting to these situational developments, who possess a broad international perspective and concern for and understanding of the international situation and its development. Chinese education's "three orientations" (toward modernization, toward the world, and toward the future) were also issued in response to adapting to this change.

In the twenty-first century, our country's reform and opening up will progress deeper and international exchanges will be further expanded. Cultural and educational dealings, led by economic dealings, will become increasingly frequent, and all aspects of education such as its objectives, content, methods, means, and so on will adapt to the future needs of internationalization. In regard to educational content (curriculum), a focus on internationalization will become even more prominent.

First of all, the popularity of foreign languages education will be greatly increased. In order to enable the members of society to better adapt to the needs of international exchanges, the proportion of courses in foreign languages (especially English) in secondary schools and universities will be further increased and primary schools will gradually begin to offer courses in foreign languages.

Second, educational institutions will further open up to the international community. In the twenty-first century, our country will attract even more foreign students to study the Chinese language and culture. We will also recruit even more foreign scholars to teach foreign languages and culture, the international flavor within school campuses will become even stronger, and the setting up of curricula will also consider this feature.

Furthermore, the construction of courses will further adapt to the needs of internationalization. Internationalization does not only mean an understanding of foreign language and culture, but more importantly it is the formation of a moral character and style that considers issues from the perspective of the interests of all of humanity and from a global perspective, understands the international community, and cares and is tolerant of different cultures. This requires that in constructing courses, attention needs to be placed on the cultivation of an international spirit, especially humanities subjects such as Chinese, history, geography, philosophy, and so on, which need to strengthen the pervasiveness of their internationalized content.

Finally, curriculum reform will gradually bring our courses in line with correlating courses overseas. At every stage of schooling—university, secondary, and primary—one of the trends in changes to course content has been toward drawing closer to international standards; this is especially the case for university courses such as international economics, international law, and natural science subjects, which may very likely make great use of original teaching materials that are commonly used internationally.

Additionally, the internationalization of curriculum research is also one of the characteristics of our country's development of educational science for the twenty-first century. In Chinese modern history, from the thinking of the "gradual introduction of Western learning to the East" in regard to educational subjects to the emergence and development of Chinese modern pedagogy, Chinese education has gone through a complicated and rough process. History has proven that if our country's educational sciences were to restrict themselves to a designated area and close themselves off to the outside, then they would lack the ability to "engage in dialogue" with all the countries in the world and would be unable to attain genuine and healthy development. Therefore, curriculum research will also further carry out comparative research on setting up a curriculum, curriculum design, curriculum implementation, and curriculum evaluation, in accordance with international regulations. On the current basis of being comparatively more focused on researching the current situation of overseas curriculum development, we must pay even more attention to exploring the universal rules in regard to reform of the curricula of the world and provide a multidimensional frame of reference for curriculum reform.

3. Localization as the Trait of Curriculum Reform

The trend of having localization be the trait of Chinese curriculum reform will further focus on the traditional cultural characteristics of the Chinese nation and strengthen the development and research of local teaching materials.

Internationalization is not at all "Westernization," and it is also not at all the discarding of the characteristics of our country's education. Having the individuality of our country's education fall into oblivion would causes the development and curriculum reform of our country's education to follow blindly behind the steps of every Western country. It will instead focus on the internationalization of "localization," with our country's culture for its context and China's national circumstances for its basic internationalization. National curriculum reform cannot be separated from national cultural traditions, because the traditional accumulated wisdom that exists within an awareness of national culture has an important impact on curriculum reform; traditions are linked to the past, present, and future.

At the same time as adapting to internationalization, many countries also have strengthened their localization efforts in regard to curriculum reform, placing their country's traditional cultural education in a very important position. For example, Swedish advocate for and organizer of educational reform Professor Torston Husén believes that basic courses that embody a country's cultural traditions, such as literature, history, and so on, cannot be weakened at any time and instead must be strengthened. The newest scientific and technological achievements should be appropriately absorbed on this basis, and these two aspects should be properly combined. Japanese school education, while focusing on learning and absorbing the value orientations of Western culture, also emphasizes cultivating modern

Japanese people to inherit and carry forward the traditional culture and Eastern Confucian ethics and morals of loyalty to one's country, loyalty to one's company, and loyalty to one's duties and handles the relationship between inheritance and innovation, assimilating and discarding, more appropriately. In regard to compiling course content, Japan attaches more importance to localized content. For example, within Japanese history textbooks, the proportion of ancient, modern, domestic, and foreign content is scientifically organized in accordance with their own country's national circumstances.

The twenty-first-century society will be an internationalized society with highly developed technology. It is precisely because of this that we must strengthen the education of traditional cultures and, especially important, carry forward the nation's fine culture. This type of "strongly rooted" localization trend will be particularly focused on in our country's future society. China is a civilized and ancient country with a long-standing culture; traditional culture has a long history that goes back into the dim and distant past, and is both vast and profound, within which are many brilliant ideas that are our treasured riches. Reform must be based on examining the past from the present, which allows fine traditional culture to serve modernization. In this present age, two of the world's great ways of thinking—scientism and humanism—should coordinate their development. The traditional cultural ideology on education, which is based on humanism and ethical standards within the cultural system of Chinese Confucianism, will bring its active function to the era. Western scholars who are concerned with Chinese traditional culture also place a particular emphasis on content in regard to this aspect.

Since ancient times, Chinese people have a persistent mainland national self-consciousness and nostalgic sentiments for their own country and hometown, thinking that "bright is the moon over my home village." From the line in Lu You's poem, "in the evening, Venus collects up rays of light, I desire to sacrifice my life for the country, but alas! There are no battlefields" to Gu Yanwu's famous saying, "the rise and fall of the nation concerns everyone," all without exception reflect strong patriotic passion. Our country is a civilized and ancient country with thousands of years' worth of history and splendid culture. We have accumulated a rich spiritual heritage, and how to enhance our national culture and continue to carry it forward will be an issue that our country's twenty-first-century educational reform must regard seriously. History has repeatedly shown people that the more "localized" something is, is often also the more "internationalized" it is, and the more worldwide significance it possesses.

The localization trend in our country's curriculum reform for the twenty-first century will be expressed in the following few aspects.

First, the Chinese language education, which acts as a symbol of localization, will receive a lot of attention. Since the beginning of the 1990s, in the Chinese mainland and the Southeast Asia region, the demand for Chinese language education is continually increasing. The craze for learning the Chinese language will continue for a long time, and it is very likely that a large number of bilingual schools will emerge.

Second, within the system of school education and social education, Chinese cultural courses, as well as content with Chinese characteristics, will account for a large proportion of the courses offered. In March 1991, the top leaders of our government sent a letter to the heads of the State Commission of Education that advocated the dissemination of "China's splendid five thousand years of culture." With regard to this notice, the State Commission of Education requires students to be taught to "know about our country's major accomplishments in areas such as literature and art, science and technology, philosophy, ethics and morals, education, military affairs, foreign relations and so on, as well as to know about the far-reaching impact that our country has had on the history of humanity and to establish a sense of national self-esteem, self-confidence and pride." Seen in this light, the component occupied by Chinese cultural courses in the school education system should be gradually increased. Within the social education system, along with the increase of people's leisure time, a large number of various forms of Chinese cultural education groups have been created, such as Chinese Qigong, Chinese martial arts, Chinese calligraphy, traditional Chinese medicine and health, and so on. These groups not only attract many Chinese people but will also play a role in strongly radiating this culture to other countries in the world.

Third, curriculum form and content will also be further localized. Ancient China's teaching materials, with their wealth of compiled experiences as well as excellent templates, have provided curriculum reform with things to inherit and learn from. The *Three-Character Textbook, Thousand-Character Reader, Standards for Students, Hurriedly Written Essays, Words Given to Children, Five-Character Lessons*, and other concise and comprehensive elementary teaching materials are easy to read aloud clearly, easy to remember, and far superior to many other teaching materials for children. In curriculum reform of the twenty-first century, it is possible to learn from the successful experiences of ancient times, enabling the compilation of teaching resources to have even more local flavor.

Last, the localization of curriculum research will also be strengthened. Chinese-American psychologist Ovid Tzeng once said when discussing the localization issue of Chinese psychology science that completely adopting the use of Western psychology methods to research Chinese psychology is an illusion. He said: "At a time when traditional intelligence tests are already under attack due to racial and cultural differences, our primary and secondary schools are still reprinting large volumes of these scales to test students; at a time when scholars have repeatedly warned against the abuse of intelligence testing due to a lack of consideration for situational and cultural aspects, our education units are repeatedly using the results of these tests as the standards for students' placements in classes. Education authorities' careless actions harm people, harm situations and harm the country." Similarly, at the same time as emphasizing the internationalization of educational research (including curriculum research), we will also pay more attention to the localization of research methods, we will widely adopt the strengths of many schools of thought and maintain our own characteristics in regard to aspects such as the choice of curriculum research topics, methods, and so on, and furthermore, we will gradually form curriculum theory that has Chinese characteristics.

Since the reform and opening up, our country's curriculum reform has continually become more profound and has achieved many accomplishments. However, on the whole, the shackles and influence of the planned institutional model still exist. Much of the teaching content and curriculum system is still out of date, lags behind, and is incompatible with the present-day developments in science and technology, economy, and society. The personnel required for the twenty-first century are all high-quality and innovative people. Faced with the urgent needs of the times, we must increase the degree of our country's curriculum reform.

4. Diversification as the Direction of Curriculum Reform

The trend of having diversification as the direction in Chinese curriculum reform will realistically carry out the curriculum management policies at the national level, local level, and school level. Teachers will go from being the executors of a single curriculum to becoming curriculum developers.

Among the postwar curriculum reforms of basic education, America's curriculum reform was the earliest and the most striking. The important guiding ideology of curriculum reform this time was to emphasize the unity of the country's foundation and to form a nationwide modern curriculum with unified teaching content. However, the development of a large-scale national curriculum did not achieve the desired results and was dogged by criticism. In the early 1970s, scholars pointed out that the curriculum reforms of the 1950s and 1960s "chose to have adults dominate over students. They only knew they had to make children learn, they did not ask children what they wanted to learn. Due to the fact that the reformers were university academics, they did not have much of a connection with public schools and educational colleges and also tended to ignore the grim realities of classroom and school organization."

Based on reflections on the failure to develop a national curriculum, the development of a school-based curriculum, which corresponds with the development of a national curriculum, began to receive increasingly more attention at the beginning of the 1970s. In the 1990s, it became one of the slogans of educational reform in many countries.

In our country, Chen Xia was relatively early in noting the trend of curriculum diversification. In *Curriculum Theory* he suggested that we must properly handle "the relationship between uniform requirements and adapting to differences," indicating that "there will be diversified courses which will adapt to diversified needs." In the 1980s, this kind of exploration of curriculum diversification was implemented under the premise of a unified and centralized mechanism. In the 1990s, a school-based curriculum began to be a concern for our country's scholars. In June 1999, the National Education Work Conference determined the curriculum management policies at the three levels of State, local, and school, and the exploration of the issue of curriculum diversification entered the level of being developed by a curriculum development system.

The development of the school-based curriculum proposes new requirements of school teachers. For a long time, teachers were accustomed to organizing teaching by following a prescribed order in accordance with uniform textbooks, which emphasizes methodology and not the course. The proposal of a school-based curriculum requires teachers to not only accomplish their work in teaching lessons but also participate in curriculum development. Teachers will transform from being the executors of a single curriculum to becoming curriculum developers.

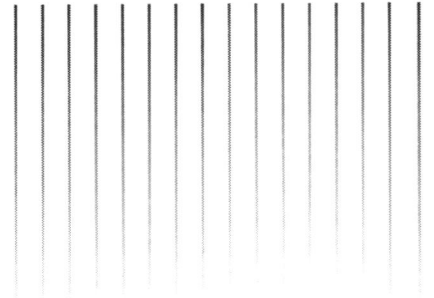

18

The Innovation and Future of Chinese Moral Education

In the new century, what sort of challenges and tasks will Chinese moral education face? What sort of trends and characteristics will emerge in the development of China's moral education? How will China's moral education system further reform and innovate? These are questions that every Chinese educator with a sense of responsibility to history, every Chinese person who fosters the Chinese civilization, and every international educational peer who respects Eastern theory and culture is extremely concerned about. They are also the questions that the research of Chinese moral education needs to urgently explore and answer.

1. The Challenges of Knowledge, the Commercial Market, and Globalization

A knowledge-based economy is beginning to take shape, the market economy system is gradually being established, the tide of globalization is surging upward and forward, and the cries for sustainable development are growing stronger and stronger. Chinese moral education will be subjected to unprecedented challenges.

"In today's world, science and technology are advancing by leaps and bounds, a knowledge-based economy is already beginning to take shape and competition in regards to national strength is becoming increasingly fierce."[1] China's economic and social development not only ushers in the common problems encountered by all the countries in the world in their development but implements a transformation from old systems to new systems and adheres to and constructs the special national circumstances of socialism with Chinese characteristics. This sort of objective social existence determines that Chinese moral education in the twenty-first century will face even more complex and grim challenges and glorious and formidable tasks. It will also constitute a basis in reality and a fundamental driving force for the future development and innovation of Chinese moral education.

The Upsurge in the Revolution of Science and Technology, the Sudden Rise of a Knowledge-Based Economy, and China's New Progress in Modernization Proposes New Requirements of the Times for Chinese Moral Education

When humanity entered the twenty-first century, a new form of economics based on knowledge production, distribution, and use was on the rapid rise, that is, the knowledge economy. According to the estimations of UN experts, in the next 30 years, or perhaps an even shorter time, the knowledge economy would fundamentally take shape within the world.[2] During this period, China on the one hand must speed up the completion of industrialization and on the other hand must also seize the opportunity and greet the arrival of the knowledge economy era. This proposes new requirements of the times for Chinese moral education. The "knowledge" of the knowledge economy includes both scientific and technological knowledge, as well as humanistic knowledge and broad spiritual, moral, and cultural knowledge such as people's ideas and behaviors, the orientations of their values, and so on. Within a knowledge economy, the latter is an important factor that similarly directly affects economic development. As a highly integrated and networked economy, the development of a knowledge economy inevitably requires the strengthening of the construction of new types of ethics and moral education, which includes content such as the ethics of science and technology, the ethics of information, economic ethics, ecological ethics, and so on, in order to protect and promote economic and social norms and its orderly operations and people's healthy and harmonious development.

The soul of the knowledge economy is innovation, and its key lies in cultivating people who are able to innovate, as Ye Shengtao has asserted: "Those who research and make use of science and technology are not computers or robots, but hundreds and thousands of living people. These hundreds and thousands of people must research well and make good use of science and technology. They must not only rely on the brilliant intelligence of science and technology, but must also rely on purity in their thinking and moral character and strength in their willpower and conduct."[3] Cultivating the innovative spirit of a new generation of citizens has especially become a prominent task for moral education. Chinese moral education must strive to adapt to the new requirements that the twenty-first-century knowledge economy and China's modernization raise for the qualities of national ideology and morals and the Chinese nation's spiritual culture.

The Construction of a Socialist Market Economy System
Produces Positive and Negative Effects for Moral Education

As we are entering the new century, China is currently in the process of further realizing its fundamental shift from a traditional planned economic system toward a socialist market economic system. In this process of change, the adjustments of all system structures and distribution methods, the full development and use of the role of the market mechanism, and the continuous liberation and development of productive forces will profoundly affect every field of social life and will greatly shock traditional value systems and ethics.

The establishment of a socialist market economy system urgently requires the strengthening of a proper orientation of political ideology. It requires that an even more reasonable concept of values be established on a series of fundamental relationships such as the relationship between morality and benefits, the individual and the collective, fairness and efficiency, competition and cooperation, rights and obligations, democracy and the rule of the law, and so on, and it calls for a new form of ethics and a new subject personality that are adapted for the market economy. These have already played and will continue to play an active role in promoting the development of Chinese moral education.

At the same time, the coexistence of a variety of economic components and distribution methods under market economy conditions, the prevailing use of the principles of material interests, strengthening of competitiveness and trends toward profits, and in addition the fact that the new system itself is not perfect, tend to produce negative effects for moral education, and it is relatively easy to form and be misguided by the values of individualism. This leads to all sorts of corruption and ugly phenomena seizing the opportunity to spread, such as a "crisis of faith," "a loss of morality," money worship, egomania, abuses of power, cheating and deception, and so on.

Chinese moral education needs both (1) to reflect the needs of the development of the market economy to promote the construction of values and ethics that are adapted for the market economy system and (2) to go beyond the limitations inherent in the market economy, to use noble moral ideals to cultivate people, and to comprehensively further bring out its proper function of leading, coordinating, and enhancing the market economy and society.

The Wave of Globalization, the Pressures of Hegemonies, and Our
Country's Expansion of Its Opening to the Outside World, Including
"Joining the WTO," Has Brought New Issues to Moral Education

After entering the new century, peace and development will continue to be mainstream in world situations. Economic, scientific and technological, and cultural exchanges and collaborations in various countries will become increasingly extensive, international exchanges will become increasingly information oriented and networked, and economic globalization will speed up. However, at the same time, competitions of national strength will also become even more intense, and the gap between the rich and the poor and unequal relationships between developing and developed countries will possibly continue to expand. Furthermore, the hegemonic threat that interferes with the internal affairs of other countries, forces a social system and ideology on others, and even uses armed forces to invade other countries still seriously exists.

Faced with this kind of situation, by further opening up to the outside world China will, on the one hand, enhance mutual understanding and friendly collaborative relations with other countries; strive for a good and peaceful international environment as well as peaceful surroundings; participate in the world economic cycle; and absorb and learn even more from the advanced science and technology, management experiences, and all other achievements of the civilizations of the world's various countries, including developed capitalist countries. On the other hand, we must also open ourselves up to risks; safeguard our national independence and dignity; persist in a form of socialism with Chinese characteristics; constantly enhance our comprehensive national strength, including the strength of our economy, national defense, and national cohesiveness; oppose hegemonies; and resist corrupt ideological culture that corrodes the people, especially the youth.

To carry out moral education under such environmental conditions necessitates moral education to face toward the world and educate people to possess an open international perspective and an understanding toward and respect for the cultural traditions of other countries. Moral education must also promote international peace and cooperation and learn the moral accomplishments of advanced civilizations of the present world. We must have our feet firmly planted in our own country, teach people to properly understand our nation's circumstances, carry on the fine cultural traditions and revolutionary traditions of the Chinese nation, vigorously carry forward the spirit of patriotism, constantly enhance our ability to discriminate and be selective in regard to various forms of foreign culture, and "unite and work hard for the achievement of the Four Modernizations and the shared ideals on rejuvenating China."[4] This is also a new issue that the era has produced for Chinese moral education.

The Responsibility to History That Ecological Protection and Sustainable Development Present to Moral Education
Along with the development of science and technology and industrialization, humanity's ability to conquer and transform nature has been greatly enhanced; however, at the same time, it has also caused unprecedented destruction of the earth's environment that we ourselves exist within. "People have already admitted that we are facing some serious ecological issues. As far as we know, these may seriously threaten the survival of humanity such as changes in the atmosphere, the destruction of the ozone layer, acid rain, radioactive pollution from nuclear power plants, water pollution, the decrease of arable land, the extinction of species of plants and animals, deforestation and the dramatic growth of the world's population. All of these force us to re-examine humanity's survival and lifestyles."[5]

The challenges raised by ecological destruction are far beyond the scope of an individual, a region, a country, or a generation; they are challenges that present and future humanity face in common. Many countries, including China, proceed from their own country's national circumstances as a starting point, earnestly implementing sustainable development strategies that mutually combine economic development and ecological protection and furthermore seek international cooperation in this regard.

It is precisely in such circumstances that UNESCO developed "learning to care" from the focus it proposed in regard to individuals "learning to be." Furthermore, it has treated this as the slogan for twenty-first-century education, emphasizing that we must teach people to extract themselves from their small spheres within which they only care about themselves and to "care about others," to "care about society and the country's political, economic and ecological interests," to "care about other species," to "care about earth's living conditions," and so on.[6] The Chinese cultural tradition of "harmony of man with nature" has received universal attention and recognition. People pay increasingly more attention to protecting the ecological environment in order to achieve the coexistence and sustainable development of people, society, and nature.

This not only expands human relationships to a relationship between humans and nature, it adds new meaning to ethics and morals and, in practice, is also deeply involved in the handling of the issue of relationships between the individual and society and the country, between a certain group of people and the whole of humanity, and between the current generation and future generations; essentially, it reflects the ethical requirements of the new century. To cultivate values with which people place the interests of the country, society, and all of humanity as a whole before their own interests; to cultivate people who will serve the people and have a sense of responsibility in regard to benefiting future generations; to transform the new code of ethics of harmoniously uniting people, society, and nature into one's own self-consciousness and the habits of a civilization—these are the responsibilities to which Chinese moral education of the twenty-first century is duty bound.

Modern Social Life and the Survival and Development of People as Individuals Highlight Various Aspects of Concern in Moral Education

From the beginning of the twenty-first century, China's economy began to take a step toward the level of moderately developed countries from the standpoint of being relatively well off. The high degree of development in modern material civilizations will further change people's social lives and the individual's survival and modes of development. Life with an abundance of materials will not necessarily bring with it a rich spiritual civilization. On the contrary, indulging in material comforts will inevitably cause people to lose their spiritual homeland and to forsake their ideals and hard working to the extent that greed will become second nature and superstition will be rife.

Modern advanced technology has created the wonders of "dialogue between man and machine" and "knowing about the whole world without leaving one's home." However, it has decreased the opportunities for people to directly interact with one another and may result in a certain degree of alienation in human relations, human indifference, and loss of humanitarianism. Modern-day work, studies, and life that are full of competition and risks, and are fast paced and constantly changing, will give people enormous psychological pressure.

Whether one's psychological quality is good or bad, whether one's ability to adapt to society is strong or weak, have become increasingly important factors in determining whether or not a person is successful. How to construct a modern spiritual homeland for the Chinese people; how to cultivate people's noble ideals, sentiments, and the quality of their will to work arduously, be honest, and self-disciplined; how to carry forward the humanistic spirit and enhance humanistic values; and how to enable people to develop robust personalities and fine psychological qualities are the prominent problems related to the people's future survival and development that Chinese moral education of the new century must be deeply concerned about.

Comprehensively Promoting the Development of Quality Education and Moral Education Itself Produces the Need for Internal Reform

At the turn of the century, in order to reach the grand goal of achieving the construction of socialist modernization and the great rejuvenation of the Chinese nation, China held the Third National Education Conference, mobilizing all of the people to deepen educational reform, comprehensively promote quality education, and implement the strategy of rejuvenating the country through science and education. This is a profound change for the entire educational cause and will inevitably spur the further development and innovation of moral education.

For a long time, due to the influence of exam-oriented education, Chinese moral education's frequent cries of "put moral education first" were ignored or distorted. The "boasting and empty words" mode of moral education, the top-heavy sequence of moral education, and the rationalism of the evaluation methods of moral education caused an obvious decline in Chinese moral education. Under these sorts of circumstances, an establishment of a moral education system based on the traditional economic and political system and the social structure would be hard pressed to gain a genuine shake-up and substantial reform.

The faults that exist in this sort of moral education system, such as its being divorced from reality, its neglect of its main subjects, its closed off and singular nature, its formalism, and so on, have become increasingly apparent and severely affect the appeal and effectiveness of moral education. Along with the development of the times, especially the comprehensive promotion of quality education, Chinese moral education has already reached a time when it must further reform and innovate. This is also the inherent need and challenge that the development of Chinese moral education in the new century assumes.

2. A Unified Structure in the Development of Moral Education

In the development of Chinese moral education in the new century, a structure will emerge that unifies the real and the transcendental, the national and the global, the subjective and the normative, the practical and the scientific, and the integral and the open.

To face the challenges and arduous tasks of the twenty-first century and to sum up both its positive and negative experiences, Chinese moral education must abide by historical materialism and dialectics, and it must walk a developmental path that is based in reality, is oriented toward the future, criticizes the idea of inheritance, and integrates innovation. It must also put its efforts into constructing a modern socialist system of moral education with Chinese characteristics. This is also one of the great trends in the development of Chinese moral education for the twenty-first century. It clearly possesses the following basic features.

The Unity of Reality and the Transcendental

This unity is in regard to the basis of moral education and its functions. In the twenty-first century, Chinese moral education will completely break away from its outdated mode of moral education that was established on the basis of the pre-existing economic system and social structure. It will abandon the "prescriptions to aid the times," of "a return to traditions" or "transplanting Western ideas," truly basing China in reality and orienting the country toward the future. In the current world environment it will use the practice of modernization in China as its foundation and be compatible with both a socialist market economy and opening up to the outside world. It will help those being educated to establish correct political orientations and values and cultivate a new code of ethics and and a positive, active, and open personality.

Through the process of reflecting and adapting to reality, Chinese moral education will also actively break through the limitations of reality, orient itself toward the future, and use moral ideals that sprout in reality but transcend reality to lead people, nurture people, and motivate people, propelling those being educated to constantly pursue even more noble spiritual states and behaviors, to improve themselves and enhance their lives, to work hard for the sake of creating common prosperity and a highly civilized society in the future, thereby fully bringing into play the significant role that moral education plays in boosting people's comprehensive development, the spiritual civilization of the Chinese nation, and the entire construction of modernization.

The Unity of the National and the Global

This unity is in regard to the origins and characteristics of moral education. Chinese moral education in the twenty-first century will be guided by Marxism, use the construction of modernization as its basis, and use "making the past serve the present" and "adapting foreign things to serve China" as its principles. It will carry on the tradition of excellence in Chinese moral education, learn from achievements of the moral education of the modern world's civilizations, and strive to open itself up to development and to blaze a new path. Chinese moral education will respect history, further tap into arranging and critiquing the inherited legacy of Chinese moral education, discard the residues of feudalism that are based on small-scale peasant economies and the autocratic monarchy system, and absorb the essence of democracy that possesses universal rationality, embodies the national spirit, and conforms to the psychological features of national culture. Chinese moral education should place even more of an emphasis on carrying forward the tradition of moral progress formed since the May Fourth Movement and integrating it into the new construction of the modern moral education system, enabling moral education to be rooted into national culture and full of Chinese characteristics.

At the same time, Chinese moral education will still have to face the world. Further strengthening exchanges and collaborations with the moral education in other countries, resisting the corrosion of corrupt ideology and culture, extensively using advanced theories of, teaching materials for, and experiences from moral education that are suitable for national circumstances, and integrating them into a modern moral education system with Chinese characteristics will enable China's moral education system to converge with the world tides and be even more with the times.

The Unity of the Subjective and the Normative

This unity is in regard to the essence and objectives of moral education. In the twenty-first century, Chinese moral education is no longer simply to preach and exert limitations on people from the outside but rather to be people focused, to treat morals as an internal need of people, to develop those being educated as the main subjects of ideological and moral growth, and to treat the construction of the virtues of its main subjects and the development of the main subjects of virtues as its fundamental objective. Therefore, it will fully respect the status of those being educated as the main subjects, earnestly implement the democratization of moral education, attach importance to stimulating the moral consciousness of those being educated, and put all of its efforts into enhancing their ability to differentiate right from wrong and good from evil, and their ability to self-educate and to put morals and ethics into practice.

At the same time, Chinese moral education will attach importance to "standard education." It will use reasonable standards as the objective requirements of socioeconomic development and the concentrated reflection of humanity's moral civilization and the spirit of group self-discipline, devoting itself to formative education of a new code of ethics that suits the needs of a socialist market economy system and construction of modernization. This includes the formative education of standards such as social morality, professional ethics, family ethics, students' daily behavior, and so on. It enables these standards to become the requirements of the main subject's innate "self-discipline," thereby forming good and civilized habits, interpersonal relations, and moral customs; establishing an even more reasonable social order for living and an even more reasonable order for one's individual life; creating a favorable environment for the development of the main subject's virtues; and enabling one to truly attain a necessary grasp on morality and on moral freedom.

The Unity of the Practical and the Scientific

This unity is in regard to the central focus and manner of moral education. Twenty-first-century Chinese moral education will change its manner of education, which is centered mainly on the theory of "indoctrination" and formalism. It will treat the actual ideological and moral problems of the practice of establishing modernization and the ethical practices of those being educated as its central focus. It will place an emphasis on guiding those being educated to consciously devote themselves to ethical practices; to combine the moral practices, experiences, and accomplishments found in participating in collective social practices and in one's individual daily life; and to persevere, repeatedly practice, and have these form into habits. Chinese moral education enables those being educated to learn and apply correct theories through the process of practice; furthermore, it transforms these theories into their own thinking and moral beliefs, implementing the unified and coordinated development of moral cognition, moral emotions, moral determination, and moral behavior on the basis of practice. To use the practices of those being educated as the fundamental standards for the inspection and evaluation of the effects of moral education continuously improves the effectiveness of moral education.

At the same time Chinese moral education is enhancing its practicality, it will also stress its scientific nature. It will emphasize cultivating those being educated not only to be driven by active emotions but also to use the rational spirit of science to carry out ethical practices and moral critiques and to apply scientific methods of advanced technological means such as observations, investigations, experimentations, case analyses, and so on, to understand the target of education, implement moral education, sum up the experiences of moral education, reveal the rules of moral education, and furthermore, under the guidance of Marxism, direct the new practices and new developments of moral education and enable the construction of moral education subjects to achieve a new level and gradually succeed in making Chinese moral education scientific.

The Unity of Integrality and Openness

This unity is in regard to the structure and system of moral education. Twenty-first-century Chinese moral education will break the singular, closed-off old structure of moral education and establish an integral and open new "great moral education" system. Based on the integrality of the development of people's quality and the diversity of factors that influence the development of people's ideological and moral qualities, Chinese moral education will focus on the overall entity and strive to enable those being educated to learn to be upright people and to be citizens who "have ideals, morals, culture, and discipline" and promote the comprehensive improvement and overall development of their qualities. To link differences and similarities and arrange the specific content and the ways and means of implementation of various stages of education, forms of scientific sequence, and overall convergence of moral education; to intrinsically combine moral education with intellectual education, physical education, aesthetic education, and other forms of education; to have moral education take up residence within all school subjects and curriculum; and furthermore, to regard the community as an important means of reliance, to enhance the strength of the organization and coordination of various forms of education, at all levels and for all types of schools, families, and societies constitutes the social networks and overall combined forces of moral education.

In the face of all types of mutual exchanges and surges of ideology and culture and the diverse, colorful, and changing modern world, Chinese moral education must not only have an overall structure but should also be an open system. In order to create an open society, within which the main subjects of ideology and morality can self-learn, be self-reliant, and be self-disciplined, it will enable those being educated to place themselves within the open educational context and process. Within its mutual opening up to the outside environment, it will constantly implement its own development and updates, and at the same time fully bring into play its function of selecting, guiding, and creating culture, thereby forming a modern education system that is full of vigor and vitality.

3. The Need for Innovative Educational Objectives in Moral Education
The new objectives system for twenty-first-century moral education has the cultivation of a new type of personality for its main subject as its core. Its basic structure can be summarized as the patriotic spirit, ethical spirit, spirit of innovation, and spirit of self-discipline.

The innovation of educational objectives in twenty-first-century Chinese moral education is needed in order to take the initiative and meet the challenges of the new era, to "face toward modernization, face toward the world, and face toward the future," to fully embody the moral philosophy of the harmonious development of people, society, and nature, with the training of new people who "have ideals, morals, culture, and discipline" as its general requirement. The new system of objectives has the cultivation of a new type of personality for its main subjects as its core; its basic structure can be summarized as four types of spirits.

The first is a patriotic spirit. Chinese moral education must first cultivate the subject awareness of those being educated as being members of the Chinese nation with a strong sense of national self-esteem, self-confidence, and deep patriotic feelings; they are to understand national history, be well acquainted with national circumstances, and consciously carry on the Chinese nation's fine cultural and revolutionary traditions. They are to ardently love the socialist motherland, connect their individual life ideals with the common ideals of the nation, and realize their own value in the struggles for the modernization cause of the motherland and the great rejuvenation of the Chinese nation. They are to carry forward the spirit of democracy, fulfill their civic duties in accordance with the law and with the attitude of being masters of their own country, exercise their civil rights, actively participate in the country's political and social life, and promote democratic and legal construction.

The second is an ethical spirit. Chinese moral education must cultivate those being educated to establish the ethics and values of the people and oneself as a whole entity, the integration of justice and profit, and the oneness of heaven and humanity. It must have those being educated consciously comply with social morality, professional ethics, family ethics, environmental ethics, and regulations, as well as common international regulations. They are to properly handle the relationships between the interests of themselves, others, the collective, and the country; to advocate collectivism and service to the people; and to enhance their spiritual state. They are to learn how to care, to cooperate, and to engage in interpersonal exchanges and international cooperation. They are to ardently love nature, cherish life, and do their duty in regard to the harmonious unity and sustainable development of people, society, and nature.

The third is the spirit of innovation. "Education has both the power to nurture the spirit of innovation and also the power to repress the spirit of innovation."[7] Chinese moral education must open up and develop the potential of those being educated and create a relaxed environment for the development of their personalities. They need to vigorously cultivate their spirit of innovation, enabling them to possess an open perspective, the concept of reform, and the pursuit of innovation. They need to be able to conduct independent thinking and rational critiques on existing knowledge and traditional ideology and morals, dare to break outmoded conventions, challenge authority, and explore the truth. They are to develop innovative personalities that are self-confident and cheerful, aggressive in competitions, eclectic, unconventional, full of imagination, and willing to be creative. Finally, moral education will enhance the psychological qualities of those being educated in regard to adapting to change, withstanding setbacks, and being tenacious and unyielding.

The fourth is the spirit of self-discipline. "Teaching is for the sake of achieving the need not to teach."[8] Chinese moral education should attach importance to inspiring the inner moral needs of those being educated and cultivate their spirit of self-improvement and their ability to self-educate and self-develop. Faced with the impact of diverse, muddled, and complicated ideology and culture, they should be able to independently judge and select, to absorb beneficial nourishments, to resist rotten decay and bad temptations; to consciously transform the progress of moral ideology and reasonable behavioral norms into their own beliefs and habits; to carry out self-reflection, self-regulation, and self-cultivation of their own thoughts, feelings, and actions; and to realistically persevere in putting the needs and aspirations of their own moral development and character improvement into practice and to realize themselves through the constant improvement of their living practices.

4. The Need for Innovative Educational Content in Moral Education

Twenty-first-century moral education must form a system for moral educational content that possesses Chinese characteristics, reflects the spirit of the times, and is life oriented and innovative.

The innovation of twenty-first-century Chinese moral educational content must be in accordance with the new objectives of Chinese moral education and the laws of the development of ideological and moral qualities of those being educated.

It must carry forward the Chinese nation's fine moral traditions and combine with what has been learned from the achievements of advanced civilizations in the modern world. It will draw close to and be concerned about the reality of the lives of those being educated, keenly reflect socioeconomic changes and cultural innovations, and form a system for moral educational content that has Chinese characteristics, reflects the spirit of the times, and is life oriented and innovative.

First, convert a strengthening of the critiques of the inheritance and creativeness of the Chinese moral traditions into an integration with and "sinicization" of what has been learned from the advanced civilizations of the world. Ancient Chinese ethics and morals have accumulated thousands of years' worth of ample content forming a perfect system, which is handed down through a great quantity of classical literature and poetry, lifestyle habits, role models, and so on; among these are things that, although they were produced in a feudal society, reflect the fine traditions of a national spirit to a certain degree.

Take, for instance, the ideology and concepts of "oneness of heaven and humanity" and "to be people-oriented," the patriotic aspirations of "the rise and fall of the nation concerns everyone," the feelings of the collective of "the world for all" and "grieve first, rejoice afterwards," the enterprising spirit of "be energetic and show promise, unceasingly strive for improvement," the principles of human relationships of "benevolence and filial piety" and "modesty and good manners," the orientation of values toward "acting ethically and not being tempted by riches" and "obligation first, interests second," the moral qualities of "honesty and keeping one's promises" and "hard work, thriftiness, and integrity," the attitude of self-cultivation of "moral, mental, or spiritual self-cultivation" and "being strict with oneself in solitude and self-discipline," and the grand righteousness of "not being corrupted by wealth or honors, not being shaken by poverty and not being cowed by power," and so on. These fine traditions must be analyzed from the perspective of today's world and the context of China's development. They must be separated from the traditional moral system based on small-scale peasant economies and a patriarchal system, beginning with distinguishing it from the interwoven dregs of feudalism, giving it new meaning that is with the times and enabling it to become an important source of modern moral educational content that has Chinese characteristics.

Carrying forwards the fine moral traditions of the Chinese nation should include carrying on and developing modern China, especially the new ideas and morals created and formed by the social changes and advancements since the May Fourth Movement, for example the rejuvenation of China; resisting aggression, establishing ideals, the notion of struggling arduously, integrating workers and peasants; to serve the people, to dedicate oneself to national liberation and the modernization of socialism; to promote democracy, oppose dictatorships, fight for freedom and equality, shoulder social responsibility, respect the independence of one's personality and pursue individual liberation and development; to hold science in high regard, eliminate superstitions, emancipate the mind, seek the truth through facts, constantly search for the truth, and reform innovation, and so on. The innovation of Chinese moral educational content needs these as a cultural source even more.

At the same time, we must also pay attention to absorbing the accomplishments of advanced civilizations of various countries in the modern world, including developed capitalist countries, especially the ideas, concepts, and ethical norms that are generally applicable to the market economy, the knowledge society, and the resolution of common ethical issues of present-day humanity. Additionally, we must change them in accordance with our country's national circumstances, causing these to be integrated with the fine moral traditions of the Chinese nation to form one entity, becoming an integral part of the educational content for Chinese moral education in the new century.

Second, break the old "curriculum" restrictions and "dogmatic" form and construct moral educational content that is life oriented. Chinese moral education must draw close to and be concerned with the individual lives and the reality of the lives of those being educated. It must closely connect the ideas, ethics, and people's everyday lives that reflect society's requirements and form educational content that is suitable for the different types of characteristics and different stages of reality of those being educated. The moral education curriculum in schools needs to break the old "curriculum" restrictions and "subject" model and to use the combination of theory, norms, and certain learning segments in students' lifestyle practices as teaching material. In addition to the visible course content, moral education must also place an emphasis on developing and using the active hidden course content within teaching activities and the environment. To do this, we must comprehensively implement quality education, improve the teaching activities and environment of school education, and minimize the factors within these that have a negative impact on students' ideas and moral character.

Chinese moral education must take root in the soil of life, integrate a concern for the individual daily lives, study lives, interactive lives, collective lives, professional lives, and so on of those being educated, and in guiding them truly bring into play its functions of affirming, regulating, and enhancing life.

Third, strengthen the innovativeness of Chinese moral educational content. It must have a system that is fundamentally relatively stable and, more importantly, it must open up to the times and to life and constantly absorb fresh ideological and moral nourishment from socioeconomic changes and cultural innovations. It must introduce all the new ideological and moral challenges, conflicts, issues, and hot topics that people encounter in their lives, letting the individuality of educators and those being educated be displayed, to develop ideological and moral critiques and innovative abilities and to achieve the continuous innovation of moral educational content.

5. The Need for Innovative Educational Methods in Moral Education

Twenty-first-century moral education must establish a system for moral educational methods that possesses Chinese characteristics and distinct features of the times, complies with regulations, and is highly effective.

The innovation of twenty-first-century Chinese moral educational methods must be in accordance with the new objectives and new content of Chinese moral education. It must summarize the experiences of moral education in history and in reality, earnestly implement fundamental principles that are subjective and practical, achieve the intrinsic combination of humanistic educational style and modern scientific and technological means, and establish a system for moral educational methods that possesses Chinese characteristics and distinct features of the times, complies with regulations, and is highly effective.

First, we are to respect the position of those being educated as being the main subjects and bring into play their role as the main subjects of moral education, thereby promoting the subjects' self-formation and self-development of ideology and morals. The innovation of Chinese moral education first lies in abolishing the model of the unidirectional inculcation of an arrogance based on one's social position. It must treat moral education as an interaction between the educator's teaching and the students' learning and furthermore, truly respect the position of those being educated as the main subjects of moral education through the implementation of self-education activities of those being educated. It must also establish relationships that are democratic and equal, allow the teachers and students to mutually benefit from the teacher's teaching, and be close and friendly, creating the necessary preconditions for the development of the personalities of those being educated as the main subjects. It must proceed from the reality of life and growth of those being educated, to guide patiently and systematically, to inspire and lead them, to awaken the moral needs and ideological awareness of those being educated and enable them to actively participate in the process of education. Optimizing the environment and sharing feelings will enable those being educated to actively bring about the internalization of ideology and morals through being imperceptibly influenced by teachings and by the heartfelt sympathetic responses of students and teachers. We must enable those being educated to learn how to self-educate and allow them to practice differentiating right from wrong in an open context with the ability to independently choose their correct values and behavior. Those being educated must also learn how to cultivate themselves in their own lives, to constantly adapt to new objective requirements in regard to ideology and morals, and to motivate, regulate, improve, transcend, and innovate themselves.

Second is the unity of moral knowledge and practice, to pay attention to guiding those being educated to consciously carry out moral practices and to use the practices of those being educated as the fundamental standards for inspecting and evaluating the effect of moral education. The innovation of Chinese moral educational methods must overcome the wrongful practices of mainly focusing on teaching through preaching and formalism. It must shift the central focus of moral education to that of guiding the practices of those being educated, treat the conscious practices of those being educated as the starting point and ending point of moral education and as the basic channel for cultivating the ideology and morals of the main subjects of moral education. It must enable those being educated in the necessary theoretical knowledge to practice conscientious studying and, furthermore, to gain profound experiences and understandings through their own practices in life, enabling them to truly transform these into their own understanding or even beliefs. It must organize opportunities for those being educated to participate in all sorts of social practices such as volunteer labor, the construction of culture, social surveys, scientific and technological services, work-study programs, military and political training, festival activities, and so on, and more importantly, to guide them to consciously put a correct ideological and moral understanding into practice in their actions anytime and anywhere in their daily lives. In accordance with actual needs, moral education can gather a certain amount of time to organize those being educated to launch certain practical activities; more importantly, we must guide them to persevere in repeatedly practicing the necessary fundamental ideology, morals, and civilized behavior of upstanding people, thereby forming good habits. We must innovate the methods of evaluation for moral education and have evaluations linked to the moral practices of those being educated, treating the improvement and enhancement of the moral practices of those being educated as the fundamental standards for measuring the development of the subject's virtues and for assessing the effects of moral education.

Third is carrying out the integration of a humanistic educational style and modern scientific and technological means. Moral education is an education that is people-oriented, uses people to educate people, and teaches people how to be upstanding. An educational style that is full of humanistic features such as inter-personal exchanges, the communication of emotions, teaching by words and deeds, the emulation of role models, the reading of classics, investigations and experiences, personal practice, self-cultivation, and so on, and possesses irreplaceable important values and unique advantages, is also in the fine traditions of Chinese moral educational methods. Twenty-first-century Chinese moral education must carry on and develop these effective educational methods well, according to new situations. At the same time, it should be concerned about the effects on moral education of modern information science and technology, such as mass media and communications, multimedia computers, the Internet, and so on, as well as modern psychological science and technology such as psychological testing and consultations. To actively develop and use these scientific and technological means for the service of moral education, to bring out the strengths that these have in cultivating a modern consciousness and personality for the main subjects, to suppress the negative effects these means may produce that are not conducive to people's healthy growth, and furthermore to intrinsically integrate these means with a humanistic educational style and to enhance the practical results of "educating a person," are some of the important aspects of innovating Chinese moral educational methods.

6. The Need for an Innovative Education System in Moral Education

Twenty-first-century moral education needs to build a moral education system that is full of the vigor and vitality of scientification, democratization, socialization, and lifelong education.

Innovation of the twenty-first-century Chinese moral education system must adapt to socioeconomic changes and reforms of the entire education system, abide by the rules of modern moral education, and build a system that the development of Chinese moral education needs, which is full of the vigor and vitality of scientification, democratization, socialization, and lifelong education.

First is the establishment of a research mechanism. The development and innovation of Chinese moral education must rely on science. It must treat launching scientific research on moral education as an important function of the organization of moral education, and furthermore, it must establish an operating mechanism for moral education, which pioneers research. It must also vigorously develop the survey research of moral education and timely grasp the trends and rules in regard to the development of young people's ideology and morals. It will form a correct decision-making and operational program for moral education and guide the practices of moral education as a whole through collecting and profiling moral education phenomena, finding examples and case studies, researching the new circumstances and issues of moral education, and carrying out experiments in moral education. It is necessary to strengthen the scientific construction of moral education, to classify the topics of moral education as important content for a country or location's planning for philosophy and social sciences and educational sciences. It will thereby cultivate a large number of moral education experts who are accomplished in scientific theory, establish the necessary moral education research institutions, construct high-level moral education subjects, and furthermore guarantee experts' wages and research funding, enabling the scientification of Chinese moral education to achieve implementation in terms of its system.

Second, Chinese moral education needs to further democratize its management system. While adhering to fundamental objectives and fundamental content of moral education for national unity, we must target the different circumstances of the different types of people from different places who are being educated. We must research and formulate concrete objectives and content for moral education, which are multilayered and diversified; develop a moral education curriculum for school that integrates the national curriculum, local curriculum, and school curriculum; and better adapt to the developmental needs of the personalities and characters of those being educated by fully bringing out the enthusiasm, advantages, and features of moral education in all schools and locations. It is necessary to implement a management system for moral education that the masses widely participate in under the leadership of the Party and government, enabling educators and those being educated to participate in its management, thereby expanding their rights to self-educate and self-manage. We will also set up a working committee and advisory board for moral education, composed of moral education experts, administrative leaders, and representatives of the masses from all different areas, who will specifically manage the moral education and provide the Party and government with important information and advice on policy decisions for moral education. Also, the evaluation system of moral education is to be reformed and its aspects of self-evaluation and public evaluation strengthened.

Third is the formation of a social network. It must turn toward all the members of society from the high ground of having raised the ideological and moral qualities of the Chinese nation and its level of spiritual civilization, with the education of young people and children as its focus, and strive to build a multilayered network for moral education and a system of lifelong education in the entire society. It is not only the educational department that must grasp moral education; other departments such as publicity, literature and art, television broadcasting, newspaper publishing, electronic information, and even public security, commercial and industrial management, and customs must similarly grasp and jointly administer moral education in cooperation. Not only must schools become fine places for educating people, but enterprises and public institutions and parts of society must play a role in moral education. Under the government's overall plan, the implementation of intimate collaborations between schools, families, and all aspects of society in the surrounding local area will form a community network for moral education. It must not only care about the healthy growth of young people and children but also systematically organize adult moral education, including the education of elderly people, forming a lifelong moral education system, thereby making Chinese moral education socialized and lifelong.

7. The Need for Innovative Teachers in Moral Education

Twenty-first-century moral education needs to create a team of moral education teachers for the new century who are ambitious, can take on the important task of educating people, and can serve as role models.

The twenty-first-century Chinese moral education teachers must enable themselves to take the initiative to adapt to and promote the development of Chinese moral education. In the practice of innovation in moral education, they must strive to achieve the innovation of themselves, creating a team of moral education teachers for the new century who are ambitious, can take on the important task of educating people, and can serve as role models.

"The educator himself must be educated."[9] Moral education teachers who were trained in the Chinese moral education of the past must however cultivate the future generation of new people, and furthermore must themselves first be educated and innovate themselves.

The innovation of Chinese moral education teachers, apart from having to adapt to the socialization and lifelong nature of moral education and forming a structure for the teaching ranks that combines full-time and part-time teachers, mutually complements the functions of each other and is grand in scale. What is more important is that it must fundamentally transform the function and role of moral education teachers. It must enable the function of moral education teachers to shift, from monodirectional teaching of ideological and moral conclusions due to "lecturing on doctrine," to caring, guiding, and helping those being educated to achieve the self-development of their ideological and moral qualities and at the same time as this process, enable themselves to also be educated and achieve development. Thus, the role of moral education teachers must also accordingly shift from indoctrinators and controllers who are placed above those being educated to mentors and people of exemplary character for the development of the main virtues of those being educated.

To this end, Chinese moral education teachers must strive to achieve the innovation and improvement of their own qualities. They must have a broad perspective, a correct outlook on the world, and correct methodology in regard to the twenty-first-century world and China's socioeconomic development and cultural changes. They must have a clear awareness of their own task of educating people and establish socialist modern moral education ideals and concepts with Chinese characteristics; they must also constantly strengthen their own ideological culture and moral cultivation in an open environment and truly be able to enlighten the minds of those being educated and be their role models. Finally, they must systematically master the knowledge and skills of modern moral education and improve the innovative wisdom and practical abilities of moral education.

Whether the development and innovation of Chinese moral education is successful may in the end depend on whether Chinese moral education teachers are able to innovate.

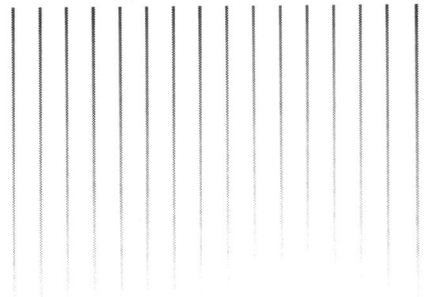

19

The Future Prospects of the Reform of Chinese Teachers

To strengthen education, we must first strengthen teachers. According to the Ministry of Education, our country currently has 17 million educators; among these are more than 13.9 million full-time teachers who work at various types and levels of schools. They are an important force in promoting the scientific development of the educational cause and in enhancing the quality of education. Strengthening the teaching ranks and raising the quality of teaching are the expectations of the broad masses of people, and educational reform and development are an even more urgent need.

Quality education has been talked about for many years, but why has it not been truly implemented up till now? In addition to the misalignment of the government's role and the bias of examination and evaluation mechanisms, as well as society's part in adding fuel to the fire, one extremely important factor is a lack of teachers who are able to truly implement quality education. Especially since the implementation of free compulsory education, the quality of teachers in rural villages will directly affect the quality of basic education there. All in all, the key to putting quality education into effect lies in its teachers and in the quality of the teachers. High-quality teachers will possess a correct concept of education, a profound knowledge system, and good teacher-student relationships; they will inevitably know how to face all students, research the overall circumstances of all students in aspects such as the students' morals, intellect, and physical health and fitness; explore educational methods that are suitable for students' healthy mental and physical development; and thus their teaching is also bound to be quality education. Conversely, low-quality teachers will not understand the true meaning of education, will not consciously learn and undertake advanced studies, and will not work in accordance with the requirements of quality education; they may consciously or unconsciously pursue test scores to the extent that they are incapable of caring about students' mental and physical health; they explain a large number of examples to students every day, arrange a large amount of homework, and implement all kinds of tests. Their teaching will inevitably be exam-oriented education that is contrary to the purpose of quality education. To sum it all up, the quality of education does not depend on how beautiful the school buildings are nor how state-of-the-art the school facilities are, but on the quality of that person who stands at the classroom podium. Therefore, the construction of a cohort of high-level teachers is also a precondition of implementing quality education.

1. Strengthening the Teaching Ranks and the Reform of Teacher Education

From an overall perspective, the most brilliant and talented people have still not truly entered teaching, the teacher-training model is relatively simplified, and the system for teachers to continue education is not complete and its standards are not uniform. There is also a shortage of outstanding teachers in rural villages and in disadvantaged city schools, the allocation of quality teachers and resources is uneven, a small number of teachers are suffering from serious burnout, and quality overall is on the low side. Therefore, strengthening the construction of the teaching ranks and the reform of teacher education is imminent.

In recent years, under the leadership of the Party committees and governments at all levels and with the support of the entire society, the improvement of the cohort of primary and secondary school teachers has achieved new breakthroughs and new headway. First, the allocation of teacher resources has been optimized. The total number of teachers has increased, and their age composition has been further optimized with young and middle-aged teachers becoming the main body of primary and secondary school teachers. Teachers who are 45 years old and below in primary, junior high, and senior high schools account, respectively, for 69.9, 84, and 87.3 percent. Second, the overall quality of teachers has improved. The academic qualification rate of full-time teachers in kindergartens, primary schools, junior high schools, and senior high schools have reached, respectively, 96.5, 99.5, 98.7, and 94.8 percent. Among these, the improvement in the academic qualification rate of teachers in rural areas is even more apparent. Teachers who have a junior college degree or undergraduate degree have already become the bulk of the newly added teachers. Third, the strength of qualified teachers in rural villages has been enhanced. Through the Project for Ad Hoc Posts for Rural Compulsory Education Teachers and Rural School Master's Teacher Training Plan, urban teachers' provision of assistance for rural education, and teacher-training internship programs that bring education to underdeveloped areas and other operations, rural education personnel were replenished and strengthened. Fourth, teacher training is completely in full swing. The central government has allocated RMB550 million of special funds for the implementation of the National Training Plan (the National Plan for Training Primary and Secondary School Teachers) in 2010; altogether, 1.15 million primary and secondary school teachers were trained, among whom rural teachers account for 95.6 percent. Fifth, teachers' professional ethics have managed to be valued. Through a series of educational activities such as the nationwide nomination of a teaching and education model and the dissemination of learning that promoted the theme of teachers' professional ethics and learning to put measures such as the Primary and Secondary School Teachers' Professional Code of Ethics into practice, the construction of teachers' professional ethics received further interest and attention, causing many outstanding teaching groups to emerge.

However, we should clearly see that our present building up of the teaching profession still faces many problems and difficulties.

First, the most brilliant and talented people have still not truly entered the teaching ranks. The best education must have the most brilliant teachers. In history, the best periods for educational development are always the periods when the most brilliant and talented people in society become teachers. However, in view of the current situation, our most brilliant senior high and university graduates tend not to choose teaching as their career. In the past few years, although we have attracted brilliant students to enroll in teacher training through a series of measures such as free teacher training, increasing teachers' salary based on performance, and so on, the situation has not changed all that much. In comparison, one of the secrets behind the sudden emergence of Finnish education in the past few years is its relatively high level of entry into the profession, which ensures the basic qualifications of teachers. The minimum academic qualification for Finnish schoolteachers of compulsory education is a master's degree. Teachers must receive at least five years of higher education before it is possible for them to attain this qualification; furthermore, the teaching profession is the number one career aspiration of senior high graduates, and the competition for entrance into teacher education courses has increased tenfold.

Second, the teacher-training model is relatively simplified. We have adopted a model of training teachers in teacher-training colleges that is relatively singular and closed off; it lacks a pipeline to attract outstanding university students to undertake the teaching profession. In the curriculum for teacher-training education, courses in educational theory and teaching skills are seriously underrepresented, with course content generally limited to the three old subjects of pedagogy, psychology, and teaching materials and methods. Furthermore, the class hours these subjects take up in general are only 160 hours, less than 5 percent of all courses. The design of these courses lacks an in-depth study into the patterns of teacher growth, especially in regard to their professional identity and professional development, and it basically does not take teachers' professional reading and writing into consideration. In the training of educational skills, there are even fewer opportunities. The time allocated for education internships is also seriously insufficient, with only

4 to 6 weeks, which is a far cry from the 15 weeks of internship time in countries such as England and America.

Third, the system for the continuing education of teachers is not complete and its standards are not uniform. In recent years, our country's continuing education for teachers has made considerable progress, but there are still problems such as deviations from the objectives, the fact that the structure is simplified, teacher quality that is not high, outdated content, methods falling behind the times, and an incomplete incentives mechanism. For example, in terms of the training objectives, emphasis is placed on raising the level of academic qualifications, while the training of ability is taken lightly; emphasis is placed on knowledge transferral, while the improvement of teachers' professional ethics is taken lightly; emphasis is placed on the continuing education of teachers with academic qualifications that do not meet the standards, while the continuing education of teachers with academic qualifications that meet the standards is taken lightly, and so on. In regard to institutional settings, relative to the large and complete network for teacher training and further studies for the continuing education of teachers in foreign countries, our country is still basically limited to universities, colleges of education, and teacher-training schools, clearly demonstrating the flaws of a singular system. We still mainly use traditional classroom teaching methods as well as the "rote learning method" and the "cramming method" to teach. Teaching methods that can truly improve the teachers' teaching skills, techniques, and practical management abilities—and moreover are lively, active, and highly practical—are rarely put to use. A large part of the training content repeats the curriculum that has been developed by normal colleges; for teachers who already have experiences in teaching, its level of instructiveness is not very strong. We have yet to establish a complete mechanism for self-training and research, incentives, and assessment. There is a lot of mandatory training and very little elective training; this, to a very large extent, influences the initiative and enthusiasm of teachers' participation in continuing education, causing many teachers to view continuing education as a commitment that they are obliged to do.

Fourth, there is a shortage of brilliant teachers in rural and disadvantaged urban schools; the resource allocation of quality teachers is unbalanced. Although the country has continually increased its investments in education, the educational gap between remote rural villages and ethnic minority regions versus developed regions is still evident. According to the survey of 50 countries conducted by the National Assessment of Educational Quality Centre, the gap in the quality of education between rural and urban schools is still very large. Although the country has adopted many methods to stabilize the number of rural teachers, the phenomenon of "the peacock flies southeast" is still becoming more and more critical. According to the survey of the Department of Education on the Guangxi Zhuang Autonomous Region, in the Twelfth Five-Year Plan period" the number of unfiled teaching positions in the region's rural primary and secondary schools (including kindergartens) reached more than 86,000 people. In many rural schools there is a serious shortage of full-time teachers in subjects such as foreign languages, music, art, physical health, geography, history, biology, and so on. In the urban areas, it is also very common for the brilliant teachers to be concentrated in prestigious schools, leading to the widening of the gap between schools and the craze for selecting schools despite repeated prohibition efforts.

Fifth, the burnout of a small number of teachers is serious and overall quality is on the low side. If you were to do an Internet search on "occupational burnout," as much as 80 percent of the content is related to teachers. In other words, within the groups as a whole who have a tendency toward burning out, the teachers have put forth the strongest voices. Teachers' working hours are long, the demands required of them are high, the targets of their teaching are complex, and the pressure they have is great, causing many teachers to experience a sense of burning out. This burnout is the result of collusion between exam-oriented ideology and market-oriented ideology and also leads to separating teachers from students, colleagues, and life and knowledge as well as isolation between themselves and society. In regard to just the teacher-student relationship, teachers mostly use authority and test scores to threaten children, or, the means of utilitarian teacher's love and profane success as a form of enticement to control students. The teacher-student relationship involves control and being controlled, and inculcating and being inculcated, rather than a friendly and natural teacher-student relationship. In regard to relationships between colleagues, in the face of test scores, bonuses, salaries, and job titles, teachers have practically become antagonistic competitors with one another. Although there are also teaching and research activities in their teaching lives, there is, however, no genuine teaching and research; although there are teaching and administrative staff general assemblies, there is, however, no genuine sense of public activities with colleagues; teachers have become unrelated strangers living under the same roof.

2. The Need to Change the Training Model for Teacher Education
I propose launching a 3 + 1 model for teaching colleges and exploring a 4 + 1 model, reforming the education courses and teaching methods at teaching colleges, strengthening internships for teacher education, and regarding education research papers as a bachelor's thesis for preservice teachers.

With the trends in integration and expansion in the scale of teachers' colleges, the training of teachers has weakened to a certain extent. Therefore, we propose the following suggestions for the reform of teacher education.

Promote a 3 + 1 Model for Teaching Colleges and Explore a 4 + 1 Model
The so-called 3 + 1 model refers to having students who are studying for an undergraduate degree in teaching, under the same conditions for their four years of schooling, to systematically study common compulsory courses and specialized compulsory courses, as well as common elective courses and specialized elective courses, for their first three years of the degree course and to use their final year to concentrate on studying the educational curriculum subjects, to carry out teacher training and internships, and to complete their graduation project or thesis.

Because the education courses are spread out over quite a few semesters at the teaching colleges in our country and thus are stretched out for far too long, they are unable to attract enough attention from students, basic concepts and basic theory learned are easily forgotten, and educational theory and practice are separated from one another. Students often focus their attention on theory in their majors and do not take educational theory seriously; thus the educational objectives of offering these courses are far from being achieved, directly and negatively influencing students' cultivation of educational theory, improvements in their practical teaching abilities, and also the quality of preservice teachers. Instead, concentrating education courses in the final year of a teaching degree will enable students to become highly aware of the importance of educational courses from an ideological perspective and the fact that the ability to teach is a teacher's most important ability; due to the close links between the subjects, the fact that their prevalence is strong and their set up is clear prompts the further enhancement of students' awareness of their roles as future teachers, while also changing the relatively relaxed learning circumstances of the previous four-year preservice teacher model.

The 4 + 1 education model for normal colleges implies the merging of independently set up normal colleges and comprehensive universities with professional education and is a departure from vocational education. Educational courses and training in teaching skills as a form of vocational education will be offered by specialized institutions as preservice training for new teachers. Under this model students would need to simultaneously attain an undergraduate diploma and a teacher-training certificate in order to attain their teaching qualification. This institute should be responsible for the continuing education of new teachers while also being one of the conditions for teaching promotions. The 4 + 1 model is suitable for training high school teachers.

Reform the Education Courses of Normal Colleges

The education courses offered by our current teaching colleges usually only include subjects such as public psychology, pedagogy, teaching methodologies in various subjects, and teaching internships. They are already unable to meet the needs of reality and possess many problems: (1) Education courses have not been arranged in their proper position of importance. The categories of courses are too singular (known as the "three old courses"), there are few training courses on professional teaching skills and few contact hours (approximately 5 to 6 percent of the total number of contact hours), with the proportion of contact hours being seriously out of balance. (2) In regard to teaching materials, there have been no major breakthroughs in the framework of basic theory and the pedagogical function of teaching materials is insufficient. (3) The teaching content is seriously out of touch with reality (the realities of teacher-training education and the realities of basic education). (4) Teaching content insufficiently reflects the characteristics of the times; it does not sufficiently summarize the new situations, new issues, and new experiences occurring within our country's reform of education since the reform and opening up. It also insufficiently sums up what has been learned from present-day international educational theories and empirical studies. (5) There is a lack of overall research and coordination in regard to the overlapping, repetition, and permeation of the setup of content and related disciplines, resulting in the scientific nature and validity of the courses being affected.

In order to reform the setup of education courses to meet the needs of the twenty-first century in terms of training teaching personnel, a comprehensive reform of the existing curriculum should be carried out. The new curriculum setup should include the following four aspects:

1. *Foundation courses in education.* Change courses in public pedagogy and psychology to the three courses of foundational education, teaching and learning psychology, and educational theory.
2. *Courses in professional teaching skills.* This includes oral training for teachers, training in writing regulations and skills, subject pedagogy, and modern educational technology.
3. *Lecture courses on education (as an elective).* This includes a number of courses such as class management, student evaluation, counseling, and so on.
4. *Courses in educational practice.* This includes teaching practicums, educational investigations, reports on outstanding principles, teachers and class patrons who are at the forefront of education, and so on. The design of this course focuses on the integration of educational theory and practice and also focuses on cultivating students' ability to teach.

Reform the Teaching Methods of Education Courses in Normal Colleges

Compared to Western developed countries, the teaching methods of our country's education courses appear to be excessively rigid, with the preaching theory of "teachers talk, students listen" as its main form of teaching. Before students begin their teaching practicums, they basically have not entered the educational teaching context before, and this causes students to have great difficulties in consciously using theory to analyze and solve problems. In view of this, the focus of educational reform of the teaching methods at normal colleges is to properly handle the relationships between the role that teachers play in leading and the role that students play as the main subjects, classroom teaching and extracurricular practicums, teaching materials, and the reform of basic education as well as theoretical learning and practice. Examples are arranging for students to launch classroom discussions and debates, to host reading forums, and to carry out classroom teaching scenarios and teaching evaluations; integrating education and teaching theory; making on-site observations of teaching and playing the recordings of the classroom teachings of outstanding primary and secondary school teachers; having students carry out analyses and evaluations of the teaching objectives, teaching methods, and teaching procedures used in these factual recordings of teaching from a theoretical perspective; compiling standardized lesson plans; prompting students to transform knowledge of the psychology of teaching and learning into teaching skills as soon as possible; inviting external outstanding primary and secondary school principals, teachers, and class patrons to introduce students to excellence in teaching and their experiences working as class patrons; transforming the role of teachers in education courses; requiring teachers to enter the front lines of secondary schools and understand the secondary school students and the process and contents of secondary school teaching. Furthermore, it requires teachers to investigate the problems within secondary school teaching and to carry out appropriate educational research. This will enable teachers to have very close ties with the reality of secondary schooling and to provide guidance for preservice teachers in regard to educational theory and practice. The effectiveness of teaching will significantly improve and at the same time will fully bring into play the role of the teachers' communication as the bridge between preservice teachers and primary and secondary education teaching practices, further deepening the perceptual awareness of preservice teachers toward primary and secondary schools.

Strengthen the Teaching Internships of Teaching Colleges
At present, there exist problems of varying degrees in the guidance of preservice teaching internships in the following five areas: (1) the objectives for guiding preservice teaching internships are not clear and evaluations are not standardized; (2) the qualifications of internship teacher guides lack rigid standards and regulations; (3) there is a certain bias that exists in regard to the contents of internship guidance; (4) the tendency to formalize the process guiding internships is relatively serious; and (5) the guidance of teaching internships has a tendency to be simplified. Therefore, we suggest that the internship guidance must be strengthened and outstanding teacher guides need to be selected, a reasonable internship program needs to be formulated, and the outstanding teachers in the schools offering internships need to be fully brought into play.

Regard Education Research Papers as a Bachelor's Thesis for Preservice Teachers
Regarding education research papers as a bachelor's thesis is an effective way of strengthening the didacticism of preservice teacher education. Allowing preservice teachers to carry out educational investigations and to write up research papers can greatly enhance their teaching awareness henceforth, prompting them to take the initiative during teaching practicums to prepare themselves for teaching.

3. The Need to Strengthen Teachers' Continuing Education
I recommend perfecting the legal system for continuing education for teachers in China; establishing a system for determining the qualifications of Chinese teachers' continuing education; setting up a base, website, library, and resource center for video images for continuing education for Chinese teachers; organizing a cohort of overseers for Chinese continuing education; and establishing commercial market mechanisms for Chinese continuing education and training.

The establishment of continuing education as a type of education system is the result of educational changes. In recent years, at the same time that our country's continuing education for teachers has achieved great results, many problems still exist, and these problems severely restrict the growth of education and improvements in the quality of education. Here, we put forward the following suggestions in regard to our country's continuing education for teachers:

1. *Establish and perfect a legal system for the continuing education of Chinese teachers.* The two laws (Teachers Law of the People's Republic of China and the Education Law of the People's Republic of China) provide only general stipulations for teachers' continuing education from an overall perspective and make only preliminary changes to the lawless situation of teachers' continuing education in China. In contrast, they lack clear stipulations in regard to specific problems in teachers' continuing education. Therefore, the country must formulate operable legislation for teacher training as soon as possible and should have clear explanations of aspects in continuing education such as funding sources, establishment of training institutions, assessment methods, determination of training certificates, what sort of training and under what sort of circumstances should different teachers receive training, and so on. Only by gradually perfecting our country's legal system for teachers' continuing education can we truly set the continuing education of teachers in our country on the track toward legalization and enable teachers' training to be mandatory, serious, stable, and effective.

2. *Establish a system for determining the teacher qualifications of Chinese teachers' continuing education.* Under determining teacher qualifications for teachers' continuing education, our country should speed up the pace and draw on the stipulations for teacher qualifications and system for appointments within the Teachers Law. Furthermore, it should extensively absorb experiences from abroad and make clear stipulations on aspects such as the level that the teaching qualifications of continuing education for teachers should achieve, the period of validity in regard to teachers' teaching ability and teaching qualifications, and so on. Finally, it should strive to establish a relatively complete system for determining teacher qualifications in regard to teachers' continuing education within three to five years.

3. *Establish a base for Chinese teachers' continuing education.* In the present day, where knowledge is increasingly becoming synthesized, teachers need to have not only deep expert knowledge but also extensive interrelated knowledge; undoubtedly, prestigious universities and comprehensive universities will have more of a distinct advantage in this respect. Additionally, a base for teachers' continuing education can also be accomplished in primary and secondary schools. Some famous primary and secondary schools are in reality educational centers for local culture. They have a relatively strong base of disciplines and a large cohort of great teachers who are highly experienced and teach at a high standard. Thus, having these primary and secondary schools carry out continuing education and training for teachers would make it targeted, and tangible results would be easy to achieve. In addition, as long as conditions permit,

specialized teacher training and research centers can also be established. These centers will hire first-rate master teachers to engage in dialogues with teachers in accordance with the specialized topic of teaching and learning. Through exchanges with master teachers, teachers' pursuit of ideals will be inspired and their latent abilities and creativity will be stimulated.

4. *Establish a network for Chinese teachers' continuing education, fully make use of Internet resources, and provide an abundance of continuing education resources for the vast number of teachers.* The administrative department of education should set up a national network for teachers' continuing education, optimize and centralize all of the country's best teaching resources, and provide teachers with a vast space to learn knowledge and access information, thereby promoting changes in teaching styles, methods, and models. Additionally, the advantages of the flexibility and dynamic nature of nongovernment Internet companies' resources can be made use of, and their participation in the construction of a network for teachers' continuing education can be extensively absorbed. Changes can also be carried out on the foundation of preexisting websites, for example Education Online (http://www.eduol.cn), "China's largest online teacher training college."

5. *Establish a library for Chinese teachers' continuing education and provide teachers with nourishment for the mind.* At present, the contents of the teaching resources used in our country are outdated compared with developed countries, they are behind by about 10 years, and thus strengthening the translating and compiling of teaching resources and the updating of the content has become an urgent matter. At the same time, experts should be organized to research and investigate a reading list for teachers' continuing education, screen foreign and Chinese educational classics, and provide teachers with a wide range of reading materials, which will broaden their knowledge base and enrich their spiritual world.

6. *Establish resource centers for video images of famous Chinese educators.* The brilliant lectures and classroom teaching of present-day educators should be recorded and be of service to the nation's training institutions, making "resource sharing" a reality. This plan would thereby avoid the situation in which brilliant educators bustle about and busy themselves dealing with various lectures and activities by enabling them to have sufficient time and energy to research teaching and learning. In addition, the establishment of resource centers for video images also provides schools in remote areas and some disadvantaged schools with a channel for engaging in dialogue with master educators, helping the teachers at these schools to gain access to educational information as quickly as possible, to grasp advanced educational philosophy and teaching methods, and to constantly improve their quality of teaching through observing and emulating these great educators.

7. *Set up a cohort of overseers for Chinese continuing education.* Many brilliant teachers at the forefront of educational work have an abundance of teaching experiences; however, due to their lack of literacy in regard to basic educational

theory, it is difficult to elevate their experiences into theorized knowledge and form a concrete teaching model. At this time, expert guidance and help is needed to assist them in overcoming the "plateauing phenomenon" after reaching their peak and to also help them to become expert and academic teachers as quickly as possible. This work was previously undertaken only sporadically by a small number of college and university teachers and some researchers, but in the present day, the administrative department for education should come forward and tutor a number of outstanding teachers in a focused way, thereby bringing out beneficial scale effects.

8. *Establish commercial market mechanisms for the Chinese teachers' continuing education and training.* The targets of continuing education are from many and varied departments and levels and have different needs. However, the current government policy is to have the higher authorities designate training locations and training content; schools and teachers do not have any rights to choose, and this administrative monopoly is bringing inefficiency to educational work. There is a commonly held sense of resentment toward this type of mandatory training. In order to deal with inspections by higher authorities, teachers will report to the training locations but immediately leave, frequently causing the phenomenon where the number of people who actually attend training does not even reach half of the numbers who should be attending. Therefore, schools and teachers should be given the right to choose the training bases and the content of training and moreover to independently make choices in accordance with their own needs. The administrative department of education should increase the necessary monitoring, as the result of such measures is that all training bases will undoubtedly do everything possible to improve the quality of their training in order to attract students. Only by being market oriented can there be pressure; only by having pressure can there be impetus. Therefore, the establishment of market mechanisms for continuing education and training is imperative.

4. The Focus of Reform on the Enhancement of the Quality cf Rural Teachers

I suggest that the strengthening of the rural teaching ranks be undertaken from two aspects: replenishing the quantity of teachers and enhancing the quality of the teachers. The best teachers should be enticed to go to rural villages, and the training of rural teachers should be strengthened.

The *National Outline for Medium and Long Term Educational Reform and Development* clearly promotes fairness as the National Policy for Basic Education; furthermore, it puts forward that the key to fairness in education lies in fair opportunities, the basic requirement being to safeguard citizens' right to an education in accordance with the law. Its focus is to promote the balanced development of compulsory education and assistance of disadvantaged groups. Its fundamental measures are to reasonably allocate teaching resources and to be inclined toward rural regions, remote and poor areas, and ethnic minority regions, accelerating the closing of the gap in education.

In actual fact, the key to fairness in education lies in the rural villages. At present, education in rural villages has already become the shortest plank of wood in the "wooden bucket" of Chinese education. In many cities, our education's "hardware" (buildings, facilities, and so on) and "software" (personnel, management, and so on) are not inferior to those of some developed countries, but in rural villages, generally speaking, the level of our educational development is relatively low. In recent years I have visited many rural schools. We have discovered that after the exclusions from agricultural taxes, the tuition and miscellaneous school fees during the compulsory education stage, textbook fees, and accommodation fees for rural disadvantaged students were a burden on the parents. Although there has been great development and changes made to rural education, it is not as if fundamental changes to perceptions have occurred as people had expected. On the contrary, in some places the atrophy of rural schools is more serious, to the extent that in some villages the "hollowing out" phenomenon has reached a stage where schools would be hard pressed to continue.

The key to rural education lies in the teachers of rural villages. Why is rural education atrophying? One of the important reasons is that rural villages do not have good teachers. Some excellent teachers have all gone to county towns and big cities, which is why schools in county towns are overcrowded.

Teachers in rural villages are the most important force in Chinese education. According to statistics, in 2009 there were 10.64 million full-time teachers in regular primary and secondary schools nationally, among whom 5.6334 million were primary school teachers, 3.5134 million junior high teachers, and 1.4933 million were senior high teachers. In regard to the urban-rural distribution, 2.1807 million teachers taught in cities, 3.7299 million taught in county towns, and 4.7295 million taught in rural villages, with primary and secondary school teachers below the level of county towns accounting for 79.5 percent of teachers. This is why we say that without improvements to the quality of teachers in rural villages, there would be no cohort of high-quality Chinese teachers; without the development of rural education, there would be no modernizing of Chinese education. The key to the development of rural education lies in enhancing the quality of the rural teaching cohort.

Problems in the construction of the rural teaching cohort are mainly approached from two different aspects: replenishing the quantity of teachers and enhancing the quality of teachers. In regard to quantity, the crux is the need to attract excellent teachers to rural villages. In recent years, the administrative department of education has put in a lot of work on this aspect, such as recruiting 124,000 teachers with special posts to work in more than 900 counties and 15,000 rural schools in the western region, promoting the support of rural teachers by urban teachers, and so on. Such measures should continue to be implemented. However, at the same time, I believe what is even more important is that a regular mechanism for replenishing the quantity of teachers should be established. I think that there are two extremely important points. The first is that the current system of free education for preservice teachers needs to be reformed. It should draw from the approach taken by having university students act as village officials and attract the most brilliant university students to teach in rural villages. It should thoroughly remove students' worries back at home and enable them to truly be able to stay, leave if they want, and work well. In other words, not to give funding at the time when preservice students enroll, but to select those university students who have the will to serve rural villages from among the most brilliant graduates and exempt their tuition fees from normal universities after fulfilling three years of service in rural areas. After three years, they will be allowed the freedom of choice and given points in the admission process for postgraduate students or civil servants. If they decide to stay on in rural villages, they will be provided relocation fees, research and training fees, and so on. The second point is that a group of volunteers who are retired teachers needs to be organized to solve the issue of qualified teachers. Nationally, there are many retired teachers and personnel for science and technology, most of whom are physically healthy and have exceptional professional skills. If such a group can be organized and regularly head out to rural regions where they are most needed to devote their efforts, they can to a certain extent solve the issue of teacher shortages in rural areas.

In the construction of a cohort of rural teachers, the cohort of kindergarten teachers needs to be especially strengthened and the overall quality of rural kindergarten teachers improved. Currently, the staff to child ratio (teaching and administrative staff to children) in our country's kindergartens is 1 to 17.8, with the ratio being 1 to 9.7 in cities, 1 to 17.2 in county towns, and 1 to 36.5 ratio in rural villages; the latter far exceed the ratio of between 1 to 7 and 1 to 8 as stipulated by "Standards Compiled for All-Day and Residential Kindergartens." The shortage of kindergarten teachers has already become a bottleneck in restricting the development of the rural preschool education profession. Therefore, the proper running of local midrange normal schools for kindergarten teachers and the teaching of the specialized field of preschool education at colleges and universities needs to be vigorously promoted. The establishment of local teaching colleges for kindergarten teachers should be supported and the scale for free tuition for preservice teachers majoring in preschool education should be expanded. At the same time as implementing training programs for rural kindergarten teachers, training for all kindergarten teachers in all areas needs to be promoted, professional standards need to be issued, and so on.

In regard to enhancing the quality of teachers, the administrative department of education has also done a lot of work, such as recruiting more than 4,500 brilliant undergraduate students in total to teach in rural villages since the 2004 implementation of the Rural School Education Masters Training Plan. In 2010 it began investing RMB550 million in the national training plan, with the focus also being to strengthen the fostering of rural teaching staff. Many private institutions and nongovernmental organizations (NGOs) have also done a lot of highly effective work, such as Operation Burning Candle, which drew on the resources of New Oriental to train foreign languages teachers in rural villages and achieved very good results.

However, I believe that apart from these sorts of "in and out" training, the most critical thing is that the rules should be in accordance with teachers' professional development and providing systematic and comprehensive training for rural teachers. In accord with the explorations by the New Graduate School of Education in recent years in locations such as Guizhou's Fenggang county and Sichuan's Beichuan county, I believe that for the growth of a good teacher there are actually three important points. We have titled them the "lucky three treasures" of teachers' professional development: professional reading, professional writing, and the professional development community. For professional reading, it is to stand on the shoulders of master educators and to move forward. We have specially developed a professional reading map for teachers, created a new online teaching college network, and encouraged teachers to engage in dialogues about those great educational classics. For professional writing, it is to stand on our own shoulders and rise up. We have specially developed narrative studies in teacher education, begun constructing a library of typical cases in Chinese education, and encouraged teachers to live brilliantly, do things brilliantly, and write brilliantly and to write their own life stories; For the professional development community, it is to stand on the shoulders of the collective and take flight. Through such forms as online education we have enabled teachers to break the limitations of time and space and to carry out in-depth exchanges and collaborations. From looking at the actual circumstances in which the majority of nearly 1,000 students of our online teaching college are teachers from rural primary and secondary schools, there are indeed rules with which the growth of rural teachers complies.

From looking at the practices of several private institutions as well as our own explorations, we see that paying attention to the power of society and promoting the construction of a rural teaching cohort is highly effective. I hope that the administrative department of education can promptly pay attention to and sum up the experiences of these people and furthermore give support in aspects such as funding, enabling the whole society to care about and support the construction of a cohort of rural teachers.

"Education as the foundation" is a project of vital and lasting importance; the grand plan for education uses quality as its requirement; quality education uses teachers as its foundation. We must attach great importance to the cultivation and creation of a batch of high-quality teachers, as only by relentlessly putting time and effort into each stage can we truly implement quality within education's future.

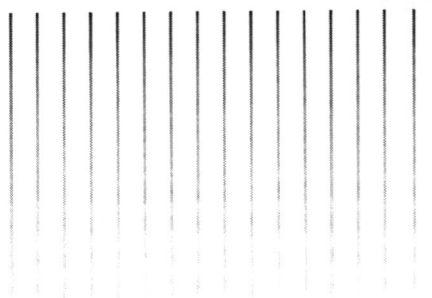

20

The Future Prospects of Chinese Education

Since entering the twenty-first century, the knowledge-based economy, which has advanced technology at its core, has already taken up a position of leadership in economic development. The importance of human resources is far greater than that of other eras; the country's comprehensive national strength and international competitiveness will increasingly depend on the development of education, the progress of science and technology, and the level of knowledge innovation. In the twenty-first-century context whereby the development of high-quality education is increasingly being regarded as the fundamental national policy for social and economic development by all countries, Chinese education will also promote the progress and development of the entire Chinese nation with a brand-new attitude. In looking ahead to the future of Chinese education, what developmental trends and characteristics will there be?

1. Improvements to the Quality of Education Will Be Increasingly Valued

The foundational role of education and its strategic status will become more prominent. Chinese education will focus not only on expanding the scale of education but also on improving the quality of education.

The socioeconomic development of all of the world's countries in the twentieth century, especially the reality of the sudden rise of developing countries as well as the postwar economic miracles of countries such as Japan, has already caused people to more and more profoundly and consciously come to realize that the

306

development of society and the economy increasingly relies on the advancement of science and technology and improvements in the quality of workers. At the turn of the century, countries such as America, Germany, France, Japan, and Singapore have adopted several proactive measures and countermeasures in regard to adapting education to the developments of the new century. These measures and countermeasures are based on a fundamental understanding: in the international competition of the twenty-first century, whoever manages to triumph in education will also triumph in gaining dominance and the position of leadership among the world's countries. As a developing country, if China wants to stand among the leading world powers, it must also be firmly rooted in the foundations of educational development.

In the twentieth century, due to the limitations of various conditions, many people in our country could not fully enjoy the right to an education. However, in the development of Chinese education in the twenty-first century, under the joint efforts of the whole society, investments in education will increasingly grow, the legal system and institutions for education will further improve, and inequality of education will greatly decrease. In the mid and later period of the twenty-first century, the whole society will become a society where everyone loves education and everyone has access to an education; it will be an educational paradise with a rich cultural atmosphere. The popularization of higher education that we have always dreamed about will have become a reality in the twenty-first century and the great strategy of "rejuvenating the country through science and education," will truly be realized. Through the influence and nurturing of education, the Chinese people as a whole will appear before the people of the world with a brand-new mental outlook.

In the twenty-first century, the quality education that we have constantly cried out for and pursued over the past many years will achieve a deeper level of development and furthermore will become the main theme of twenty-first-century educational reform and development. Under the guidance of quality education, our country will establish a complete quality education system and achieve world-class standards in education. Students will be liberated from the shackles of exams; all students will be able to achieve the maximum degree of development in terms of their personalities and latent talents, enabling them to joyfully and actively enjoy the new flavors that the education of the new century brings, within an educational atmosphere that allows them to harmoniously develop both physically and mentally. Education will shift from focusing on cultivating "one-dimensional people" who possess only one vocational skill for adaptation to an industrial society, to cultivating universally talented people who are able to adapt to a rapidly changing society. Under the guidance of the contents and teaching methods of science education, people's passion and ability to innovate will have achieved an enormous amount of development. Improvements in the quality of education will further strengthen the cohesiveness of the Chinese nation and reveal the wisdom and capabilities of the Chinese people.

Along with the growing importance that society attaches to education, the social and economic status of teachers will also be elevated. The wages and treatment of university teachers will be improved substantially, and this profession will rise to the top of the ranks in social status. Primary and secondary school teaching will also increasingly become a profession that people respect. The elevation of the status of teachers and the extensive implementation of teaching certifications will cause the competition for teaching jobs to become increasingly intense. The appointment system for all staff will also enable the quality of teachers to continually improve.

2. Informatization Will Change the Chinese Education Model
China will be taking a step into an information society; the new technological revolution of education will greatly change the Chinese education model.

Informatization is one of the basic characteristics of social development in the new century. The famous futurist Alvin Toffler believes that no matter how chaotic and disorderly the future seems to the present, one of its significant features is the expansion and rapid spread of knowledge. New scientific theories and technical knowledge have to be updated every day; yesterday's themes from science fiction novels have already become a reality today. Industrial, commercial, and financial industries are increasingly dependent on market and technical information; information warfare between companies increasingly becomes fiercer and has already become a matter of life and death. Contention between countries has also increasingly shifted from striving for military might to a technology race. Whoever possesses a large amount of knowledge will be able to triumph in the new century.

The information society of the twenty-first century will lead to the new technological revolution of education and the functions of computers will be greatly enhanced. In the wake of computers' entrance into classrooms and homes, schools will extensively adopt the use of computers, and educational teaching software systems in every subject area will be widely developed and used. The three education systems of education at school, at home, and in society may be linked through a computer network. To adapt to this, education on information processing will be further strengthened at every learning stage; teachers will actively and flexibly use a variety of information media machines and teaching resources to help and guide students to learn. The teaching style that was mainly based on lecturing may change to become a style mainly based on teachers assisting as facilitators and students using the means of information to obtain knowledge.

The popularity of multimedia computers further enhances the charm of self-studying, the traditional classroom education mode will be thoroughly subverted, and in many regions in China a large number of "open schools," in its true sense, will emerge. In these kinds of schools, learning is not subjected to the constraints of time, and through modern communication means students can "deliver" homework to teachers and teachers can also give explanations on problems and "issue" exam papers, lesson handouts, and homework to students. Students and teachers can have heart-to-heart chats and discuss issues at an appointed time. In the not too distant future, e-textbooks will be universal, various forms of educational websites will be established one after another, and various types of schools at all stages of education will shape their school's image through educational networks and strive to gain outstanding students. Interschool learning will become a possibility, the new form of an interschool joint diploma will become a reality, and new forms of online universities similar to the Khan Academy will also emerge.

The information society will not cause the demise of schools, as no matter how brilliant computers are, they still cannot replace living and breathing teachers. Furthermore, with the proliferation of computers, problems such as students playing video games and neglecting their studies will also arise. Therefore, future Chinese education will also have to face new problems such as how to guard against the negative effects of an information society and strive to establish a new education system that can effectively use information technology.

3. The Internationalization of Education Will Greatly Accelerate

The process of the internationalization of China's economy will be greatly accelerated and the international flavor of education will also become more apparent as a new educational landscape for international understanding will emerge.

In the new century, modern transportation and communication technology will be highly developed; economic, scientific and technological, cultural, and educational exchanges will be further expanded; links between all countries will become more and more intimate; and contact between any countries and regions on earth will become both quick and convenient, as if they were in the same village. No one country can be completely isolated from the international community and survive and develop long-term, as every country is opening up and automatically integrating itself into the international community. This will become an important feature of the new century.

In the international community of the new century, the solutions to many problems will no longer be within the capabilities of one country or a few countries; instead, they will depend on the collaborative efforts of all countries. In other words, only proceeding from the point of view of all of humanity, actively contributing to the peace and prosperity of humanity by solving all sorts of the earth's problems, and participating in the creation of a culture for humanity that will enable the normal functioning of the ecosystems of the universe's vessel, "Planet Earth," to be maintained and allow the coexistence of nature, people, and machines—only by doing all this can the healthy and stable development of the international community be possible.

The new century's international community will also have an important impact on China's education as a new educational landscape for international understanding will emerge, and cultural and educational exchanges, with economic exchanges as their figurehead, will become increasingly frequent. Furthermore, various aspects of education such as its objectives, content, methods, means, and so on will meet the requirements of internationalization.

First, the proliferation rate of foreign languages education will greatly increase and foreign languages education will be generally offered starting from primary school. A large number of bilingual schools will emerge, and in urban areas this will become a leading mode of education. The proportion of foreign language courses in secondary schools will be further increased, and university courses will use teaching materials written in foreign languages.

Second, educational institutions will further open themselves up to the international community. Internationally renowned educational institutions will enter China one after another, and a large number of models for running schools through international cooperation, such as the University of Nottingham in Ningbo, the Xi'an Jiaotong University–Liverpool University, and the New York University Shanghai, will emerge. At the same time, China will attract even more foreign students to come and learn the Chinese language and culture, and there will be increasingly more foreign students who will come to China to study science and technology. Our country will also recruit even more foreign scholars to teach, the international flavor on campus will become even more intense, and international schools will emerge in great numbers.

Again, education in international understanding will be further strengthened. Internationalization does not mean only the understanding and mastery of a foreign language, as what is more important is to form a character and style that considers issues first from the interests of all of humanity and a global perspective, understands the international community, and is concerned about and tolerant of foreign cultures. Therefore, education in international understanding will be further strengthened in schools, focusing on the cultivation of an international spirit.

What is worth mentioning is that in the future, a large number of "dumbbell scholars" will emerge in Chinese education. They will travel back and forth between China and other countries, engaging in teaching and research at overseas academic institutions and carrying out entrepreneurship and development in domestic science and technology industrial parks. They will bring back advanced science and technology, market information, and management models from overseas and engage domestically in the research, development, and production of high-tech products, with products then being sold once again overseas. I personally think that around the 2020s the return of Chinese students who have been studying abroad will peak. Students who have returned from studying overseas will play a role as the new force in China's economic construction and social development in the twenty-first century.

Of course, internationalization does not mean "Westernization" and is not the abandoning of the characteristics of Chinese education. While it strengthens education in international understanding, China's future education must pay even more attention to education about the Chinese nation's traditions and focus on unearthing the outstanding traditions of educational culture.

4. Education Will Attach More Importance to Serving People's Development of Themselves

Education in China will further go beyond the role of being a tool for political or economic development and serve people's development of themselves and the enrichment of people's spiritual lives. The inherent charm of education will even more be able to fully reveal itself.

At the moment, China is gradually entering the status of a "mature" society. The important feature of a mature society is the increase in leisure time and the desire for a spiritual life. Enriching people's leisure time and satisfying people's spiritual needs are naturally tasks that education is duty bound to undertake. Education will not only undertake the political and economic functions of "rejuvenating the country" and "enriching the people" but will instead place more importance on its fundamental function in nurturing people. An advocate of lifelong education, Paul Lengrand, early on revealed education's significance in regard to enriching people's spiritual lives and satisfying people's leisure time when he said:

> In our era, there is still one factor that plays a decisive role—the increase of leisure time. For generations, it was the privilege of a minority of people. At present, leisure time has already become something that hundreds and millions of workers can attain and brings about a new frontier in their lives. It is publicly known to people that in the not too distant future, the members of our society will have more and more time to use for rest and recreation compared to the time spent on undertaking work. This then raises the question of what they will do with their leisure time, with the answer being that a part of it will be spent on education. The first point is that education must be carried out for the sake of leisure time, that is to say, people must be prepared and furthermore, undertake training so that they will valuably use this sort of freely allocated time; the second point is that leisure time must provide people with education, that is to say, people are able, and furthermore, should, use a large proportion of their free nights, weekends and also their few weeks or even months of holidays, for intellectual activities, learning, research and for arousing their desire for knowledge and enabling them to undertake various artistic activities.

In the mature society of the future, the concept of dividing a person's life into school, work, and retirement will be phased out and schools will no longer be the place where students are prepared for everything in their lives, as education will be linked to a person's entire life. In other words, future education will be an education that is society-based learning and a learning-based society, mutually supplemented by formal and informal education and an education that is undertaken from the cradle to the grave.

In the new era, China's social education (community education) facilities will be greatly developed. Educational institutions at all levels will formally set up coordinated organizations for social education, and educational facilities such as libraries, museums, science and technology museums, educational facilities for young people, educational facilities for women, sports facilities, and places similar to civic halls (municipal halls) overseas will also play a role in lifelong education.

5. The Education Industry Will Have a Greater and Faster Development

The Chinese market economy system will further improve, people's demand for education will become increasingly stronger; furthermore, a trend in diversification will emerge and the process of the industrialization of education will further accelerate.

Together with the gradual development and maturity of our country's market economy in the 1990s, education has already liberated itself from the original closed model of a planned economy, gradually becoming market oriented. Education has already begun to break the structures and systems arranged by the State, a new kind of diversified educational development model is forming, and, as the subject of education, schools are also gradually becoming aware of their own dominant position in the market economy and society. Accompanying the further maturation of the market economy in the future century, the trend of acceleration of the industrialization process of education will appear. People's material standard of living will further improve, and the traditional social mentality of hoping that one's child succeeds, as well as the continual expansion in the size of the population, will determine that the education market will have considerable potential and a large amount of space to expand.

First, with the issuing of the *National Outline for Medium and Long Term Educational Reform and Development*, the future of private schools will have a relatively large amount of growth, especially as noncompulsory education and various forms of non-State schools will rapidly emerge in all sorts of places. By virtue of advantages such as their state-of-the-art educational facilities, flexible school mechanisms, and high wages for teachers, they attract a considerable number of students. This, to a very large extent, alleviates the pressure in regard to educational investments at all levels of the government. More funding will be used to invest and transform State-owned schools, thereby improving the overall quality of Chinese school education.

Second, various industries that revolve around education, such as teaching facilities, tutoring, teaching materials and teaching references, school uniforms, school supplies, and so on, will become intensely competitive, and all sorts of organizations, both within and outside of education, will form all kinds of industry groups. The education industry will become an important force within the industrial structure.

Again, educational institutions will be more involved in all areas of society and freely sweep across the main battlefield of economic construction. Not only will a large number of university and college corporate groups emerge, such as the Peking University Founder Group Corp., Shenyang Neu-Alpine Software Co.

Ltd., and Tsinghua Unisplendour Co. Ltd.; listed educational companies such as New Oriental, Xueda Education Group, and Ambow Education Holding Ltd. will also emerge. Science and technology industrial parks of colleges and universities themselves will also appear in China, and famous colleges and universities will venture outside of their school gates and districts even more. The industry revenue of some colleges and universities will surpass the government's allocated funds for the first time and become the main source of funding for schools. Some enterprises run by primary and secondary schools will further shake up the industry, with some "little giants" in the basic education industry prominently emerging, such as Goodbaby International Holdings Ltd., Wahaha Commercial Co., Ltd., and the Wuzhong Group. At the same time, the majority of schools will implement a separation between the school and enterprises; principals will no longer be only "money" oriented, but also "education" oriented and should invest their entire physical and mental selves into the management of the school.

With the increase in the country's economic strength, some "fake privately operated companies" at all levels of the government will gradually withdraw from the market and will provide truly private schools with space to develop; at the same time, the government will increase the strength of its support for privately run schools in the field of basic education and increase its purchasing of the products of public services in the field of education so that the education industry will further develop.

6. Education Will Further Pursue the Unity of a Scientific and Humanistic Spirit

In the wake of the development of science and technology in a newer and more advanced direction, the field of education will further pursue the harmony between a scientific and humanistic spirit and seek the unity of democratization and legalization. Education will become a powerful weapon for humanity's self-restraint and self-improvement.

In the new century, natural science and the field of science and technology will have many new breakthroughs. At the same time people are enjoying the fruits of advanced technology, they will also be faced with unprecedented challenges. Deforestation, desertification, serious pollution, the devastation of acid rain, the greenhouse effect, the ozone layer crisis, the dramatic population increase, the issue of cloning, the extinction of certain species, and so on are all issues that seriously threaten the survival of humanity. Therefore, education in the new century will attach more importance to the harmony between the scientific and humanistic spirit and will also attach more importance to the cultivation of morals and ethics. Educating students to care about humanity and society and to learn how to be upright people will become the main theme of Chinese education in the twenty-first century. Sustainable development education with content such as the environment, resources, population, and so on will permeate all levels of schooling and all school subjects. The legacy of human civilization and the essence of traditional morality will once again achieve widespread interest.

Along with the continuous advancement in the process of social democratization, the maturation and development of people's awareness of democracy, democratic environment, and the democratization of education will increasingly be valued. The theme of the fight for equality in educational opportunities in various Chinese regions will change from the right to an education to for the right to a better education. Therefore, the proper running of every school will become one of the missions of all levels of government. Improving the standards of disadvantaged schools will become an important part of the reform of basic education. Within the schools, teacher-student relationships will become further democratized. More and more teachers have consciously become aware of the fact that democratic teacher-student relationships will enable the process of education to be lively and active and guarantee that students' creative spirit and creativity will be fully developed. Teachers and students will also increasingly become more involved in the management affairs of the school, with autonomous organizations of teachers and students playing an even greater role.

To be compatible with democratization, customized education will also become a beautiful part of the Chinese educational landscape. More schools will begin to abandon the views and practices of standardization and unification. Instead, they will focus on pursuing their own characteristics in running a school and their own educational style. In the educational process, even more teachers will become aware that the true meaning of education is to fully tap into the latent capabilities of every student, form the unique personalities of students, and give full play to students' creativity.

In order to protect the healthy development of the educational cause, legalization will also become a major trait of Chinese education. Chinese educational legislation will become more complete, rigorous, and systematic, and law enforcement will be more stringent. The actions of educators and of the administrative department of education will be more strictly carried out in accordance with the relevant laws. By the 2020s, the system of laws and regulations for Chinese education will be quite complete, and furthermore will ensure the healthy development of the educational cause with its authoritativeness.

Education is the cornerstone of national rejuvenation and social progress. It is the fundamental channel for improving the quality of the country's citizens and promoting the comprehensive development of people. It is entrusted with the hopes of millions and millions of families for a better life. To strengthen a country, education must first be strengthened. I firmly believe that in accordance with the overall deployment of *The National Outline for Medium and Long Term Educational Reform and Development*, the socialist educational cause, which is full of vitality, vigor, and Chinese characteristics, will definitely take upon itself this important historic task in the process of achieving the great rejuvenation of the Chinese nation!

Postscript

In July 2011, the fourth edition of *My Vision on Education*, which is the sixth volume of *Zhu Yongxin's Works on the New Education*, was published by China Renmin University Press.

In October 2011, the illustrated version of *My Vision on Education* was published by the Culture and Art Publishing House. The editor in charge was Wen Longyu, who was formerly with Lijiang Publishing Company. After she transferred to the Culture and Art Publishing House, she also strove to have this book once more published by the publishing house that she works for. Therefore, this illustrated edition only retains the first 10 chapters of the fourth edition; the contents of the latter 10 chapters have been removed and the two appendices "Culture, Establishes a Soul for the School" and "Enrich the Life of a Teacher" have been added as well as some pictures.

Therefore, this revised *My Vision on Education* should be the sixth edition.

Apart from removing the appendix "To Have the 'Truth' Revealed," Chapter 16, "The Direction of Reform in Chinese Higher Education," and Chapter 19, "The Future Prospects of the Reform of Chinese Teachers," have at the same time undergone a rather large amount of supplementing and modifying. Related adjustments have also been made on the contents of other chapters, while reverifications of quotations in parts of the book have also been carried out. Taking into consideration the need for a translated English edition and the requirements of academic norms, the sixth edition has also added an index of subjects and references for the entire book.

I have always wished that, through repeatedly thinking over my work, it could be revised to the point of perfection. However, each time it is revised, my heart always skips a beat and I cannot help but always blame myself: why can't I just buckle down and use a sufficient amount of time to seriously polish this? In actual fact, I vow to myself every time that I will calmly take the time to revise this, but due to the dual pressures of government affairs and work, all I can manage to do in the end is to make the most of my spare time and strive to do the best under the conditions at the time. Perhaps it is impossible to find the sufficient time to polish this old piece as much as I like before I retire.

Thus, I have always been urged by publishing houses to race forward, and this time I have again been urged to come racing out due to the compilation of an English edition.

Whether it is at a slow walk or a fast run, this book will be continually improved. Many thoughts and much collected material can only be added to book in the future.

Zhu Yongxin

Notes

Chapter 1

1. Lu Jie, "The Return to True Education—On the Essential of Moral Education," *Journal of East China Normal University* (Education Sciences), 2001, p. 4.
2. Romain Rolland, *Beethoven the Creator*, translated by Fu Lei (Hefei: Anhui Literature and Arts Publishing House, 1999).

Chapter 2

1. Vasyl Sukhomlinsky, *Recommendations for Teachers*, translated by Du Diankun (Beijing: Educational Science Press, 1984).
2. Tao Xingzhi, "Primary School Teachers and Democratic Movements," in *The Complete Works of Tao Xingzhi* (Chengdu: Sichuan Education Publishing Company, 1991), 4:635.

Chapter 4

1. *K. Marx and F. Engel's' Theory on Art*, 1st ed. (Beijing: People's Literature Press, 1966), 4:393.
2. Zong Baihua, *Walking Aesthetics* (Shanghai: Shanghai People's Publishing House, 2005), 459.
3. Vasyl Sukhomlinsky, *To Children I Give My Heart* (Tianjin: Tianjin People's Publishing House, 1969), 49–50.
4. Edmondo De Amicis, *Cuore (Heart): An Italian Schoolboy's Journal*, translated by Xia Mianzun (Hainan: Nanhai Press, 2011), 20–21.
5. Cai Yuanpei, "General Education and Vocational Training," *The Education Magazine* 13, no. 1 (1920): 12.

Chapter 6

1. You Qiangui: *In Search of a Bucolic Primary School* (Beijing: China Friendship Press, 1999).
2. Tetsuko Kuroyanagi: *Totto-Chan: The Little Girl at the Window*, translated by Zhao Yujiao (Hainan: Nanhai Publishing Company, 1982), 250.

Chapter 7

1. Xie Shengyu, "Using Love to Create Sentences, *Teachers' Outlook*, 1997 (5).

Chapter 8

1. Xu Jialu, *The 'Wei An' Works: Xu Jialu on Education* (Beijing: Educational Science Press, 2002).

Chapter 9

1. UNESCO, *Learning: The Treasure Within*, 1st ed. (Beijing: Educational Science Publishing House, 1996), 3. (UNESCO's report submitted by Jacques Delors, former president of the International Commission on Education for the Twenty-first Century)

Chapter 11

1. Sui Tiangui, "The Connotations and Standards of Modernization," *Education Outlook*, 1996 (1).
2. Alex Inkeles, *The Modernization of People*, translated by Yin Lujun (Chengdu: Sichuan People's Publishing Press, 1985), 4–8.
3. D. H. Smith and A. Inkeles, "The O.M. Scale: A Comparative Sociopsychological Measure of Individual Modernity," *Sociometry*, 1966 (29), 353–377.
4. J. A.Kahl, *The Measurement of Modernization: A Study of Values in Brazil and Mexico* (Austin: University of Texas Press,1968), 18–51.
5. Yang Guoshu, ed., *Chinese Values—A Social Sciences View* (Taipei: Laurel Book Co., 1993), 65–119.
6. See Lu Jie, "Modernization, the Modernization of People and the Modernization of Moral Education," *Jiangsu Educational Research*, 1997 (1).
7. Inkeles, *The Modernization of People*, 97.
8. Yang Dongping, "The Modernization of Education: The Great Duty that Transcends Centuries," *Explorations of Modernization in Education*, 1996 (2).
9. Cited in "The Modernization of Education: Concepts, Ideas and Countermeasures," *Jiangsu Educational Research*, 1996 (6).
10. Zhou Defan, "Strategic Choices to Transcend Centuries—Some Thoughts on Education Modernization Projects in My Province, in *Jiangsu Educational Research*, 1995 (4).

Chapter 12

1. Liu Dachun, *The Knowledge Economy and China's Necessary Response* (Beijing: China Economic Publishing House, 1998).
2. "The Open Challenge Issued by Harvard's Principal," *China Education Daily*, May 4, 1998.
3. Jin Ma, Preface, *Theory on Innovative Wisdom* (Beijing: China Youth Press, 1991), 4.

Chapter 13

1. Hans Joachim Morganthau, Cheng Chaoze, *Puzzles in China's Economic Growth* (Shanghai: Shanghai Jiao Tong University Press, 2004); Zhao Yining, "The Leap of China's Comprehensive National Strength," *Outlook News Weekly*, September 27, 1999 (39).
2. Sun Yulan and Xu Yuliang, eds., *Ethnopsychology* (Beijing: Knowledge Press, 1990), 40.
3. Diao Pei'e, *Educational Culture* (Nanjing: Jiangsu Education Press, 1992), 121.
4. Sun and Xu, *Ethnopsychology*, 113.
5. See *The Analects*—Ji Shi.
6. Li Kangping, "Traditional and Contemporary Modern Education for the National Spirit," in *International Understanding of Education Heading Towards the 21st Century*, ed. Zhu Yongxin (Nanjing: Jiangsu Education Press, 1995).

7. Academy of Social Sciences, Psychological and Education Research Division, Central Government of the Soviet Communist Party, *Social Psychology and Pedagogy Within the Workings of the Party*, translated by Shi Minde and He Delin (Nanning: Guangxi People's Publishing House, 1986), 69.

8. Diao Pei'e, *Educational Culture* (Nanjing: Jiangsu Education Press, 1992), 108.

9. Nakamura Hajime, *An Essay on Comparative Thinking*, translated by Wu Zhen (Hangzhou: Zhejiang People's Press, 1987), 38.

10. Deng Xiaoping, speech at the National Conference on Education, May 1985.

11. Theodore W. Schultz, *The Economic Value of Education*, translated by Cao Yanting (Changchun: Jilin People's Press, 1982), 70.

12. John Sheehan, *The Economics of Education*, translated by Zheng Yiyong (Beijing: Educational Science Press, 1981), 46.

13. Wang Fengxian, ed., *Introduction to Patriotic and Communist Education of Primary and Secondary School Students* (Beijing: Educational Science Press, 1987), 332.

Chapter 14

1. "Hold High the Great Banner of Socialism with Chinese Characteristics and Strive for New Victories in Building a Moderately Prosperous Society in All Respects," *People's Daily*, October 25, 2007.

2. Amartya Sen, *Development as Freedom*, translated by Ren Ze and Yu Zhen (Beijing: Renmin University of China Press, 2002), 2.

3. Chen Zhili, "Education Also Requires Sustainable Development," China Education and Research Computer Network, http://www.edu.cn/20020108/3016699.shtml.

4. Liu Haoguang, "The Further Increases in the Economic and Education Gap Between the Eastern and Western Regions and Rural and Urban Regions," *China Education Daily*, March 6, 2004.

5. Central Educational and Research Institute, *2001 Research Reports on China's Development of Basic Education* (Beijing: Education Science Press, 2002), 121.

6. Mu Yifei, "Education Equality Calls Out for the Highest School Standards to Be Limited," *China Youth Daily*, February 25, 2004.

7. Liu Tiefang, *Escape and Return to One's Hometown* (Fuzhou: Fujian Education Press, 2008), 15.

8. National Statistics Bulletin on Education Career Development 2009, accessed August 4, 2010 [Ministry of Education's website].

9. "Hold High the Great Banner."

10. Fu Weili, "A Scientific Outlook on Development as the Threshold to an Education that Satisfies the People," *Journal of the Chinese Society of Education*, 2008 (1).

11. Yuan Zhenguo, "Implementing the Comprehensive, Coordinated and Sustainable Development of Education," *China Education Daily*, July 26, 2008.

12. Ibid.

13. Ibid.

Chapter 18

1. See CPC Central Committee and the State Council, *Decision on Deepening Educational Reform and Promoting Quality Education*.

2. See Wu Jisong, *The Knowledge Economy* (Beijing: Beijing Science and Technology Press, 1998).

3. *The Works of Ye Shengtao* (Nanjing: Jiangsu Education Press, 1991), 11:253.
4. See CPC Central Committee, *Outline on the Implementation of Education in Patriotism.*
5. National Education Development Research Center of the State Commission of Education, the Chinese National Commission for UNESCO, *The Future Problems and Challenges Facing Education: The Collected Works of the International Symposium on Towards 21st Century Education* (Beijing: People's Press, 1991), 18.
6. Ibid., 19.
7. International Commission on the Development of Education: *Learning to Be,* translated by East China Normal University, Institute of Comparative Education (Beijing: Education and Science Press, 1996), 188.
8. *The Works of Ye Shengtao* (Nanjing: Jiangsu Education Press, 1991), 11:297.
9. *The Selected Works of Marx and Engels,* 2nd ed. (Beijing: People's Publishing House, 1995), 1:11.

References

Adler, Alfred. *The Education of Children*. Translated by Peng Zhengmei and Peng Lili. Shanghai: Shanghai People's Publishing House, 2005.

Altbach, Philip G. *Comparative Higher Education: Knowledge, the University, and Development*. Beijing: People's Education Press, 2001.

Berk, Laura E. *Child Development*. 5th ed. Translated by Wu Ying. Nanjing: Jiangsu Education Publishing House, 2002.

Bollnow, Otto Friedrich. *Education and Anthropology*. Translated by Li Qilong. Shanghai: East China Normal University Press, 1999.

Cai Keyong. *Where Is China's Education Going in the 21st Century?* Changchun: Jilin People's Publishing House, 2001.

Chen Jianxiang and Sang Xinmin. *Dialogue on Educational Philosophy*. Shijiazhuang: Hebei Education Press, 1996.

Cheng Fangping and Mao Zuhuan. *Report on Educational Issues in China*. Beijing: China Social Sciences Press, 2002.

Chinese Central Institute of Educational Sciences. *2001 Research Report on the Development of China's Basic Education*. Beijing: Educational Science Publishing House, 2002.

Chu Hongqi. *The Path of Modernization for Education*. Beijing: Educational Science Publishing House, 1996.

Clark, Ron. *The Essential 55*. Translated by Wang Ying. Beijing: Electronics Industry Publishing House, 2009.

De Amicis, Edmondo. *Cuore: The Heart of a Boy*. Translated by Xia Mianzun. Hainan: Nanhai Publishing Company, 2011.

Diao Pei'e. *Educational Culture*. Nanjing: Jiangsu Education Press, 1992.

Du Yanyan and David Sun. "The Optimal Choices for Regional Educational Development in Poverty Stricken Areas." *Journal of Liaoning Educational Research*, 1999 (3).

Esquith, Rafe. *Teach Like Your Hair's on Fire: The Methods and Madness Inside Room 56*. Translated by Bian Nana. Beijing: China City Press, 2009.

Fang Jiansen. *Higher Education Developmental Theory and Practice in China*. Shanghai: Fudan University Press, 1999.

Finser, Torin M. *School as a Journey: The Eight-Year Odyssey of a Waldorf Teacher and His Class*. Translated by Wu Bei. Beijing: People's Literature Publishing House, 2006.

Fu Weili. "An Education that Satisfies the People in View of the Scientific Concept of Development." *Journal of the Chinese Society of Education*, 2008 (1).

Gu Minyuan. *The Cultural Foundation of Chinese Education*. Taiyuan: Shanxi Education Press, 2004.

Gunter, Mary Alice, Thomas H. Estes, and Jan Hasbrouck Schwab. *Instruction: A Models Approach*. 4th ed. Translated by Yin Yanqiu. Nanjing: Jiangsu Education Publishing House, 2006.

He Xiaozhong. *Idol Subcultures and the Education of Young People Through the Use of Role Models*. Nanchang: Jiangxi People's Publishing House, 2004.

Huang Shuguang, Wang Lunxin, and Yuan Wenhui. *The Cultural Mission of China's Reform of Basic Education*. Beijing: Educational Science Publishing House, 2001.

Inkeles, Alex. *Becoming Modern*. Translated by Yin Lujun. Chengdu: Sichuan People's Publishing House, 1985.

International Commission on Education for the Twenty-first Century. *Learning: The Treasure Within*. Translated by the Chinese branch of the UNESCO Headquarters. Beijing: Educational Science Publishing House, 1996.

Krishnamurti, Jiddu. *Freedom of the Soul*. Translated by Liao Shide. Beijing: Jiuzhou Press, 2005.

Li Zhenxi. *Love and Education*. Guilin: Lijiang Publishing House, 2007.

Li Zhongsen. "The Connotations of a Scientific Outlook on Development." *Wen Wei Po*, March 15, 2004 (10).

Liao Shenzhan et al. "From a Multi-disciplinary Mode to a Interdisciplinary Mode." *Educational Science*, 2000 (3).

Ling Longhua. "Education Concerns Life." *Jiangsu Education*, 2002 (8).

Liu Dehua. *Dignity of Humanity in Education*. Guilin: Guangxi Normal University Press, 2003.

Liu Haoguang. "The Further Increases in the Economic and Education Gap Between the Eastern and Western Regions and Rural and Urban Regions." *China Education Daily*, March 3, 2004.

Liu Jinghai. *Success Education*. Fuzhou: Fuzhou Education Press, 2001.

Lu Jie. "Modernization, People's Modernization and Moral Education's Modernization." *Jiangsu Education Research*, 1997 (1).

Morin, Edgar. *Complexity Theory and Educational Issues*. Translated by Chen Yizhuang. Beijing: Peking University Press, 2004.

Mu Yifei. "Education Equality Calls Out for the Highest School Standards to Be Limited." *China Youth Daily*, February 25, 2004.

Neill, A. S. *Summerhill School*. Translated by Wang Kenan. Hainan: Nanhai Publishing Company, 2006.

Noll, James. *Clashing Views on Educational Issues*. 14th ed. New York: McGraw-Hill, 2008.

Ornstein, Allen C., and Daniel U. Levine. *Foundations of Education*. 8th ed. Translated by Yang Shubing et al. Nanjing: Jiangsu Education Publishing House, 2003.

Palmer, Parker J. *The Courage to Teach: Exploring the Inner Landscape*. Translated by Wu Guozhen and Yu Wei. Shanghai: East China Normal University Press, 2005.

Peng Keshan. "Constructions Problems in Regards to China's Land Resources and Ecological Environment." *Urban Planning Forum*, 1999 (2).

People's Daily Commentators. "Hold High the Great Banner of Socialism with Chinese Characteristics and Strive for New Victories in Building a Moderately Prosperous Society in All Respects." *People's Daily*, October 25, 2007.

People's Daily Commentators. "A Significant and Urgent Political Task—on the Further Studying and Implementation of General Secretary Hu Jintao's Important Speech on September 19." *People's Daily*, September 26, 2008.

Qian Liqun and Liu Tiefang. *Rural China and Rural Education*. Fuzhou: Fujian Education Press, 2008.

Ressekh, Shapour, and George Vaideanu. *The Contents of Education: A Worldwide View of Their Development from the Present to the Year 2000*. Translated by Zhou Nanzhao and Sang Xinmin. Beijing: Educational Science Publishing House, 1996.

Regional Educational Research on Sustainable Development. "Research on the Sustainable Development of Regional Education." *Chinese Population, Resources and Environment*, 2000 (1).

Schultz, Theodore W. *The Economic Value of Education*. Translated by Cao Yanting. Changchun: Jilin People's Publishing House, 1982.

Sheehan, John. *The Economics of Education*. Translated by Zheng Yiyong. Beijing: Educational Science Publishing House, 1981.

Shi Shuchen. "The Humanistic Value of Environmental Education." *Journal of Langfang Teachers College*, 2002 (9).

Shi Zhongying. *Introduction to Educational Philosophy*. Beijing: Beijing Normal University Press, 2004.

Su Xuanliang. "The Current Problems in Rural Education and Countermeasures to Solve Them." *Education Exploration*, 2003 (2).

Sui Tiangui. "The Connotations and Standards of Modernization." *Education Watch*, 1996 (1).

Sukhomlinsky, Vasyl. *Recommendations for Teachers*. Translated by Du Diankun. Beijing: Educational Science Publishing House, 1984.

Tang Dehai. "Extensive Discussion on the Vulnerable Groups Within the Field of Pedagogy." *Journal of Educational Development and Research*, 2000 (8).

Tian Baojun et al. "Research on the Educational Problems of Disadvantaged Social Groups." *Tribune of Social Sciences*, 2002 (11).

Tian Jianguo. "Establishing a Developmental Outlook on Science Education." *China Education Daily*, April 21, 2004 (4).

Toffler, Alvin. *Future Shock*. Translated by Cai Shenzhang. Beijing: CITIC Publishing House, 2006.

Toffler, Alvin. *Powershift*. Translated by Wu Yingchun et al. Beijing: CITIC Publishing House, 2006.

UNESCO, International Commission on the Development of Education. *Learning to Be*. Translated by East China Normal University, Institute of Comparative Education. Beijing: Education and Science Press, 1996.

Wang Kunqing. *Spirit and Education*. Shanghai: Shanghai Education Press, 2002.

Wang Xiaohui and Zhao Zhongjian. *For the Issues and Prospects of 21st Century Education*. Beijing: Educational Science Publishing House, 2002.

Xia Shaoping. "Reflections and Theoretical Conceptions on China's Rural Education Under the Vision of Lifelong Education." *Journal of Henan Vocation-Technical Teachers College*, 2001 (6).

Xiao Chuan. *The Ideals and Beliefs of Education*. Shanghai: Yuelu Publishing House, 2002.

Xiao Dongbo and Zhu Yongxin. *Education and the Chinese National Cohesiveness*. Zhengzhou: Daxiang Press, 2005.

Xie Shengyu. "Using Love to Create Sentences." *Teachers' Outlook*, 1997 (5).

Xu Jialu. *The Works of Wei An: Xu Jialu on Education*. Beijing: Educational Science Publishing House, 2002.

Xu Ming et al. *The Cultural Development of Contemporary China*. Beijing: Encyclopedia of China Publishing House, 2008.

Yang Dongping. *The Ideals and Reality of Fairness in Chinese Education*. Beijing: Peking University Press, 2006.

Yang Dongping. "The Modernization of Education: The Great Mission of Stepping Across the Centuries." *Explorations on the Modernization of Education*, 1996 (2).

Yang Zhousong. "Initial Explorations on the Globalization Theory." *Journal of Educational Research*, 93.

Ye Zhishan and Ye Zhimei. *The Collected Works of Ye Shengtao*. Nanjing: Jiangsu Education Press, 2005.

Yi Lianyun. *Rebuild the Spiritual Home for Schools*. Beijing: Educational Science Publishing House, 2003.

You Qiangui. *In Search of a Bucolic Primary School*. Beijing: China Friendship Press, 1999.

Yuan Zhenguo. "The Scientific Outlook on Development and the Selection of Education Policies." *Educational Research*, 2004 (4).

Zhang Minjie. *Research on Disadvantaged Social Groups in China*. Changchun: Changchun Publishing House, 2003.

Zhang Renjie. *Comparative History Studies on Chinese and Overseas Education*. Modern Volume. Jinan: Shandong Education Press, 1997.

Zhao Jianwei. *The Education Disease: An Interrogation of Present-Day Education*. Beijing: China Society Press, 2003.

Zheng Jinzhou. *Educational and Cultural Studies*. Beijing: People's Publishing House, 2000.

Zhong Wanjuan and Yang Runyong. "Discussions on the Formulation of Regional Education Policies." *Educational Science*, 2003 (6).

Zhu Yongxin. *The History of Chinese and Foreign Educational Thought*. Nanjing: Nanjing University Press, 2000.

Zhu Yongxin. "How to Run Education to the Satisfaction of the People." *China Education Daily*, August 2, 2008 (3).

Zhu Yongxin. *The Miracle of Education: 17 Touching Stories About Education*. Shanghai: Shanghai Education Press, 2010.

Zhu Yongxin. *Recordings of the Moral Thoughts of Famous Chinese Class Patrons*. Nanjing: Jiangsu Education Press, 2000.

Zhu Yongxin. *Recordings of the Thoughts of Famous Chinese Principals in Regards to Running a School*. Nanjing: Jiangsu Education Press, 2000.

Zhu Yongxin. *Recordings of the Thoughts on Teaching of Famous Chinese Teachers of Distinction*. Nanjing: Jiangsu Education Press, 2000.

Zhu Yongxin. *Review and Reflection Series on 60 Years of Education in the New China*. Tianjin: Tianjin Education Press, 2010.

Zhu Yongxin. *The Scientific Outlook on Development and Chinese Educational Reform*. Rev. ed. Fuzhou: Fujian Education Press, 2009.

Zhu Yongxin, *Theories on Innovative Education*. Nanjing: Jiangsu Education Press, 2001.

Zhu Yongxin. *What Is Chinese Education Lacking*. Suzhou: Suzhou University Press, 2003.

Zhu Yongxin, Cheng Jinkuan, and Bao Yinchu. *Chinese Moral Education*. Suzhou: Suzhou University Press, 2004.

Zhu Yongxin and Xu Qingyu. *A Philosophical Exploration of Educational Issues*. Suzhou: Suzhou University Press, 2003.

Zhu Yongxin and Xu Yadong. *The Outlooks of Chinese Educators for the 21st Century*. Taiyuan: Shanxi Education Press, 1997.

Zhu Yongxin and Yuan Zhenguo. *Chinese Teachers: The Practice of Professional Quality*. Nanjing: Jiangsu Education Press, 2003.

Index

About the Author

Zhu Yongxin is deputy secretary and a member of the standing committee of the Chinese People's Political Consultative Conference (CPPCC), vice chairman of the Association for Promoting Democracy (CAPD), and vice president of the Chinese Society of Education (CSE). He also works as a professor and PhD supervisor in Suzhou University. A key figure in the New Education Reform in China, he has won several prestigious awards for his groundbreaking work.

CPSIA information can be obtained at www.ICGtesting.com
Printed in the USA
LVOW12s1418250414

383276LV00005B/9/P